MAGGIE:
A GIRL OF THE STREETS

AN AUTHORITATIVE TEXT
BACKGROUNDS AND SOURCES
THE AUTHOR AND THE NOVEL
REVIEWS AND CRITICISM

STEPHEN CRANE

MAGGIE: A GIRL OF THE STREETS

(A STORY OF NEW YORK) (1893)

AN AUTHORITATIVE TEXT
BACKGROUNDS AND SOURCES
THE AUTHOR AND THE NOVEL
REVIEWS AND CRITICISM

→» «←

Edited by
THOMAS A. GULLASON

UNIVERSITY OF RHODE ISLAND

W • W • NORTON & COMPANY
New York   *London*

Daniel Aaron: "Howells' 'Maggie,' " *The New England Quarterly*, Vol. 38 (March 1965), pp. 85–90. Reprinted by permission of the author and the publisher.

Lars Åhnebrink: from *The Beginnings of Naturalism in American Fiction, 1891–1903* (Uppsala: American Institute, Uppsala University, 1950; New York: Russell & Russell, 1961). Reprinted by permission of Russell & Russell.

Frank Bergon: from *Stephen Crane's Artistry* (New York: Columbia University Press, 1975), pp. 71–76. Reprinted by permission of the publisher.

John Berryman: from *Stephen Crane*. Copyright © 1950 William Sloane Associates; copyright © renewed 1977 Kate Berryman. Reprinted with the permission of Farrar, Straus & Giroux, Inc.

Joseph X. Brennan: "Ironic and Symbolic Structure in Crane's *Maggie*," © 1962 by The Regents of the University of California. Reprinted from *Nineteenth-Century Fiction*, Vol. 16, No. 4 (March 1962), pp. 305–15, by permission of The Regents and Joseph X. Brennan.

Stephen Crane: from *Stephen Crane: Letters*, ed. R. W. Stallman and Lillian Gilkes (New York: New York University Press, 1960).

Marcus Cunliffe: "Stephen Crane and the American Background of *Maggie*," *American Quarterly* (Spring 1955), pp. 35–44. Copyright © 1955, Trustees of the University of Pennsylvania. Reprinted by permission of the author and the publisher.

David Fitelson: "Stephen Crane's *Maggie* and Darwinism," *American Quarterly* (Summer 1964), pp. 182–86. Copyright © 1964, Trustees of the University of Pennsylvania. Reprinted by permission of the author and the publisher.

Donald B. Gibson: from *The Fiction of Stephen Crane*, copyright © 1968 by Southern Illinois University Press. Reprinted by permission of the Southern Illinois University Press.

Thomas A. Gullason: "Tragedy and Melodrama in Stephen Crane's *Maggie*." Copyright © 1978 by Thomas A. Gullason.

Thomas A. Gullason: from "The Sources of Stephen Crane's *Maggie*," *Philological Quarterly*, Vol. 38, No. 4 (October 1959), pp. 497–502. Reprinted by permission of the publisher.

Arno Karlen: "The Craft of Stephen Crane," © 1974 by the University of Georgia, originally appeared in the Fall 1974 issue of *The Georgia Review*, and is reprinted by permission of *The Georgia Review*.

Joseph Katz: "The *Maggie* Nobody Knows," *Modern Fiction Studies*, Vol. 12, No. 2 (Summer 1966), pp. 203–12. Copyright © 1966 by Purdue Research Foundation, West Lafayette, Indiana, U.S.A.

Jay Martin: from *Harvests of Change: American Literature 1865–1914*. Reprinted by permission of Jay Martin © 1968.

Janet Overmyer: "The Structure of Crane's *Maggie*," *The University of Kansas City Review*, Vol. 29, No. 1 (Autumn 1962), pp. 71–72. Reprinted by courtesy of The Editors of *New Letters*, The University of Missouri-Kansas City, and the author.

Hershel Parker and Brian Higgins: "Maggie's 'Last Night': Authorial Design and Editorial Patching," *Studies in the Novel*, Vol. 10, No. 1 (Spring 1978), 64–75. Reprinted by permission of the publisher.

Donald Pizer: "Stephen Crane's 'Maggie' and American Naturalism," *Criticism*, Vol. 7, No. 2 (1965), pp. 168–75. Copyright © 1965 The Wayne State University Press. Reprinted by permission of the author and the publisher.

Katherine G. Simoneaux: "Color Imagery in Crane's *Maggie: A Girl of the Streets*," *CLA Journal*, Vol. 18 (September 1974), pp. 91–100. Reprinted by permission of The College Language Association and the author.

Eric Solomon: selections from *Stephen Crane: From Parody to Realism* (Cambridge, Mass.: Harvard University Press, 1966). Copyright © 1966 by The President and Fellows of Harvard College. Reprinted by permission of the publisher.

William Bysshe Stein: "New Testament Inversions in Crane's *Maggie*," *Modern Language Notes* (April 1958), pp. 268–72. Copyright © 1958 The Johns Hopkins University Press. Reprinted by permission of the author and the publisher.

Charles Child Walcutt: from *American Literary Naturalism: A Divided Stream* (Minneapolis: University of Minnesota Press, 1956). Copyright © 1956 by the University of Minnesota. Reprinted by permission of the publisher.

Library of Congress Cataloging in Publication Data
Crane, Stephen, 1871–1900.
Maggie, a girl of the streets.
(A Norton critical edition)
Bibliography: p.
I. Gullason, Thomas A. II. Title.
PZ3.C852Maf 1979 [PS1449.C85]   813'.4   78-24596
ISBN 0-393-01222-0
ISBN 0-393-95024-7 pbk.

Dedicated
to the Memory of
the Reverend Jonathan Townley Crane
(1819–1880)
and
Mary Helen Peck Crane
(1827–1891),
the parents of
STEPHEN CRANE

Contents

Preface

Stephen Crane's first novel, *Maggie: A Girl of the Streets* (*A Story of New York*), written under the pseudonym Johnston Smith, was published at his own expense in early 1893 because no commercial publisher would touch it. Even his hired and still-unknown publisher, a firm specializing in religious and medical texts, presumably refused to have its imprint on such a shocking and "cruel" book. Of the eleven hundred copies printed, Crane gave away a hundred and sold only a handful. *Maggie* was stillborn. But it won Crane two powerful champions whom he called his "literary fathers," Hamlin Garland and William Dean Howells. His second novel, *The Red Badge of Courage* (1895), was a phenomenal bestseller and acclaimed—then and now—as a great American novel. Only because of this was *Maggie* officially published in 1896, by D. Appleton and Company, though Crane had to make some concessions and revisions.

Neither the 1893 *Maggie* (reprinted in this volume) nor the 1896 *Maggie* is a great American novel. Yet it remains an important novel for many reasons. More starkly than *The Red Badge*, it presents the essence of Crane's art and vision, where he flourishes a radically new lifestyle in writing and seeing and feeling. Its avant-garde techniques of impressionism, symbolism, and irony, and its perception of reality signal the spirit of modern American literature found in Crane's disciples of the 1920s—Sherwood Anderson and Ernest Hemingway. It is the first major naturalistic novel in America. (Unfortunately, the naturalistic novel has never had a fair hearing; moreover, *Maggie* is no mere handbook of naturalism, but a highly individualized and highly stylized work of art.) It made the city, with its slum dwellers and social problems, a fit subject for serious literary study, when the novel of the 1890s was still generally regarded as escapist fare, as mere entertainment. It helped to liberate the American novel, for in its satiric portraits of sacred institutions (like the Church), its profanity, crude slang, violence, prostitution, and degradation, *Maggie* was battling the genteel realism and romance of the day, along with the tight censorship imposed by publishers and public alike. It prepared the way for Theodore Dreiser's *Sister Carrie* (1900), which also suffered at the hands of censorship; and for the muckraking movement that began in the early 1900s.

In other ways, Stephen Crane's *Maggie* has assumed a special status in American culture. It epitomizes the young man's first novel, the "genius of youth" (Crane began writing *Maggie* at nineteen as a student at Syracuse University). It is the "new" novel, the "antinovel" of its day. It is the work of an "angry young man," the "rebel" challenging conventions and traditions. It is the "experimental novel," for basically as in his other major works—*The Red Badge*, "The Open Boat" (1897), "The Monster" (1898), "The Blue Hotel" (1898)—Crane in *Maggie* was working in a relatively new genre, Henry James's "blest nouvelle," the short novel, which still defies definition. The importance of *Maggie*, then, lies in what it promised and accomplished in both intrinsic and extrinsic terms. It is the great "seminal" novel.

Stephen Crane's family world and his private life add to his long-lived appeal and glamour. He was the fourteenth and last child of the Methodist minister, Jonathan Townley Crane, and Mary Helen Peck Crane, daughter of the well-known Methodist minister, George Peck. Both parents were prolific writers and doers. They were zealous crusaders against drinking, smoking, dancing, gambling, and other sins. The Reverend Crane wrote distinguished tracts and volumes like *An Essay on Dancing* (1848) and *Arts of Intoxication* (1870); he also delivered a popular talk, "The Teachings of Science about Alcoholic Liquors." His wife presented an illustrated lecture, "The Effects of Alcohol upon the Organs and Tissues of the Body," and was president of the Woman's Christian Temperance Union (WCTU) of Port Jervis, New York, and later of Asbury Park and Ocean Grove, New Jersey. She faithfully attended the annual national conventions of the WCTU held in various parts of the country.

As Stephen Crane grew up, he became the wayward son, indulging in many of the sins that his parents had warred against. He was a chainsmoker, and in his bohemian days in New York City, he was alleged to have tried opium and to have consorted with prostitutes. He defended a prostitute, Dora Clark, in court. Later he eloped with Cora Taylor, the madam of a bawdyhouse in Jacksonville, Florida; there is no record that they ever married.

Beneath his bohemian veneer, Stephen Crane had the crusading instincts of his parents and many of their values. While he did say that "preaching is fatal to art in literature," he drew large lessons: the terror and waste of slum life in *Maggie*; the stupidity and meaninglessness of war and violence in *The Red Badge*. His parents would have been proud of these humanistic ends but shocked by the "profane" and "vulgar" means he used. The touching and pathetic discord between Stephen Crane and his mother is partially revealed in his third novel, *George's Mother* (1896).

The fact that Stephen Crane did so much in such a brief life of twenty-eight years (1871–1900) also makes him appealing and glamorous. As a youth he resided in idyllic and rural communities (Port Jervis and Asbury Park), next to nature, hunting and fishing and swimming. In New York City, he was a reporter for several of the leading newspapers; then a foreign correspondent, covering both the Greco-Turkish War and the Spanish-American War. He was an expatriate in England, enjoying the friendship and respect of major literary figures such as Joseph Conrad and Henry James. With all his movements and activities, he was still able to produce six novels, more than a hundred short stories and sketches, two volumes of poetry, plays, news reports, and war dispatches. In the end, he was the artist dying young of tuberculosis in a sanatorium in Badenweiler, Germany. Stephen Crane remains the "genius" of his generation and the "wonder boy" of American literature.

Many libraries and individuals have been of inestimable help in the preparation of this volume. I want to express my deep appreciation to the staffs at the Library of Congress, Harvard, Princeton, Brown, Rutgers, Columbia, Drew University (especially Kenneth E. Rowe and Donald Vorp), the Boston Public Library, the New York Public Library, the New Jersey Historical Society at Newark, the National Woman's Christian Temperance Union in Evanston, Illinois, the Interlibrary Loan Department (Roberta Doran and Vicki Burnett) and the Audiovisual Services Center (Peter J. Hicks III and Roger Merola) at the University of Rhode Island. A special thanks to the contributors whose essays are reproduced in this volume; to Harold Kuebler and Doubleday & Company, Inc.; and to my son, Edward, my wife, Betty, and my mother, Rebecca Sahagian Gullason, for their interest and encouragement.

I want also to acknowledge the guidance and wisdom provided by the editorial staff at W. W. Norton & Company, especially John W. N. Francis and Emily Garlin, who helped and advised at all stages of this undertaking.

THOMAS A. GULLASON

The Text of
Maggie: A Girl of the Streets
(A Story of New York) (1893)

Chapter I

A very little boy stood upon a heap of gravel for the honor of Rum Alley. He was throwing stones at howling urchins from Devil's Row[1] who were circling madly about the heap and pelting at him.

His infantile countenance was livid with fury. His small body was writhing in the delivery of great, crimson[2] oaths.

"Run, Jimmie, run! Dey'll get yehs," screamed a retreating Rum Alley child.

"Naw," responded Jimmie with a valiant roar, "dese micks[3] can't make me run."

Howls of renewed wrath went up from Devil's Row throats. Tattered gamins on the right made a furious assault on the gravel heap. On their small, convulsed faces there shone the grins of true assassins. As they charged, they threw stones and cursed in shrill chorus.

The little champion of Rum Alley stumbled precipitately down the other side. His coat had been torn to shreds in a scuffle, and his hat was gone. He had bruises on twenty parts of his body, and blood was dripping from a cut in his head. His wan features wore a look of a tiny, insane demon.[4]

On the ground, children from Devil's Row closed in on their antagonist. He crooked his left arm defensively about his head and fought with cursing fury. The little boys ran to and fro, dodging, hurling stones and swearing in barbaric trebles.

From a window of an apartment house that upreared its form from amid squat, ignorant stables, there leaned a curious woman. Some laborers, unloading a scow at a dock at the river,[5] paused for a moment and regarded the fight. The engineer of a passive tugboat hung lazily to a railing and watched. Over on the Island,[6] a worm of

1. Rum Alley and Devil's Row are apparently fictitious places; they assume symbolic importance. Rum Alley may have been suggested to Crane by the chapter, "The Reign of Rum," in Jacob Riis's *How the Other Half Lives*, below, and by the long-lived prohibition work of his parents. (His father wrote *Arts of Intoxication* and his mother served as president of local chapters of the Woman's Christian Temperance Union [WCTU].) Crane repeated the theme of alcoholism in his third novel, *George's Mother* (1896).
2. In the 1896 *Maggie*, published by D. Appleton and Company, "crimson" was deleted. Color is a significant aspect of Crane's art and vision. See Joseph J. Kwiat, "Stephen Crane and Painting," *American Quarterly*, IV (Winter 1952), 331-38; and Robert L. Hough, "Crane and Goethe: A Forgotten Relationship," *Nineteenth-Century Fiction*, XVII (September 1962), 135-48. For color imagery in *Maggie*, see the essay by Katherine Simoneaux, below.
3. Derogatory slang, from "Michael," for a person of Irish descent and usually of the laboring class. Variant of Michael—"Mike"—appears elsewhere in the novel. In the 1896 *Maggie*, "micks" was changed to "mugs."

4. References to "demon," "assassins," "barbaric," and later "fiends" reflect the melodramatic and nightmare reality of the slum world. Crane employs a mixed style in *Maggie*—drawing on the Bible, the epic, romance, naturalism, melodrama, irony, and parody—to capture the nature of things and various attitudes toward existence. See Leonard Lutwack, "Mixed and Uniform Prose Styles in the Novel," *The Journal of Aesthetics and Art Criticism*, XVIII (March 1960), 350-57.
5. The East River, a tidal strait connecting Upper New York Bay with Long Island Sound (about sixteen miles in length) and separating the western end of Long Island (Brooklyn and Queens) from Manhattan Island and the Bronx.
6. In the 1890s, the "Island," located in the East River and extending from 51st to 86th Streets in Manhattan, was known as Blackwell's Island. Here the City of New York maintained a penitentiary, various hospitals, and almshouses. Later it was called Welfare Island; now it is Roosevelt Island. Though referred to as a naturalist, Crane often avoids the literal documentation and close details of a more typical naturalist like Theodore Dreiser.

4 · *Maggie: A Girl of the Streets*

yellow convicts came from the shadow of a grey ominous building and crawled slowly along the river's bank.

A stone had smashed into Jimmie's mouth. Blood was bubbling over his chin and down upon his ragged shirt. Tears made furrows on his dirt-stained cheeks. His thin legs had begun to tremble and turn weak, causing his small body to reel. His roaring curses of the first part of the fight had changed to a blasphemous chatter.

In the yells of the whirling mob of Devil's Row children there were notes of joy like songs of triumphant savagery. The little boys seemed to leer gloatingly at the blood upon the other child's face.

Down the avenue came boastfully sauntering a lad of sixteen years, although the chronic sneer of an ideal manhood already sat upon his lips.[7] His hat was tipped with an air of challenge over his eye. Between his teeth, a cigar stump was tilted at the angle of defiance. He walked with a certain swing of the shoulders which appalled the timid. He glanced over into the vacant lot in which the little raving boys from Devil's Row seethed about the shrieking[8] and tearful child from Rum Alley.

"Gee!" he murmured with interest. "A scrap. Gee!"

He strode over to the cursing circle, swinging his shoulders in a manner which denoted that he held victory in his fists. He approached at the back of one of the most deeply engaged of the Devil's Row children.

"Ah, what deh hell,"[9] he said, and smote the deeply-engaged[1] one on the back of the head. The little boy fell to the ground and gave a hoarse, tremendous howl. He scrambled to his feet, and perceiving, evidently, the size of his assailant, ran quickly off, shouting alarms. The entire Devil's Row party followed him. They came to a stand a short distance away and yelled taunting oaths at the boy with the chronic sneer. The latter, momentarily, paid no attention to them.

"What deh hell, Jimmie?" he asked of the small champion.

Jimmie wiped his blood-wet features with his sleeve.

"Well, it was dis way, Pete, see! I was goin' teh lick dat Riley kid and dey all pitched on me."

Some Rum Alley children now came forward. The party stood for a moment exchanging vainglorious remarks with Devil's Row. A few stones were thrown at long distances, and words of challenge passed

---

7. Frequent device of Crane's, not to name his characters immediately or often (in this case Pete). To Crane, people were more important as types and symbols than as individuals.
8. Sample of Crane's fondness for alliteration ("seethed," "shrieking"), for poetic effects in his prose. Crane's best poetry can be found in his best prose, like "The Open Boat," and not in his poems.
9. For the 1896 *Maggie*, Crane made various changes or concessions. "Hell" became "h——

ll" or "h——l" and "damn" became "d——n." Sometimes these words were removed entirely.
1. The hyphen in "deeply-engaged" was removed in the 1896 *Maggie*, thus blurring Crane's epithet (compound adjective) and his ironic use of the epic tradition, classical and medieval. Note references to "shouting alarms," "warriors," "catapultian," "flails," and to epic ideals like "honor" and "valor." See Warren D. Anderson, "Homer and Stephen Crane," *Nineteenth-Century Fiction*, XIX (June 1964), 77–86.

between small warriors. Then the Rum Alley contingent turned slowly in the direction of their home street. They began to give, each to each, distorted versions of the fight. Causes of retreat in particular cases were magnified. Blows dealt in the fight were enlarged to catapultian power, and stones thrown were alleged to have hurtled with infinite accuracy. Valor grew strong again, and the little boys began to swear with great spirit.

"Ah, we blokies² kin lick deh hull damn Row," said a child, swaggering.

Little Jimmie was striving to stanch³ the flow of blood from his cut lips. Scowling, he turned upon the speaker.

"Ah, where deh hell was yeh when I was doin' all deh fightin'?" he demanded. "Youse kids makes me tired."

"Ah, go ahn," replied the other argumentatively.

Jimmie replied with heavy contempt. "Ah, youse can't fight, Blue Billie!⁴ I kin lick yeh wid one han'."

"Ah, go ahn," replied Billie again.

"Ah," said Jimmie threateningly.

"Ah," said the other in the same tone.

They struck at each other, clinched, and rolled over on the cobble stones.

"Smash 'im, Jimmie, kick deh damn guts out of 'im,"⁵ yelled Pete, the lad with the chronic sneer, in tones of delight.

The small combatants pounded and kicked, scratched and tore. They began to weep and their curses struggled in their throats with sobs. The other little boys clasped their hands and wriggled their legs in excitement. They formed a bobbing circle about the pair.

A tiny spectator was suddenly agitated.

"Cheese it, Jimmie, cheese it! Here comes yer fader," he yelled.

The circle of little boys instantly parted. They drew away and waited in ecstatic awe for that which was about to happen. The two little boys fighting in the modes of four thousand years ago, did not hear the warning.

Up the avenue there plodded slowly a man with sullen eyes. He was carrying a dinner pail and smoking an apple-wood pipe.

As he neared the spot where the little boys strove, he regarded them listlessly.⁶ But suddenly he roared an oath and advanced upon the rolling fighters.

"Here, you Jim, git up, now, while I belt yer life out, you damned disorderly brat."

---

2. Slang for "fellows." In other places in the novel, the term "blokies" (also "blokes") is almost always used contemptuously.
3. Stop or check.
4. Blue Billie, Maggie, and Pete reappear in Crane's companion novel of the slums, *George's Mother*.

5. In the 1896 *Maggie*, the violence of "kick deh damn guts out of 'im," was changed to "kick d' face off 'im!"
6. Besides the fights and near fights, Crane also creates the atmosphere of passivity and indifference.

He began to kick into the chaotic mass on the ground. The boy Billie felt a heavy boot strike his head. He made a furious effort and disentangled himself from Jimmie. He tottered away, damning.

Jimmie arose painfully from the ground and confronting his father, began to curse him. His parent kicked him. "Come home, now," he cried, "an' stop yer jawin', er I'll lam[7] the everlasting head off yehs."

They departed. The man paced placidly along with the apple-wood emblem of serenity between his teeth. The boy followed a dozen feet in the rear. He swore luridly, for he felt that it was degradation[8] for one who aimed to be some vague soldier, or a man of blood with a sort of sublime license, to be taken home by a father.

Chapter II

Eventually they entered into a dark region where, from a careening building, a dozen gruesome[9] doorways gave up loads of babies to the street and the gutter. A wind of early autumn raised yellow dust from cobbles and swirled it against an hundred windows. Long streamers of garments fluttered from fire-escapes. In all unhandy places there were buckets, brooms, rags and bottles. In the street infants played or fought with other infants or sat stupidly in the way of vehicles. Formidable women, with uncombed hair and disordered dress, gossiped while leaning on railings, or screamed in frantic quarrels. Withered persons, in curious postures of submission to something, sat smoking pipes in obscure corners. A thousand odors of cooking food came forth to the street. The building quivered and creaked from the weight of humanity stamping about in its bowels.

A small ragged girl dragged a red, bawling infant along the crowded ways. He was hanging back, baby-like, bracing his wrinkled, bare legs.

The little girl cried out: "Ah, Tommie,[1] come ahn. Dere's Jimmie and fader. Don't be a-pullin' me back."

She jerked the baby's arm impatiently. He fell on his face, roaring. With a second jerk she pulled him to his feet, and they went on. With the obstinacy of his order, he protested against being dragged in a chosen direction. He made heroic endeavors to keep on his legs, denounce his sister and consume a bit of orange peeling which he chewed between the times of his infantile orations.

---

7. Slang for "wallop" or "beat."
8. One of the themes of the novel; foreshadows Maggie's later degradation.
9. This word is repeated several times, as well as set descriptions, to sketch one Rum Alley tenement building, which comes to represent life in the slums. Crane may have known the history of the Tenement House Commission of 1884, which reported on the cramped, unsanitary, and unsafe tenement buildings; another commission was formed in 1894, one year after the publication of *Maggie*.
1. Though he appears only briefly in the novel, Tommie reappears in other slum tales by Crane: "An Ominous Baby," "A Great Mistake," and "A Dark-Brown Dog."

As the sullen-eyed man, followed by the blood-covered boy, drew near, the little girl burst into reproachful cries. "Ah, Jimmie, youse bin fightin' agin."

The urchin swelled disdainfully.

"Ah, what deh hell, Mag. See?"

The little girl upbraided him. "Youse allus fightin', Jimmie, an' yeh knows it puts mudder out when yehs come home half dead, an' it's like we'll all get a poundin'."

She began to weep. The babe threw back his head and roared at his prospects.

"Ah, what deh hell!" cried Jimmie. "Shut up er I'll smack yer mout'. See?"

As his sister continued her lamentations, he suddenly swore and struck her. The little girl reeled and, recovering herself, burst into tears and quaveringly cursed him. As she slowly retreated her brother advanced dealing her cuffs. The father heard and turned about.

"Stop that, Jim, d'yeh hear? Leave yer sister alone on the street. It's like I can never beat any sense into yer damned wooden head."

The urchin raised his voice in defiance to his parent and continued his attacks. The babe bawled tremendously, protesting with great violence. During his sister's hasty manoeuvres, he was dragged by the arm.

Finally the procession plunged into one of the gruesome doorways. They crawled up dark stairways and along cold, gloomy halls. At last the father pushed open a door and they entered a lighted room in which a large woman was rampant.

She stopped in a career from a seething stove to a pan-covered table. As the father and children filed in she peered at them.

"Eh, what? Been fightin' agin, by Gawd!"[2] She threw herself upon Jimmie. The urchin tried to dart behind the others and in the scuffle the babe, Tommie, was knocked down. He protested with his usual vehemence, because they had bruised his tender shins against a table leg.

The mother's massive shoulders heaved with anger. Grasping the urchin by the neck and shoulder she shook him until he rattled. She dragged him to an unholy sink, and, soaking a rag in water, began to scrub his lacerated face with it. Jimmie screamed in pain and tried to twist his shoulders out of the clasp of the huge arms.

The babe sat on the floor watching the scene, his face in contortions like that of a woman at a tragedy.[3] The father, with a newly-ladened pipe in his mouth, crouched on a backless chair near the

2. In the 1896 *Maggie*, "by Gawd!" was deleted ("Gawd" was also deleted elsewhere; sometimes it was softened to "Gee") probably because it was considered blasphemous.

3. Crane draws on dramatic form—tragedy and melodrama—in *Maggie*. The tenement neighbors act as a "chorus."

stove. Jimmie's cries annoyed him. He turned about and bellowed at his wife:

"Let the damned kid alone for a minute, will yeh, Mary? Yer allus poundin' 'im. When I come nights I can't git no rest 'cause yer allus poundin' a kid. Let up, d'yeh hear? Don't be allus poundin' a kid."

The woman's operations on the urchin instantly increased in violence. At last she tossed him to a corner where he limply lay cursing and weeping.

The wife put her immense hands on her hips and with a chieftain-like stride approached her husband.

"Ho," she said, with a great grunt of contempt. "An' what in the devil are you stickin' your nose for?"

The babe crawled under the table and, turning, peered out cautiously. The ragged girl retreated and the urchin in the corner drew his legs carefully beneath him.

The man puffed his pipe calmly and put his great mudded[4] boots on the back part of the stove.

"Go teh hell," he murmured, tranquilly.

The woman screamed and shook her fists before her husband's eyes. The rough yellow of her face and neck flared suddenly crimson. She began to howl.

He puffed imperturbably at his pipe for a time, but finally arose and began to look out at the window into the darkening chaos of back yards.

"You've been drinkin', Mary," he said. "You'd better let up on the bot', ol' woman, or you'll git done."

"You're a liar. I ain't had a drop," she roared in reply.

They had a lurid altercation, in which they damned each other's souls with frequence.[5]

The babe was staring out from under the table, his small face working in his excitement.

The ragged girl went stealthily over to the corner where the urchin lay.

"Are yehs hurted much, Jimmie?" she whispered timidly.

"Not a damn bit! See?" growled the little boy.

"Will I wash deh blood?"

"Naw!"

"Will I—"

"When I catch dat Riley kid I'll break 'is face! Dat's right! See?"

He turned his face to the wall as if resolved to grimly bide his time.

In the quarrel between husband and wife, the woman was victor. The man grabbed his hat and rushed from the room, apparently

4. Becomes "muddied" in the 1896 *Maggie*.   5. Sentence reduced to "They had a lurid altercation" in the 1896 *Maggie*.

determined upon a vengeful drunk. She followed to the door and thundered at him as he made his way down-stairs.

She returned and stirred up the room until her children were bobbing about like bubbles.

"Git outa deh way," she persistently bawled, waving feet with their dishevelled shoes near the heads of her children. She shrouded herself, puffing and snorting, in a cloud of steam at the stove, and eventually extracted a frying-pan full of potatoes that hissed.

She flourished it. "Come teh yer suppers, now," she cried with sudden exasperation. "Hurry up, now, er I'll help yeh!"

The children scrambled hastily. With prodigious clatter they arranged themselves at table. The babe sat with his feet dangling high from a precarious infant chair and gorged his small stomach. Jimmie forced, with feverish rapidity, the grease-enveloped pieces between his wounded lips. Maggie, with side glances of fear of interruption, ate like a small pursued tigress.[6]

The mother sat blinking at them. She delivered reproaches, swallowed potatoes and drank from a yellow-brown bottle. After a time her mood changed and she wept as she carried little Tommie into another room and laid him to sleep with his fists doubled in an old quilt of faded red and green grandeur. Then she came and moaned by the stove. She rocked to and fro upon a chair, shedding tears and crooning miserably to the two children about their "poor mother" and "yer fader, damn 'is soul."

The little girl plodded between the table and the chair with a dish-pan on it. She tottered on her small legs beneath burdens of dishes.

Jimmie sat nursing his various wounds. He cast furtive glances at his mother. His practised eye perceived her gradually emerge from a muddled mist of sentiment until her brain burned in drunken heat. He sat breathless.

Maggie broke a plate.

The mother started to her feet as if propelled.

"Good Gawd," she howled. Her eyes glittered on her child with sudden hatred. The fervent red of her face turned almost to purple. The little boy ran to the halls, shrieking like a monk[7] in an earthquake.

He floundered about in darkness until he found the stairs. He stumbled, panic-stricken, to the next floor. An old woman opened a door. A light behind her threw a flare on the urchin's quivering face.

6. Animal imagery reinforces Crane's view of slum life as a jungle. See Mordecai and Erin Marcus, "Animal Imagery in *The Red Badge of Courage*," *Modern Language Notes*, LXXIV (February 1959), 108–11.

7. Religious imagery adds another dimension to the novel. Compare with the monk image that opens Chapter XIX. See William Bysshe Stein, "New Testament Inversions in Crane's *Maggie*," below.

"Eh, Gawd, child, what is it dis time? Is yer fader beatin' yer mudder, or yer mudder beatin' yer fader?"[8]

Chapter III

Jimmie and the old woman listened long in the hall. Above the muffled roar of conversation, the dismal wailings of babies at night, the thumping of feet in unseen corridors and rooms, mingled with the sound of varied hoarse shoutings in the street and the rattling of wheels over cobbles, they heard the screams of the child and the roars of the mother die away to a feeble moaning and a subdued bass muttering.

The old woman was a gnarled and leathery personage who could don, at will, an expression of great virtue. She possessed a small music box capable of one tune, and a collection of "God bless yehs" pitched in assorted keys of fervency. Each day she took a position upon the stones of Fifth Avenue,[9] where she crooked her legs under her and crouched immovable and hideous, like an idol. She received daily a small sum in pennies. It was contributed, for the most part, by persons who did not make their homes in that vicinity.

Once, when a lady had dropped her purse on the sidewalk, the gnarled woman had grabbed it and smuggled it with great dexterity beneath her cloak. When she was arrested she had cursed the lady into a partial swoon, and with her aged limbs, twisted from rheumatism, had almost kicked the stomach[1] out of a huge policeman whose conduct upon that occasion she referred to when she said: "The police, damn 'em."

"Eh, Jimmie, it's cursed shame," she said. "Go, now, like a dear an' buy me a can,[2] an' if yer mudder raises 'ell all night yehs can sleep here."

Jimmie took a tendered tin-pail and seven pennies and departed. He passed into the side door of a saloon and went to the bar. Straining up on his toes he raised the pail and pennies as high as his arms would let him. He saw two hands thrust down and take them. Directly the same hands let down the filled pail and he left.

In front of the gruesome doorway he met a lurching figure. It was his father, swaying about on uncertain legs.

8. This chapter, like others, ends in irony. Here Crane exposes the chronic pattern of adult life (the Johnsons).

9. The fashionable street of New York City (in Manhattan), beginning at Washington Square and ending at the Harlem River. Borders Central Park from 59th to 110th Streets.

1. In the 1896 *Maggie*, "had almost kicked the stomach" was changed to "had kicked the breath."

2. Can of beer or "growler." Jacob Riis campaigned to stop slum children from purchasing beer for adults. See his *How the Other Half Lives*, below; also see Stephen Crane's "The Broken-Down Van," below.

"Give me deh can. See?" said the man, threateningly.

"Ah, come off! I got dis can fer dat ol' woman an' it 'ud be dirt[3] teh swipe it. See?" cried Jimmie.

The father wrenched the pail from the urchin. He grasped it in both hands and lifted it to his mouth. He glued his lips to the under edge and tilted his head. His hairy throat swelled until it seemed to grow near his chin. There was a tremendous gulping movement and the beer was gone.

The man caught his breath and laughed. He hit his son on the head with the empty pail. As it rolled clanging into the street, Jimmie began to scream and kicked repeatedly at his father's shins.

"Look at deh dirt what yeh done me," he yelled. "Deh ol' woman 'ill be raisin' hell."

He retreated to the middle of the street, but the man did not pursue. He staggered toward the door.

"I'll club hell outa yeh[4] when I ketch yeh," he shouted, and disappeared.

During the evening he had been standing against a bar drinking whiskies and declaring to all comers, confidentially: "My home reg'lar livin' hell! Damndes' place! Reg'lar hell! Why do I come an' drin' whisk' here thish way? 'Cause home reg'lar livin' hell!"

Jimmie waited a long time in the street and then crept warily up through the building. He passed with great caution the door of the gnarled woman, and finally stopped outside his home and listened.

He could hear his mother moving heavily about among the furniture of the room. She was chanting in a mournful voice, occasionally interjecting bursts of volcanic wrath at the father, who, Jimmie judged, had sunk down on the floor or in a corner.

"Why deh blazes don' chere try teh keep Jim from fightin'? I'll break yer jaw," she suddenly bellowed.

The man mumbled with drunken indifference. "Ah, wha' deh hell. W'a's odds? Wha' makes kick?"

"Because he tears 'is clothes, yeh damn fool," cried the woman in supreme wrath.

The husband seemed to become aroused. "Go teh hell," he thundered fiercely in reply. There was a crash against the door and something broke into clattering fragments. Jimmie partially suppressed a howl and darted down the stairway. Below he paused and listened. He heard howls and curses, groans and shrieks, confusingly in chorus as if a battle were raging. With all was the crash of splintering furniture. The eyes of the urchin glared in fear that one of them would discover him.

---

3. In several places, references to "dirt" or "contamination" suggest the moral awareness or hypocritical postures of the people of the slums.

4. The violence of "I'll club hell outa yeh" was reduced to "I'll paste yeh" in the 1896 *Maggie*.

Curious faces appeared in doorways, and whispered comments passed to and fro. "Ol' Johnson's raisin' hell agin."

Jimmie stood until the noises ceased and the other inhabitants of the tenement had all yawned and shut their doors. Then he crawled up-stairs with the caution of an invader of a panther den. Sounds of labored breathing came through the broken door-panels. He pushed the door open and entered, quaking.

A glow from the fire threw red hues over the bare floor, the cracked and soiled plastering, and the overturned and broken furniture.

In the middle of the floor lay his mother asleep. In one corner of the room his father's limp body hung across the seat of a chair.

The urchin stole forward. He began to shiver in dread of awakening his parents. His mother's great chest was heaving painfully. Jimmie paused and looked down at her. Her face was inflamed and swollen from drinking. Her yellow brows shaded eye-lids that had grown blue. Her tangled hair tossed in waves over her forehead. Her mouth was set in the same lines of vindictive hatred that it had, perhaps, borne during the fight. Her bare, red arms were thrown out above her head in positions of exhaustion, something, mayhap, like those of a sated villain.

The urchin bended[5] over his mother. He was fearful lest she should open her eyes, and the dread within him was so strong, that he could not forbear to stare, but hung as if fascinated over the woman's grim face.

Suddenly her eyes opened. The urchin found himself looking straight into that expression, which, it would seem, had the power to change his blood to salt. He howled piercingly and fell backward.

The woman floundered for a moment, tossed her arms about her head as if in combat, and again began to snore.

Jimmie crawled back in the shadows and waited. A noise in the next room had followed his cry at the discovery that his mother was awake. He grovelled in the gloom, the eyes from out his drawn face riveted upon the intervening door.

He heard it creak, and then the sound of a small voice came to him. "Jimmie! Jimmie! Are yehs dere?" it whispered. The urchin started. The thin, white face of his sister looked at him from the doorway of the other room. She crept to him across the floor.

The father had not moved, but lay in the same death-like sleep. The mother writhed in uneasy slumber, her chest wheezing as if she were in the agonies of strangulation. Out at the window a florid moon was peering over dark roofs, and in the distance the waters of a river[6] glimmered pallidly.

---

5. Characteristic of Crane to use "bended." Changed to "bent" in the 1896 *Maggie*. 6. East River (see first footnote 5 in Chapter I).

The small frame of the ragged girl was quivering. Her features were haggard from weeping, and her eyes gleamed from fear. She grasped the urchin's arm in her little trembling hands and they huddled in a corner. The eyes of both were drawn, by some force, to stare at the woman's face, for they thought she need only to awake and all fiends would come from below.

They crouched until the ghost-mists of dawn appeared at the window, drawing close to the panes, and looking in at the prostrate, heaving body of the mother.

Chapter IV

The babe, Tommie, died. He went away in a white, insignificant coffin, his small waxen hand clutching a flower that the girl, Maggie, had stolen from an Italian.

She and Jimmie lived.[7]

The inexperienced fibres of the boy's eyes were hardened at an early age. He became a young man of leather. He lived some red years without laboring. During that time his sneer became chronic. He studied human nature in the gutter, and found it no worse than he thought he had reason to believe it. He never conceived a respect for the world, because he had begun with no idols that it had smashed.

He clad his soul in armor by means of happening hilariously in at a mission church where a man composed his sermons of "yous."[8] While they got warm at the stove, he told his hearers just where he calculated they stood with the Lord. Many of the sinners were impatient over the pictured depths of their degradation. They were waiting for soup-tickets.

A reader of words of wind-demons might have been able to see the portions of a dialogue pass to and fro between the exhorter and his hearers.

"You are damned," said the preacher. And the reader of sounds might have seen the reply go forth from the ragged people: "Where's our soup?"

Jimmie and a companion sat in a rear seat and commented upon the things that didn't concern them, with all the freedom of English gentlemen. When they grew thirsty and went out their minds confused the speaker with Christ.

Momentarily, Jimmie was sullen with thoughts of a hopeless alti-

---

7. These two paragraphs reveal Crane's understated staccato style, foreshadowing the Hemingway style of the 1920s.

8. At this point, the following was added to the 1896 *Maggie*: "Once a philosopher asked this man why he did not say 'we' instead of 'you.' The man replied, 'What?'"

tude where grew fruit. His companion said that if he should ever meet God[9] he would ask for a million dollars and a bottle of beer.

Jimmie's occupation for a long time was to stand on street-corners and watch the world go by, dreaming blood-red dreams at the passing of pretty women. He menaced mankind at the intersections of streets.

On the corners he was in life and of life. The world was going on and he was there to perceive it.

He maintained a belligerent attitude toward all well-dressed men. To him fine raiment was allied to weakness, and all good coats covered faint hearts. He and his order were kings, to a certain extent, over the men of untarnished clothes, because these latter dreaded, perhaps, to be either killed or laughed at.

Above all things he despised obvious Christians and ciphers with the chrysanthemums of aristocracy in their button-holes. He considered himself above both of these classes. He was afraid of neither the devil nor the leader of society.

When he had a dollar in his pocket his satisfaction with existence was the greatest thing in the world. So, eventually, he felt obliged to work. His father died and his mother's years were divided up into periods of thirty days.[1]

He became a truck driver. He was given the charge of a painstaking pair of horses and a large rattling truck. He invaded the turmoil and tumble of the down-town streets and learned to breathe maledictory defiance at the police who occasionally used to climb up, drag him from his perch and beat him.

In the lower part of the city he daily involved himself in hideous tangles. If he and his team chanced to be in the rear he preserved a demeanor of serenity, crossing his legs and bursting forth into yells when foot-passengers took dangerous dives beneath the noses of his champing horses. He smoked his pipe calmly for he knew that his pay was marching on.

If in the front and the key-truck of chaos, he entered terrifically into the quarrel that was raging to and fro among the drivers on their high seats, and sometimes roared oaths and violently got himself arrested.

After a time his sneer grew so that it turned its glare upon all things. He became so sharp that he believed in nothing. To him the police were always actuated by malignant impulses and the rest of the world was composed, for the most part, of despicable creatures who were all trying to take advantage of him and with whom, in defense, he was obliged to quarrel on all possible occasions. He

---

9. In the 1896 *Maggie*, "meet God" was changed to "go to heaven."

1. Note how Crane reflects the calloused world of *Maggie* by treating the father's death as an incidental fact.

himself occupied a down-trodden position that had a private but distinct element of grandeur in its isolation.

The most complete cases of aggravated idiocy were, to his mind, rampant upon the front platforms of all of the street cars. At first his tongue strove with these beings, but he eventually was superior. He became immured like an African cow.[2] In him grew a majestic contempt for those strings of street cars that followed him like intent bugs.

He fell into the habit, when starting on a long journey, of fixing his eye on a high and distant object, commanding his horses to begin, and then going into a sort of a trance of observation. Multitudes of drivers might howl in his rear, and passengers might load him with opprobrium, he would not awaken until some blue policeman turned red and began to frenziedly tear bridles and beat the soft noses of the responsible horses.

When he paused to contemplate the attitude of the police toward himself and his fellows, he believed that they were the only men in the city who had no rights. When driving about, he felt that he was held liable by the police for anything that might occur in the streets, and was the common prey of all energetic officials. In revenge, he resolved never to move out of the way of anything, until formidable circumstances, or a much larger man than himself forced him to it.

Foot-passengers were mere pestering flies with an insane disregard for their legs and his convenience. He could not conceive their maniacal desires to cross the streets. Their madness smote him with eternal amazement. He was continually storming at them from his throne. He sat aloft and denounced their frantic leaps, plunges, dives and straddles.

When they would thrust at, or parry, the noses of his champing horses, making them swing their heads and move their feet, disturbing a solid dreamy repose, he swore at the men as fools, for he himself could perceive that Providence had caused it clearly to be written, that he and his team had the unalienable right to stand in the proper path of the sun chariot, and if they so minded, obstruct its mission or take a wheel off.

And, perhaps, if the god-driver had an ungovernable desire to step down, put up his flame-colored[3] fists and manfully dispute the right of way, he would have probably been immediately opposed by a scowling mortal with two sets of very hard knuckles.

It is possible, perhaps, that this young man would have derided, in an axle-wide alley, the approach of a flying ferry boat. Yet he achieved a respect for a fire engine. As one charged toward his truck,

---

2. Sentence dropped in 1896 *Maggie*.

3. Another Homeric epithet (see second footnote

1 in Chapter I). Not hyphenated in 1893 *Maggie* but hyphenated in 1896 *Maggie*.

he would drive fearfully upon a sidewalk, threatening untold people with annihilation. When an engine would strike a mass of blocked trucks, splitting it into fragments, as a blow annihilates a cake of ice, Jimmie's team could usually be observed high and safe, with whole wheels, on the sidewalk. The fearful coming of the engine could break up the most intricate muddle of heavy vehicles at which the police had been swearing for the half of an hour.

A fire engine was enshrined in his heart as an appalling thing that he loved with a distant dog-like devotion. They had been known to overturn street cars. Those leaping horses, striking sparks from the cobbles in their forward lunge, were creatures to be ineffably admired. The clang of the gong pierced his breast like a noise of remembered war.

When Jimmie was a little boy, he began to be arrested. Before he reached a great age, he had a fair record.

He developed too great a tendency to climb down from his truck and fight with other drivers. He had been in quite a number of miscellaneous fights, and in some general barroom rows that had become known to the police. Once he had been arrested for assaulting a Chinaman. Two women in different parts of the city, and entirely unknown to each other, caused him considerable annoyance by breaking forth, simultaneously, at fateful intervals, into wailings about marriage and support and infants.

Nevertheless, he had, on a certain star-lit evening, said wonderingly and quite reverently: "Deh moon looks like hell, don't it?"

Chapter V

The girl, Maggie, blossomed in a mud puddle. She grew to be a most rare and wonderful production of a tenement district, a pretty girl.

None of the dirt of Rum Alley seemed to be in her veins. The philosophers up-stairs, down-stairs and on the same floor, puzzled over it.

When a child, playing and fighting with gamins in the street, dirt disguised[4] her. Attired in tatters and grime, she went unseen.

There came a time, however, when the young men of the vicinity said: "Dat Johnson goil is a puty good looker." About this period her brother remarked to her: "Mag, I'll tell yeh dis! See? Yeh've edder got teh go teh hell[5] or go teh work!" Whereupon she went to work, having the feminine aversion of going to hell.[6]

4. Several modern editions of *Maggie* wrongly print this as "disgusted."
5. Interestingly, the 1896 *Maggie* becomes more explicit: "go on d' toif" (turf, i.e., walk the streets as a prostitute) replaces "go teh hell."
6. In the 1896 *Maggie*, "of going to hell" was changed to "to the alternative."

By a chance, she got a position in an establishment where they made collars and cuffs. She received a stool and a machine in a room where sat twenty girls of various shades of yellow discontent. She perched on the stool and treadled at her machine all day, turning out collars, the name of whose brand could be noted for its irrelevancy to anything in connection with collars. At night she returned home to her mother.

Jimmie grew large enough to take the vague position of head of the family. As incumbent of that office, he stumbled up-stairs late at night, as his father had done before him. He reeled about the room, swearing at his relations, or went to sleep on the floor.

The mother had gradually arisen to that degree of fame that she could bandy words with her acquaintances among the police-justices. Court-officials called her by her first name. When she appeared they pursued a course which had been theirs for months. They invariably grinned and cried out: "Hello, Mary, you here again?" Her grey head wagged in many a court. She always besieged the bench with voluble excuses, explanations, apologies and prayers. Her flaming face and rolling eyes were a sort of familiar sight on the Island.[7] She measured time by means of sprees, and was eternally swollen and dishevelled.

One day the young man, Pete, who as a lad had smitten the Devil's Row urchin in the back of the head and put to flight the antagonists of his friend, Jimmie, strutted upon the scene. He met Jimmie one day on the street, promised to take him to a boxing match in Williamsburg,[8] and called for him in the evening.

Maggie observed Pete.

He sat on a table in the Johnson home and dangled his checked legs with an enticing nonchalance. His hair was curled down over his forehead in an oiled bang. His rather pugged nose seemed to revolt from contact with a bristling moustache of short, wire-like hairs. His blue double-breasted coat, edged with black braid, buttoned close to a red puff tie, and his patent-leather shoes looked like murder-fitted weapons.[9]

His mannerisms stamped him as a man who had a correct sense of his personal superiority. There was valor and contempt for circumstances in the glance of his eye. He waved his hands like a man of the world, who dismisses religion and philosophy, and says "Fudge."[1] He had certainly seen everything and with each curl of

---

7. Blackwell's Island (see first footnote 6 in Chapter I).
8. Formerly Williamsburgh, an incorporated city on the eastern shore of the East River that was merged into Brooklyn in 1855.
9. This description of Pete suggests the Bowery B'hoy (Boy), a tough of the Lower East Side who dressed as a "dandy." Manhattan's Lower East Side was a four-square-mile triangle bounded roughly by Fourteenth Street on the north, the Bowery on the west, and the East River on the east.
1. Exclamation of contempt suggesting "bunk" or "nonsense." Changed to "Rats!" in 1896 *Maggie*.

his lip, he declared that it amounted to nothing. Maggie thought he must be a very elegant and graceful bartender.

He was telling tales to Jimmie.

Maggie watched him furtively, with half-closed eyes, lit with a vague interest.

"Hully gee! Dey makes me tired," he said. "Mos' e'ry day some farmer[2] comes in an' tries teh run deh shop. See? But dey gits t'rowed right out! I jolt dem right out in deh street before dey knows where dey is! See?"

"Sure," said Jimmie.

"Dere was a mug come in deh place deh odder day wid an idear he wus goin' teh own deh place! Hully gee, he wus goin' teh own deh place! I see he had a still on[3] an' I didn' wanna giv 'im no stuff, so I says: 'Git deh hell outa here an' don' make no trouble,' I says like dat! See? 'Git deh hell outa here an' don' make no trouble'; like dat. 'Git deh hell outa here,' I says. See?"

Jimmie nodded understandingly. Over his features played an eager desire to state the amount of his valor in a similar crisis, but the narrator proceeded.

"Well, deh blokie he says: 'T'hell wid it! I ain' lookin' for no scrap,' he says (See?), 'but' he says, 'I'm 'spectable cit'zen an' I wanna drink an' purtydamnsoon, too.' See? 'Deh hell,' I says. Like dat! 'Deh hell,' I says. See? 'Don' make no trouble,' I says. Like dat. 'Don' make no trouble.' See? Den deh mug he squared off an' said he was fine as silk wid his dukes (See?) an' he wanned a drink damnquick. Dat's what he said. See?"

"Sure," repeated Jimmie.

Pete continued. "Say, I jes' jumped deh bar an' deh way I plunked[4] dat blokie was great. See? Dat's right! In deh jaw! See? Hully gee, he t'rowed a spittoon true deh front windee. Say, I taut I'd drop dead. But deh boss, he comes in after an' he says, 'Pete, yehs done jes' right! Yeh've gota keep order an' it's all right.' See? 'It's all right,' he says. Dat's what he said."

The two held a technical discussion.

"Dat bloke was a dandy," said Pete, in conclusion, "but he hadn' oughta made no trouble. Dat's what I says teh dem: 'Don' come in here an' make no trouble,' I says, like dat. 'Don' make no trouble.' See?"

As Jimmie and his friend exchanged tales descriptive of their prowess, Maggie leaned back in the shadow. Her eyes dwelt wonderingly and rather wistfully upon Pete's face. The broken furniture, grimy walls, and general disorder and dirt of her home of a sudden appeared

2. Disparaging slang for a "stupid person," a "greenhorn."

3. Slang for "inebriated" or "drunk."

4. Slang for "hit" or "strike a blow."

before her and began to take a potential aspect. Pete's aristocratic person looked as if it might soil. She looked keenly at him, occasionally, wondering if he was feeling contempt. But Pete seemed to be enveloped in reminiscence.

"Hully gee," said he, "dose mugs can't phase me. Dey knows I kin wipe up deh street wid any t'ree of dem."

When he said, "Ah, what deh hell," his voice was burdened with disdain for the inevitable and contempt for anything that fate might compel him to endure.

Maggie perceived that here was the beau ideal of a man. Her dim thoughts were often searching for far away lands where, as God says, the little hills sing together in the morning. Under the trees of her dream-gardens there had always walked a lover.[5]

Chapter VI

Pete took note of Maggie.

"Say, Mag, I'm stuck on yer shape. It's outa sight," he said, parenthetically, with an affable grin.

As he became aware that she was listening closely, he grew still more eloquent in his descriptions of various happenings in his career. It appeared that he was invincible in fights.

"Why," he said, referring to a man with whom he had had a misunderstanding, "dat mug scrapped like a damn dago.[6] Dat's right. He was dead easy. See? He taut he was a scrapper! But he foun' out diff'ent! Hully gee."

He walked to and fro in the small room, which seemed then to grow even smaller and unfit to hold his dignity, the attribute of a supreme warrior. That swing of the shoulders that had frozen the timid when he was but a lad had increased with his growth and education at the ratio of ten to one. It, combined with the sneer upon his mouth, told mankind that there was nothing in space which could appall him. Maggie marvelled at him and surrounded him with greatness. She vaguely tried to calculate the altitude of the pinnacle from which he must have looked down upon her.

"I met a chump deh odder day way up in deh city," he said. "I was goin' teh see a frien' of mine. When I was a-crossin' deh street deh chump runned plump inteh me, an' den he turns aroun' an' says, 'Yer insolen' ruffin,' he says, like dat. 'Oh, gee,' I says, 'oh, gee, go teh hell and git off deh eart',' I says, like dat. See? 'Go teh hell an' git off deh eart',' like dat. Den deh blokie he got wild. He says I was

---

5. Portions of last two sentences are suggestive biblical echoes from Psalms 98:8, 96:12, and 65:12.

6. Derogatory slang for one of Latin descent and of the working class. Here probably an Italian, one of the large immigrant groups in the Lower East Side in the 1890s.

a contempt'ble scoun'el, er somet'ing like dat, an' he says I was doom' teh everlastin' pe'dition an' all like dat. 'Gee,' I says, 'gee! Deh hell I am,' I says. 'Deh hell I am,' like dat. An' den I slugged 'im. See?"

With Jimmie in his company, Pete departed in a sort of a blaze of glory from the Johnson home. Maggie, leaning from the window, watched him as he walked down the street.

Here was a formidable man who disdained the strength of a world full of fists. Here was one who had contempt for brass-clothed power; one whose knuckles could defiantly ring against the granite of law. He was a knight.

The two men went from under the glimmering street-lamp and passed into shadows.

Turning, Maggie contemplated the dark, dust-stained walls, and the scant and crude furniture of her home. A clock, in a splintered and battered oblong box of varnished wood, she suddenly regarded as an abomination. She noted that it ticked raspingly. The almost vanished flowers in the carpet-pattern, she conceived to be newly hideous. Some faint attempts she had made with blue ribbon, to freshen the appearance of a dingy curtain, she now saw to be piteous.

She wondered what Pete dined on.

She reflected upon the collar and cuff factory. It began to appear to her mind as a dreary place of endless grinding. Pete's elegant occupation brought him, no doubt, into contact with people who had money and manners. It was probable that he had a large acquaintance of pretty girls. He must have great sums of money to spend.

To her the earth was composed of hardships and insults. She felt instant admiration for a man who openly defied it. She thought that if the grim angel of death should clutch his heart, Pete would shrug his shoulders and say: "Oh, ev'ryt'ing goes."

She anticipated that he would come again shortly. She spent some of her week's pay in the purchase of flowered cretonne for a lambrequin.[7] She made it with infinite care and hung it to the slightly-careening mantel, over the stove, in the kitchen. She studied it with painful anxiety from different points in the room. She wanted it to look well on Sunday night when, perhaps, Jimmie's friend would come. On Sunday night, however, Pete did not appear.

Afterward the girl looked at it with a sense of humiliation. She was now convinced that Pete was superior to admiration for lambrequins.

A few evenings later Pete entered with fascinating innovations in his apparel. As she had seen him twice and he had different suits on

---

7. Cretonne is a colorfully printed fabric of heavy unglazed cotton, linen, or rayon. A lambrequin is a drapery or curtain, usually hung from the edge of a shelf or above a window or doorway.

each time, Maggie had a dim impression that his wardrobe was prodigiously extensive.

"Say, Mag," he said, "put on yer bes' duds Friday night an' I'll take yehs teh deh show. See?"

He spent a few moments in flourishing his clothes and then vanished, without having glanced at the lambrequin.

Over the eternal collars and cuffs in the factory Maggie spent the most of three days in making imaginary sketches of Pete and his daily environment. She imagined some half dozen women in love with him and thought he must lean dangerously toward an indefinite one, whom she pictured with great charms of person, but with an altogether contemptible disposition.

She thought he must live in a blare of pleasure. He had friends, and people who were afraid of him.

She saw the golden glitter of the place where Pete was to take her. An entertainment of many hues and many melodies where she was afraid she might appear small and mouse-colored.

Her mother drank whiskey all Friday morning. With lurid face and tossing hair she cursed and destroyed furniture all Friday afternoon.[8] When Maggie came home at half-past six her mother lay asleep amidst the wreck of chairs and a table. Fragments of various household utensils were scattered about the floor. She had vented some phase of drunken fury upon the lambrequin. It lay in a bedraggled heap in the corner.

"Hah," she snorted, sitting up suddenly, "where deh hell yeh been? Why deh hell don' yeh come home earlier? Been loafin' 'round deh streets. Yer gettin' teh be a reg'lar devil."

When Pete arrived Maggie, in a worn black dress, was waiting for him in the midst of a floor strewn with wreckage. The curtain at the window had been pulled by a heavy hand and hung by one tack, dangling to and fro in the draft through the cracks at the sash. The knots of blue ribbons appeared like violated flowers.[9] The fire in the stove had gone out. The displaced lids and open doors showed heaps of sullen grey ashes. The remnants of a meal, ghastly, like dead flesh, lay in a corner. Maggie's red mother, stretched on the floor, blasphemed and gave her daughter a bad name.

Chapter VII

An orchestra of yellow silk women and bald-headed men on an elevated stage near the centre of a great green-hued hall, played a

8. The constant breaking of furniture in the Johnson household has been pointed out by some critics as unnaturalistic and unreal.

9. Foreshadows Maggie's seduction. Earlier she was identified with "blossomed."

popular waltz.[1] The place was crowded with people grouped about little tables. A battalion of waiters slid among the throng, carrying trays of beer glasses and making change from the inexhaustible vaults of their trousers pockets. Little boys, in the costumes of French chefs, paraded up and down the irregular aisles vending fancy cakes. There was a low rumble of conversation and a subdued clinking of glasses. Clouds of tobacco smoke rolled and wavered high in air about the dull gilt of the chandeliers.

The vast crowd had an air throughout of having just quitted labor. Men with calloused hands and attired in garments that showed the wear of an endless trudge[2] for a living, smoked their pipes contentedly and spent five, ten, or perhaps fifteen cents for beer. There was a mere sprinkling of kid-gloved men who smoked cigars purchased elsewhere. The great body of the crowd was composed of people who showed that all day they strove with their hands. Quiet Germans, with maybe their wives and two or three children, sat listening to the music, with the expressions of happy cows. An occasional party of sailors from a war-ship, their faces pictures of sturdy health, spent the earlier hours of the evening at the small round tables. Very infrequent tipsy men, swollen with the value of their opinions, engaged their companions in earnest and confidential conversation. In the balcony, and here and there below, shone the impassive faces of women. The nationalities of the Bowery[3] beamed upon the stage from all directions.

Pete aggressively walked up a side aisle and took seats with Maggie at a table beneath the balcony.

"Two beehs!"

Leaning back he regarded with eyes of superiority the scene before them. This attitude affected Maggie strongly. A man who could regard such a sight with indifference must be accustomed to very great things.

It was obvious that Pete had been to this place many times before, and was very familiar with it. A knowledge of this fact made Maggie feel little and new.

He was extremely gracious and attentive. He displayed the consideration of a cultured gentleman who knew what was due.

1. One of the three hall scenes which chart Maggie's degradation and downfall; others open Chapters XII and XIV. (See Janet Overmyer, "The Structure of Crane's *Maggie*," below.) This "great green-hued hall" was probably Atlantic Garden, where were planted trees and flowers. It was a well-known and reputable beer-garden of the day in the Bowery serving up to four thousand customers in an evening, especially Germans and their families. Women were featured in the or-chestra, which played Strauss and other music (here a "popular waltz").

2. Wearisome labor, plodding.

3. Located in the Lower East Side in Manhattan, the Bowery in Crane's day began at Chatham Square and extended as far as Cooper Square on Eighth Street, where Third and Fourth Avenues begin. Between 1880 and 1900 there were more and more saloons, concert and dance halls, dime museums, low-class theaters and dives, cheap lodging houses, and pawnshops in the Bowery.

"Say, what deh hell? Bring deh lady a big glass! What deh hell use is dat pony?"[4]

"Don't be fresh, now," said the waiter, with some warmth, as he departed.

"Ah, git off deh 'eart'," said Pete, after the other's retreating form.

Maggie perceived that Pete brought forth all his elegance and all his knowledge of high-class customs for her benefit. Her heart warmed as she reflected upon his condescension.

The orchestra of yellow silk women and bald-headed men gave vent to a few bars of anticipatory music and a girl, in a pink dress with short skirts, galloped upon the stage. She smiled upon the throng as if in acknowledgment of a warm welcome, and began to walk to and fro, making profuse gesticulations and singing, in brazen soprano tones, a song, the words of which were inaudible. When she broke into the swift rattling measures of a chorus some half-tipsy men near the stage joined in the rollicking refrain and glasses were pounded rhythmically upon the tables. People leaned forward to watch her and to try to catch the words of the song. When she vanished there were long rollings of applause.

Obedient to more anticipatory bars, she reappeared amidst the half-suppressed cheering of the tipsy men. The orchestra plunged into dance music and the laces of the dancer fluttered and flew in the glare of gas jets. She divulged the fact that she was attired in some half dozen skirts. It was patent that any one of them would have proved adequate for the purpose for which skirts are intended. An occasional man bent forward, intent upon the pink stockings. Maggie wondered at the splendor of the costume and lost herself in calculations of the cost of the silks and laces.

The dancer's smile of stereotyped enthusiasm was turned for ten minutes upon the faces of her audience. In the finale she fell into some of those grotesque attitudes which were at the time popular among the dancers in the theatres up-town, giving to the Bowery public the phantasies of the aristocratic theatre-going public, at reduced rates.

"Say, Pete," said Maggie, leaning forward, "dis is great."

"Sure," said Pete, with proper complacence.

A ventriloquist followed the dancer. He held two fantastic dolls on his knees. He made them sing mournful ditties and say funny things about geography and Ireland.

"Do dose little men talk?" asked Maggie.

"Naw," said Pete, "it's some damn fake. See?"

Two girls, on the bills as sisters, came forth and sang a duet that is heard occasionally at concerts given under church auspices. They

---

4. Small drinking glass.

supplemented it with a dance which of course can never be seen at concerts given under church auspices.

After the duettists had retired, a woman of debatable age sang a negro melody. The chorus necessitated some grotesque waddlings supposed to be an imitation of a plantation darkey, under the influence, probably, of music and the moon. The audience was just enthusiastic enough over it to have her return and sing a sorrowful lay,[5] whose lines told of a mother's love and a sweetheart who waited and a young man who was lost at sea under the most harrowing circumstances. From the faces of a score or so in the crowd, the self-contained look faded. Many heads were bent forward with eagerness and sympathy. As the last distressing sentiment of the piece was brought forth, it was greeted by that kind of applause which rings as sincere.

As a final effort, the singer rendered some verses which described a vision of Britain being annihilated by America,[6] and Ireland bursting her bonds. A carefully prepared crisis was reached in the last line of the last verse, where the singer threw out her arms and cried, "The star-spangled banner." Instantly a great cheer swelled from the throats of the assemblage of the masses.[7] There was a heavy rumble of booted feet thumping the floor. Eyes gleamed with sudden fire, and calloused hands waved frantically in the air.

After a few moments' rest, the orchestra played crashingly, and a small fat man burst out upon the stage. He began to roar a song and stamp back and forth before the foot-lights, wildly waving a glossy silk hat and throwing leers, or smiles, broadcast. He made his face into fantastic grimaces until he looked like a pictured devil on a Japanese kite. The crowd laughed gleefully. His short, fat legs were never still a moment. He shouted and roared and bobbed his shock of red wig until the audience broke out in excited applause.

Pete did not pay much attention to the progress of events upon the stage. He was drinking beer and watching Maggie.

Her cheeks were blushing with excitement and her eyes were glistening. She drew deep breaths of pleasure. No thoughts of the atmosphere of the collar and cuff factory came to her.

When the orchestra crashed finally, they jostled their way to the sidewalk with the crowd. Pete took Maggie's arm and pushed a way for her, offering to fight with a man or two.

They reached Maggie's home at a late hour and stood for a moment in front of the gruesome doorway.

"Say, Mag," said Pete, "give us a kiss for takin' yeh teh deh show, will yer?"

5. Narrative ballad usually dealing with love or adventure.
6. Reflects some of the anti-British feelings of the 1890s, including Crane's, who satirized British imperialism in "A Foreign Policy, in Three Glimpses" (1891?).
7. Here the 1896 *Maggie* adds ", most of them of foreign birth."

Maggie laughed, as if startled, and drew away from him.

"Naw, Pete," she said, "dat wasn't in it."

"Ah, what deh hell?" urged Pete.

The girl retreated nervously.

"Ah, what deh hell?" repeated he.

Maggie darted into the hall, and up the stairs. She turned and smiled at him, then disappeared.

Pete walked slowly down the street. He had something of an astonished expression upon his features. He paused under a lamp-post and breathed a low breath of surprise.

"Gawd," he said, "I wonner if I've been played fer a duffer."[8]

Chapter VIII

As thoughts of Pete came to Maggie's mind, she began to have an intense dislike for all of her dresses.

"What deh hell ails yeh? What makes yeh be allus fixin' and fussin'? Good Gawd," her mother would frequently roar at her.

She began to note, with more interest, the well-dressed women she met on the avenues. She envied elegance and soft palms. She craved those adornments of person which she saw every day on the street, conceiving them to be allies of vast importance to women.

Studying faces, she thought many of the women and girls she chanced to meet, smiled with serenity as though forever cherished and watched over by those they loved.

The air in the collar and cuff establishment strangled her. She knew she was gradually and surely shrivelling in the hot, stuffy room. The begrimed windows rattled incessantly from the passing of elevated trains. The place was filled with a whirl of noises and odors.[9]

She wondered as she regarded some of the grizzled women in the room, mere mechanical contrivances sewing seams and grinding out, with heads bended over their work, tales of imagined or real girlhood happiness, past drunks, the baby at home, and unpaid wages. She speculated how long her youth would endure. She began to see the bloom upon her cheeks as valuable.

She imagined herself, in an exasperating future, as a scrawny woman with an eternal grievance. Too, she thought Pete to be a very fastidious person concerning the appearance of women.

She felt she would love to see somebody entangle their fingers in the oily beard of the fat foreigner who owned the establishment. He was a detestable creature. He wore white socks with low shoes.

8. Slang for "stupid person" or "fool."
9. This paragraph more clearly suggests a sweatshop of the day than does the previous description of Maggie's place of employment. See Riis's *How the Other Half Lives*, below.

He sat all day delivering orations, in the depths of a cushioned chair. His pocket-book deprived them of the power of retort.

"What een hell do you sink I pie fife dolla a week for? Play? No, py damn!"

Maggie was anxious for a friend to whom she could talk about Pete. She would have liked to discuss his admirable mannerisms with a reliable mutual friend. At home, she found her mother often drunk and always raving.

It seems that the world had treated this woman very badly, and she took a deep revenge upon such portions of it as came within her reach. She broke furniture as if she were at last getting her rights. She swelled with virtuous indignation as she carried the lighter articles of household use, one by one under the shadows of the three gilt balls,[1] where Hebrews chained them with chains of interest.[2]

Jimmie came when he was obliged to by circumstances over which he had no control. His well-trained legs brought him staggering home and put him to bed some nights when he would rather have gone elsewhere.

Swaggering Pete loomed like a golden sun to Maggie. He took her to a dime museum[3] where rows of meek freaks astonished her. She contemplated their deformities with awe and thought them a sort of chosen tribe.

Pete, raking[4] his brains for amusement, discovered the Central Park Menagerie and the Museum of Arts.[5] Sunday afternoons would sometimes find them at these places. Pete did not appear to be particularly interested in what he saw. He stood around looking heavy, while Maggie giggled in glee.

Once at the Menagerie he went into a trance of admiration before the spectacle of a very small monkey threatening to thrash a cageful because one of them had pulled his tail and he had not wheeled about quickly enough to discover who did it. Ever after Pete knew that monkey by sight and winked at him, trying to induce him to fight with other and larger monkeys.

At the Museum, Maggie said, "Dis is outa sight."

"Oh hell," said Pete, "wait till next summer an' I'll take yehs to a picnic."

While the girl wandered in the vaulted rooms, Pete occupied himself in returning stony stare for stony stare, the appalling scrutiny of the watch-dogs of the treasures. Occasionally he would remark in loud tones: "Dat jay[6] has got glass eyes," and sentences of the sort.

1. Pawnshop.
2. Like Riis and others, Crane here reflects the ethnic stereotypes of the day. (Also note the descriptions of Maggie's employer.)
3. Popular amusement centers of the day with wax figures, mechanized contrivances, and panoramic views.
4. Changed to "racking" in the 1896 *Maggie*.
5. The Central Park Menagerie (Zoological Garden), located on the east side of Central Park, opposite the Fifth Avenue and 64th Street entrance. This building and several others housed collections of animals, birds, and reptiles. The Metropolitan Museum of Art, located on Fifth Avenue and 82nd Street.
6. Slang for "stupid person," "inexperienced."

When he tired of this amusement he would go to the mummies and moralize over them.

Usually he submitted with silent dignity to all which he had to go through, but, at times, he was goaded into comment.

"What deh hell," he demanded once. "Look at all dese little jugs! Hundred jugs in a row! Ten rows in a case an' 'bout a t'ousand cases! What deh blazes use is dem?"

Evenings during the week he took her to see plays in which the brain-clutching heroine was rescued from the palatial home of her guardian, who is cruelly after her bonds, by the hero with the beautiful sentiments. The latter spent most of his time out at soak in pale-green snow storms, busy with a nickel-plated revolver, rescuing aged strangers from villains.[7]

Maggie lost herself in sympathy with the wanderers swooning in snow storms beneath happy-hued church windows. And a choir within singing "Joy to the World." To Maggie and the rest of the audience this was transcendental realism. Joy always within, and they, like the actor, inevitably without. Viewing it, they hugged themselves in ecstatic pity of their imagined or real condition.

The girl thought the arrogance and granite-heartedness of the magnate of the play was very accurately drawn. She echoed the maledictions that the occupants of the gallery showered on this individual when his lines compelled him to expose his extreme selfishness.

Shady persons in the audience revolted from the pictured villainy of the drama. With untiring zeal they hissed vice and applauded virtue. Unmistakably bad men evinced an apparently sincere admiration for virtue.

The loud gallery was overwhelmingly with the unfortunate and the oppressed. They encouraged the struggling hero with cries, and jeered the villain, hooting and calling attention to his whiskers. When anybody died in the pale-green snow storms, the gallery mourned. They sought out the painted misery and hugged it as akin.

In the hero's erratic march from poverty in the first act, to wealth and triumph in the final one, in which he forgives all the enemies that he has left, he was assisted by the gallery, which applauded his generous and noble sentiments and confounded the speeches of his opponents by making irrelevant but very sharp remarks. Those actors who were cursed with villainy parts were confronted at every turn by the gallery. If one of them rendered lines containing the most subtile distinctions between right and wrong, the gallery was immediately aware if the actor meant wickedness, and denounced him accordingly.

The last act was a triumph for the hero, poor and of the masses,

7. Crane's satirical view of the popular melodramas of the day. See his "Some Hints for Play-Makers" (November 4, 1893).

the representative of the audience, over the villain and the rich man, his pockets stuffed with bonds, his heart packed with tyrannical purposes, imperturbable amid suffering.

Maggie always departed with raised spirits from the showing places of the melodrama. She rejoiced at the way in which the poor and virtuous eventually surmounted the wealthy and wicked. The theatre made her think. She wondered if the culture and refinement she had seen imitated, perhaps grotesquely, by the heroine on the stage, could be acquired by a girl who lived in a tenement house and worked in a shirt factory.

Chapter IX

A group of urchins were intent upon the side door of a saloon. Expectancy gleamed from their eyes. They were twisting their fingers in excitement.

"Here she comes," yelled one of them suddenly.

The group of urchins burst instantly asunder and its individual fragments were spread in a wide, respectable half-circle about the point of interest. The saloon door opened with a crash, and the figure of a woman appeared upon the threshold. Her grey hair fell in knotted masses about her shoulders. Her face was crimsoned and wet with perspiration. Her eyes had a rolling glare.

"Not a damn cent more of me money will yehs ever get, not a damn cent. I spent me money here fer t'ree years an' now yehs tells me yeh'll sell me no more stuff! T'hell wid yeh, Johnnie Murckre! 'Disturbance'? Disturbance be damned! T'hell wid yeh, Johnnie—"

The door received a kick of exasperation from within and the woman lurched heavily out on the sidewalk.

The gamins in the half-circle became violently agitated. They began to dance about and hoot and yell and jeer. Wide dirty grins spread over each face.

The woman made a furious dash at a particularly outrageous cluster of little boys. They laughed delightedly and scampered off a short distance, calling out over their shoulders to her. She stood tottering on the curb-stone and thundered at them.

"Yeh devil's kids," she howled, shaking red fists. The little boys whooped in glee. As she started up the street they fell in behind and marched uproariously. Occasionally she wheeled about and made charges on them. They ran nimbly out of reach and taunted her.

In the frame of a gruesome doorway she stood for a moment cursing them. Her hair straggled, giving her crimson features a look of insanity. Her great fists quivered as she shook them madly in the air.

The urchins made terrific noises until she turned and disappeared. Then they filed quietly in the way they had come.

The woman floundered about in the lower hall of the tenement house and finally stumbled up the stairs. On an upper hall a door was opened and a collection of heads peered curiously out, watching her. With a wrathful snort the woman confronted the door, but it was slammed hastily in her face and the key was turned.

She stood for a few minutes, delivering a frenzied challenge at the panels.

"Come out in deh hall, Mary Murphy, damn yeh, if yehs want a row.[8] Come ahn, yeh overgrown terrier, come ahn."

She began to kick the door with her great feet. She shrilly defied the universe to appear and do battle. Her cursing trebles brought heads from all doors save the one she threatened. Her eyes glared in every direction. The air was full of her tossing fists.

"Come ahn, deh hull damn gang of yehs, come ahn," she roared at the spectators. An oath or two, cat-calls, jeers and bits of facetious advice were given in reply. Missiles clattered about her feet.

"What deh hell's deh matter wid yeh?" said a voice in the gathered gloom, and Jimmie came forward. He carried a tin dinner-pail in his hand and under his arm a brown truckman's apron done in a bundle. "What deh hell's wrong?" he demanded.

"Come out, all of yehs, come out," his mother was howling. "Come ahn an' I'll stamp yer damn brains under me feet."[9]

"Shet yer face, an' come home, yeh damned old fool," roared Jimmie at her. She strided up to him and twirled her fingers in his face. Her eyes were darting flames of unreasoning rage and her frame trembled with eagerness for a fight.

"T'hell wid yehs! An' who deh hell are yehs? I ain't givin' a snap of me fingers fer yehs," she bawled at him. She turned her huge back in tremendous disdain and climbed the stairs to the next floor.

Jimmie followed, cursing blackly. At the top of the flight he seized his mother's arm and started to drag her toward the door of their room.

"Come home, damn yeh," he gritted between his teeth.

"Take yer hands off me! Take yer hands off me," shrieked his mother.

She raised her arm and whirled her great fist at her son's face. Jimmie dodged his head and the blow struck him in the back of the neck. "Damn yeh," gritted he again. He threw out his left hand and writhed his fingers about her middle arm. The mother and the son began to sway and struggle like gladiators.

---

8. Quarrel or fight.

9. In the 1896 *Maggie*, "damn brains under me feet" was changed to "faces tru d' floor."

"Whoop!" said the Rum Alley tenement house. The hall filled with interested spectators.

"Hi, ol' lady, dat was a dandy!"

"T'ree to one on deh red!"

"Ah, stop yer damn scrappin'!"

The door of the Johnson home opened and Maggie looked out. Jimmie made a supreme cursing effort and hurled his mother into the room. He quickly followed and closed the door. The Rum Alley tenement swore disappointedly and retired.

The mother slowly gathered herself up from the floor. Her eyes glittered menacingly upon her children.

"Here, now," said Jimmie, "we've had enough of dis. Sit down, an' don' make no trouble."

He grasped her arm, and twisting it, forced her into a creaking chair.

"Keep yer hands off me," roared his mother again.

"Damn yer ol' hide," yelled Jimmie, madly. Maggie shrieked and ran into the other room. To her there came the sound of a storm of crashes and curses. There was a great final thump and Jimmie's voice cried: "Dere, damn yeh, stay still." Maggie opened the door now, and went warily out. "Oh, Jimmie."

He was leaning against the wall and swearing. Blood stood upon bruises on his knotty fore-arms where they had scraped against the floor or the walls in the scuffle. The mother lay screeching on the floor, the tears running down her furrowed face.

Maggie, standing in the middle of the room, gazed about her. The usual upheaval of the tables and chairs had taken place. Crockery was strewn broadcast in fragments. The stove had been disturbed on its legs, and now leaned idiotically to one side. A pail had been upset and water spread in all directions.

The door opened and Pete appeared. He shrugged his shoulders. "Oh, Gawd," he observed.

He walked over to Maggie and whispered in her ear. "Ah, what deh hell, Mag? Come ahn and we'll have a hell of a time."

The mother in the corner upreared her head and shook her tangled locks.

"Teh hell wid him and you," she said, glowering at her daughter in the gloom. Her eyes seemed to burn balefully. "Yeh've gone teh deh devil, Mag Johnson, yehs knows yehs have gone teh deh devil. Yer a disgrace teh yer people, damn yeh. An' now, git out an' go ahn wid dat doe-faced jude[1] of yours. Go teh hell wid him, damn yeh, an' a good riddance. Go teh hell an' see how yeh likes it."

Maggie gazed long at her mother.

---

1. Probably suggests "dude," for Pete is concerned about his clothes and appearance. Note that he is called "doe-faced."

"Go teh hell now, an' see how yeh likes it. Git out. I won't have sech as yehs in me house! Get out, d'yeh hear! Damn yeh, git out!"

The girl began to tremble.

At this instant Pete came forward. "Oh, what deh hell, Mag, see," whispered he softly in her ear. "Dis all blows over. See? Deh ol' woman 'ill be all right in deh mornin'. Come ahn out wid me! We'll have a hell of a time."

The woman on the floor cursed. Jimmie was intent upon his bruised fore-arms. The girl cast a glance about the room filled with a chaotic mass of debris, and at the red, writhing body of her mother.

"Go teh hell an' good riddance."[2]

She went.

Chapter X

Jimmie had an idea it wasn't common courtesy for a friend to come to one's home and ruin one's sister. But he was not sure how much Pete knew about the rules of politeness.

The following night he returned home from work at rather a late hour in the evening. In passing through the halls he came upon the gnarled and leathery old woman who possessed the music box. She was grinning in the dim light that drifted through dust-stained panes. She beckoned to him with a smudged forefinger.

"Ah, Jimmie, what do yehs t'ink I got onto las' night. It was deh funnies' t'ing I ever saw," she cried, coming close to him and leering. She was trembling with eagerness to tell her tale. "I was by me door las' night when yer sister and her jude feller came in late, oh, very late. An' she, the dear, she was a-cryin' as if her heart would break, she was. It was deh funnies' t'ing I ever saw. An' right out here by me door she asked him did he love her, did he. An' she was a-cryin' as if her heart would break, poor t'ing. An' him, I could see by deh way what he said it dat she had been askin' orften, he says: 'Oh, hell, yes,' he says, says he, 'Oh, hell, yes.'"

Storm-clouds swept over Jimmie's face, but he turned from the leathery old woman and plodded on up-stairs.

"Oh, hell, yes," called she after him. She laughed a laugh that was like a prophetic croak. "'Oh, hell, yes,' he says, says he, 'Oh, hell, yes.'"

There was no one in at home. The rooms showed that attempts had been made at tidying them. Parts of the wreckage of the day before had been repaired by an unskilful hand. A chair or two and the table, stood uncertainly upon legs. The floor had been newly swept. Too, the blue ribbons had been restored to the curtains, and

2. This sentence becomes "Git th' devil outa here" in the 1896 *Maggie*.

the lambrequin, with its immense sheaves of yellow wheat and red roses of equal size, had been returned, in a worn and sorry state, to its position at the mantel. Maggie's jacket and hat were gone from the nail behind the door.

Jimmie walked to the window and began to look through the blurred glass. It occurred to him to vaguely wonder, for an instant, if some of the women of his acquaintance had brothers.

Suddenly, however, he began to swear.

"But he was me frien'! I brought 'im here! Dat's deh hell of it!"

He fumed about the room, his anger gradually rising to the furious pitch.

"I'll kill deh jay! Dat's what I'll do! I'll kill deh jay!"

He clutched his hat and sprang toward the door. But it opened and his mother's great form blocked the passage.

"What deh hell's deh matter wid yeh?" exclaimed she, coming into the rooms.

Jimmie gave vent to a sardonic curse and then laughed heavily.

"Well, Maggie's gone teh deh devil! Dat's what! See?"

"Eh?" said his mother.

"Maggie's gone teh deh devil! Are yehs deaf?" roared Jimmie, impatiently.

"Deh hell she has," murmured the mother, astounded.

Jimmie grunted, and then began to stare out at the window. His mother sat down in a chair, but a moment later sprang erect and delivered a maddened whirl of oaths. Her son turned to look at her as she reeled and swayed in the middle of the room, her fierce face convulsed with passion, her blotched arms raised high in imprecation.

"May Gawd curse her forever," she shrieked. "May she eat nothin' but stones and deh dirt in deh street. May she sleep in deh gutter an' never see deh sun shine agin. Deh damn—"

"Here, now," said her son. "Take a drop on yourself."[3]

The mother raised lamenting eyes to the ceiling.

"She's deh devil's own chil', Jimmie," she whispered. "Ah, who would t'ink such a bad girl could grow up in our fambly, Jimmie, me son. Many deh hour I've spent in talk wid dat girl an' tol' her if she ever went on deh streets I'd see her damned. An' after all her bringin' up an' what I tol' her and talked wid her, she goes teh deh bad, like a duck teh water."

The tears rolled down her furrowed face. Her hands trembled.

"An' den when dat Sadie MacMallister next door to us was sent teh deh devil by dat feller what worked in deh soap-factory, didn't I tell our Mag dat if she—"

---

3. Sentence changed to "Go fall on yerself, an' quit dat" in the 1896 *Maggie*.

"Ah, dat's anudder story," interrupted the brother. "Of course, dat Sadie was nice an' all dat—but—see—it ain't dessame as if—well, Maggie was diff'ent—see—she was diff'ent."

He was trying to formulate a theory that he had always unconsciously held, that all sisters, excepting his own, could advisedly be ruined.

He suddenly broke out again. "I'll go t'ump hell outa deh mug what did her deh harm. I'll kill 'im! He t'inks he kin scrap, but when he gits me a-chasin' 'im he'll fin' out where he's wrong, deh damned duffer. I'll wipe up deh street wid 'im."

In a fury he plunged out of the doorway. As he vanished the mother raised her head and lifted both hands, entreating.

"May Gawd curse her forever," she cried.

In the darkness of the hallway Jimmie discerned a knot of women talking volubly. When he strode by they paid no attention to him.

"She allus was a bold thing," he heard one of them cry in an eager voice. "Dere wasn't a feller come teh deh house but she'd try teh mash[4] 'im. My Annie says deh shameless t'ing tried teh ketch her feller, her own feller, what we useter know his fader."

"I could a' tol' yehs dis two years ago," said a woman, in a key of triumph. "Yessir, it was over two years ago dat I says teh my ol' man, I says, 'Dat Johnson girl ain't straight,' I says. 'Oh, hell,' he says. 'Oh, hell.' 'Dat's all right,' I says, 'but I know what I knows,' I says, 'an' it 'ill come out later. You wait an' see,' I says, 'you see.'"

"Anybody what had eyes could see dat dere was somethin' wrong wid dat girl. I didn't like her actions."

On the street Jimmie met a friend. "What deh hell?" asked the latter.

Jimmie explained. "An' I'll t'ump 'im till he can't stand."

"Oh, what deh hell," said the friend. "What's deh use! Yeh'll git pulled in! Everybody 'ill be onto it! An' ten plunks![5] Gee!"

Jimmie was determined. "He t'inks he kin scrap, but he'll fin' out diff'ent."

"Gee," remonstrated the friend. "What deh hell?"

Chapter XI

On a corner a glass-fronted building shed a yellow glare upon the pavements. The open mouth of a saloon called seductively to passengers to enter and annihilate sorrow or create rage.

The interior of the place was papered in olive and bronze tints of imitation leather. A shining bar of counterfeit massiveness extended down the side of the room. Behind it a great mahogany-appearing

---

4. Slang for "entice" or "flirt with."   5. Slang for "dollars."

sideboard reached the ceiling. Upon its shelves rested pyramids of shimmering glasses that were never disturbed. Mirrors set in the face of the sideboard multiplied them. Lemons, oranges and paper napkins, arranged with mathematical precision, sat among the glasses. Many-hued decanters of liquor perched at regular intervals on the lower shelves. A nickel-plated cash register occupied a position in the exact centre of the general effect. The elementary senses of it all seemed to be opulence and geometrical accuracy.

Across from the bar a smaller counter held a collection of plates upon which swarmed frayed fragments of crackers, slices of boiled ham, dishevelled bits of cheese, and pickles swimming in vinegar. An odor of grasping, begrimed hands and munching mouths pervaded.

Pete, in a white jacket, was behind the bar bending expectantly toward a quiet stranger. "A beeh," said the man. Pete drew a foam-topped glassful and set it dripping upon the bar.

At this moment the light bamboo doors at the entrance swung open and crashed against the siding. Jimmie and a companion entered. They swaggered unsteadily but belligerently toward the bar and looked at Pete with bleared and blinking eyes.

"Gin," said Jimmie.

"Gin," said the companion.

Pete slid a bottle and two glasses along the bar. He bended his head sideways as he assiduously polished away with a napkin at the gleaming wood. He had a look of watchfulness upon his features.

Jimmie and his companion kept their eyes upon the bartender and conversed loudly in tones of contempt.

"He's a dindy[6] masher, ain't he, by Gawd?" laughed Jimmie.

"Oh, hell, yes," said the companion, sneering widely. "He's great, he is. Git onto deh mug on deh blokie. Dat's enough to make a feller turn hand-springs in 'is sleep."

The quiet stranger moved himself and his glass a trifle further away and maintained an attitude of oblivion.

"Gee! ain't he hot stuff!"

"Git onto his shape! Great Gawd!"

"Hey," cried Jimmie, in tones of command. Pete came along slowly, with a sullen dropping of the under lip.

"Well," he growled, "what's eatin' yehs?"

"Gin," said Jimmie.

"Gin," said the companion.

As Pete confronted them with the bottle and the glasses, they laughed in his face. Jimmie's companion, evidently overcome with merriment, pointed a grimy forefinger in Pete's direction.

---

6. Changed to "dandy" in the 1896 *Maggie*.

"Say, Jimmie," demanded he, "what deh hell is dat behind deh bar?"

"Damned if I knows," replied Jimmie. They laughed loudly. Pete put down a bottle with a bang and turned a formidable face toward them. He disclosed his teeth and his shoulders heaved restlessly.

"You fellers can't guy[7] me," he said. "Drink yer stuff an' git out an' don' make no trouble."

Instantly the laughter faded from the faces of the two men and expressions of offended dignity immediately came.

"Who deh hell has said anyt'ing teh you," cried they in the same breath.

The quiet stranger looked at the door calculatingly.

"Ah, come off," said Pete to the two men. "Don't pick me up for no jay. Drink yer rum an' git out an' don' make no trouble."

"Oh, deh hell," airily cried Jimmie.

"Oh, deh hell," airily repeated his companion.

"We goes when we git ready! See!" continued Jimmie.

"Well," said Pete in a threatening voice, "don' make no trouble."

Jimmie suddenly leaned forward with his head on one side. He snarled like a wild animal.

"Well, what if we does? See?" said he.

Dark blood flushed into Pete's face, and he shot a lurid glance at Jimmie.

"Well, den we'll see whose[8] deh bes' man, you or me," he said.

The quiet stranger moved modestly toward the door.

Jimmie began to swell with valor.

"Don' pick me up fer no tenderfoot.[9] When yeh tackles me yeh tackles one of deh bes' men in deh city. See? I'm a scrapper, I am. Ain't dat right, Billie?"

"Sure, Mike," responded his companion in tones of conviction.

"Oh, hell," said Pete, easily. "Go fall on yerself."

The two men again began to laugh.

"What deh hell is dat talkin'?" cried the companion.

"Damned if I knows," replied Jimmie with exaggerated contempt.

Pete made a furious gesture. "Git outa here now, an' don' make no trouble. See? Youse fellers er lookin' fer a scrap an' it's damn likely yeh'll fin' one if yeh keeps on shootin' off yer mout's. I know yehs! See? I kin lick better men dan yehs ever saw in yer lifes. Dat's right! See? Don' pick me up fer no stuff er yeh might be jolted out in deh street before yeh knows where yeh is. When I comes from behind dis bar, I t'rows yehs bote inteh deh street. See?"

"Oh, hell," cried the two men in chorus.

---

7. Slang for "make fun of," "ridicule."
8. Changed to "who's" in 1896 *Maggie*.

9. Inexperienced person; novice.

The glare of a panther came into Pete's eyes. "Dat's what I said! Unnerstan'?"

He came through a passage at the end of the bar and swelled down upon the two men. They stepped promptly forward and crowded close to him.

They bristled like three roosters. They moved their heads pugnaciously and kept their shoulders braced. The nervous muscles about each mouth twitched with a forced smile of mockery.

"Well, what deh hell yer goin' teh do?" gritted Jimmie.

Pete stepped warily back, waving his hands before him to keep the men from coming too near.

"Well, what deh hell yer goin' teh do?" repeated Jimmie's ally. They kept close to him, taunting and leering. They strove to make him attempt the initial blow.

"Keep back, now! Don' crowd me," ominously said Pete.

Again they chorused in contempt. "Oh, hell!"

In a small, tossing group, the three men edged for positions like frigates contemplating battle.

"Well, why deh hell don' yeh try teh t'row us out?" cried Jimmie and his ally with copious sneers.

The bravery of bull-dogs sat upon the faces of the men. Their clenched fists moved like eager weapons.

The allied two jostled the bartender's elbows, glaring at him with feverish eyes and forcing him toward the wall.

Suddenly Pete swore redly. The flash of action gleamed from his eyes. He threw back his arm and aimed a tremendous, lightning-like blow at Jimmie's face. His foot swung a step forward and the weight of his body was behind his fist. Jimmie ducked his head, Bowery-like, with the quickness of a cat. The fierce, answering blows of him and his ally crushed on Pete's bowed head.

The quiet stranger vanished.

The arms of the combatants whirled in the air like flails. The faces of the men, at first flushed to flame-colored anger, now began to fade to the pallor of warriors in the blood and heat of a battle. Their lips curled back and stretched tightly over the gums in ghoul-like grins. Through their white, gripped teeth struggled hoarse whisperings of oaths. Their eyes glittered with murderous fire.

Each head was huddled between its owner's shoulders, and arms were swinging with marvelous rapidity. Feet scraped to and fro with a loud scratching sound upon the sanded floor. Blows left crimson blotches upon pale skin. The curses of the first quarter minute of the fight died away. The breaths of the fighters came wheezingly from their lips and the three chests were straining and heaving. Pete at intervals gave vent to low, labored hisses, that sounded like a desire to kill. Jimmie's ally gibbered at times like a wounded maniac. Jimmie was silent, fighting with the face of a sacrificial priest. The rage of fear shone in all their eyes and their blood-colored fists swirled.

At a tottering moment a blow from Pete's hand struck the ally and he crashed to the floor. He wriggled instantly to his feet and grasping the quiet stranger's beer glass from the bar, hurled it at Pete's head.

High on the wall it burst like a bomb, shivering fragments flying in all directions. Then missiles came to every man's hand. The place had heretofore appeared free of things to throw, but suddenly glass and bottles went singing through the air. They were thrown point blank at bobbing heads. The pyramid of shimmering glasses, that had never been disturbed, changed to cascades as heavy bottles were flung into them. Mirrors splintered to nothing.

The three frothing creatures on the floor buried themselves in a frenzy for blood. There followed in the wake of missiles and fists some unknown prayers, perhaps for death.

The quiet stranger had sprawled very pyrotechnically out on the sidewalk. A laugh ran up and down the avenue for the half of a block.

"Dey've t'rowed a bloke inteh deh street."

People heard the sound of breaking glass and shuffling feet within the saloon and came running. A small group, bending down to look under the bamboo doors, watching the fall of glass, and three pairs of violent legs, changed in a moment to a crowd.

A policeman came charging down the sidewalk and bounced through the doors into the saloon. The crowd bended and surged in absorbing anxiety to see.

Jimmie caught first sight of the on-coming interruption. On his feet he had the same regard for a policeman that, when on his truck, he had for a fire engine. He howled and ran for the side door.

The officer made a terrific advance, club in hand. One comprehensive sweep of the long night stick threw the ally to the floor and forced Pete to a corner. With his disengaged hand he made a furious effort at Jimmie's coat-tails. Then he regained his balance and paused.

"Well, well, you are a pair of pictures. What in hell yeh been up to?"

Jimmie, with his face drenched in blood, escaped up a side street, pursued a short distance by some of the more law-loving, or excited individuals of the crowd.

Later, from a corner safely dark, he saw the policeman, the ally and the bartender emerge from the saloon. Pete locked the doors and then followed up the avenue in the rear of the crowd-encompassed policeman and his charge.

On first thoughts Jimmie, with his heart throbbing at battle heat, started to go desperately to the rescue of his friend, but he halted.

"Ah, what deh hell?" he demanded of himself.

Chapter XII

In a hall of irregular shape sat Pete and Maggie drinking beer. A submissive orchestra dictated to by a spectacled man with frowsy hair and a dress suit, industriously followed the bobs of his head and the waves of his baton. A ballad singer, in a dress of flaming scarlet, sang in the inevitable voice of brass. When she vanished, men seated at the tables near the front applauded loudly, pounding the polished wood with their beer glasses. She returned attired in less gown, and sang again. She received another enthusiastic encore. She reappeared in still less gown and danced. The deafening rumble of glasses and clapping of hands that followed her exit indicated an overwhelming desire to have her come on for the fourth time, but the curiosity of the audience was not gratified.

Maggie was pale. From her eyes had been plucked all look of self-reliance. She leaned with a dependent air toward her companion. She was timid, as if fearing his anger or displeasure. She seemed to beseech tenderness of him.

Pete's air of distinguished valor had grown upon him until it threatened stupendous dimensions. He was infinitely gracious to the girl. It was apparent to her that his condescension was a marvel.

He could appear to strut even while sitting still and he showed that he was a lion of lordly characteristics by the air with which he spat.

With Maggie gazing at him wonderingly, he took pride in commanding the waiters who were, however, indifferent or deaf.

"Hi, you, git a russle[1] on yehs! What deh hell yehs lookin' at? Two more beehs, d'yeh hear?"

He leaned back and critically regarded the person of a girl with a straw-colored wig who upon the stage was flinging her heels in somewhat awkward imitation of a well-known danseuse.[2]

At times Maggie told Pete long confidential tales of her former home life, dwelling upon the escapades of the other members of the family and the difficulties she had to combat in order to obtain a degree of comfort. He responded in tones of philanthropy. He pressed her arm with an air of reassuring proprietorship.

"Dey was damn jays," he said, denouncing the mother and brother.

The sound of the music which, by the efforts of the frowsy-headed leader, drifted to her ears through the smoke-filled atmosphere, made

---

1. Slang for "move," "hustle." 2. Female ballet dancer.

the girl dream. She thought of her former Rum Alley environment and turned to regard Pete's strong protecting fists. She thought of the collar and cuff manufactory and the eternal moan of the proprietor: "What een hell do you sink I pie fife dolla a week for? Play? No, py damn." She contemplated Pete's man-subduing eyes and noted that wealth and prosperity was indicated by his clothes. She imagined a future, rose-tinted, because of its distance from all that she previously had experienced.

As to the present she perceived only vague reasons to be miserable. Her life was Pete's and she considered him worthy of the charge. She would be disturbed by no particular apprehensions, so long as Pete adored her as he now said he did. She did not feel like a bad woman. To her knowledge she had never seen any better.

At times men at other tables regarded the girl furtively. Pete, aware of it, nodded at her and grinned. He felt proud.

"Mag, yer a bloomin' good-looker," he remarked, studying her face through the haze. The men made Maggie fear, but she blushed at Pete's words as it became apparent to her that she was the apple of his eye.

Grey-headed men, wonderfully pathetic in their dissipation, stared at her through clouds. Smooth-cheeked boys, some of them with faces of stone and mouths of sin, not nearly so pathetic as the grey heads, tried to find the girl's eyes in the smoke wreaths. Maggie considered she was not what they thought her. She confined her glances to Pete and the stage.

The orchestra played negro melodies and a versatile drummer pounded, whacked, clattered and scratched on a dozen machines to make noise.

Those glances of the men, shot at Maggie from under half-closed lids, made her tremble. She thought them all to be worse men than Pete.

"Come, let's go," she said.

As they went out Maggie perceived two women seated at a table with some men. They were painted and their cheeks had lost their roundness. As she passed them the girl, with a shrinking movement, drew back her skirts.

Chapter XIII

Jimmie did not return home for a number of days after the fight with Pete in the saloon. When he did, he approached with extreme caution.

He found his mother raving. Maggie had not returned home. The parent continually wondered how her daughter could come to such a pass. She had never considered Maggie as a pearl dropped unstained into Rum Alley from Heaven, but she could not conceive how it was possible for her daughter to fall so low as to bring disgrace upon her family. She was terrific in denunciation of the girl's wickedness.

The fact that the neighbors talked of it, maddened her. When women came in, and in the course of their conversation casually asked, "Where's Maggie dese days?" the mother shook her fuzzy head at them and appalled them with curses. Cunning hints inviting confidence she rebuffed with violence.

"An' wid all deh bringin' up she had, how could she?" moaningly she asked of her son. "Wid all deh talkin' wid her I did an' deh t'ings I tol' her to remember? When a girl is bringed up deh way I bringed up Maggie, how kin she go teh deh devil?"

Jimmie was transfixed by these questions. He could not conceive how under the circumstances his mother's daughter and his sister could have been so wicked.

His mother took a drink from a squdgy³ bottle that sat on the table. She continued her lament.

"She had a bad heart, dat girl did, Jimmie. She was wicked teh deh heart an' we never knowed it."

Jimmie nodded, admitting the fact.

"We lived in deh same house wid her an' I brought her up an' we never knowed how bad she was."

Jimmie nodded again.

"Wid a home like dis an' a mudder like me, she went teh deh bad," cried the mother, raising her eyes.

One day, Jimmie came home, sat down in a chair and began to wriggle about with a new and strange nervousness. At last he spoke shamefacedly.

"Well, look-a-here, dis t'ing queers us! See? We're queered! An' maybe it 'ud be better if I—well, I t'ink I kin look 'er up an'—maybe it 'ud be better if I fetched her home an'—"

The mother started from her chair and broke forth into a storm of passionate anger.

"What! Let 'er come an' sleep under deh same roof wid her mudder agin! Oh, yes, I will, won't I? Sure? Shame on yehs, Jimmie Johnson, fer sayin' such a t'ing teh yer own mudder—teh yer own mudder! Little did I t'ink when yehs was a babby playin' about me feet dat ye'd grow up teh say sech a t'ing teh yer mudder—yer own mudder. I never taut—"

Sobs choked her and interrupted her reproaches.

"Dere ain't nottin' teh raise sech hell about," said Jimmie. "I on'y says it 'ud be better if we keep dis t'ing dark, see? It queers us! See?"

3. Squat.

His mother laughed a laugh that seemed to ring through the city and be echoed and re-echoed by countless other laughs. "Oh, yes, I will, won't I! Sure!"

"Well, yeh must take me fer a damn fool," said Jimmie, indignant at his mother for mocking him. "I didn't say we'd make 'er inteh a little tin angel, ner nottin', but deh way it is now she can queer us! Don' che see?"

"Aye, she'll git tired of deh life atter a while an' den she'll wanna be a-comin' home, won' she, deh beast! I'll let 'er in den, won' I?"

"Well, I didn' mean none of dis prod'gal bus'ness anyway," explained Jimmie.

"It wasn't no prod'gal dauter, yeh damn fool," said the mother. "It was prod'gal son,[4] anyhow."

"I know dat," said Jimmie.

For a time they sat in silence. The mother's eyes gloated on a scene her imagination could call before her. Her lips were set in a vindictive smile.

"Aye, she'll cry, won' she, an' carry on, an' tell how Pete, or some odder feller, beats 'er an' she'll say she's sorry an' all dat an' she ain't happy, she ain't, an' she wants to come home agin, she does."

With grim humor, the mother imitated the possible wailing notes of the daughter's voice.

"Den I'll take 'er in, won't I, deh beast. She kin cry 'er two eyes out on deh stones of deh street before I'll dirty deh place wid her. She abused an' ill-treated her own mudder— her own mudder what loved her an' she'll never git anodder chance dis side of hell."

Jimmie thought he had a great idea of women's frailty, but he could not understand why any of his kin should be victims.

"Damn her," he fervidly said.

Again he wondered vaguely if some of the women of his acquaintance had brothers. Nevertheless, his mind did not for an instant confuse himself with those brothers nor his sister with theirs. After the mother had, with great difficulty, suppressed the neighbors, she went among them and proclaimed her grief. "May Gawd forgive dat girl," was her continual cry. To attentive ears she recited the whole length and breadth of her woes.

"I bringed 'er up deh way a dauter oughta be bringed up an' dis is how she served me! She went teh deh devil deh first chance she got! May Gawd forgive her."

When arrested for drunkenness she used the story of her daughter's downfall with telling effect upon the police-justices. Finally one of them said to her, peering down over his spectacles: "Mary, the records of this and other courts show that you are the mother of forty-

4. In the biblical parable of the Prodigal Son (Luke 15:11–32).

two daughters who have been ruined. The case is unparalleled in the annals of this court, and this court thinks—"

The mother went through life shedding large tears of sorrow. Her red face was a picture of agony.

Of course Jimmie publicly damned his sister that he might appear on a higher social plane. But, arguing with himself, stumbling about in ways that he knew not, he, once, almost came to a conclusion that his sister would have been more firmly good had she better known why. However, he felt that he could not hold such a view. He threw it hastily aside.

Chapter XIV

In a hilarious hall there were twenty-eight tables and twenty-eight women and a crowd of smoking men.[5] Valiant noise was made on a stage at the end of the hall by an orchestra composed of men who looked as if they had just happened in. Soiled waiters ran to and fro, swooping down like hawks on the unwary in the throng; clattering along the aisles with trays covered with glasses; stumbling over women's skirts and charging two prices for everything but beer, all with a swiftness that blurred the view of the cocoanut palms and dusty monstrosities painted upon the walls of the room. A bouncer,[6] with an immense load of business upon his hands, plunged about in the crowd, dragging bashful strangers to prominent chairs, ordering waiters here and there and quarreling furiously with men who wanted to sing with the orchestra.

The usual smoke cloud was present, but so dense that heads and arms seemed entangled in it. The rumble of conversation was replaced by a roar. Plenteous oaths heaved through the air. The room rang with the shrill voices of women bubbling o'er with drink-laughter. The chief element in the music of the orchestra was speed. The musicians played in intent fury. A woman was singing and smiling upon the stage, but no one took notice of her. The rate at which the piano, cornet and violins were going, seemed to impart wildness to the half-drunken crowd. Beer glasses were emptied at a gulp and conversation became a rapid chatter. The smoke eddied and swirled like a shadowy river hurrying toward some unseen falls. Pete and Maggie entered the hall and took chairs at a table near the door. The

5. Probably a concert saloon, like the hall in Chapter XII, though seedier. A lower-class establishment usually found in basements of buildings and providing coarse music and entertainment. Crane has a woman at every table. This suggests the "waitresses" in concert saloons who drank with customers and received a percentage on the drinks they sold. For a different reading of this scene, see Sholom J. Kahn, "Stephen Crane and Whitman: A Possible Source for 'Maggie,'" *Walt Whitman Review*, VII (December 1961), 75–77.
6. Employee whose job included ejecting disorderly patrons.

woman who was seated there made an attempt to occupy Pete's attention and, failing, went away.

Three weeks had passed since the girl had left home. The air of spaniel-like dependence had been magnified and showed its direct effect in the peculiar off-handedness and ease of Pete's ways toward her.

She followed Pete's eyes with hers, anticipating with smiles gracious looks from him.

A woman of brilliance and audacity, accompanied by a mere boy, came into the place and took seats near them.

At once Pete sprang to his feet, his face beaming with glad surprise.

"By Gawd,[7] there's Nellie," he cried.

He went over to the table and held out an eager hand to the woman.

"Why, hello, Pete, me boy, how are you," said she, giving him her fingers.

Maggie took instant note of the woman. She perceived that her black dress fitted her to perfection. Her linen collar and cuffs were spotless. Tan gloves were stretched over her well-shaped hands. A hat of a prevailing fashion perched jauntily upon her dark hair. She wore no jewelry and was painted with no apparent paint. She looked clear-eyed through the stares of the men.

"Sit down, and call your lady-friend over," she said cordially to Pete. At his beckoning Maggie came and sat between Pete and the mere boy.

"I thought yeh were gone away fer good," began Pete, at once. "When did yeh git back? How did dat Buff'lo bus'ness turn out?"

The woman shrugged her shoulders. "Well, he didn't have as many stamps[8] as he tried to make out, so I shook him, that's all."

"Well, I'm glad teh see yehs back in deh city," said Pete, with awkward gallantry.

He and the woman entered into a long conversation, exchanging reminiscences of days together. Maggie sat still, unable to formulate an intelligent sentence upon the conversation and painfully aware of it.

She saw Pete's eyes sparkle as he gazed upon the handsome stranger. He listened smilingly to all she said. The woman was familiar with all his affairs, asked him about mutual friends, and knew the amount of his salary.

She paid no attention to Maggie, looking toward her once or twice and apparently seeing the wall beyond.

The mere boy was sulky. In the beginning he had welcomed with acclamations the additions.

---

7. Changed to "Hully gee," in 1896 *Maggie*.   8. Slang for "money" (especially paper money).

"Let's all have a drink! What'll you take, Nell? And you, Miss what's-your-name. Have a drink, Mr.———, you, I mean."

He had shown a sprightly desire to do the talking for the company and tell all about his family. In a loud voice he declaimed on various topics. He assumed a patronizing air toward Pete. As Maggie was silent, he paid no attention to her. He made a great show of lavishing wealth upon the woman of brilliance and audacity.

"Do keep still, Freddie! You gibber like an ape, dear,"[9] said the woman to him. She turned away and devoted her attention to Pete.

"We'll have many a good time together again, eh?"

"Sure, Mike," said Pete, enthusiastic at once.

"Say," whispered she, leaning forward, "let's go over to Billie's and have a heluva time."

"Well, it's dis way! See?" said Pete. "I got dis lady frien' here."

"Oh, t'hell with her," argued the woman.

Pete appeared disturbed.

"All right," said she, nodding her head at him. "All right for you! We'll see the next time you ask me to go anywheres with you."

Pete squirmed.

"Say," he said, beseechingly, "come wid me a minit an' I'll tell yer why."

The woman waved her hand.

"Oh, that's all right, you needn't explain, you know. You wouldn't come merely because you wouldn't come, that's all there is of it."

To Pete's visible distress she turned to the mere boy, bringing him speedily from a terrific rage. He had been debating whether it would be the part of a man to pick a quarrel with Pete, or would he be justified in striking him savagely with his beer glass without warning. But he recovered himself when the woman turned to renew her smilings. He beamed upon her with an expression that was somewhat tipsy and inexpressibly tender.

"Say, shake that Bowery jay," requested he, in a loud whisper.

"Freddie, you are so droll," she replied.

Pete reached forward and touched the woman on the arm.

"Come out a minit while I tells yeh why I can't go wid yer. Yer doin' me dirt, Nell! I never taut ye'd do me dirt, Nell. Come on, will yer?" He spoke in tones of injury.

"Why, I don't see why I should be interested in your explanations," said the woman, with a coldness that seemed to reduce Pete to a pulp.

His eyes pleaded with her. "Come out a minit while I tells yeh."

The woman nodded slightly at Maggie and the mere boy, "'Scuse me."

9. Changed to "You talk like a clock," in the 1896 *Maggie*.

The mere boy interrupted his loving smile and turned a shrivelling glare upon Pete. His boyish countenance flushed and he spoke, in a whine, to the woman:

"Oh, I say, Nellie, this ain't a square deal, you know. You aren't goin' to leave me and go off with that duffer, are you? I should think—"

"Why, you dear boy, of course I'm not," cried the woman, affectionately. She bended over and whispered in his ear. He smiled again and settled in his chair as if resolved to wait patiently.

As the woman walked down between the rows of tables, Pete was at her shoulder talking earnestly, apparently in explanation. The woman waved her hands with studied airs of indifference. The doors swung behind them, leaving Maggie and the mere boy seated at the table.

Maggie was dazed. She could dimly perceive that something stupendous had happened. She wondered why Pete saw fit to remonstrate with the woman, pleading for forgiveness with his eyes. She thought she noted an air of submission about her leonine Pete. She was astounded.

The mere boy occupied himself with cock-tails and a cigar. He was tranquilly silent for half an hour. Then he bestirred himself and spoke.

"Well," he said, sighing, "I knew this was the way it would be." There was another stillness. The mere boy seemed to be musing.

"She was pulling m'leg. That's the whole amount of it," he said, suddenly. "It's a bloomin' shame the way that girl does. Why, I've spent over two dollars in drinks to-night. And she goes off with that plug-ugly who looks as if he had been hit in the face with a coin-die.[1] I call it rocky treatment for a fellah like me. Here, waiter, bring me a cock-tail and make it damned strong."

Maggie made no reply. She was watching the doors. "It's a mean piece of business," complained the mere boy. He explained to her how amazing it was that anybody should treat him in such a manner. "But I'll get square with her, you bet. She won't get far ahead of yours truly, you know," he added, winking. "I'll tell her plainly that it was bloomin' mean business. And she won't come it over me with any of her 'now-Freddie-dears.' She thinks my name is Freddie, you know, but of course it ain't. I always tell these people some name like that, because if they got onto your right name they might use it sometime. Understand? Oh, they don't fool me much."

Maggie was paying no attention, being intent upon the doors. The mere boy relapsed into a period of gloom, during which he exterminated a number of cock-tails with a determined air, as if replying

---

1. Hard metal device for coining money.

defiantly to fate. He occasionally broke forth into sentences composed of invectives joined together in a long string.

The girl was still staring at the doors. After a time the mere boy began to see cobwebs just in front of his nose. He spurred himself into being agreeable and insisted upon her having a charlotte-russe[2] and a glass of beer.

"They's gone," he remarked, "they's gone." He looked at her through the smoke wreaths. "Shay, lil' girl, we mightish well make bes' of it. You ain't such bad-lookin' girl, y'know. Not half bad. Can't come up to Nell, though. No, can't do it! Well, I should shay not! Nell fine-lookin' girl! F—i—n—ine. You look damn bad longsider her, but by y'self ain't so bad. Have to do anyhow. Nell gone. On'y you left. Not half bad, though."

Maggie stood up.

"I'm going home," she said.

The mere boy started.

"Eh? What? Home," he cried, struck with amazement. "I beg pardon, did hear say home?"

"I'm going home," she repeated.

"Great Gawd, what hava struck," demanded the mere boy of himself, stupefied.

In a semi-comatose state he conducted her on board an up-town car, ostentatiously paid her fare, leered kindly at her through the rear window and fell off the steps.

Chapter XV

A forlorn woman went along a lighted avenue. The street was filled with people desperately bound on missions. An endless crowd darted at the elevated station stairs and the horse cars were thronged with owners of bundles.

The pace of the forlorn woman was slow. She was apparently searching for some one. She loitered near the doors of saloons and watched men emerge from them. She scanned furtively the faces in the rushing stream of pedestrians. Hurrying men, bent on catching some boat or train, jostled her elbows, failing to notice her, their thoughts fixed on distant dinners.

The forlorn woman had a peculiar face. Her smile was no smile. But when in repose her features had a shadowy look that was like a sardonic grin, as if some one had sketched with cruel forefinger indelible lines about her mouth.

Jimmie came strolling up the avenue. The woman encountered him with an aggrieved air.

2. Dessert of sponge cake with whipped cream or custard filling.

"Oh, Jimmie, I've been lookin' all over fer yehs—," she began.

Jimmie made an impatient gesture and quickened his pace.

"Ah, don't bodder me! Good Gawd!" he said, with the savageness of a man whose life is pestered.

The woman followed him along the sidewalk in somewhat the manner of a suppliant.

"But, Jimmie," she said, "yehs told me ye'd—"

Jimmie turned upon her fiercely as if resolved to make a last stand for comfort and peace.

"Say, fer Gawd's sake, Hattie, don' foller me from one end of deh city teh deh odder. Let up, will yehs! Give me a minute's res', can't yehs? Yehs makes me tired, allus taggin' me. See? Ain' yehs got no sense? Do yehs want people teh get onto me? Go chase yerself, fer Gawd's sake."

The woman stepped closer and laid her fingers on his arm. "But, look-a-here—"

Jimmie snarled. "Oh, go teh hell."

He darted into the front door of a convenient saloon and a moment later came out into the shadows that surrounded the side door. On the brilliantly lighted avenue he perceived the forlorn woman dodging about like a scout. Jimmie laughed with an air of relief and went away.

When he arrived home he found his mother clamoring. Maggie had returned. She stood shivering beneath the torrent of her mother's wrath.

"Well, I'm damned," said Jimmie in greeting.

His mother, tottering about the room, pointed a quivering forefinger.

"Lookut her, Jimmie, lookut her. Dere's yer sister, boy. Dere's yer sister. Lookut her! Lookut her!"

She screamed in scoffing laughter.

The girl stood in the middle of the room. She edged about as if unable to find a place on the floor to put her feet.

"Ha, ha, ha," bellowed the mother. "Dere she stands! Ain' she purty? Lookut her! Ain' she sweet, deh beast? Lookut her! Ha, ha, lookut her!"

She lurched forward and put her red and seamed hands upon her daughter's face. She bent down and peered keenly up into the eyes of the girl.

"Oh, she's jes' dessame as she ever was, ain' she? She's her mudder's purty darlin' yit, ain' she? Lookut her, Jimmie! Come here, fer Gawd's sake, and lookut her."

The loud, tremendous sneering of the mother brought the denizens of the Rum Alley tenement to their doors. Women came in the hallways. Children scurried to and fro.

"What's up? Dat Johnson party on anudder tear?"[3]

"Naw! Young Mag's come home!"

"Deh hell yeh say?"

Through the open doors curious eyes stared in at Maggie. Children ventured into the room and ogled her, as if they formed the front row at a theatre. Women, without, bended toward each other and whispered, nodding their heads with airs of profound philosophy. A baby, overcome with curiosity concerning this object at which all were looking, sidled forward and touched her dress, cautiously, as if investigating a red-hot stove. Its mother's voice rang out like a warning trumpet. She rushed forward and grabbed her child, casting a terrible look of indignation at the girl. _

Maggie's mother paced to and fro, addressing the doorful of eyes, expounding like a glib showman at a museum. Her voice rang through the building.

"Dere she stands," she cried, wheeling suddenly and pointing with dramatic finger. "Dere she stands! Lookut her! Ain' she a dindy? An' she was so good as to come home teh her mudder, she was! Ain' she a beaut'? Ain' she a dindy? Fer Gawd's sake!"

The jeering cries ended in another burst of shrill laughter.

The girl seemed to awaken. "Jimmie—"

He drew hastily back from her.

"Well, now, yer a hell of a t'ing, ain' yeh?" he said, his lips curling in scorn. Radiant virtue sat upon his brow and his repelling hands expressed horror of contamination.

Maggie turned and went.

The crowd at the door fell back precipitately. A baby falling down in front of the door, wrenched a scream like a wounded animal from its mother. Another woman sprang forward and picked it up, with a chivalrous air, as if rescuing a human being from an on-coming express train.

As the girl passed down through the hall, she went before open doors framing more eyes strangely microscopic, and sending broad beams of inquisitive light into the darkness of her path. On the second floor she met the gnarled old woman who possessed the music box.

"So," she cried, " 'ere yehs are back again, are yehs? An' dey've kicked yehs out? Well, come in an' stay wid me teh-night. I ain' got no moral standin'."

From above came an unceasing babble of tongues, over all of which rang the mother's derisive laughter.

---

3. Slang for "rampage" or "spree."

Chapter XVI

Pete did not consider that he had ruined Maggie. If he had thought that her soul could never smile again, he would have believed the mother and brother, who were pyrotechnic[4] over the affair, to be responsible for it.

Besides, in his world, souls did not insist upon being able to smile. "What deh hell?"

He felt a trifle entangled. It distressed him. Revelations and scenes might bring upon him the wrath of the owner of the saloon, who insisted upon respectability of an advanced type.

"What deh hell do dey wanna raise such a smoke[5] about it fer?" demanded he of himself, disgusted with the attitude of the family. He saw no necessity for anyone's losing their equilibrium merely because their sister or their daughter had stayed away from home.

Searching about in his mind for possible reasons for their conduct, he came upon the conclusion that Maggie's motives were correct, but that the two others wished to snare him. He felt pursued.

The woman of brilliance and audacity whom he had met in the hilarious hall showed a disposition to ridicule him.

"A little pale thing with no spirit," she said. "Did you note the expression of her eyes? There was something in them about pumpkin pie and virtue. That is a peculiar way the left corner of her mouth has of twitching, isn't it? Dear, dear, my cloud-compelling Pete, what are you coming to?"

Pete asserted at once that he never was very much interested in the girl. The woman interrupted him, laughing.

"Oh, it's not of the slightest consequence to me, my dear young man. You needn't draw maps for my benefit. Why should I be concerned about it?"

But Pete continued with his explanations. If he was laughed at for his tastes in women, he felt obliged to say that they were only temporary or indifferent ones.

The morning after Maggie had departed from home, Pete stood behind the bar. He was immaculate in white jacket and apron and his hair was plastered over his brow with infinite correctness. No customers were in the place. Pete was twisting his napkined fist slowly in a beer glass, softly whistling to himself and occasionally holding the object of his attention between his eyes and a few weak beams of sunlight that had found their way over the thick screens and into the shaded room.

With lingering thoughts of the woman of brilliance and audacity, the bartender raised his head and stared through the varying cracks

4. Resembling fireworks.　　　　5. Slang for "anger" or "fuss."

between the swaying bamboo doors. Suddenly the whistling pucker faded from his lips. He saw Maggie walking slowly past. He gave a great start, fearing for the previously-mentioned eminent respectability of the place.

He threw a swift, nervous glance about him, all at once feeling guilty. No one was in the room.

He went hastily over to the side door. Opening it and looking out, he perceived Maggie standing, as if undecided, on the corner. She was searching the place with her eyes.

As she turned her face toward him Pete beckoned to her hurriedly, intent upon returning with speed to a position behind the bar and to the atmosphere of respectability upon which the proprietor insisted.

Maggie came to him, the anxious look disappearing from her face and a smile wreathing her lips.

"Oh, Pete—," she began brightly.

The bartender made a violent gesture of impatience.

"Oh, my Gawd," cried he, vehemently. "What deh hell do yeh wanna hang aroun' here fer? Do yeh wanna git me inteh trouble?" he demanded with an air of injury.

Astonishment swept over the girl's features. "Why, Pete! yehs tol' me—"

Pete glanced profound irritation. His countenance reddened with the anger of a man whose respectability is being threatened.

"Say, yehs makes me tired. See? What deh hell deh yeh wanna tag aroun' atter me fer? Yeh'll git me inteh trouble wid deh ol' man an' dey'll be hell teh pay! If he sees a woman roun' here he'll go crazy an' I'll lose me job! See? Ain' yehs got no sense? Don' be allus bodderin' me. See? Yer brudder come in here an' raised hell an' deh ol' man hada put up fer it! An' now I'm done! See? I'm done."

The girl's eyes stared into his face. "Pete, don' yeh remem—"

"Oh, hell," interrupted Pete, anticipating.

The girl seemed to have a struggle with herself. She was apparently bewildered and could not find speech. Finally she asked in a low voice: "But where kin I go?"

The question exasperated Pete beyond the powers of endurance. It was a direct attempt to give him some responsibility in a matter that did not concern him. In his indignation he volunteered information.

"Oh, go teh hell," cried he. He slammed the door furiously and returned, with an air of relief, to his respectability.

Maggie went away.

She wandered aimlessly for several blocks. She stopped once and asked aloud a question of herself: "Who?"

A man who was passing near her shoulder, humorously took the questioning word as intended for him.

"Eh? What? Who? Nobody! I didn't say anything," he laughingly said, and continued his way.

Soon the girl discovered that if she walked with such apparent aimlessness, some men looked at her with calculating eyes. She quickened her step, frightened. As a protection, she adopted a demeanor of intentness as if going somewhere.

After a time she left rattling avenues and passed between rows of houses with sternness and stolidity stamped upon their features. She hung her head for she felt their eyes grimly upon her.

Suddenly she came upon a stout gentleman in a silk hat and a chaste black coat, whose decorous row of buttons reached from his chin to his knees. The girl had heard of the Grace of God and she decided to approach this man.[6]

His beaming, chubby face was a picture of benevolence and kind-heartedness. His eyes shone good-will.

But as the girl timidly accosted him, he gave a convulsive movement and saved his respectability by a vigorous side-step. He did not risk it to save a soul. For how was he to know that there was a soul before him that needed saving?

Chapter XVII

Upon a wet evening, several months after the last chapter, two interminable rows of cars, pulled by slipping horses, jangled along a prominent side-street. A dozen cabs, with coat-enshrouded drivers, clattered to and fro. Electric lights, whirring softly, shed a blurred radiance. A flower dealer, his feet tapping impatiently, his nose and his wares glistening with rain-drops, stood behind an array of roses and chrysanthemums. Two or three theatres emptied a crowd upon the storm-swept pavements. Men pulled their hats over their eyebrows and raised their collars to their ears. Women shrugged impatient shoulders in their warm cloaks and stopped to arrange their skirts for a walk through the storm. People having been comparatively silent for two hours burst into a roar of conversation, their hearts still kindling from the glowings of the stage.

The pavements became tossing seas of umbrellas. Men stepped forth to hail cabs or cars, raising their fingers in varied forms of polite request or imperative demand. An endless procession wended toward elevated stations. An atmosphere of pleasure and prosperity seemed to hang over the throng, born, perhaps, of good clothes and of having just emerged from a place of forgetfulness.

In the mingled light and gloom of an adjacent park, a handful of

6. A clergyman.

wet wanderers, in attitudes of chronic dejection, was scattered among the benches.

A girl of the painted cohorts of the city went along the street. She threw changing glances at men who passed her, giving smiling invitations to men of rural or untaught pattern and usually seeming sedately unconscious of the men with a metropolitan seal upon their faces.

Crossing glittering avenues, she went into the throng emerging from the places of forgetfulness. She hurried forward through the crowd as if intent upon reaching a distant home, bending forward in her handsome cloak, daintily lifting her skirts and picking for her well-shod feet the dryer spots upon the pavements.

The restless doors of saloons, clashing to and fro, disclosed animated rows of men before bars and hurrying barkeepers.

A concert hall gave to the street faint sounds of swift, machine-like music, as if a group of phantom musicians were hastening.

A tall young man, smoking a cigarette with a sublime air, strolled near the girl. He had on evening dress, a moustache, a chrysanthemum, and a look of ennui, all of which he kept carefully under his eye. Seeing the girl walk on as if such a young man as he was not in existence, he looked back transfixed with interest. He stared glassily for a moment, but gave a slight convulsive start when he discerned that she was neither new, Parisian, nor theatrical. He wheeled about hastily and turned his stare into the air, like a sailor with a searchlight.

A stout gentleman, with pompous and philanthropic whiskers, went stolidly by, the broad of his back sneering at the girl.

A belated man in business clothes, and in haste to catch a car, bounced against her shoulder. "Hi, there, Mary, I beg your pardon! Brace up, old girl." He grasped her arm to steady her, and then was away running down the middle of the street.

The girl walked on out of the realm of restaurants and saloons. She passed more glittering avenues and went into darker blocks than those where the crowd travelled.

A young man in light overcoat and derby hat received a glance shot keenly from the eyes of the girl. He stopped and looked at her, thrusting his hands in his pockets and making a mocking smile curl his lips. "Come, now, old lady," he said, "you don't mean to tell me that you sized me up for a farmer?"

A laboring man marched along with bundles under his arms. To her remarks, he replied: "It's a fine evenin', ain't it?"

She smiled squarely into the face of a boy who was hurrying by with his hands buried in his overcoat, his blonde locks bobbing on his youthful temples, and a cheery smile of unconcern upon his lips. He turned his head and smiled back at her, waving his hands.

"Not this eve—some other eve!"

A drunken man, reeling in her pathway, began to roar at her. "I ain' ga no money, dammit," he shouted, in a dismal voice. He lurched on up the street, wailing to himself, "Dammit, I ain' ga no money. Damn ba' luck. Ain' ga no more money."

The girl went into gloomy districts near the river, where the tall black factories shut in the street and only occasional broad beams of light fell across the pavements from saloons. In front of one of these places, from whence came the sound of a violin vigorously scraped, the patter of feet on boards and the ring of loud laughter, there stood a man with blotched features.

"Ah, there," said the girl.

"I've got a date," said the man.

Further on in the darkness she met a ragged being with shifting, blood-shot eyes and grimy hands. "Ah, what deh hell? T'ink I'm a millionaire?"

She went into the blackness of the final block. The shutters of the tall buildings were closed like grim lips. The structures seemed to have eyes that looked over her, beyond her, at other things. Afar off the lights of the avenues glittered as if from an impossible distance. Street car bells jingled with a sound of merriment.

When almost to the river[7] the girl saw a great figure.[8] On going forward she perceived it to be a huge fat man in torn and greasy garments. His grey hair straggled down over his forehead. His small, bleared eyes, sparkling from amidst great rolls of red fat, swept eagerly over the girl's upturned face. He laughed, his brown, disordered teeth gleaming under a grey, grizzled moustache from which beer-drops dripped. His whole body gently quivered and shook like that of a dead jelly fish. Chuckling and leering, he followed the girl of the crimson legions.

At their feet the river appeared a deathly black hue. Some hidden factory sent up a yellow glare, that lit for a moment the waters lapping oilily against timbers. The varied sounds of life, made joyous by distance and seeming unapproachableness, came faintly and died away to a silence.

Chapter XVIII

In a partitioned-off section of a saloon sat a man with a half dozen women, gleefully laughing, hovering about him. The man had ar-

---

7. East River (see first footnote 5, Chapter I). Note how Crane has telescoped time in this chapter.

8. This entire paragraph was deleted in the 1896 *Maggie*. See Hershel Parker and Brian Higgins, "Maggie's 'Last Night': Authorial Design and Editorial Patching," below.

rived at that stage of drunkenness where affection is felt for the universe.

"I'm good f'ler, girls," he said, convincingly. "I'm damn good f'ler. An'body treats me right, I allus trea's zem right! See?"

The women nodded their heads approvingly. "To be sure," they cried in hearty chorus. "You're the kind of a man we like, Pete. You're outa sight![9] What yeh goin' to buy this time, dear?"

"An't'ing yehs wants, damn it," said the man in an abandonment of good will. His countenance shone with the true spirit of benevolence. He was in the proper mode[1] of missionaries. He would have fraternized with obscure Hottentots.[2] And above all, he was overwhelmed in tenderness for his friends, who were all illustrious.

"An't'ing yehs wants, damn it," repeated he, waving his hands with beneficent recklessness. "I'm good f'ler, girls, an' if an'body treats me right I—here," called he through an open door to a waiter, "bring girls drinks, damn it. What 'ill yehs have, girls? An't'ing yehs wants, damn it!"

The waiter glanced in with the disgusted look of the man who serves intoxicants for the man who takes too much of them. He nodded his head shortly at the order from each individual, and went.

"Damn it," said the man, "we're havin' heluva time. I like you girls! Damn'd if I don't! Yer right sort! See?"

He spoke at length and with feeling, concerning the excellencies of his assembled friends.

"Don' try pull man's leg, but have a heluva time! Das right! Das way teh do! Now, if I sawght yehs tryin' work me fer drinks, wouldn' buy damn t'ing! But yer right sort, damn it! Yehs know how ter treat a f'ler, an' I stays by yehs 'til spen' las' cent! Das right! I'm good f'ler an' I knows when an'body treats me right!"

Between the times of the arrival and departure of the waiter, the man discoursed to the women on the tender regard he felt for all living things. He laid stress upon the purity of his motives in all dealings with men in the world and spoke of the fervor of his friendship for those who were amiable. Tears welled slowly from his eyes. His voice quavered when he spoke to them.

Once when the waiter was about to depart with an empty tray, the man drew a coin from his pocket and held it forth.

"Here," said he, quite magnificently, "here's quar'."

The waiter kept his hands on his tray.

"I don' want yer money," he said.

The other put forth the coin with tearful insistence.

"Here, damn it," cried he, "tak't! Yer damn goo' f'ler an' I wan' yehs tak't!"

9. Slang for "remarkable" or "incredible."
1. Changed to "mood" in 1896 *Maggie*.
2. A South African people.

"Come, come, now," said the waiter, with the sullen air of a man who is forced into giving advice. "Put yer mon in yer pocket! Yer loaded an' yehs on'y makes a damn fool of yerself."

As the latter passed out of the door the man turned pathetically to the women.

"He don' know I'm damn goo' f'ler," cried he, dismally.

"Never you mind, Pete, dear," said a woman of brilliance and audacity, laying her hand with great affection upon his arm. "Never you mind, old boy! We'll stay by you, dear!"

"Das ri'," cried the man, his face lighting up at the soothing tones of the woman's voice. "Das ri', I'm damn goo' f'ler an' w'en anyone trea's me ri', I treats zem ri'! Shee!"

"Sure!" cried the women. "And we're not goin' back on you, old man."

The man turned appealing eyes to the woman of brilliance and audacity. He felt that if he could be convicted of a contemptible action he would die.

"Shay, Nell, damn it, I allus trea's yehs shquare, didn' I? I allus been goo' f'ler wi' yehs, ain't I, Nell?"

"Sure you have, Pete," assented the woman. She delivered an oration to her companions. "Yessir, that's a fact. Pete's a square fellah, he is. He never goes back on a friend. He's the right kind an' we stay by him, don't we, girls?"

"Sure," they exclaimed. Looking lovingly at him they raised their glasses and drank his health.

"Girlsh," said the man, beseechingly, "I allus trea's yehs ri', didn' I? I'm goo' f'ler, ain', I, girlsh?"

"Sure," again they chorused.

"Well," said he finally, "le's have nozzer drink, zen."

"That's right," hailed a woman, "that's right. Yer no bloomin' jay! Yer spends yer money like a man. Dat's right."

The man pounded the table with his quivering fists.

"Yessir," he cried, with deep earnestness, as if someone disputed him. "I'm damn goo' f'ler, an' w'en anyone trea's me ri', I allus trea's—le's have nozzer drink."

He began to beat the wood with his glass.

"Shay," howled he, growing suddenly impatient. As the waiter did not then come, the man swelled with wrath.

"Shay," howled he again.

The waiter appeared at the door.

"Bringsh drinksh," said the man.

The waiter disappeared with the orders.

"Zat f'ler damn fool," cried the man. "He insul' me! I'm ge'man! Can' stan' be insul'! I'm goin' lickim when comes!"

"No, no," cried the women, crowding about and trying to subdue him. "He's all right! He didn't mean anything! Let it go! He's a good fellah!"

"Din' he insul' me?" asked the man earnestly.

"No," said they. "Of course he didn't! He's all right!"

"Sure he didn' insul' me?" demanded the man, with deep anxiety in his voice.

"No, no! We know him! He's a good fellah. He didn't mean anything."

"Well, zen," said the man, resolutely, "I'm go' 'pol'gize!"

When the waiter came, the man struggled to the middle of the floor.

"Girlsh shed you insul' me! I shay damn lie! I 'pol'gize!"

"All right," said the waiter.

The man sat down. He felt a sleepy but strong desire to straighten things out and have a perfect understanding with everybody.

"Nell, I allus trea's yeh shquare, din' I? Yeh likes me, don' yehs, Nell? I'm goo' f'ler?"

"Sure," said the woman of brilliance and audacity.

"Yeh knows I'm stuck on yehs, don' yehs, Nell?"

"Sure," she repeated, carelessly.

Overwhelmed by a spasm of drunken adoration, he drew two or three bills from his pocket, and, with the trembling fingers of an offering priest, laid them on the table before the woman.

"Yehs knows, damn it, yehs kin have all got, 'cause I'm stuck on yehs, Nell, damn't, I—I'm stuck on yehs, Nell—buy drinksh— damn't—we're havin' heluva time—w'en anyone trea's me ri'—I— damn't, Nell—we're havin' heluva—time."

Shortly he went to sleep with his swollen face fallen forward on his chest.

The women drank and laughed, not heeding the slumbering man in the corner. Finally he lurched forward and fell groaning to the floor.

The women screamed in disgust and drew back their skirts.

"Come ahn," cried one, starting up angrily, "let's get out of here."

The woman of brilliance and audacity stayed behind, taking up the bills and stuffing them into a deep, irregularly-shaped pocket. A guttural snore from the recumbent man caused her to turn and look down at him.

She laughed. "What a damn fool," she said, and went.

The smoke from the lamps settled heavily down in the little compartment, obscuring the way out. The smell of oil, stifling in its intensity, pervaded the air. The wine from an overturned glass dripped softly down upon the blotches on the man's neck.

Chapter XIX

In a room a woman sat at a table eating like a fat monk in a picture.

A soiled, unshaven man[3] pushed open the door and entered.

"Well," said he, "Mag's dead."

"What?" said the woman, her mouth filled with bread.

"Mag's dead," repeated the man.

"Deh hell she is," said the woman. She continued her meal. When she finished her coffee she began to weep.

"I kin remember when her two feet was no bigger dan yer t'umb, and she weared worsted boots," moaned she.

"Well, whata dat?" said the man.

"I kin remember when she weared worsted boots," she cried.

The neighbors began to gather in the hall, staring in at the weeping woman as if watching the contortions of a dying dog. A dozen women entered and lamented with her. Under their busy hands the rooms took on that appalling appearance of neatness and order with which death is greeted.

Suddenly the door opened and a woman in a black gown rushed in with outstretched arms. "Ah, poor Mary," she cried, and tenderly embraced the moaning one.

"Ah, what ter'ble affliction is dis," continued she. Her vocabulary was derived from mission churches. "Me poor Mary, how I feel fer yehs! Ah, what a ter'ble affliction is a disobed'ent chil'."

Her good, motherly face was wet with tears. She trembled in eagerness to express her sympathy. The mourner sat with bowed head, rocking her body heavily to and fro, and crying out in a high, strained voice that sounded like a dirge[4] on some forlorn pipe.

"I kin remember when she weared worsted boots an' her two feets was no bigger dan yer t'umb an' she weared worsted boots, Miss Smith," she cried, raising her streaming eyes.

"Ah, me poor Mary," sobbed the woman in black. With low, coddling cries, she sank on her knees by the mourner's chair, and put her arms about her. The other women began to groan in different keys.

"Yer poor misguided chil' is gone now, Mary, an' let us hope it's fer deh bes'. Yeh'll fergive her now, Mary, won't yehs, dear, all her disobed'ence? All her t'ankless behavior to her mudder an' all her badness? She's gone where her ter'ble sins will be judged."

The woman in black raised her face and paused. The inevitable sunlight came streaming in at the windows and shed a ghastly cheerfulness upon the faded hues of the room. Two or three of the

---

3. Note reference to Jimmie as a "man." As in Chapter XVII, Crane has telescoped time. 4. Hymn or choral song of mourning.

spectators were sniffling, and one was loudly weeping. The mourner arose and staggered into the other room. In a moment she emerged with a pair of faded baby shoes held in the hollow of her hand.

"I kin remember when she used to wear dem," cried she. The women burst anew into cries as if they had all been stabbed. The mourner turned to the soiled and unshaven man.

"Jimmie, boy, go git yer sister! Go git yer sister an' we'll put deh boots on her feets!"

"Dey won't fit her now, yeh damn fool," said the man.

"Go git yer sister, Jimmie," shrieked the woman, confronting him fiercely.

The man swore sullenly. He went over to a corner and slowly began to put on his coat. He took his hat and went out, with a dragging, reluctant step.

The woman in black came forward and again besought the mourner.

"Yeh'll fergive her, Mary! Yeh'll fergive yer bad, bad chil'! Her life was a curse an' her days were black an' yeh'll fergive yer bad girl? She's gone where her sins will be judged."

"She's gone where her sins will be judged," cried the other women, like a choir at a funeral.

"Deh Lord gives and deh Lord takes away," said the woman in black, raising her eyes to the sunbeams.

"Deh Lord gives and deh Lord takes away," responded the others.

"Yeh'll fergive her, Mary!" pleaded the woman in black. The mourner essayed to speak but her voice gave way. She shook her great shoulders frantically, in an agony of grief. Hot tears seemed to scald her quivering face. Finally her voice came and arose like a scream of pain.

"Oh, yes, I'll fergive her! I'll fergive her!"

A Note on the Text

The 1893 *Maggie*, reproduced in this Norton Critical Edition, was published by an unknown printer of religious and medical texts. The second and revised *Maggie* was published by D. Appleton and Company in 1896. The recent CEAA (Center for Editions of American Authors) edition of *Maggie* (*The Works of Stephen Crane*, ed. Fredson Bowers [Charlottesville: The University Press of Virginia, 1969], vol. 1) was intended as a definitive text, to supersede both the 1893 and 1896 editions of the novel. Instead, to some textual scholars, it has turned out to be a third *Maggie*. For a sampling of the criticism, see Donald Pizer, "On the Editing of Modern American Texts," *Bulletin of the New York Public Library*, LXXV (March 1971), 147–53; and his review of the Virginia *Maggie* in *Modern Philology*, LXVIII (November 1970), 212–14. Also see Hershel Parker and Brian Higgins, "Maggie's 'Last Night,' " below; and David J. Nordloh, "On Crane Now Edited: The University of Virginia Edition of *The Works of Stephen Crane*," *Studies in the Novel*, X (Spring 1978), 103–19.

The list which follows gives the typographical and other errors in the 1893 edition that have been silently corrected in the current text. The words and phrases in boldface (with page and line numbers) are as given in this Norton Critical Edition; they are followed by the words and phrases as they appeared in the 1893 edition.

4.12	**manhood** manood		18.38	**See?"** See."
4.19	**interest. "A** interest, "A		18.41	**grimy** grimey
4.35	**forward.** foward.		19.6	**t'ree** tree
5.29	**Jimmie** Jimmy		19.15	**sight,"** sight,'
7.4	**disdainfully** distainfully		19.22	**taut** tau't
7.6	**him.** him,		20.1	**somet'ing** someting
8.38	**"Will I—"** "Will I"—		20.7	**of a world** of world
9.2	**down-stairs** down stairs		23.7	**benefit.** benefit
10.12	**music box** music-box		23.15	**half-tipsy** half tipsy
12.1	**doorways** door-ways		23.35	**"dis is** "dis it
12.5	**up-stairs** upstairs		26.6	**admirable** amirable
12.37	**doorway** door-way		26.15	**obliged** oblgied
14.6	**perceive it.** perceive it		26.29	**thrash** trash
14.14	**chrysanthemums** chrisanthemums		26.33	**monkeys.** monkeys
14.23	**breathe** breath		27.19	**ecstatic** ecstastic
14.29	**foot-passengers** foot passengers		28.6	**theatre** theater
15.37	**flame-colored** flame colored		28.16	**half-circle** half circle
16.1	**sidewalk** side-walk		28.18	**Her grey** He gray
16.5	**sidewalk** side-walk		28.24	**'Disturbance'?** 'Disturbance?'
16.8	**fire engine** fire-engine		29.18	**Missiles** Missles
16.10	**street cars** street-cars		29.20	**a tin** tin a
17.19	**Island** island		29.25	**yeh damned** yer damned
17.32	**shoes looked** shoes, looked		29.27	**frame** framed
18.7	**But dey** But deh		30.5	**damn** dam
18.15	**trouble';** trouble;'		30.20	**door now,** now, door
18.18	**similar** similiar		31.11	**riddance."** riddance.
18.21	**'spectable** spectable		31.21	**t'ink** tink
18.35	**hadn'** had'n'		31.22	**t'ing** ting

31.26	**t'ing**	ting
31.28	**by**	be
31.29–30	**'Oh, hell, yes,' . . . 'Oh, hell, yes.''**	"Oh, hell, yes," . . . "Oh, hell, yes."
31.32	**up-stairs**	up stairs
32.35	**t'ink**	tink
33.8	**t'inks**	tinks
33.10	**'im.''**	'im.
33.21	**"Yessir,**	"Yesir,
33.24	**it 'ill**	it'ill
33.29	**t'ump**	tump
33.30	**use!**	use!"
33.34	**friend. "What**	friend, "What
34.7	**centre**	center
34.12	**begrimed**	begrimmed
35.29	**Billie?"**	Billie?
35.33	**talkin'?''**	talkin?"
35.41	**bote**	boat
36.1	**eyes.**	eyes
36.10	**hands**	hand
37.9	**missiles**	missles
37.16	**missiles**	missles
37.21	**t'rowed**	trowed
38.28	**yehs lookin'**	yeh's lookin'
38.40	**smoke-filled**	smoked-filled
39.21	**Smooth-cheeked**	Smooth cheeked
39.39	**home.**	home
40.32	**an'—''**	an—"
40.38	**t'ink**	tink
40.42	**nottin'**	nottin
41.3	**won't**	wont
41.6	**nottin',**	nottin,
41.10	**anyway,''**	anyway,
41.39	**police-justices**	police justices
42.20	**an immense**	a immense
42.42	**" 'Scuse**	"Scuse
45.1	**shrivelling**	shriveling
45.28–29	**coin-die**	coin-dye
46.9	**bad-lookin'**	bad lookin'
46.12	**gone.**	gone
46.12	**On'y**	O'ny
46.16	**look-a-here**	look-a here
46.27–28	**forefinger**	fore-finger
46.46	**hallways**	hall-ways
46.22	**her.**	her
46.30	**on-coming**	oncoming
49.10	**wanna**	wanna'
49.10	**fer?**	fer?
51.1	**didn't**	did'nt
51.8	**sternness**	sterness
51.20	**chapter,**	chapter
52.9	**forgetfulness**	forgetness
52.43	**hands**	hand
53.15	**grimy**	grimey
53.15	**T'ink**	Tink
53.19	**eyes**	eyet
54.8	**"An't'ing**	"An'thin'
54.13	**"An't'ing**	"An'thing
54.16	**An't'ing**	An'thing
54.16	**wants,**	want,
54.27	**treat**	treata
54.37	**Magnificently,**	magnificently
55.12	**Me**	me'
55.43	**damn**	dam
56.4	**didn't!**	didn't?
56.5	**me?''**	me,"
56.16	**din'**	din
56.26	**heluva**	heleva
56.42	**glass**	glasss
57.9	**t'umb**	tumb
57.23	**chil'.''**	chile."
57.29	**t'umb**	tumb
57.35	**it's**	its
57.37	**t'ankless**	tankless

Backgrounds and Sources

New York City Locales Mentioned in *Maggie*

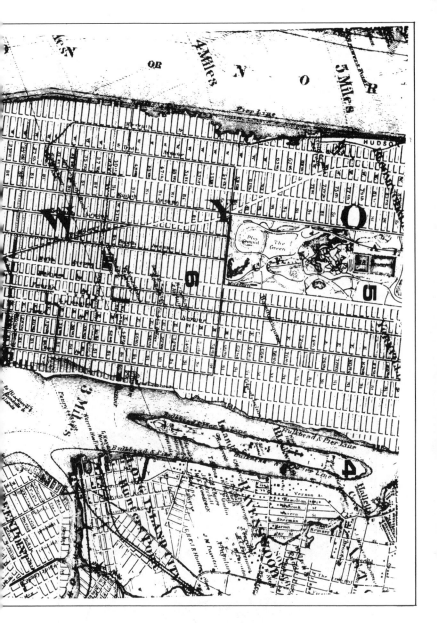

1. *The Bowery*
2. *The East River*
3. *Williamsburg*
4. *Blackwell's Island*
5. *Central Park*
6. *Fifth Avenue*

63

Lower Manhattan (Including the Bowery)

64

CHARLES LORING BRACE

From *The Dangerous Classes of New York; and Twenty Years' Work Among Them* †

A girl street-rover is to my mind the most painful figure in all the unfortunate crowd of a large city. With a boy, "Arab of the streets," one always has the consolation that, despite his ragged clothes and bed in a box or hay-barge, he often has a rather good time of it, and enjoys many of the delicious pleasures of a child's roving life, and that a fortunate turn of events may at any time make an honest, industrious fellow of him. At heart we cannot say that he is much corrupted; his sins belong to his ignorance and his condition, and are often easily corrected by a radical change of circumstances. The oaths, tobacco-spitting, and slang, and even the fighting and stealing of a street-boy, are not so bad as they look. Refined influences, the checks of religion, and a fairer chance for existence without incessant struggle, will often utterly eradicate these evil habits, and the rough, thieving New York vagrant make an honest, hard-working Western pioneer. It is true that sometimes the habit of vagrancy and idling may be too deeply worked in him for his character to speedily reform; but, if of tender years, a change of circumstances will nearly always bring a change of character.

With a girl-vagrant it is different. She feels homelessness and friendlessness more; she has more of the feminine dependence on affection; the street-trades, too, are harder for her, and the return at night to some lonely cellar or tenement-room, crowded with dirty people of all ages and sexes, is more dreary. She develops body and mind earlier than the boy, and the habits of vagabondism stamped on her in childhood are more difficult to wear off.

† From Chapter X, "Street Girls: Their Sufferings and Crimes," in *The Dangerous Classes of New York; and Twenty Years' Work Among Them*, by Charles Loring Brace (New York: Wynkoop & Hallenbeck, Publishers, 1872), pp. 114–19. Charles Loring Brace (1826–90) gave up his theological studies in order to do missionary work among the delinquents of New York City. He helped found the Children's Aid Society in 1853 and was widely and affectionately known as the "children's friend." He was deeply admired by Jacob Riis (who mentioned his work in *How the Other Half Lives*), and it was Riis who may have influenced Stephen Crane's *Maggie*. For further discussion of Loring, see Marcus Cunliffe, "Stephen Crane and the American Background of *Maggie*," below. On Riis, see Thomas A. Gullason, "A Minister, a Social Reformer, and *Maggie*," below.

Then the strange and mysterious subject of sexual vice comes in. It has often seemed to me one of the most dark arrangements of this singular world that a female child of the poor should be permitted to start on its immortal career with almost every influence about it degrading, its inherited tendencies overwhelming toward indulgence of passion, its examples all of crime or lust, its lower nature awake long before its higher, and then that it should be allowed to soil and degrade its soul before the maturity of reason, and beyond all human possibility of cleansing![1]

For there is no reality in the sentimental assertion that the sexual sins of the lad are as degrading as those of the girl. The instinct of the female is more toward the preservation of purity, and therefore her fall is deeper—an instinct grounded in the desire of preserving a stock, or even the necessity of perpetuating our race.

Still, were the indulgences of the two sexes of a similar character—as in savage races—were they both following passion alone, the moral effect would not perhaps be so different in the two cases. But the sin of the girl soon becomes what the Bible calls "a sin against one's own body," the most debasing of all sins. She soon learns to offer for sale that which is in its nature beyond all price, and to feign the most sacred affections, and barter with the most delicate instincts. She no longer merely follows blindly and excessively an instinct; she perverts a passion and sells herself. The only parallel case with the male sex would be that in some Eastern communities which are rotting and falling to pieces from their debasing and unnatural crimes. When we hear of such disgusting offenses under any form of civilization, whether it be under the Rome of the Empire, or the Turkey of to-day, we know that disaster, ruin, and death, are near the State and the people.

This crime, with the girl, seems to sap and rot the whole nature. She loses self-respect, without which every human being soon sinks to the lowest depths; she loses the habit of industry, and cannot be taught to work. Having won her food at the table of Nature by unnatural means, Nature seems to cast her out, and henceforth she cannot labor. Living in a state of unnatural excitement, often worked up to a high pitch of nervous tension by stimulants, becoming weak in body and mind, her character loses fixedness of purpose and tenacity and true energy. The diabolical women who support and plunder her, the vile society she keeps, the literature she reads, the business she has chosen or fallen into, serve continually more and more to degrade and defile her. If, in a moment of remorse, she flee away and take honest work, her weakness and bad habits follow her;

---

1. References to "cleansing," to "dirty" above, and later to "polluted" were characteristic ways in which ministers dramatized the world of sin, corruption, and regeneration. In *Maggie*, Crane continually refers to "dirt" and "contamination." [*Editor.*]

she is inefficient, careless, unsteady, and lazy; she craves the stimulus and hollow gayety of the wild life she has led; her ill name dogs her; all the wicked have an instinct of her former evil courses; the world and herself are against reform, and, unless she chance to have a higher moral nature or stronger will than most of her class, or unless Religion should touch even her polluted soul, she soon falls back, and gives one more sad illustration of the immense difficulty of a fallen woman rising again.

The great majority of prostitutes,[2] it must be remembered, have had no romantic or sensational history, though they always affect this. They usually relate, and perhaps even imagine, that they have been seduced from the paths of virtue suddenly and by the wiles of some heartless seducer. Often they describe themselves as belonging to some virtuous, respectable, and even wealthy family. Their real history, however, is much more commonplace and matter-of-fact. They have been poor women's daughters, and did not want to work as their mothers did; or they have grown up in a tenement-room, crowded with boys and men, and lost purity before they knew what it was; or they have liked gay company, and have had no good influences around them, and sought pleasure in criminal indulgences; or they have been street-children, poor, neglected, and ignorant, and thus naturally and inevitably have become depraved women. Their sad life and debased character are the natural outgrowth of poverty, ignorance, and laziness. The number among them who have "seen better days," or have fallen from heights of virtue, is incredibly small. They show what fruits neglect in childhood, and want of education and of the habit of labor, and the absence of pure examples, will inevitably bear. Yet in their low estate they always show some of the divine qualities of their sex. The physicians in the Blackwell's Island Hospital[3] say that there are no nurses so tender and devoted to the sick and dying as these girls. And the honesty of their dealings with the washerwomen and shopkeepers, who trust them while in their vile houses, has often been noted.

The words of sympathy and religion always touch their hearts, though the effect passes like the April cloud. On a broad scale, probably no remedy that man could apply would ever cure this fatal disease of society. It may, however, be diminished in its ravages, and prevented in a large measure. The check to its devastations in a laboring or poor class will be the facility of marriage, the opening of new channels of female work, but, above all, the influences of education and Religion.

* * *

2. It is interesting to note that discussions of sex and prostitution were tolerated in non-fiction works and in periodical essays but not so readily in a fiction like *Maggie*. [*Editor.*]

3. Located in the East River and extending from 51st to 86th Streets in Manhattan. Here New York City maintained various hospitals, almshouses, and a penitentiary. [*Editor.*]

REVEREND THOMAS DE WITT TALMAGE

From *The Evil Beast* †

* * *

Will the time never come when this nation shall rise up higher than partisanship, and cast its suffrage for sober men?

The fact is, that the two million of dollars which the liquor-dealers raised for the purpose of swaying State and National legislation has done its work, and the nation is debauched. Higher than legislatures or the Congress of the United States is the Whiskey Ring!

The Sabbath has been sacrificed to the rum traffic. To many of our people, the best day of the week is the worst. Bakers must keep their shops closed on the Sabbath. It is dangerous to have loaves of bread going out on Sunday. The shoe store is closed: severe penalty will attack the man who sells boots on the Sabbath. But down with the window-shutters of the grog-shops! Our laws shall confer particular honor upon the rum traffickers. All other trades must stand aside for these. Let our citizens who have disgraced themselves by trading in clothing, and hosiery, and hardware, and lumber, and coal, take off their hats to the rum-seller, elected to particular honor. It is unsafe for any other class of men to be allowed license for Sunday work. But swing out your signs, O ye traffickers in the peace of families, and in the souls of immortal men! Let the corks fly, and the beer foam, and the rum go tearing down the half-consumed throat of the inebriate. God does not see! Does he? Judgment will never come! Will it?

People say, "Let us have more law to correct this evil." We have more law now than we execute. In what city is there a mayoralty that dare do it? The fact is, that there is no advantage in having the law higher than public opinion. What would be the use of the Maine Law[1] in New York? Neal Dow, the Mayor of Portland, came out with a posse and threw the rum of the city into the street. But I do not

---

† From the pamphlet *The Evil Beast: A Sermon,* by Reverend Thomas De Witt Talmage (New York: National Temperance Society and Publication House, 1871), pp. 7–11, 13–15. Reverend Talmage (1832–1902) was the controversial head of the Central Presbyterian Church in Brooklyn (1869–94) and drew the largest audiences of any minister of his day. His dynamic sermons appeared in 3,500 newspapers each week and he made extensive lecture tours each year. He spoke at Ocean Grove, New Jersey, in 1891 and at Asbury Park, New Jersey, in 1892, when Stephen Crane resided there and served as a news correspondent for the *New York Tribune.* See Marcus Cunliffe, "Stephen Crane and the American Background of *Maggie,*" below, for further discussion of Talmage.,

1. Sometime in the 1890s, Stephen Crane wrote a sketch, "The Camel," in which he satirized the Maine Law, prohibiting the sale of alcohol in the State. "The Camel" was not published during Crane's lifetime. It first appeared in *The Complete Short Stories and Sketches of Stephen Crane,* ed. Thomas A. Gullason (New York: Doubleday and Company, 1963). [*Editor.*]

believe there are three mayors in the United States with his courage or nobility of spirit.

I do not know but that God is determined to let drunkenness triumph, and the husbands and sons of thousands of our best families be destroyed by this vice, in order that our people, amazed and indignant, may rise up and demand the extermination of this municipal crime. There is a way of driving down the hoops of a barrel so tight that they break.

We are, in this country, at this time, trying to regulate this evil by a tax on whiskey. You might as well try to regulate the Asiatic cholera or the small-pox by taxation. The men who distil liquors are, for the most part, unscrupulous, and the higher the tax, the more inducement to illicit distillation. New York produces forty thousand gallons of whiskey every twenty-four hours, and the most of it escapes the tax. The most vigilant officials fail to discover the cellars and vaults and sheds where this work is done.

Oh! the folly of trying to restrain an evil by government tariff! If every gallon of whiskey made—if every flask of wine produced, should be taxed a thousand dollars, it would not be enough to pay for the tears it has wrung from the eyes of widows and orphans, nor for the blood it has dashed on the Christian church, nor for the catastrophe of the millions it has destroyed for ever.

I sketch two houses in this street. The first is bright as home can be. The father comes at nightfall, and the children run out to meet him. Luxuriant evening meal. Gratulation, and sympathy, and laughter. Music in the parlor. Fine pictures on the wall. Costly books on the stand. Well-clad household. Plenty of everything to make home happy.

House the second: Piano sold yesterday by the sheriff. Wife's furs at pawnbroker's shop. Clock gone. Daughters' jewelry sold to get flour. Carpets gone off the floor. Daughters in faded and patched dresses. Wife sewing for the stores. Little child with an ugly wound on her face, struck in an angry blow. Deep shadow of wretchedness falling in every room. Door-bell rings. Little children hide. Daughters turn pale. Wife holds her breath. Blundering step in the hall. Door opens. Fiend, brandishing his fist, cries, "Out! out! What are you doing here?"

Did I call this house the second? No; it is the same house. Rum transformed it. Rum embruted the man. Rum sold the shawl. Rum tore up the carpets. Rum shook its fist. Rum desolated the hearth. *Rum* changed that paradise into a hell![2]

* * *

2. The Johnson family, in *Maggie*, resides in Rum Alley. Both parents drink and so does the son Jimmie later. The image of the brewery appears in Crane's other New York City novel, *George's Mother* (1896). [*Editor.*]

I have shown you the EVIL BEAST. The question is, Who will hunt him down, and how shall we shoot him? I answer, First, by getting our children right on this subject. Let them grow up with an utter aversion to strong drink. Take care how you administer it even as medicine. If you find that they have a natural love for it, as some have, put in a glass of it some horrid stuff, and make it utterly nauseous. Teach them, as faithfully as you do the catechism, that rum is a fiend. Take them to the almshouse, and show them the wreck and ruin it works. Walk with them into the homes that have been scourged by it. If a drunkard hath fallen into a ditch, take them right up where they can see his face, bruised, savage, and swollen, and say, "Look, my son. Rum did that!" Looking out of your window at some one who, intoxicated to madness, goes through the street, brandishing his fist, blaspheming God, a howling, defying, shouting, reeling, raving, and foaming maniac, say to your son, "Look; that man was once a child like you." As you go by the grog-shop, let them know that that is the place where men are slain, and their wives made paupers, and their children slaves. Hold out to your children all warnings, all rewards, all counsels, lest in after-days they break your heart and curse your gray hairs.

A man laughed at my father for his scrupulous temperance principles, and said: "I am more liberal than you. I always give my children the sugar in the glass after we have been taking a drink."

Three of his sons have died drunkards, and the fourth is imbecile through intemperate habits.

Again, we will battle this evil at the ballot-box. How many men are there who can rise above the feelings of partisanship, and demand that our officials shall be sober men?

I maintain that the question of sobriety is higher than the question of availability; and that, however eminent a man's services may be, if he have habits of intoxication, he is unfit for any office in the gift of a Christian people. Our laws will be no better than the men who make them.

Spend a few days at Harrisburg, or Albany, or Washington, and you will find out why, upon these subjects, it is impossible to get righteous enactments.

REVEREND THOMAS DE WITT TALMAGE

From *The Night Sides of City Life*†

* * *

For several Sabbath mornings I have pointed out to you the fountains of municipal corruption, and this morning I propose to show you what are the means for the rectification of those fountains. There are four or five kinds of salt that have a cleansing tendency. So far as God may help me this morning, I shall bring a cruse[1] of salt to the work, and empty it into the great reservoir of municipal crime, sin, shame, ignorance, and abomination.

In this work of cleansing our cities, I have first to remark that *there is a work for the broom and the shovel that nothing else can do.*[2] There always has been an intimate connection between iniquity and dirt. The filthy parts of the great cities are always the most iniquitous parts. The gutters and the pavements of the Fourth Ward, New York, illustrate and symbolize the character of the people in the Fourth Ward.

The first thing that a bad man does when he is converted is thoroughly to wash himself. There were, this morning, on the way to the different churches, thousands of men in proper apparel who, before their conversion, were unfit in their Sabbath dress. When on the Sabbath I see a man uncleanly in his dress, my suspicions in regard to his moral character are aroused, and they are always well founded. So as to allow no excuse for lack of ablution, God has cleft the continents with rivers and lakes, and has sunk five great oceans, and all the world ought to be clean. Away, then, with the dirt from our cities, not only because the physical health needs an ablution, but because all the great moral and religious interests of the cities demand it as a positive necessity. A filthy city always has been and always will be a wicked city.

Another corrective influence that we would bring to bear upon the evils of our great cities is *a Christian printing-press*. The newspapers of any place are the test of its morality or immorality. The newsboy who runs along the street with a roll of papers under his arm is a

† From Chapter X, "The Reservoirs Salted," in *The Night Sides of City Life*, by Reverend Thomas De Witt Talmage (Chicago: J. Fairbanks & Co., 1878), pp. 128–34, 137–38. For discussions of Talmage, see his *The Evil Beast*, above, and Marcus Cunliffe, "Stephen Crane and the American Background of *Maggie*," below.
1. A small jar or pot. [*Editor*.]

2. Philanthropists and ministers like Charles Loring Brace and the Reverend Talmage, along with reformers and crusading newspapers, helped to create a new field for fiction, the city and the slums. Like Brace before him, Talmage links the city to "dirt," "iniquity," and "cleansing." In *Maggie*, Crane makes literal and symbolic use of "dirt" and "contamination." [*Editor*.]

tremendous force that cannot be turned aside nor resisted, and at his every step the city is elevated or degraded. This hungry, all-devouring American mind must have something to read, and upon editors and authors and book-publishers and parents and teachers rest the responsibility of what they shall read. Almost every man you meet has a book in his hand or a newspaper in his pocket. What book is it you have in your hand? What newspaper is it you have in your pocket? Ministers may preach, reformers may plan, philan-thropists may toil for the elevation of the suffering and the criminal, but until all the newspapers of the land and all the booksellers of the land set themselves against an iniquitous literature—until then we will be fighting against fearful odds. Every time the cylinders of Harper or Appleton or Ticknor or Peterson or Lippincott[3] turn, they make the earth quake. From them goes forth a thought like an angel of light to feed and bless the world, or like an angel of darkness to smite it with corruption and sin and shame and death. May God by His omnipotent Spirit purify and elevate the American printing-press!

I go on further and say that *we must depend upon the school for a great deal of correcting influence*. Community can no more afford to have ignorant men in its midst than it can afford to have uncaged hyenas. Ignorance is the mother of hydra-headed crime. Thirty-one per cent of all the criminals of New York State can neither read nor write. Intellectual darkness is generally the precursor of moral dark-ness. I know there are educated outlaws—men who, through their sharpness of intellect, are made more dangerous. They use their fine penmanship in signing other people's names, and their science in ingenious burglaries, and their fine manners in adroit libertinism. They go their round of sin with well-cut apparel, and dangling jew-elry, and watches of eighteen karats, and kid gloves. They are refined, educated, magnificent villains. But that is the exception. It is gen-erally the case that the criminal classes are as ignorant as they are wicked. For the proof of what I say, go into the prisons and the penitentiaries, and look upon the men and women incarcerated. The dishonesty in the eye, the low passion in the lip, are not more conspicuous than the ignorance in the forehead. The ignorant classes are always the dangerous classes.[4] Demagogues marshal them. They are helmless, and are driven before the gale.

*　*　*

Still further: *reformatory societies are an important element in the rectification of the public fountains*. Without calling any of them by name, I refer more especially to those which recognize the physical as well as the moral woes of the world. There was pathos and a great

3. Some of the important publishing houses of the day. [*Editor.*]

4. An echo of Charles Loring Brace's *The Dan-gerous Classes of New York* (see above). [*Editor.*]

deal of common sense in what the poor woman said to Dr. Guthrie
when he was telling her what a very good woman she ought to be.
"Oh," she said, "if you were as hungry and cold as I am, you could
think of nothing else." I believe the great want of our city is the
Gospel and something to eat! Faith and repentance are of infinite
importance; but they cannot satisfy an empty stomach! You have to
go forth in this work with the bread of eternal life in your right hand,
and the bread of this life in your left hand, and then you can touch
them, imitating the Lord Jesus Christ, who first broke the bread and
fed the multitude in the wilderness, and then began to preach,
recognizing the fact that while people are hungry they will not listen,
and they will not repent.[5] We want more common sense in the
distribution of our charities; fewer magnificent theories, and more
hard work. In the last war, a few hours after the battle of Antietam,
I had a friend who was moving over the field, and who saw a good
Christian man distributing tracts. My friend said to him: "This is no
time to distribute tracts. There are three thousand men around here
who are bleeding to death, who have not had bandages put on. Take
care of their bodies, then give them tracts." That was well said. Look
after the woes of the body, and then you will have some success in
looking after the woes of the soul.

Still further: *the great remedial influence is the Gospel of Christ*.
Take that down through the lanes of suffering. Take that down amid
the hovels of sin. Take that up amid the mansions and palaces of
your city. That is the salt that can cure all the poisoned fountains of
public iniquity. Do you know that in this cluster of three cities, New
York, Jersey City, and Brooklyn, there are a great multitude of
homeless children? You see I speak more in regard to the youth and
the children of the country, because old villains are seldom reformed,
and therefore I talk more about the little ones. They sleep under the
stoops, in the burned-out safe, in the wagons in the streets, on the
barges, wherever they can get a board to cover them. And in the
summer they sleep all night long in the parks. Their destitution is
well set forth by an incident. A city missionary asked one of them:
"Where is your home?" Said he: "I don't have no home, sir." "Well,
where are your father and mother?" "They are dead, sir." "Did you
ever hear of Jesus Christ?" "No, I don't think I ever heard of him."
"Did you ever hear of God?" "Yes, I've heard of God. Some of the
poor people think it kind of lucky at night to say something over
about that before they go to sleep. Yes, sir, I've heard of him." Think
of a conversation like that in a Christian city.

How many are waiting for you to come out in the spirit of the
Lord Jesus Christ and rescue them from the wretchedness here! A

5. Like Talmage, Crane in *Maggie* was critical of unrealistic and naive ministers. See the mission church preacher in Chapter IV of *Maggie*. [*Editor.*]

man was trying to talk with a group of these outcasts, and read the Bible, and trying to comfort them, and he said: "My dear boys, when your father and your mother forsake you, who will take you up?" They shouted "The perlice, sir; the perlice?" Oh that the Church of God had arms long enough and hearts warm enough to take them up. How many of them there are! As I was thinking of the subject this morning, it seemed to me as though there was a great brink, and that these little ones with cut and torn feet were coming on toward it. And here is a group of orphans. O fathers and mothers, what do you think of these fatherless and motherless little ones? No hand at home to take care of their apparel, no heart to pity them. Said one little one, when the mother died: "Who will take care of my clothes now?" The little ones are thrown out in this great, cold world. They are shivering on the brink like lambs on the verge of a precipice. Does not your blood run cold as they go over it?

And here is another group that come on toward the precipice. They are the children of besotted parents. They are worse off than orphans. Look at that pale cheek: woe bleached it. Look at that gash across the forehead; the father struck it. Hear that heart-piercing cry: a drunken mother's blasphemy compelled it. And we come out and we say: "O ye suffering, peeled and blistered ones, we come to help you." "Too late!" cry thousands of voices. "The path we travel is steep down, and we can't stop. Too late!" and we catch our breath and we make a terrific outcry. "Too late!" is echoed from the garret to the cellar, from the gin-shop and from the brothel. "Too late!" It *is* too late, and they go over.

Here is another group, an army of neglected children. They come on toward the brink, and every time they step ten thousand hearts break. The ground is red with the blood of their feet. The air is heavy with their groans. Their ranks are being filled up from all the houses of iniquity and shame. Skeleton Despair pushes them on toward the brink. The death-knell has already begun to toll, and the angels of God hover like birds over the plunge of a cataract. While these children are on the brink they halt, and throw out their hands, and cry: "Help! help!" O church of God, will you help? Men and women bought by the blood of the Son of God, will you help? while Christ cries from the heavens: "Save them from going down; I am the ransom."

* * *

For this vast multitude, are we willing to go forth from this morning's service and see what we can do, employing all the agencies I have spoken of for the rectification of the poisoned fountains? We live in a beautiful city. The lines have fallen to us in pleasant places, and we have a goodly heritage; and any man who does not like a residence in Brooklyn, must be a most uncomfortable and unreasonable man. But, my friends, the material prosperity of a city is not its chief glory. There may be fine houses and beautiful streets, and that all be the garniture of a sepulcher. Some of the most prosperous cities of the world have gone down, not one stone left upon another. But a city may be in ruins long before a tower has fallen, or a column has crumbled, or a tomb has been defaced. When in a city the churches of God are full of cold formalities and inanimate religion; when the houses of commerce are the abode of fraud and unholy traffic; when the streets are filled with crime unarrested and sin unenlightened and helplessness unpitied—that city is in ruins, though every church were a St. Peter's, and every moneyed institution were a Bank of England, and every library were a British Museum, and every house had a porch like that of Rheims and a roof like that of Amiens and a tower like that of Antwerp, and traceried windows like those of Freiburg.

My brethren, our pulses beat rapidly the time away, and soon we will be gone; and what we have to do for the city in which we live we must do right speedily, or never do it at all. In that day, when those who have wrapped themselves in luxuries and despised the poor, shall come to shame and everlasting contempt, I hope it may be said of you and me that we gave bread to the hungry, and wiped away the tear of the orphan, and upon the wanderer of the street we opened the brightness and benediction of a Christian home; and then, through our instrumentality, it shall be known on earth and in heaven, that Mary Lost became Mary Found!

JACOB RIIS

From *How the Other Half Lives*†

Introduction

* * *

It is ten years and over, now, since that line divided New York's population evenly. To-day three-fourths of its people live in the

† From *How the Other Half Lives: Studies Among the Tenements of New York*, by Jacob A. Riis (New York: Charles Scribner's Sons, 1890), pp. 2–3, 179–80, 182–83, 185–86, 210–13, 215–21, 234–35. The Danish immigrant Jacob Riis (1849–1914) was a police reporter for the *New York Tribune*. President Theodore Roosevelt called him "the most useful citizen in New York"; to others he was the "great emancipator" of the slums. One of the earliest muckraking books, *How the Other Half Lives* (published in November 1890) focused on the Lower East Side slums and did "more than anything else to prepare the way for the housing investigations and new tenement-house codes of the next decade." Beginning in 1890, Riis abandoned regular newspaper work and became a free-lance journalist, active reformer, and lecturer. Not only Riis's locale and subject may have inspired Stephen Crane, his use of the short vignette may have influenced Crane's style in the 1893 *Maggie*. For Riis's relationship with Crane, see Thomas A. Gullason, "A Minister, a Social Reformer, and *Maggie*," below.

tenements, and the nineteenth century drift of the population to the cities is sending ever-increasing multitudes to crowd them. The fifteen thousand tenant houses that were the despair of the sanitarian in the past generation have swelled into thirty-seven thousand, and more than twelve hundred thousand persons call them home. The one way out he saw—rapid transit to the suburbs—has brought no relief. We know now that there is no way out; that the "system" that was the evil offspring of public neglect and private greed has come to stay, a storm-centre forever of our civilization. Nothing is left but to make the best of a bad bargain.

What the tenements are and how they grow to what they are, we shall see hereafter. The story is dark enough, drawn from the plain public records, to send a chill to any heart. If it shall appear that the sufferings and the sins of the "other half," and the evil they breed, are but as a just punishment upon the community that gave it no other choice, it will be because that is the truth. The boundary line lies there because, while the forces for good on one side vastly outweigh the bad—it were not well otherwise—in the tenements all the influences make for evil; because they are the hot-beds of the epidemics that carry death to rich and poor alike; the nurseries of pauperism and crime that fill our jails and police courts; that throw off a scum of forty thousand human wrecks to the island asylums and workhouses year by year; that turned out in the last eight years a round half million beggars to prey upon our charities; that maintain a standing army of ten thousand tramps with all that that implies; because, above all, they touch the family life with deadly moral contagion. This is their worst crime, inseparable from the system. That we have to own it the child of our own wrong does not excuse it, even though it gives it claim upon our utmost patience and tenderest charity.

* * *

Chapter XV. The Problem of the Children

The problem of the children becomes, in these swarms, to the last degree perplexing. Their very number make one stand aghast. I have already given instances of the packing of the child population in East Side tenements. They might be continued indefinitely until the array would be enough to startle any community. For, be it remembered, these children with the training they receive—or do not receive— with the instincts they inherit and absorb in their growing up, are to be our future rulers, if our theory of government is worth anything. More than a working majority of our voters now register from the tenements. I counted the other day the little ones, up to ten years or so, in a Bayard Street tenement that for a yard has a triangular space in the centre with sides fourteen or fifteen feet long, just room enough for a row of ill-smelling closets at the base of the triangle and a hydrant at the apex. There was about as much light in this "yard" as in the average cellar. I gave up my self-imposed task in despair when I had counted one hundred and twenty-eight in forty families. Thirteen I had missed, or not found in. Applying the average for the forty to the whole fifty-three, the house contained one hundred and seventy children. It is not the only time I have had to give up such census work. I have in mind an alley—an inlet rather to a row of rear tenements—that is either two or four feet wide according as the wall of the crazy old building that gives on it bulges out or in. I tried to count the children that swarmed there, but could not. Sometimes I have doubted that anybody knows just how many there are about. Bodies of drowned children turn up in the rivers right along in summer whom no one seems to know anything about. When last spring some workmen, while moving a pile of lumber on a North River pier, found under the last plank the body of a little lad crushed to death, no one had missed a boy, though his parents afterward turned up. The truant officer assuredly does not know, though he spends his life trying to find out, somewhat illogically, perhaps, since the department that employs him admits that thousands of poor children are crowded out of the schools year by year for want of room. There was a big tenement in the Sixth Ward, now happily appropriated by the beneficent spirit of business that blots out so many foul spots in New York—it figured not long ago in the official reports as "an out-and-out hog-pen"—that had a record of one hundred and two arrests in four years among its four hundred and seventy-eight tenants, fifty-seven of them for drunken and disorderly conduct. I do not know how many children there were in it, but the inspector reported that he found only seven in the whole house who owned that they went to school. The rest gathered all the instruction they received running for beer for their elders.[1] Some of them claimed the "flat" as their home as a mere matter of form. They slept in the streets at night. The official came upon a little party of four drinking beer out of the cover of a milk-can in the hallway. They were of the seven good boys and proved their claim to the title by offering him some.

*   *   *

With such human instincts and cravings, forever unsatisfied, turned into a haunting curse; with appetite ground to keenest edge by a hunger that is never fed, the children of the poor grow up in joyless homes to lives of wearisome toil that claims them at an age when the play of their happier fellows has but just begun. Has a yard

---

1. See "The Reign of Rum," below, for Riis's shock and indignation at this errand slum children had to perform. Note that Jimmie, in Chapter III of *Maggie*, runs a similar errand. [*Editor.*]

of turf been laid and a vine been coaxed to grow within their reach, they are banished and barred out from it as from a heaven that is not for such as they. I came upon a couple of youngsters in a Mulberry Street yard a while ago that were chalking on the fence their first lesson in "writin'." And this is what they wrote: "Keeb of te Grass." They had it by heart, for there was not, I verily believe, a green sod within a quarter of a mile. Home to them is an empty name. Pleasure? A gentleman once catechized a ragged class in a down-town public school on this point, and recorded the result: Out of forty-eight boys twenty had never seen the Brooklyn Bridge that was scarcely five minutes' walk away, three only had been in Central Park, fifteen had known the joy of a ride in a horse-car. The street, with its ash-barrels and its dirt, the river that runs foul with mud, are their domain. What training they receive is picked up there. And they are apt pupils. If the mud and the dirt are easily reflected in their lives, what wonder? Scarce half-grown, such lads as these confront the world with the challenge to give them their due, too long withheld, or————. Our jails supply the answer to the alternative.

* * *

Nothing is now better understood than that the rescue of the children is the key to the problem of city poverty, as presented for our solution to-day; that character may be formed where to reform it would be a hopeless task. The concurrent testimony of all who have to undertake it at a later stage: that the young are naturally neither vicious nor hardened, simply weak and undeveloped, except by the bad influences of the street, makes this duty all the more urgent as well as hopeful. Helping hands are held out on every side. To private charity the municipality leaves the entire care of its proletariat of tender years, lulling its conscience to sleep with liberal appropriations of money to foot the bills. Indeed, it is held by those whose opinions are entitled to weight that it is far too liberal a paymaster for its own best interests and those of its wards. It deals with the evil in the seed to a limited extent in gathering in the outcast babies from the streets. To the ripe fruit the gates of its prisons, its reformatories, and its workhouses are opened wide the year round. What the showing would be at this end of the line were it not for the barriers wise charity has thrown across the broad highway to ruin— is building day by day—may be measured by such results as those quoted above in the span of a single life.

Chapter XVIII. *The Reign of Rum*

Where God builds a church the devil builds next door—a saloon, is an old saying that has lost its point in New York. Either the devil was on the ground first, or he has been doing a good deal more in the way of building. I tried once to find out how the account stood, and counted to 111 Protestant churches, chapels, and places of worship of every kind below Fourteenth Street, 4,065 saloons. The worst half of the tenement population lives down there, and it has to this day the worst half of the saloons. Uptown the account stands a little better, but there are easily ten saloons to every church to-day. I am afraid, too, that the congregations are larger by a good deal; certainly the attendance is steadier and the contributions more liberal the week round, Sunday included. Turn and twist it as we may, over against every bulwark for decency and morality which society erects, the saloon projects its colossal shadow, omen of evil wherever it falls into the lives of the poor.

Nowhere is its mark so broad or so black. To their misery it sticketh closer than a brother, persuading them that within its doors only is refuge, relief. It has the best of the argument, too, for it is true, worse pity, that in many a tenement-house block the saloon is the one bright and cheery and humanly decent spot to be found. It is a sorry admission to make, that to bring the rest of the neighborhood up to the level of the saloon would be one way of squelching it; but it is so. Wherever the tenements thicken, it multiplies. Upon the direst poverty of their crowds it grows fat and prosperous, levying upon it a tax heavier than all the rest of its grievous burdens combined. It is not yet two years since the Excise Board made the rule that no three corners of any street-crossing, not already so occupied, should thenceforward be licensed for rum-selling. And the tardy prohibition was intended for the tenement districts. Nowhere else is there need of it. One may walk many miles through the homes of the poor searching vainly for an open reading-room, a cheerful coffee-house, a decent club that is not a cloak for the traffic in rum. The dramshop yawns at every step, the poor man's club, his forum and his haven of rest when weary and disgusted with the crowding, the quarrelling, and the wretchedness at home. With the poison dealt out there he takes his politics, in quality not far apart. As the source, so the stream. The rumshop turns the political crank in New York. The natural yield is rum politics. Of what that means, successive Boards of Aldermen, composed in a measure, if not of a majority, of dive-keepers, have given New York a taste. The disgrace of the infamous "Boodle Board"[2] will be remembered until some corruption even fouler crops out and throws it into the shade.

What relation the saloon bears to the crowds, let me illustrate by a comparison. Below Fourteenth Street were, when the Health Department took its first accurate census of the tenements a year and a half ago, 13,220 of the 32,390 buildings classed as such in the whole

2. The corrupt Board of Aldermen during the era of William Marcy Tweed (1823–78), "boss" of   New York City. [*Editor.*]

city. Of the eleven hundred thousand tenants, not quite half a million, embracing a host of more than sixty-three thousand children
under five years of age, lived below that line. Below it, also, were
234 of the cheap lodging-houses accounted for by the police last
year, with a total of four millions and a half of lodgers for the
twelvemonth, 59 of the city's 110 pawnshops, and 4,065 of its 7,884
saloons. The four most densely peopled precincts, the Fourth, Sixth,
Tenth, and Eleventh, supported together in round numbers twelve
hundred saloons, and their returns showed twenty-seven per cent.
of the whole number of arrests for the year. The Eleventh Precinct,
that has the greatest and the poorest crowds of all—it is the Tenth
Ward—and harbored one-third of the army of homeless lodgers and
fourteen per cent. of all the prisoners of the year, kept 485 saloons
going in 1889. It is not on record that one of them all failed for want
of support. A number of them, on the contrary, had brought their
owners wealth and prominence. From their bars these eminent citizens stepped proudly into the councils of the city and the State. The
very floor of one of the bar-rooms, in a neighborhood that lately
resounded with the cry for bread of starving workmen, is paved with
silver dollars!

* * *

With the exception of these free lances that treat the law openly
with contempt, the saloons all hang out a sign announcing in fat
type that no beer or liquor is sold to children. In the down-town
"morgues" that make the lowest degradation of tramp-humanity pan
out a paying interest, as in the "reputable resorts" uptown where
Inspector Byrnes's[3] men spot their worthier quarry elbowing citizens
whom the idea of associating with a burglar would give a shock they
would not get over for a week, this sign is seen conspicuously displayed. Though apparently it means submission to a beneficent law,
in reality the sign is a heartless, cruel joke. I doubt if one child in a
thousand, who brings his growler[4] to be filled at the average New
York bar, is sent away empty-handed, if able to pay for what he
wants. I once followed a little boy, who shivered in bare feet on a
cold November night so that he seemed in danger of smashing his
pitcher on the icy pavement, into a Mulberry Street saloon where
just such a sign hung on the wall, and forbade the barkeeper to serve
the boy. The man was as astonished at my interference as if I had
told him to shut up his shop and go home, which in fact I might
have done with as good a right, for it was after 1 A.M., the legal
closing hour. He was mighty indignant too, and told me roughly to
go away and mind my business, while he filled the pitcher. The law
prohibiting the selling of beer to minors is about as much respected

3. Thomas Byrnes, Chief Inspector of Police in New York City. [*Editor.*]   4. A can or pitcher used to carry beer. [*Editor.*]

in the tenement-house districts as the ordinance against swearing. Newspaper readers will recall the story, told little more than a year ago, of a boy who after carrying beer a whole day for a shopful of men over on the East Side, where his father worked, crept into the cellar to sleep off the effects of his own share in the rioting. It was Saturday evening. Sunday his parents sought him high and low; but it was not until Monday morning, when the shop was opened, that he was found, killed and half-eaten by the rats that overran the place.

All the evil the saloon does in breeding poverty and in corrupting politics; all the suffering it brings into the lives of its thousands of innocent victims, the wives and children of drunkards it sends forth to curse the community; its fostering of crime and its shielding of criminals—it is all as nothing to this, its worst offence. In its affinity for the thief there is at least this compensation that, as it makes, it also unmakes him. It starts him on his career only to trip him up and betray him into the hands of the law, when the rum he exchanged for his honesty has stolen his brains as well. For the corruption of the child there is no restitution. None is possible. It saps the very vitals of society; undermines its strongest defences, and delivers them over to the enemy. Fostered and filled by the saloon, the "growler" looms up in the New York street boy's life, baffling the most persistent efforts to reclaim him. There is no escape from it; no hope for the boy, once its blighting grip is upon him. Thenceforward the logic of the slums, that the world which gave him poverty and ignorance for his portion "owes him a living," is his creed, and the career of the "tough" lies open before him, a beaten track to be blindly followed to a bad end in the wake of the growler.

Chapter XIX. The Harvest of Tares[5]

* * *

Along the water-fronts, in the holes of the dock-rats, and on the avenues, the young tough finds plenty of kindred spirits. Every corner has its gang, not always on the best of terms with the rivals in the next block, but all with a common programme: defiance of law and order, and with a common ambition: to get "pinched," *i.e.*, arrested, so as to pose as heroes before their fellows. A successful raid on the grocer's till is a good mark, "doing up" a policeman cause for promotion. The gang is an institution in New York. The police deny its existence while nursing the bruises received in nightly battles with it that tax their utmost resources. The newspapers chronicle its doings daily, with a sensational minuteness of detail that does its share toward keeping up its evil traditions and inflaming the ambition

5. Biblical allusion to Matthew 13:25. Harmful or destructive elements, like weeds growing among wheat. [*Editor.*]

of its members to be as bad as the worst. The gang is the ripe fruit of tenement-house growth. It was born there, endowed with a heritage of instinctive hostility to restraint by a generation that sacrificed home to freedom, or left its country for its country's good. The tenement received and nursed the seed. The intensity of the American temper stood sponsor to the murderer in what would have been the common "bruiser" of a more phlegmatic clime. New York's tough represents the essence of reaction against the old and the new oppression, nursed in the rank soil of its slums. Its gangs are made up of the American-born sons of English, Irish, and German parents. They reflect exactly the conditions of the tenements from which they sprang. Murder is as congenial to Cherry Street or to Battle Row, as quiet and order to Murray Hill. The "assimilation" of Europe's oppressed hordes, upon which our Fourth of July orators are fond of dwelling, is perfect. The product is our own.

Such is the genesis of New York's gangs. Their history is not so easily written. It would embrace the largest share of our city's criminal history for two generations back, every page of it dyed red with blood. The guillotine Paris set up a century ago to avenge its wrongs was not more relentless, or less discriminating, than this Nemesis of New York. The difference is of intent. Murder with that was the serious purpose; with ours it is the careless incident, the wanton brutality of the moment. Bravado and robbery are the real purposes of the gangs; the former prompts the attack upon the policeman, the latter that upon the citizen. Within a single week last spring, the newspapers recorded six murderous assaults on unoffending people, committed by young highwaymen in the public streets. How many more were suppressed by the police, who always do their utmost to hush up such outrages "in the interests of justice," I shall not say. There has been no lack of such occurrences since, as the records of the criminal courts show. In fact, the past summer has seen, after a period of comparative quiescence of the gangs, a reawakening to renewed turbulence of the East Side tribes, and over and over again the reserve forces of a precinct have been called out to club them into submission. It is a peculiarity of the gangs that they usually break out in spots, as it were. When the West Side is in a state of eruption, the East Side gangs "lie low," and when the toughs along the North River are nursing broken heads at home, or their revenge in Sing Sing, fresh trouble breaks out in the tenements east of Third Avenue. This result is brought about by the very efforts made by the police to put down the gangs. In spite of local feuds, there is between them a species of ruffianly Freemasonry that readily admits to full fellowship a hunted rival in the face of the common enemy. The gangs belt the city like a huge chain from the Battery to Harlem—the collective name of the "chain gang" has been given to their scattered groups in the belief that a much closer connection exists between them than commonly supposed—and the ruffian for whom the East Side has become too hot, has only to step across town and change his name, a matter usually much easier for him than to change his shirt, to find a sanctuary in which to plot fresh outrages. The more notorious he is, the warmer the welcome, and if he has "done" his man he is by common consent accorded the leadership in his new field.

From all this it might be inferred that the New York tough is a very fierce individual, of indomitable courage and naturally as blood-thirsty as a tiger. On the contrary he is an arrant coward. His instincts of ferocity are those of the wolf rather than the tiger. It is only when he hunts with the pack that he is dangerous. Then his inordinate vanity makes him forget all fear or caution in the desire to distinguish himself before his fellows, a result of his swallowing all the flash literature and penny-dreadfuls he can beg, borrow, or steal—and there is never any lack of them—and of the strongly dramatic element in his nature that is nursed by such a diet into rank and morbid growth. He is a queer bundle of contradictions at all times. Drunk and foul-mouthed, ready to cut the throat of a defenceless stranger at the toss of a cent, fresh from beating his decent mother black and blue to get money for rum,[6] he will resent as an intolerable insult the imputation that he is "no gentleman." Fighting his battles with the coward's weapons, the brass-knuckles and the deadly sand-bag, or with brick-bats from the housetops, he is still in all seriousness a lover of fair play, and as likely as not, when his gang has downed a policeman in a battle that has cost a dozen broken heads, to be found next saving a drowning child or woman at the peril of his own life. It depends on the angle at which he is seen, whether he is a cowardly ruffian, or a possible hero with different training and under different social conditions. Ready wit he has at all times, and there is less meanness in his make-up than in that of the bully of the London slums; but an intense love of show and applause, that carries him to any length of bravado, which his twin-brother across the sea entirely lacks. I have a very vivid recollection of seeing one of his tribe, a robber and murderer before he was nineteen, go to the gallows unmoved, all fear of the rope overcome, as it seemed, by the secret, exultant pride of being the centre of a first-class show, shortly to be followed by that acme of tenement-life bliss, a big funeral. He had his reward. His name is to this day a talisman among West Side

6. This very mother will implore the court with tears, the next morning, to let her renegade son off. A poor woman, who claimed to be the widow of a soldier, applied to the Tenement-house Relief Committee of the King's Daughters last summer, to be sent to some home, as she had neither kith nor kin to care for her. Upon investigation it was found that she had four big sons, all toughs, who beat her regularly and took from her all the money she could earn or beg; she was "a respectable woman, of good habits," the inquiry developed, and lied only to shield her rascally sons.

ruffians, and is proudly borne by the gang of which, up till the night when he "knocked out his man," he was an obscure though aspiring member.

*　*　*

Chapter XX. The Working Girls of New York

Of the harvest of tares, sown in iniquity and reaped in wrath, the police returns tell the story. The pen that wrote the "Song of the Shirt"[7] is needed to tell of the sad and toil-worn lives of New York's working-women. The cry echoes by night and by day through its tenements:

> Oh, God! that bread should be so dear,
> And flesh and blood so cheap!

Six months have not passed since at a great public meeting in this city, the Working Women's Society[8] reported: "It is a known fact that men's wages cannot fall below a limit upon which they can exist, but woman's wages have no limit, since the paths of shame are always open to her. It is simply impossible for any woman to live without assistance on the low salary a saleswoman earns, without depriving herself of real necessities. . . It is inevitable that they must in many instances resort to evil." It was only a few brief weeks before that verdict was uttered, that the community was shocked by the story of a gentle and refined woman who, left in direst poverty to earn her own living alone among strangers, threw herself from her attic window, preferring death to dishonor. "I would have done any honest work, even to scrubbing," she wrote, drenched and starving, after a vain search for work in a driving storm. She had tramped the streets for weeks on her weary errand, and the only living wages that were offered her were the wages of sin. The ink was not dry upon her letter before a woman in an East Side tenement wrote down her reason for self-murder: "Weakness, sleeplessness, and yet obliged to work. My strength fails me. Sing at my coffin: 'Where does the soul find a home and rest?'" Her story may be found as one of two typical "cases of despair" in one little church community, in the *City Mission Society's Monthly* for last February. It is a story that has many parallels in the experience of every missionary, every police reporter and every family doctor whose practice is among the poor.

*　*　*

---

7. A poem written in 1843 by the English poet, Thomas Hood. Riis quotes two lines from it. [*Editor.*]

8. This society was formed in 1888 to unionize women workers, to protect women and children from ruthless employers, and to end the use of tenements as manufacturing shops. [*Editor.*]

JACOB RIIS

From *The Children of the Poor*†

* * *

In other words, the child is a creature of environment, of opportunity, as children are everywhere. And the environment here has been bad, as it was and is in the lands across the sea that sent him to us. Our slums have fairly rivalled, and in some respects outdone, the older ones after which they patterned. Still, there is a difference, the difference between the old slum and the new. The hopelessness, the sullen submission of life in East London as we have seen it portrayed, has no counterpart here; neither has the child born in the gutter and predestined by the order of society, from which there is no appeal, to die there. We have our Lost Tenth to fill the trench in the Potter's Field[1]; quite as many wrecks at the finish, perhaps, but the start seems fairer in the promise. Even on the slums the doctrine of liberty has set its stamp. To be sure, for the want of the schooling to decipher it properly, they spell it license there, and the slip makes trouble. The tough and his scheme of levying tribute are the result. But the police settle that with him, and when it comes to a choice, the tough is to be preferred to the born pauper any day. The one has the making of something in him, unpromising as he looks; seen in a certain light he may even be considered a hopeful symptom. The other is just so much dead loss. The tough is not born: he is made. The all-important point is the one at which the manufacture can be stopped.

So rapid and great are the changes in American cities, that no slum has yet had a chance here to grow old enough to distil its deadliest poison. New York has been no exception. But we cannot always go at so fast a pace. There is evidence enough in the crystallization of the varying elements of the population along certain lines, no longer as uncertain as they were, that we are slowing up already. Any observer of the poor in this city is familiar with the appearance among them of that most distressing and most dangerous symptom, the home-feeling for the slum that opposes all efforts at betterment with dull indifference. Pauperism seems to have grown faster of late than even the efforts put forth to check it. We have witnessed this

† From Chapter 1, "The Problem of the Children," in *The Children of the Poor*, by Jacob A. Riis (New York: Charles Scribner's Sons, 1892), pp. 4–7. *The Children of the Poor* was published in October 1892. Its tone was at once more aggressive and more positive than *How the Other Half Lives*. For background on Jacob Riis, see *How the Other Half Lives*, above.

1. A place for the burial of poor or unknown persons. [*Editor.*]

past winter a dozen times the spectacle of beggars extorting money by threats or violence without the excuse which a season of exceptional distress or hardship might have furnished. Further, the raid in the last Legislature upon the structure of law built up in a generation to regulate and keep the tenements within safe limits, shows that fresh danger threatens in the alliance of the slum with politics. Only the strongest public sentiment, kept always up to the point of prompt action, avails to ward off this peril. But public sentiment soon wearies of such watch-duty, as instanced on this occasion, when several bills radically remodelling the tenement-house law and repealing some of its most beneficent provisions, had passed both houses and were in the hands of the Governor before a voice was raised against them, or anyone beside the politicians and their backers seemed even to have heard of them. And this hardly five years after a special commission of distinguished citizens had sat an entire winter under authority of the State considering the tenement-house problem,[2] and as the result of its labors had secured as vital the enactment of the very law against which the raid seemed to be chiefly directed!

The tenement and the saloon, with the street that does not always divide them, form the environment that is to make or unmake the child. The influence of each of the three is bad. Together they have power to overcome the strongest resistance. But the child born under their evil spell has none such to offer. The testimony of all to whom has fallen the task of undoing as much of the harm done by them as may be, from the priest of the parish school to the chaplain of the penitentiary, agrees upon this point, that even the tough, with all his desperation, is weak rather than vicious. He promises well, he even means well; he is as downright sincere in his repentance as he was in his wrong-doing; but it doesn't prevent him from doing the very same evil deed over again the minute he is rid of restraint. He would rather be a saint than a sinner; but somehow he doesn't keep in the *rôle* of saint, while the police help perpetuate the memory of his wickedness. After all, he is not so very different from the rest of us. Perhaps that, with a remorseful review of the chances he has had, may help to make a fellow-feeling for him in us.

That is what he needs. The facts clearly indicate that from the environment no improvement in the child is to be expected. There has been progress in the way of building the tenements of late years, but they swarm with greater crowds than ever—good reason why they challenge the pernicious activity of the politician; and the old rookeries[3] disappear slowly. In the relation of the saloon to the child there has been no visible improvement, and the street is still his

2. A Tenement House Commission had been formed in 1884 to review the conditions in the tenements of New York City. Riis's exposé in *How the Other Half Lives* (1890) was instrumental in the formation of another commission in 1894. [*Editor.*]

3. Crowded tenements. [*Editor.*]

refuge. It is, then, his opportunities outside that must be improved if relief is to come. We have the choice of hailing him man and brother or of being slugged and robbed by him. It ought not to be a hard choice, despite the tatters and the dirt, for which our past neglect is in great part to blame. Plenty of evidence will be found in these pages to show that it has been made in the right spirit already, and that it has proved a wise choice. No investment gives a better return to-day on the capital put out than work among the children of the poor.

* * *

BENJAMIN ORANGE FLOWER

From *Civilization's Inferno*†

It is difficult to over-estimate the gravity of the problem presented by those compelled to exist in the slums of our populous cities, even when considered from a purely economic point of view. From the midst of this commonwealth of degradation there goes forth a moral contagion, scourging society in all its ramifications, coupled with an atmosphere of physical decay—an atmosphere reeking with filth, heavy with foul odors, laden with disease. In time of any contagion the social cellar becomes the hot-bed of death, sending forth myriads of fatal germs which permeate the air for miles around, causing thousands to die because society is too short-sighted to understand that the interest of its humblest member is the interest of all. The slums of our cities are the reservoirs of physical and moral death, an enormous expense to the state, a constant menace to society, a reality whose shadow is at once colossal and portentous. In time of social upheavals they will prove magazines of destruction; for, while revolution will not originate in them, once let a popular uprising take form and the cellars will re-inforce it in a manner more terrible than words can portray. Considered ethically, the problem is even more embarrassing and deplorable; here, as nowhere else in civilized

† From Chapter II, "Society's Exiles," in *Civilization's Inferno; Or, Studies in the Social Cellar*, by Benjamin Orange Flower (Boston: Arena Publishing Co., 1893), pp. 23–29. Benjamin Flower (1858–1918), called the father of the muckrakers, planned to enter the ministry but turned to journalism instead. He founded the radical magazine *The Arena* (Boston) in 1889 and edited it until December 1896, then again at a later period. His journal furthered the cause of the "new realism" in literature and "protest" writing. While *Civilization's Inferno* was published the same year as the 1893 *Maggie*, its ideas, along with many others by other hands, were published as early as 1889 in the *Arena*. A sampling follows: "Certain Convictions as to Poverty" (December 1889), "Poverty and Crime in our Great Cities" (December 1889), "Rum and Rum Power" (March 1890), "Working Girls" (August 1890), "Morality and Environment" (April 1891), "The Woes of the New York Working-Girl" (December 1891), "Two Hours in the Social Cellar" (April 1892), "Evictions in New York's Tenement Houses" (December 1892), "The Tenement House Problem in New York" (April 1893).

society, thousands of our fellowmen are exiled from the enjoyments of civilization, forced into life's lowest stratum of existence, branded with that fatal word, "scum." If they seek to rise, society shrinks from them; they seem of another world; they are driven into the darkness of a hopeless existence and viewed much as were lepers in olden times. Over their heads perpetually rests the dread of eviction, of sickness and of failure to obtain employment, making existence a perpetual nightmare, from which death alone brings release. Say not that they do not feel this; I have talked with them; I have seen the agony born of a fear which rests heavy on their souls, a fear stamped in their wrinkled faces and peering forth from great pathetic eyes. For them winter has real terror, for they possess neither clothes to keep comfortable the body, nor means with which to properly warm their miserable tenements. Summer is scarcely less frightful, with its stifling heat acting on myriad germs of disease and producing fever, which frequently ends in death, or, what is still more dreaded, chronic invalidism. Starvation, misery and vice, trinity of despair, haunt their every step. The Golden Rule—the foundation of true civilization, the keynote of human happiness—reaches not their wretched quarters. Placed by society under the ban, life is one long and terrible night. But tragic as is the fate of the present generation, still more appalling is the picture when we contemplate the thousands of little waves of life yearly washed into the cellar of being; fragile, helpless innocents, responsible in no way for their presence or environment, yet condemned to a fate more frightful than the beasts of the field; human beings wandering in the dark, existing in the sewer, ever feeling the crushing weight of the gay world above, which thinks little and cares less for them. Infinitely pathetic is their lot.

The causes which have operated to produce these conditions are numerous and complex, the most apparent being the immense influx of immigration from the crowded centres of the Old World; the glamor of city life, which has allured thousands from the country, fascinating them from afar much as the gaudy colors and tinsel before the footlights dazzle the vision of a child; the rapid growth of the saloon, rendered well-nigh impregnable by the wealth of the liquor power; the wonderful labor-saving inventions, which in the hands of greed and avarice, instead of mitigating the burdens of the people, have greatly augmented them, by glutting the market with labor; the opportunities given by the government through grants, special privileges and protective measures for rapid accumulation of wealth by the few; the power which this wealth has given its possessors over the less fortunate; the spread of that fevered mental condition which subjects all finer feelings and holier aspirations to the acquisition of gold and the gratification of carnal appetites, and which is manifest in such a startling degree in the gambler's world, which to dignify we call the realm of speculation; the desire for vulgar ostentation and luxurious indulgence—in a word the fever for gold which has permeated the social atmosphere, fatally infecting hundreds of thousands of our people, chilling their hearts, benumbing their consciences, choking all divine impulses and refined sensibilities; the cowardice and lethargy of the Church, which has grown rich in gold and poor in the possession of moral energy,[1] which no longer dares to denounce the money changers, or alarm those who day by day are anaesthetizing their own souls, while adding to the misery of the world. The Church has become, to a great extent, subsidized by gold, saying in effect, "I am rich and increased in goods and have need of nothing," apparently ignorant of the fact that she "is wretched, poor, blind and naked," that she has signally failed in her true mission—that of establishing on earth an ideal brotherhood. Instead of lifting her children into that lofty spiritual realm where each feels the misery of his brother, she has so far surrendered to the mammon of unrighteousness that, without the slightest fear of having their consciences disturbed, men, in their soft-cushioned pews, find comfort while wringing from ten to twenty per cent. profit from their fellowmen in the wretched tenement districts. I refer not to the many noble exceptions, but I indict the great body of wealthy and fashionable churches, whose ministers do not know and take no steps to find out the misery that results from the avarice of their parishioners. Then again back of all this is the defective education which has developed all save character in man; education which has trained the brain but shriveled the soul. Last, but by no means least, is land speculation, which has resulted in keeping large tracts of land idle which otherwise would have blossomed with happy homes. To these influences we must add the general ignorance of the people regarding the nature, extent and growing proportions of the misery and want in the New World which is spreading like an Eastern plague in the filth of an Oriental city.

It is not my present purpose to dwell further on the causes which have produced these conditions. I wish to bring home to the mind and heart of the reader a true conception of life in the slums, by citing typical cases, illustrating a condition prevalent in every great city of the Union and increasing in its extent every year.   *   *   *

1. Note the strong attack on the Church by Flower. Crane also attacks the Church, but more obliquely. See Chapters IV and XVI of *Maggie*. [*Editor.*]

LARS ÅHNEBRINK

[Zola as Literary Model for *Maggie*]†

* * *

It is above all in Crane's slum stories that the kinship between Zola and Crane is felt. We know that Crane had steeped himself in the Bowery atmosphere, and that he drew directly from his experiences for stories[1]; nevertheless a few of Zola's novels seem to have been a source of inspiration and a literary model for some of Crane's own stories. It is probable that Crane's reading of Zola confirmed in part what he saw and felt about life in the New York slums. Beer has it that *Maggie* "was not absolute reporting. He [Crane] had invented its small plot and only two incidents of the story were from the life— the fight in the saloon and the destruction of Maggie's lambrequin by her mother."[2] If this is true, then it is even more likely that Crane may have drawn on his reading for inspiration.

Actually, *Maggie* comes close to the theme and method of *L'Assommoir*. Both authors described a good woman's way toward ultimate destruction, and both told their stories with frankness and objectivity, yet with a certain degree of sympathy for their heroines.[3] The slum environment together with a weak temperament was in part responsible for the inevitable catastrophe; both novels gave evidence of the curse of alcohol not only for the individual but for society at large.

The two writers not only laid their stories in the slums of great cities—Paris and New York—but they were also eager to depict these areas in an accurate and truthful fashion. When discussing Zola and Garland, we observed how extensively Zola portrayed the locale of the story, the milieu of the characters (exterior, interior, and social). Crane appears to have used a similar technique. It is probably no mere coincidence that he opened his tale by describing a street scene, just as Zola had done in *L'Assommoir*. Crane introduced the atmosphere of the slum district by depicting a fight between the ragged urchins of Rum Alley and Devil's Row.[4] Moreover, he sketched the

---

† From *The Beginnings of Naturalism in American Fiction*, by Lars Åhnebrink (Upsala, Sweden: A.-B. Lundequistska Bokhandeln, 1950), pp. 250–53, 255–56, 257–58, 259, 261–62, 263–64. Reprinted by Russell & Russell (New York, 1961).
1. See pp. 92–93. Note also the discussion of the slums in the early nineties. See pp. 77–80. [Page references are to the Åhnebrink work.—*Editor*.]

2. Thomas Beer, *Stephen Crane* (Garden City, N.Y., 1927), p. 98.
3. Note also both writers' attempt at recording the vulgar language of their characters. [*L'Assommoir* was available in an American translation in 1879.—*Editor*.]
4. Note the symbolic use of the names of the streets: Zola's "rue de la Goutte-d'Or" and Crane's "Rum Alley."

sordid area close to the harbor—"squat ignorant stables," laborers unloading a scow at a dock by the river, and "a worm of yellow convicts" crawling slowly along an island.[5] Then he proceeded to describe in greater detail the tenement house where Maggie lived. It is worth noting that Crane, like Zola and Garland, delineated the tenement by letting two of his characters enter the building: * * * The passage[6] should be compared with Zola's description of the tenement house on the "rue de la Goutte-d'Or".[7] We note the same emphasis on gloom, decay, and general misery; the atmosphere is equally vulgar and revolting in both cases. The imagery of the last sentence of the quotation has a Zolaesque flavor.

The two rooms occupied by the Johnsons were on a par with those in which the Coupeau family lived after they had to give up the laundry. Everything gave evidence of lack of taste, poverty, and general decay. The neighbors gossiped, quarreled, and drank. The Johnson household was not a happy one. Both parents were confirmed drunkards, who fought with each other regularly and beat their children, Maggie, Jim, and Tommie, at every opportunity. The home was a "reg'lar livin' hell." The following passage[8] gives an idea of the milieu in which the three children grew up. * * * The passage[9] may be compared with Zola's description of the homecoming of the drunkard Bijard. Both episodes illustrate admirably the demoralizing effect of alcohol on the mind of the individual. Note that neither Zola nor Crane actually described the fight as seen; both implied by means of sounds that a battle was going on. The devastating effects of the fight were then disclosed to the reader by the writers in scenes that are similar in tone and general atmosphere. Both depicted the two combatants[1] prostrate on the floor in the midst of their wrecked pieces of furniture. * * * The passages quoted[2] indicate that the milieu in which Maggie and Jim grew up was like that in which the Bijard children had to live. It is probable that the Bijard household[3] served to some extent as a model for Crane's description of the Johnson family. Further and even more definite evidence seems to confirm such an assumption. Père Bijard

5. *The Work of Stephen Crane*, 12 vols., ed. Wilson Follett (New York, 1925–27), X, 138. Hereafter *Work*.
6. The first paragraph of Chapter II in *Maggie*. [*Editor.*]
7. See pp. 240–41. Cf. also the similarity between Crane's and Garland's descriptions of the tenements. Note, for instance, the "gruesome doorways." See p. 242 of this study. [The page numbers refer to Åhnebrink's book.—*Editor.*]
8. The end of the first paragraph, Chapter II, *Maggie*. [*Editor.*]
9. In Chapter III of *Maggie*, beginning with "There was a crash . . ." and ending with "Her bare, red arms were . . . like those of a sated villain." [*Editor.*]

1. Note the difference between the two wives. Mme Bijard was a naturally good and hard-working woman, who never beat her children and who took to drinking as an antidote to her husband's viciousness, while Mrs. Johnson was a slovenly woman who did not care at all for her family.
2. From *Œuvres complètes*, 50 vols., ed. François Bernouard (Paris, 1927–29), VIII, 198–200 [hereafter *Œuvres*]; *Work*, X, 150–51; and *Œuvres*, VIII, 199–200. [*Editor.*]
3. The Coupeau household, particularly in its decay, may perhaps also have served as a model. Note that Coupeau beat his children, Nana and Étienne, on several occasions. Mrs. Johnson's degeneration has points in common with that of Gervaise.

was a drunkard, a sadist, an unmitigated beast who, on the rare occasions when he worked, always had a bottle of alcohol beside him from which he took large draughts. When intoxicated he was extremely cruel, and he managed to kill both his good, hard-working wife and his little daughter Lalie[4] by systematic ill-usage. This brute of a father seems to have been in Crane's mind when creating the Johnsons, particularly Mrs. Johnson. She was, in fact, as beastly and degraded as Bijard when drunk; and both were drunk most of the time and succeeded in terrifying their children to the same degree. In both characters, who were portrayed with indignant exaggeration, the authors denounced the alcoholist in no uncertain terms.

Originally, the Johnson and the Bijard family had had three children,[5] respectively, the eldest of whom were daughters, Maggie and Lalie. The girls resemble each other in certain respects. Both were idealized. Despite the fact that they lived in the slum sections of the city, they were unsullied by their environment. In that respect Maggie stood in marked contrast to her brother Jim who, in the typical pattern of naturalistic writing, followed in the footsteps of his father and became a drunkard in the manner of Coupeau, whose father had also been a drunkard. Moreover, despite the fact that the girls were often hungry and still more often beaten by their drunken parents, they remained incredibly kind and patient. They were almost like saints; terrified, but inured by many previous experiences of the same kind, they witnessed with resignation the fights between their parents. When her mother died, Lalie, aged eight, took care of the house and the two small children, Henriette and Jules. In like manner Maggie acted as the little mother of Jim and Tommie when Mrs. Johnson was in jail, or too drunk to be able to take care of her family.   *   *   *

*   *   *

For Maggie's development from child to a young girl, Crane seems to have found another model in *L'Assommoir*, namely Nana. Like Nana, Maggie was pretty and a most rare product of a tenement district. Of both girls it may be said with equal justice that they "blossomed in a mud-puddle."[6] They differed, however, in that Nana "était dans le vice comme un poisson dans l'eau,"[7] while Maggie was basically innocent. In addition, Maggie lacked Nana's sensuality. Two episodes, especially, link the girls together. When Nana was fifteen she took a position in a workshop where artificial flowers were made. Likewise, Maggie went to work in a collar-and-cuff factory. The descriptions of the workplaces display fundamental similarities as well as typical dissimilarities. In both establishments the workers were women, and in both places the environment was equally de-

---

4. In *Maggie* Tommie died, presumably of ill-usage.
5. Note that the Coupeau family consisted of three children, Claude, Étienne, and Nana.
6. *Work*, X, 156.
7. *Œuvres*, VIII, 375.

moralizing. Zola emphasized particularly the moral decay of the women workers, while Crane showed more restraint and merely hinted at it. Crane wanted, it seems, to demonstrate that factories turned human beings into machines, and that everything worked against Maggie, whose ruin was thus justified.   *   *   *

With the appearance of a suitor, vague dreams of a life of splendor loomed before the two girls.[8] Soon they wearied of their jobs. Meanwhile conditions in their homes became unbearable, their parents being drunk almost every day. It should be remembered that, as their degradation proceeded, Coupeau and Gervaise spent the evenings at the saloon or fighting in the dismal little room that was now their home. The climax was reached one Saturday. When Nana returned home from work, she found her parents completely drunk and the room in great disorder. Unable to stand this kind of life any longer, she went away to join her lover: *   *   *   Crane has a similar motivation for Maggie's flight from her home. Jim had been fighting with his drunken mother, and the room was in a chaotic upheaval. Then Pete, Maggie's lover, appeared in the midst of the debris, and Maggie, unable to stand the strain of the environment any more, abandoned her home:

*   *   *

It has been said above that Maggie as a child resembled Lalie, and that as a young girl she had points in common with Nana. It is probable that Crane had Gervaise Coupeau in mind when he created the last phase of Maggie's life. The downfall of Maggie is related to that of Gervaise. Temperamentally, the two women belonged to the same type.   *   *   *   To Maggie, Pete was the "ideal man," a "knight." In reality, both Lantier[9] and Pete were good-for-nothings, veritable dandies and lady-killers, who later deserted the women seduced by them.

One episode[1] in particular links Gervaise with Maggie. Toward the end of *L'Assommoir* there is a scene depicting Gervaise, starving and degraded, walking aimlessly up and down the streets, accosting several men in the manner of a prostitute.   *   *   *   Crane has a similar scene in the next to last chapter of his novel. When Maggie saw no way out she was, like Gervaise, forced to walk the streets. There is the same contrast between the heroine's gloomy mood and desperate need on the one hand, and the atmosphere of pleasure and wealth radiating from the places of amusement on the street on the other. The methods used by Zola and Crane in depicting the episodes are almost identical.   *   *   *

*   *   *

8. This is a reference to Maggie and Nana. [*Editor.*]

9. Gervaise's lover. [*Editor.*]

1. The visit which Pete and Maggie paid to the museum (*Work*, X, 170) is reminiscent of that of Coupeau and Gervaise (*Œuvres*, VIII, 77 ff.). Moreover, Crane's "hilarious hall" (pp. 194 ff.) recalls somewhat Zola's "cafe-concert" (pp. 276 ff.). (Cf. Albert J. Salvan, *Zola aux États-Unis* (Providence, R.I., 1943), p. 162.

The tragedy of Gervaise and Maggie was that, despite their moral lapses, they were naturally good and virtuous women, whose ruin was brought about by the brutal impact of circumstances and environment on weak temperaments.

Some of the parallels recorded here may have been accidental, but taken together they confirm the assumption that Crane was indebted to *L'Assommoir* in his first novel as to plot, characterization, technique, episodes, and particulars. Despite the borrowings, almost always used with restraint, *Maggie* bears the unmistakable stamp of Crane's individual temperament, his conciseness, brevity, and artistry.

* * *

MARCUS CUNLIFFE

Stephen Crane and the American Background of *Maggie*†

* * *

The most obvious place to search is not Europe but America: not Zola's Paris but Crane's New York. We can find little in fiction that can be regarded as a lead. But perhaps a clue—a genuine one—is provided by two sketches of the Bowery, "An Experiment in Misery" and "The Men in the Storm," that Crane wrote in 1893, not long after *Maggie* was published. They are documentary pieces, although the former is presented as a story. The latter was printed in B. O. Flower's *Arena*, a periodical that devoted much of its space to social problems of the day. And it is here, surely, that Crane's sources might lie, not necessarily in the *Arena* itself, but in the mass of literature produced by Americans on the evils of slum-life: ill-health, intemperance, immorality and the like. This kind of literature was in being long before the muckrakers; indeed, it can be traced back as far as the 1830's, and to the writings of such reformers as Edwin Chapin and John R. McDowall, both of whom grappled with the question of poverty and vice in New York. In 1872, for example (five years before *L'Assommoir*), Charles Loring Brace published *The Dangerous Classes of New York*, a study that was the fruit of twenty years of philanthropic work. Like Zola, Brace believes that "inheritance" is a crucial factor—that "certain appetites" (especially "the appetite for liquor and of the sexual passion"), "if indulged abnormally and excessively through two or more generations, come to have an almost irresistible force, and, no doubt, modify the brain so

† From *American Quarterly*, VII (Spring 1955), 35–44.

as to constitute almost an insane condition." [1] Brace has a chapter on "Street Girls"; like Zola again, he has no illusions as to the beginning of the street-girls' career:

> They usually relate, and perhaps even imagine, that they have been seduced from the paths of virtue suddenly and by the wiles of some heartless seducer. Often they describe themselves as belonging to some virtuous, respectable, and even wealthy family. Their real history, however, is much more commonplace. . . . They have been poor women's daughters, and did not want to work as their mothers did; or they have grown up in a tenement-room, crowded with boys and men, and lost purity before they knew what it was; or they have liked gay company, and have had no good influences around them, and sought pleasure in criminal indulgences; or they have been street-children, poor, neglected, and ignorant, and thus naturally and inevitably have become depraved women. [2]

This account is embellished with an engraving called "The Street-Girl's End," in which a dejected prostitute stands at the end of a quay, peering down into the river-waters below, literally and metaphorically on the brink.

If Crane had read Brace's book (there is, alas, not the least evidence that he did), he could have got from it more, except for the fictional form, than from *L'Assommoir*. It could have supplied him with details of the New York *milieu*—and also, of course, with the idea for Maggie's suicide. Brace has quite as close a grasp on his subject as Zola; in fact, the passage just quoted could serve as a description of Zola's Nana, as she appears in *L'Assommoir* and as she is in the sequel, *Nana*. Some years after he wrote *Maggie*, Crane was to comment with equal *expertise*. He said of *Nana*, indeed:

> this girl in Zola is a real streetwalker. I mean, she does not fool around making excuses for her career. You must pardon me if I cannot agree that every painted woman on the streets of New York was brought there by some evil man. [3]

But this is not what Maggie is like. Crane's view of her differs entirely from that of Zola or Brace. For the implication of *Maggie* is that "some evil man" is directly responsible for the fallen woman's plight. Maggie *is* "seduced from the paths of virtue . . . by the wiles of some heartless seducer" (Pete). Her brother Jimmie has also seduced a girl, only to abandon the unfortunate creature. If Crane

1. Coupeau's horrible death in *L'Assommoir* is presented by Zola as the result of a hereditary weakness for liquor which induces insanity. Unlike Zola, however, Brace takes comfort from "the action of the great law of 'Natural Selection,'" which, "in regard to the human race, is always toward temperance and virtue," since "the vicious and sensual and drunken die earlier," or produce fewer children, "and so yield place to the sober elements of society." *The Dangerous Classes of New York* (New York, 1872), pp. 43–44.
2. Brace, pp. 117–18.
3. Quoted in Robert W. Stallman, ed., *Stephen Crane: An Omnibus* (New York: Knopf, 1952), p. 675. Hereafter Stallman.

later came to think otherwise, at this time he imagined Maggie as essentially the victim of circumstance. Nana is "dans le vice comme un poisson dans l'eau." Maggie, on the other hand, is pure: "None of the dirt of Rum Alley seemed to be in her veins." In part, Crane's treatment of her is naturalistic—"Say, Pete, dis is great" is a sample of her conversation—but in other respects it is not. Altogether, Maggie is a somewhat unreal creature, and her life as a prostitute is handled by Crane with a marked lack of certainty. In chapter XVII, which culminates in her death, we see Maggie as:

> a girl of the painted cohorts of the city. She threw changing glances at men who passed her, giving smiling invitations to those of rural or untaught pattern and usually seeming sedately unconscious of the men with a metropolitan seal upon their faces.

For Crane, this is a peculiarly heavy-handed passage. At any rate, it presents Maggie as an experienced prostitute, who has apparently overcome her initial scruples. Moreover, she seems to have been reasonably successful, since she is wearing a "handsome cloak" and has "well-shod feet." Why, then, does she commit suicide?

Even less convincing is "Nellie," the "woman of brilliance and audacity" to whom Pete returns after he has grown tired of Maggie. Nell, when we first see her, speaks like the others:

> "Why, hello, Pete, me boy, how are you?"

But before long, trying to show that she has a certain vulgar sophistication, Crane overdoes it and allows her to describe Maggie as: "A little pale thing with no spirit. . . . Did you notice the expression in her eyes? There was something in them about pumpkin pie and virtue. . . . Dear, dear, Pete, what are you coming to?" And when Pete disclaims interest in Maggie, Nell replies (almost like a character in Henry James), "Oh, it's not of the slightest consequence to me, my dear young man."

This is the writing of an inexperienced author who is guessing at his subject, which he only knows about from hearsay, or from his reading. And the tone is not that of Zola, nor of the matter-of-fact Mr. Brace, though something of them is present. There is an added ingredient: a moral, didactic motive, a slight preachiness. Thus, in the dedicatory inscriptions which state that "environment . . . frequently shapes lives regardless," Crane continues: "If one proves that theory one makes room in Heaven for all sorts of souls, notably an occasional street girl, who are not confidently expected to be there by many excellent people."[4] These could nearly be the words of a clergyman; and there were several clergymen of the period who might nearly have uttered them.

4. Quoted in Stallman, p. 594.

For instance, there was Thomas DeWitt Talmage (1832–1902),[5] who came of a New Jersey family, and who—after holding ministries at Belleville, N.J., Syracuse, and Philadelphia—was appointed in 1869 to the Central Presbyterian Church of Brooklyn. Here he rapidly acquired a fame which verged on notoriety. His sermons drew as many as five thousand people (the vast Brooklyn Tabernacle could hold them all); his words were reprinted, not only in book-form but also in newspapers throughout the English-speaking world. Talmage well understood the advantage of publicity on such a scale:

> next to the Bible, the *newspaper*—swift-winged, and everywhere present, flying over the fences, shoved under the door, tossed into the counting-house, laid on the work-bench, hawked through the cars! All read it: white, black, German, Irishman, Swiss, Spaniard, American, old and young, good and bad, sick and well, before breakfast and after tea, Monday morning, Saturday night, Sunday and week-day![6]

The newspapers, on their side, were glad to feature Talmage's sermons and lectures. As the above excerpt suggests, they were vivid and racy; and they dealt with alluringly newsworthy topics. They managed to be both moral and sensational. Collections of them sold widely under such titles as *The Abominations of Modern Society* (1872), *The Night Sides of City Life* (1878) and *The Masque Torn Off* (1880). Sometimes, as when he attacks the theatre, in *Sports That Kill* (1875), Talmage admits the charge that he is fulminating like an old-time Methodist:

> My religion is not a jelly-fish, but a vertebrate. It has backbone, and tells of God's justice as well as God's mercy; and I have not in anywise, as you know, made a compromise of public iniquities.[7]

In the *Night Sides* "Sabbath morning discourses," he recounts how "I, as a minister of religion, felt I had *a divine commission to explore the iniquities of our cities*."

Yet he tours the night-haunts of New York with a certain scientific detachment, "*as a physician goes into a small-pox hospital* or a fever-shed." He goes as a social reformer as well as a clergyman. He has evidently read his Charles Loring Brace;[8] the police who pilot him around the brothels and saloons do so with a professional aplomb; and if Talmage draws moral lessons, they are not narrow or fanatical.

5. See *Dictionary of American Biography*, XVIII, 287–88; and *Life and Teachings of Rev. T. DeWitt Talmage* (n.p., 1902), with an introduction by Russell H. Conwell: a memorial volume.
6. *Abominations of Modern Society* (London, 3rd edn., 1873), p. 138.
7. *Sports that Kill* (London: James Blackwood, n.d.), p. 56. Despite the zoological vocabulary, Talmage had no sympathy for what he called the "evolutionists": "Prefer, if you will, Darwin's 'Origin of Species' to the book of Genesis, but know that you are an infidel. As for myself, since Herbert Spencer was not present at the creation and the Lord Almighty was present, I prefer to take the divine account as to what really occurred. . . . " (*Life and Teachings*, p. 68.)
8. An anecdote of a fourteen-year-old street girl in Brace (pp. 119–21) is repeated in Talmage's *Sports that Kill* (p. 172).

He condemns the pleasure-seeking male rather than the purveyors of pleasure. In the sermon called "The Gates of Hell," after expatiating on "impure literature," "the dissolute dance," "indiscreet apparel" and "alcoholic beverage," Talmage considers the prostitute:

> Suppose one of these wanderers should knock at your door, would you admit her? Suppose you knew where she came from, would you ask her to sit down at your dining-table? Would you ask her to become the governess of your children? . . . You would not— not one of a thousand of you that would dare to do it. . . . There is not one out of five thousand that has come so near the heart of the Lord Jesus Christ as to dare to help one of these fallen souls.[9]

Are there, Talmage asks, any ways out for such a girl? One way is "the sewing-girl's garret, dingy, cold, hunger-blasted":

> Another way is the street that leads to East river, at midnight, the end of the city dock, the moon shining down on the water making it look so smooth she wonders if it is deep enough. It is. No boatman near enough to hear the plunge.[1]

This will be recognized as the situation illustrated in Brace's book.

However, Talmage indicates that there is yet another way: the way of repentance. The poor shivering prostitute of his imaginary tale, touched by a sermon (and by the words in it, "wounded for our transgressions and bruised for our iniquities"), drags herself away from the city, back to her old home in the country, where a forgiving mother greets the dying girl with the cry of *"Oh, Maggie!"*[2]

The coincidence of name is interesting. So is the similarity between Talmage's observations on the respectable disdain of his congregation, and this episode in Crane, when Maggie has been rejected by Pete and is homeless:

> Suddenly she came upon a stout gentleman in a silk hat and a chaste black coat, whose decorous row of buttons reached from his chin to his knees. The girl had heard of the grace of God and she decided to approach this man. . . . But as the girl timidly accosted him he made a convulsive movement and saved his respectability by a vigorous side-step. He did not risk it to save a soul. For how was he to know that there was a soul before him that needed saving?

Or compare another set of quotations. In his sermon, "The Massacre by Needle and Sewing-Machine" (reprinted in *Abominations of Modern Society*), Talmage says:

> To thousands of young women of New York today there is only this alternative: starvation or dishonour.

9. *Night Sides*: reprinted in England as *The Night Side of New York Life* (Wakefield: William Nicholson, n.d.), p. 42.

1. *Night Side of New York Life*, p. 43.
2. *Ibid.*, p. 47.

Maggie's brother presents the alternative to her:

> "Mag, I'll tell yeh dis! See? Yeh've eeder got t'go on d'toif er go t'work."

Like Talmage's young women, Maggie starts by choosing work, and the near-starvation it entails. As Talmage puts it:

> There are thirty-five thousand sewing girls in New York and Brooklyn. Across the darkness of this night I hear their death-groan. It is not such a cry as comes from those who are suddenly hurled out of life, but a slow, grinding, horrible wasting away. Gather them before you and look into their faces, pinched, ghastly, hunger-struck! . . . See that premature stoop in the shoulders! Hear that dry, hacking, merciless cough!

Maggie's work is equally uncongenial:

> The air in the collar-and-cuff establishment strangled her. She knew she was gradually and surely shrivelling in the hot, stuffy room. . . . She became lost in thought as she looked at some of the grizzled women in the room, mere mechanical contrivances sewing seams. . . .

According to Talmage,

> Some of the worst villains of the city are the employers of these women. They beat them down to the last penny, and try to cheat them out of that.

Maggie's companions complain of "unpaid wages." They all loathe "the fat foreigner who owned the establishment," and whose "pocketbook deprived them of the power of retort":

> "What do you sink I pie fife dolla a week for? Play? No, py tamn!"

Perhaps we can now gather together some of the loose strands of this argument. The main point of it is that Crane could easily have drawn material for *Maggie* from popular American writing of the day. I am not suggesting that we should substitute the name of DeWitt Talmage for that of Emile Zola as a certain or even a probable influence upon Crane. We have no proof that Crane had read either author, though it is hard to believe that he (or for that matter anyone who looked at the New York newspapers) could *avoid* having heard of the publicity-conscious Mr. Talmage. Talmage was a minister and a moralist, many of whose tirades (e.g., against "The Temptations of Summer Watering Places") would no doubt have struck Crane as ludicrous. Crane was markedly anti-clerical in sentiment, as several references in *Maggie* and in his correspondence make clear. Maggie's brother, for a joke, goes into

> a mission church where a man composed his sermons of "you's."

Once a philosopher asked this man why he did not say "we" instead of "you." The man replied, "What?"

And in a letter of 1896, discussing *Maggie*, Crane admits that "I am not very friendly to Christianity as seen around town."[3]

Still, friendly or not, a reader of Talmage or not, Crane is affected by the American religious heritage. To some extent, despite himself, he belongs to this heritage as Talmage does. Against the logic of his novel, Crane—as we have seen—makes Maggie commit suicide. It could be said that this is a naturalistic convention. Possibly; but is it not, even more, a moralist's convention? The wages of sin is death, for Brace, for Talmage (whether the prostitute dies by drowning, or repentant in her mother's arms), and for Crane. This kind of death is a stock finale in the moralistic writings of the era. Talmage used it at least once before, in his sermon "Winter Nights" (from *The Abominations of Modern Society*):

> And so the woman stands on the abutment of the bridge, on the moonlit night, wondering if, down under the water, there is not some quiet place for a broken heart. She takes one wild leap,— and all is over.

A search among contemporary tracts would disclose plenty of other examples.[4]

Another characteristic assumption of Talmage and his kind—in fact, a standard one in reformist literature—is that the city is the abode of temptation and sin; purity is the prerogative of rural areas. The country boy is therefore the chief victim of city snares. So, after his hasty tour of New York brothels, Talmage asserts that these establishments were full of young men "with the ruddy colour of country health on their cheeks, evidently just come to town for business. . . . They had helped gather the summer grain."[5] Crane too, it will be recalled, speaks of Maggie as confining her lures to "those of rural or untaught pattern." (One doubts whether this notion was borne out by Crane's subsequent experiences.)

In various other small ways, Crane's early work shows the effect of the general American moral-religious climate. When he refers, in *Maggie*, to "smooth-cheeked boys, some of them with faces of stone and mouths of sin," the phrase could have come from a sermon. Or take this little poem, from *Black Riders:*

3. Quoted in Stallman, p. 655.

4. See, e.g., this description of the East Side waterfront: "Women are there, too—some singing, or laughing a laugh with no merriment in it; but for the most part they . . . are silent. Now and then one who has walked with bent head and despairing eyes makes a sudden resolve; there is a swift, flying rush toward the dark water beyond, and the river closes over one more victim." Mrs. Helen Campbell, *Darkness and Daylight: or, Lights and Shadows of New York Life* (Harford, Conn., 1892), p. 214.

5. *Night Side of New York Life*, p. 15. "God pity the country lad," he continues (p. 16), "unsuspecting and easily betrayed."

I stood upon a high place,
And saw, below, many devils
Running, leaping,
And carousing in sin.
One looked up, grinning,
And said, "Comrade! Brother!"

This is a variation upon the theme of "you" and "we." Though it is ironical in aim, the religiosity it mocks is something with which Crane is closely involved.

In other words, he is anti-clerical though belonging to a clerical heritage. In his early work, I do not think he knows where he stands— whether it is religion or religiosity he disapproves of, whether he is adapting or burlesquing. He reacts against the familiar elements of his world where these seem to him hypocritical, but they shape his thought.[6] Nor is this surprising when one remembers that his own father, Jonathan Townley Crane (1819–80), was a clergyman, who held various pastorates in New Jersey and New York—

> a strict Methodist of the old stamp, filled with the sense of God's redeeming love, deeply concerned about such sins as dancing, breaking the Sabbath, reading trashy novels, playing cards, billiards, and chess, and enjoying tobacco and wine, and too innocent of the world to do more than suspect the existence of greater viciousness.[7]

Crane's mother, too, was an ardent Methodist, who came from a clerical family. Crane, praising her memory, said that "Mother was always more of a Christian than a Methodist."[8] He might have said the same of his father, whose one serious fault seems to have been his monumental innocence. What Crane was reacting against, therefore, was nothing very rigid or terrible; hence, his adolescent reversal of what he had been taught consisted in condemning *false* religion; in showing that there was "greater viciousness" than Jonathan Townley Crane ever suspected; in smoking and drinking; and in not only reading "trashy novels" but actually writing some.

In fact, Stephen Crane strives to be free of not merely a family but a national atmosphere. Its restrictions are irksome just because they are, on the whole, kindly. The American emphasis is moral, didactic, redemptive. But not bleakly so: Crane's father's dogmatism

6. When Copeland & Day, his prospective publishers, objected to some of the poems "which refer to God," in the manuscript of *Black Riders*, Crane replied: "It seems to me that you cut all the ethical sense out of the book. All the anarchy, perhaps. It is the anarchy which I particularly insist upon." (Letter of September 9, 1894, reproduced in Stallman, p. 602.) Ethics and anarchy! For Crane, the two are inseparable. On the subject of Crane's religious instincts, it is interesting to note that Stallman finds *The Red Badge of Courage* "loaded with Biblical allusions and religious symbolism" (Stallman, p. 217).
7. Article by E. F. Humphrey, *Dictionary of American Biography*, IV, 506.
8. John Berryman, *Stephen Crane* (New York: William Sloane, 1950), p. 9.

is of the serenest order. So are the sensible, "enlightened" teachings of Talmage (and Henry Ward Beecher, Lyman Abbott and the other prominent clergy of the day). There is, in America, no cleavage between religion and rationalism comparable to that in, say, France (where Zola for one was, as an agnostic, thrown into violent controversies). So, when young Crane writes with would-be savage candor of the slums, the preachers have been there before him. He cannot help borrowing some of their material. In later writing he pushes further and further away from subjects that can be encompassed by well-meaning pastors. He does so because he wants to write fiction; and fiction, in America, is still too close to didacticism—to the religious tract and the philanthropic survey.[9] "Preaching," Crane observes, "is fatal to art in literature."[1] Like other Americans after him, Crane aims at direct experience, simply rendered; the comment, if any, often takes the form of irony (as if to say, *this is the way the preachers would put it—and it's just possible they may be right*).

When Crane offered *Maggie* for publication, one suspects that it was refused partly for reasons hinted at above. Other reasons may have been that it was too short for a book, and that—for all its brilliant flashes—it is really not a very good book. But I think we must add to these the fact that it was *fiction*, which contained nothing that the reader could not find in Brace, or Talmage, or in such books as *Darkness and Daylight in New York*. Why bother to print research that had already been done more fully and factually by others?

These remarks have taken us far away from Zola and from naturalism. Perhaps too far. Perhaps Crane did know *L'Assommoir* before 1893. I still feel, though, that there are many differences between Crane's impressionistic little *nouvelle*, with its sharp poetic images and its stilted situations, and Zola's ample, crowded, easy work. *L'Assommoir* does not seem to me to *explain* Crane's novel. I think it more plausible to suppose that Crane afterwards became acquainted with the writing of Zola (and Tolstoy, etc.), and decided then, with a pardonable pride, that he and they had been going in the same direction—he more efficiently, because more economically. This may be another way of saying that naturalism is a valid category, for which we can thank the literary historian. Zola and Crane are among its exemplars. But we should set them side by side, not in a causal, "because-Zola-therefore-*Maggie*" relationship. We should study Crane as an American naturalist (and also, conceivably, as a poet *manqué*: an aspect of him that I have not discussed). In doing so, and in examining the sorts of sources indicated in this article, we

9. As many commentators have said, this is true even today: *vide* the innumerable novels about alcoholism, race relations, etc. No other country has such a quantity of them in its literature.
1. From a letter of 1897 (?), quoted in Stallman, p. 673.

may usefully remind ourselves that American naturalism has two sides. One is the obvious clash between naturalism and romanticism, a conflict defined by Grant C. Knight in *The Critical Period in American Literature* and limited to the problems of fiction. The other, less obvious, is the clash between naturalism and didacticism, a subsidiary and more complicated issue that nevertheless counts for a good deal in the development of American literature. It might even help us to understand why the division between romanticism and naturalism in America is less sharp than one might expect. For a glimpse of the Talmage followers in full array might well turn an eager young author away, toward romanticism; and, conversely, it might provoke a wilful, nascent young romantic like Crane into going one better, by achieving the same results without the choir-effects.

THOMAS A. GULLASON

[A Minister, a Social Reformer, and *Maggie*]†

For over a half-century, Stephen Crane's *Maggie* (1893) has been linked with European naturalism, particularly with Zola's *L'Assommoir.*[1] A single recent critic, Marcus Cunliffe, admits that while one can draw parallels between *Maggie* and *L'Assommoir* the most obvious place to search for possible sources "is not Europe but America: not Zola's Paris but Crane's New York." He points to such things as the social consciousness of *The Arena* (to which Crane contributed two propagandistic tales, "The Men in the Storm," and "An Ominous Baby"); Charles Loring Brace's *The Dangerous Classes of New York*; and Thomas De Witt Talmage's sermons. With no definite proof that any of the above-mentioned are influences, Cunliffe concludes: "So, when young Crane writes with would-be savage candor of the slums, the preachers have been there before him. He cannot help borrowing some of their material."[2]

I suggest that much of Stephen Crane's materials for *Maggie* did come from two never-mentioned sources: his father, the minister Jonathan Townley Crane; and the famed social reformer, Jacob Riis. Though he died in 1880 when Stephen was only eight, Jonathan Crane left behind a number of works, mostly theological, which his

† From "The Sources of Stephen Crane's *Maggie*," *Philological Quarterly*, XXXVIII (October 1959), 497–502.
1. For a discussion of Zola's so-called influence on *Maggie*, see Lars Åhnebrink, *The Beginnings of Naturalism in American Fiction* (Upsala, Sweden: A.-B. Lundequistska Bokhandeln, 1950), pp. 231–276; John Berryman, *Stephen Crane* (New York, 1950), p. 63; Oscar Cargill, *Intellectual America* (New York, 1941), pp. 85–86; and H. S. Canby *et al.*, *Literary History of the United States* (New York, 1948), II, p. 1022. Yet Crane "disliked most of Zola's work": see Thomas Beer, *Stephen Crane: A Study in American Letters* (New York, 1923), p. 147.
2. "Stephen Crane and the American Background of *Maggie*," *American Quarterly*, VII (Spring 1955), 35–36, 43.

favorite son always cherished.[3] As late as 1900 in England, young Crane kept a "shelf of books, for the most part the pious and theological works of various antecedent Stephen Cranes. He had been at some pains to gather together these alien products of his kin."[4]

There was more than enough in Jonathan Crane's writings to inspire his son to deal with the manifold problems presented in *Maggie*. In *The Annual Sermon*, for example, the minister reveals his awareness of the city slum and its effect on children:

> And while in our great cities the missionary finds no difficulty in collecting crowds of children into his school, in the worst localities, the vilest dens of murder and pollution, the Church of God ought to be very slow to give up any child as hopeless and utterly beyond the reach of good.[5]

The theme of alcoholism in *Maggie*, also central to *L'Assommoir*, could have easily been suggested by Jonathan Crane's *Arts of Intoxication* (1870). In one place, the minister notes: "The great problem of the times is, 'What shall be done to stay the ravages of intoxication?'"[6] In Chapter X of the book, he discusses the psychological effects of alcoholism on the individual: "When he is so far gone [in drinking] as to stammer in his speech and totter in his gait, and be helpless in mind and body, his sense of his wisdom, his strength, his greatness, and his goodness is at its highest point."[7] In Chapter XI, he adds: "Anger, malice, revenge, every destructive passion rages, because the palsied mind feels only the evil impulse, and cares nothing for consequences."[8]

Jonathan Crane even deals with the hereditary effects of alcoholism. There is no reference to the word "heredity" in *Maggie*, yet Stephen Crane does show how Jimmie acquires the characteristics of his inebriate parents.[9] The minister says of this aspect: "When one parent is an inebriate, the child is, in a certain degree, liable to inherit constitutional peculiarities which increase the danger of his becoming a prey to the same remorseless destroyer. Where both parents are intemperate, the danger is still greater."[1] Further:

> . . . the saddest fact of all is that his [the parent's] innocent children may inherit his scars, and feel the sharp teeth of the devourer. They may be born not only with the dangerous susceptibility of

3. See *Dictionary of American Biography*, IV, p. 506.
4. Edmund Wilson, ed. *The Shock of Recognition* (New York, 1943), p. 671.
5. *The Annual Sermon* (New York, 1858), p. 22.
6. *Arts of Intoxication* (New York, 1870), p. 3.
7. *Ibid.*, p. 145.
8. *Ibid.*, p. 165. This sentence suggests the character of the drunken Swede in "The Blue Hotel."
9. Crane seemed to be interested only in environment and its effect on character. In an inscription on a copy of *Maggie*, he said: "It is inevitable that you [Dr. Lucius L. Button] will be greatly shocked by the book but continue, please, with all possible courage, to the end. For it tries to show that environment is a tremendous thing in the world and frequently shapes lives regardless." See Robert W. Stallman, ed., *Stephen Crane: An Omnibus* (New York, 1952), p. 594. Yet his treatment of Jimmie suggests that Crane was also deeply interested in the question of heredity.
1. *Arts of Intoxication*, p. 177.

alcoholic influence, but with organizations perverted and depraved by the vice of the parent, so that they too have their paroxysms of morbid restlessness and undefinable longing, when no employment contents them, no pleasures already known to them attract, no healthful food or drink satisfies, but when the first casual taste of the intoxicant thrills them with insane rapture, and marks them for a mad career and a doom from which all human tenderness and pity toil in vain to save them.[2]

Still other materials of his father's, as important as those on the slums and alcoholism, aided young Crane. In *Popular Amusements* (1869), Jonathan Crane probably suggested one of the key themes of his son's first novel: Maggie's romantic-realistic conflict. Though she is not a novel reader, Maggie attends a play and continually acts like the dreamy working girl, "the Countess of Moonshine," whom Jonathan Crane describes as follows:

But as things are, novel-readers spend many a precious hour in dreaming out clumsy little romances of their own, in which they themselves are the beautiful ladies and the gallant gentlemen who achieve impossibilities, suffer unutterable woe for a season, and at last anchor in a boundless ocean of connubial bliss. . . . In fact, the Cinderella of the old nursery story is the true type of thousands of our novel-readers. They live a sort of double life—one in their own proper persons, and in their real homes; the other as ideal lords and ladies in dream-land.[3]

His father's works, then, besides suggesting themes, characters, and psychology could have also given Stephen Crane enough incentive to do further research on city slum conditions. For on July 10, 1892, he was in New York studying his materials firsthand. He wrote a news report which hints at the Bowery dialect and at the crude first sketches of Maggie and Jimmie:

. . . a sixteen-year-old girl without any hat and with a roll of half-finished vests under her arm crossed the front platform of the green car. As she stepped up on to the sidewalk a barber from a ten-cent shop said "Ah! there!" and she answered "smarty!" with withering scorn and went down a side street. . . . At the door he [a van driver] almost stepped on a small boy with a pitcher of beer so big that he had to set it down every half block.[4]

A second important influence on Stephen Crane's *Maggie* was Jacob Riis. The twenty-year-old Crane, as a shore correspondent at Asbury Park, heard Riis's lecture on July 24, 1892. He wrote:

2. *Ibid.*, p. 184.
3. *Popular Amusements* (New York, 1870), pp. 136–38. For references to Maggie's similar romantic yearnings, see Carl Van Doren, ed., *Stephen Crane: Twenty Stories* (New York, 1940), pp. 24, 36–37. All later references to *Maggie* are to this edition.
4. "The Broken-Down Van," *New York Tribune*, July 10, 1892, p. 8. In the novel, Maggie works in a collar and cuff factory while Jimmie carries beer to one of the tenants.

The thousands of summer visitors who have fled from the hot, stifling air of the cities to enjoy the cool sea breezes are not entirely forgetful of the unfortunates who have to stay in their crowded tenements. Jacob Riis, the author of "How the Other Half Lives," gave an illustrated lecture on the same subject in the Beach Auditorium on Wednesday evening.[5]

Crane must have been impressed by Riis's comments from *How the Other Half Lives* (1890), for they met on other occasions. Hamlin Garland recalled one meeting: "On arrival at the cafe I found that he [Theodore Roosevelt] had three other guests, William Chanler (a big-game hunter), Jacob Riis, the social worker, and Stephen Crane."[6] Theodore Roosevelt wrote to Anna Cowles on July 26, 1896: "I spent three nights in town, and the others out here; a Professor Smith, a friend of Bob's turned up, and dined with me—also Jacob Riis & Stephen Crane. . . ."[7]

It is known that Stephen Crane started writing *Maggie* in 1891 while a student at Syracuse University.[8] No one knows how much of the novel had been completed at that time, nor how many revisions were made before it was published in 1893. There is a strong possibility that Crane got some valuable details, not only from Riis's lecture and later conversations with him, but also from his clinical study of the New York slums, *How the Other Half Lives*.

How the Other Half Lives and *Maggie* show striking parallels.[9] Both contrast effectively the pathetic conditions of the slum folk and the world of the well-to-do. Both indicate that the complete disregard of the plight of the poor by the rich could lead to class war. In Riis's book, a pauper slashes his knife in the air as a feeble sign of protest against the rich; he "represented one solution of the problem of ignorant poverty versus ignorant wealth that has come down to us unsolved, the danger-cry of which we have lately heard in the shout that never should have been raised on American Soil—the shout of the 'masses against the classes'—the solution of violence." In *Maggie*, Jimmie "maintained a belligerent attitude toward all well-dressed men. To him fine raiment was allied to weakness, and all good coats covered faint hearts. . . . Above all things he despised obvious Christians and ciphers with the chrysanthemums of aristocracy in their buttonholes."

Both books deal mainly with the youth of the slum world. Riis observes the gangs of hoodlums and their "stores of broken bricks." He adds: "The gang is the ripe fruit of tenement house growth. It

5. "Summer Dwellers at Asbury Park and Their Doings," *New York Tribune*, July 24, 1892, p. 22.
6. *Roadside Meetings* (New York, 1931), p. 329.
7. Elting E. Morison *et al.*, *The Letters of Theodore Roosevelt* (Cambridge, Mass., 1951), I, p. 550.
8. Stallman, pp. 5–7.

9. Crane may have gotten the name of Maggie's neighborhood, Rum Alley, from the title of Chapter XVIII, "The Reign of Rum," in Riis's book. See *How the Other Half Lives* (New York, 1932), p. 215. All later references to Riis's book are to this edition. See excerpts from Riis, above.

was born there, endowed with a heritage of instinctive hostility to restraint by a generation that sacrificed home to freedom, or left its country for its country's good." The opening of *Maggie* has a gang war:

> A very little boy [Jimmie] stood upon a heap of gravel for the honour of Rum Alley. He was throwing stones at howling urchins from Devil's Row, who were circling madly about the heap and pelting him.
> His infantile countenance was livid with the fury of battle. His small body was writhing in the delivery of oaths.

Both writers see in gang warfare an essential cowardice. Riis says: "From all this it might be inferred that the New York tough is a very fierce individual, of indomitable courage and naturally as bloodthirsty as a tiger. On the contrary he is an arrant coward." In *Maggie*, Jimmie's gang returns to war only when the enemy has retreated:

> Then the Rum Alley contingent turned slowly in the direction of their home street. They began to give, each to each, distorted versions of the fight. Causes of retreat in particular cases were magnified. Blows dealt in the fight were enlarged to catapultian power, and stones thrown were alleged to have hurtled with infinite accuracy. Valour grew strong again, and the little boys began to brag with great spirit.

Riis analyzes the evil forces that help to destroy the young children of the slums. He complains of youths who carry pitchers of beer to their elders: "I once followed a little boy, who shivered in bare feet on a cold November night so that he seemed in danger of smashing his pitcher [for carrying beer] on the icy pavement, into a Mulberry Street saloon . . . and forbade the barkeeper to serve the boy." In *Maggie*, Jimmie goes on a similar errand: "He passed into the side door of a saloon and went to the bar. Straining up on his toes he raised the pail and pennies as high as his arms would let him. He saw two hands thrust down to take them. Directly the same hands let down the filled pail, and he left."

To both writers, the young working girls are the greatest sufferers in the slums. Riis describes in detail the sweatshops of the shirtmakers where they labor. If one of these girls does not want to deprive herself of the real necessities of life (for her salary is too small), she "must in many instances resort to evil [prostitution]." Maggie also works in a collar-and-cuff factory, and after having been rejected by her lover Pete, she turns to prostitution. Still, Riis and Crane see clear evidences of untainted goodness amidst this degradation. Riis confesses that "it is not uncommon to find sweet and innocent girls, singularly untouched by the evil around them"; they are "like jewels in a swine's snout." Crane says virtually the same thing about the younger Maggie; he characterizes her as a "flower" in a mud puddle.

Native American sources, such as these works by Jonathan Crane and Jacob Riis, served Stephen Crane well; they gave him his pessimistic bias as well as hints for characters, setting, themes, and psychology. He did not need further inspiration or other materials, like Zola's *L'Assommoir*.

DAVID FITELSON

Stephen Crane's *Maggie* and Darwinism†

Possibly the most arresting critical problem posed by Stephen Crane's first novel is that of the disposition of mind that lies behind and shapes it—the ideology, so to speak, that it communicates. The problem is especially arresting because this ideology has never been closely defined, although it is often alluded to as comprising Crane's early Naturalism. Of his ideological intentions in the novel, Crane himself has been gnomic. He observed on one occasion that "I had no other purpose in writing 'Maggie' than to show people to people as they seem to me,"[1] and on another that "[the purpose was] to show that environment is a tremendous thing in this world, and often shapes lives regardlessly."[2] The statements, I should think, are contradictory. Taken together, they are scarcely helpful.

The fact is that *Maggie: A Girl of the Streets* has inserted itself in the American tradition in a peculiar fashion: it appears to have little connection with any native fiction that preceded it, and such influence as it may have had on works that came afterward is neither certain nor, in any case, very direct. The result over the years has been a sort of critical uneasiness about its being here at all: a great many more efforts have been made to attribute it—to explain it away—than actually to examine it, a development which can scarcely be blamed on the novel itself, since it is by no means a difficult piece of writing nor does it defy fruitful analysis.[3]

More than anything else, the failure of criticism to particularize stems from a reluctance to come to grips with the novel on its own terms. When it was first published, in 1893, its sordid materials and impersonal style led most reviewers to see it as little more than a

† From *American Quarterly*, XVI (Summer 1964), 182–86.
1. Quoted in Thomas Beer, *Stephen Crane: A Study in American Letters* (New York, 1923), pp. 140–141.
2. Quoted in *Stephen Crane: An Omnibus*, ed. Robert Wooster Stallman (New York, 1952), p. xxxviii.

3. The abundance of irony in the novel might conceivably constitute a source of difficulty for some readers. V. L. Parrington (*Main Currents in American Thought*, Vol. III: *The Beginnings of Critical Realism in America* [New York, 1930], p. 328) called *Maggie* "the first ironical novel ever written by an American."

fictionalized sociological study of the slums,[4] and those critics who took note of the edition of 1896 were only slightly less unwilling to regard it as a novel.[5] The characteristic early response was one of discomfort verging on shock, and in such circumstances the novel could hardly have been expected to receive systematic analysis.[6]

In the years that followed the publication of *Maggie*, *The Red Badge of Courage* grew to be an American classic. In the resulting waves of admiration for Crane as an Impressionist[7] and a student of "the moral problem of conduct,"[8] the relatively primitive attitudes of his first novel were lost from view—it was scarcely necessary to define the ideology of *Maggie* to recognize that, whatever it was, Crane had advanced a good way beyond it. Currently, although attention is again being directed to Crane's Naturalism (he is now generally considered to have been both an Impressionist *and* a Naturalist), it is more often the sources than the motives or content of that Naturalism that are examined.[9]

Luckily, *Maggie*, unlike most of the critical commentary engendered in its wake, provides considerable specific and reliable information about its ideology. In reading the novel, one discovers that Crane is presenting characters whose lives are rigidly circumscribed by what appear to be inexorable laws. These are unenchanted lives. Their fundamental condition is violence, and this fact seems to be neither haphazard nor peculiar, but reasonable and inevitable—a condition which must necessarily prevail because the world is *governed* by violence.

A world so governed provides certain clear guidelines for the way life is to be lived within it. To the degree that a character is aware

4. Thus Hamlin Garland in the *Arena* (VIII, June 1893, xi): "It is the voice of the slums . . . the most truthful and unhackneyed study I have yet read, fragment though it is." And William Dean Howells in the *New York Press* (April 15, 1894, p. xxxvii): "There is so much realism of a certain kind in it that unfits it for general reading, but once in a while it will do to tell the truth as completely as *Maggie* does."
5. *The Literary Digest* (XIII, August 8, 1896, 459) found it "more impressionistic than real." (Such a review may have been influenced by prior experience of an impressionistic Crane—possibly via *The Red Badge of Courage*, which had appeared in the *Philadelphia Press* in 1894 and in book form in 1895, and *Black Riders*, published in 1895.) But the *Nation* (LXIII, July 2, 1896, 15) was concerned that Crane's "types are mainly human beings of the order which makes us regret the power of literature to portray them," and in London, where *The Red Badge of Courage* had already made a considerable splash, the *Bookman* (II, October 1896, 19) was favorably disposed toward what was taken to be Crane's honesty: "Mr. Crane impresses us with the conviction that he tells the truth as he knows it."

6. It was not only his subject matter that led critics to confuse Crane's fiction with sociology and journalism, nor was it merely the "realism" of his style. *The Red Badge of Courage* is much less "clinical" than *Maggie*, yet for years after it appeared Crane was assumed by many to be a combat veteran.
7. See, for example, Willa Cather's introduction to *The Work of Stephen Crane*, ed. Wilson Follett, Vol. IX: *Wounds in the Rain* (New York, 1926), pp. ix–xiv. See also D. C. Aaron, "Stephen Crane," *Hudson Review*, IV (1951), 471–74, and Joseph Kwiat, "Stephen Crane and Painting," *American Quarterly*, IV (1952), 331–38.
8. See Joseph Conrad's introduction to Beer, p. 3.
9. In the case of *Maggie*, source-seeking has been focused almost exclusively on Zola's *L'Assommoir*. See Stallman, p. 6; John Berryman, *Stephen Crane* (New York, 1950), p. 62; Lars Åhnebrink, in *The Beginnings of Naturalism in American Fiction* (Cambridge, 1950), pp. 249–64; and Marcus Cunliffe, "Stephen Crane and the American Background of *Maggie*," *American Quarterly*, VII (1955), 31–44. [See the essays by Åhnebrink and Cunliffe, above.—*Editor*.]

of the nature of the world, and more particularly, to the degree that he conducts his life in accordance with that nature—to that degree will he be a survivor of violence and free from frustration. Moreover, since there are no meaningful alternatives to a life of violence, conventional notions of morality are without application. The world of the novel provides no distinction between right and wrong action— except insofar as right action is that which insures survival. Survival *is*, in effect, the way of morality, and therefore the plight of the heroine, Maggie herself, who is less violent than the others and unable to compete successfully for survival, is no occasion for sympathy. It is merely an instance of self-destruction and failure.[1]

Clearly, if all this is so, the world of this novel resembles nothing so much as the world of the jungle, and the pattern described by the lives of its characters is that of a primordial struggle for existence. Clearly, too, the law which chiefly governs this world is the law of the survival of the fittest. Now to recite, in this fashion, some of the more shopworn and tiresome rallying cries of "evolutionism" is to come substantially within reach of a definition of the novel's ideology, for that ideology clearly corresponds to some form of evolutionary doctrine. But what is not yet clear, and what the balance of this paper will attempt to demonstrate, is that the disposition of mind that shapes the novel is closely allied with certain distinctive features of the Darwinian Idea.

That the evolutionism of *Maggie* is Darwinian rather than pre-Darwinian or non-Darwinian is not at all self-evident. The words "eat or be eaten" were spoken (and surely not for the first time) by Darwin's grandfather.[2] Diderot, in his "Thoughts for Interpreting Nature," written in 1754, had propounded the doctrine of the survival of the fittest, and the actual phrase was introduced into literature by Herbert Spencer some ten years prior to the publication of *The Origin of Species*. Darwin himself credits Malthus' *Essay on Population* with first bringing to his attention the idea of life as a struggle.[3] Nevertheless, it was unmistakably Darwin who contributed the dramatically organized idea of evolution which functions in *Maggie*. Where Malthus had attributed the discrepancy between the increase in population and that in food production to beneficent Providence, the Darwinian notion of *Natural* Selection rendered all questions of life immediately susceptible of amoral interpretation—and it is the

---

1. A radically opposed view of the novel's moral structure is submitted by Max Westbrook, "Stephen Crane's Social Ethic," *American Quarterly*, XIV (1962), 587–96. Although seeming to share my conclusions about the world of the novel, Mr. Westbrook insists that the characters are not thereby deprived of ethical responsibility. The argument is interesting but it cannot be main-tained without invoking narrative attitudes of "censure" and "implicit castigation," which I do not think are really there.

2. Cited in Jacques Barzun, *Darwin, Marx, Wagner*, 2nd rev. ed. (Garden City, N.Y., 1958), p. 58.

3. Cited in Barzun, p. 28.

amorality of the life struggle that is most visibly characteristic of *Maggie*.

Even so, to identify the novel's ideology as Darwinian is not yet to be very precise. Darwinism is at best an enormously complicated idea, in its most inclusive sense comprised as much of various institutionalized responses to Darwin's theory as it is of the particulars of the theory itself—and the instability of those particulars, incidentally, is a matter of record.[4] The species of Darwinism to which the world of *Maggie* conforms is, first of all, less "scientific" than it is popular, less investigative than it is speculative.[5] (That this is so ought to remove the burden of having to establish that Crane really understood, or for that matter even *read*, Darwin.) Secondly, and more important, it is less—a lot less—optimistic than it is pessimistic. It is clearly not the same Darwinism that James J. Hill and John D. Rockefeller had in mind when they attributed the fortunes of large businesses to the survival of the fittest (although the forms are probably not as variant as Hill and Rockefeller would no doubt have insisted). And it is less closely related still to the Darwinism which, ten years before the publication of *Maggie*, provided evidence to the *New Englander*, a conservative forum of clerical opinion, of scientific authority for the claims of theology.[6] In clear distinction from these species, the Darwinism of *Maggie* harps insistently upon the odious comparison implied by the specter of man's ancestor as "a hairy quadruped, furnished with a tail and pointed ears, probably arboreal in habits." It is a Darwinism dominated by what we are now generally inclined to regard—despite occasional demurrers from the Bible Belt—as an obsolete emphasis. That Darwin himself and, somewhat more emphatically, Huxley sought to make a distinction between the social creature, man, and the baser animals, whereby the "moral sense" of the former triumphed over his dedication to the struggle for existence, is irrelevant to the species of Darwinism to which the world of *Maggie* conforms. For in that world man is neither a "social"

4. Jacques Barzun (pp. 61–68), who considers Darwin's writings hesitant, ambiguous, obscure and self-contradictory, also notes that the precise nature of his theory varied significantly in the many revisions that were made of *The Origin of Species*. The point may be made with equal justice about *The Descent of Man*, in the final revision of which (2nd ed. revised and augmented [New York, 1898], p. 61) Darwin confesses to an increasing indecision about the factors causing evolution.

5. The distinction is neither idiosyncratic nor particularly modern. In 1873, twenty years before the appearance of *Maggie*, Louis Agassiz, the *éminence grise* of the American scientific resistance to evolution, was able to write that "'Natural selection,' 'struggle for existence,' 'survival of the fittest,' are equally familiar to those who do and those who do not understand them" ("Evolution and Permanence of Types," *Atlantic Monthly*, XXXIII [1874], 95). In the same essay (p. 101) Agassiz found occasion to regret "that the young and ardent spirits of the day give themselves to speculation rather than to close and accurate investigation." From Agassiz's point of view, the writer of *Maggie* would, of course, have to be called a young and ardent spirit.

6. "A fresh source of conviction is opened to our anticipations of immortality. It is the flattest inconsistency for an evolutionist to deny the probability of a higher future life." Cited in Richard Hofstadter, *Social Darwinism in American Thought* (Philadelphia, 1945), pp. 14–15.

112 · *Daniel Aaron*

creature nor is he endowed with more than the least suspicion of a "moral sense." In the novel, as I shall attempt to show, Crane is not so much extending Darwin's notions of animal behavior to human society as he is reducing the conduct of human beings to the level of animal behavior.

✻   ✻   ✻

DANIEL AARON

Howells' "Maggie" †

In 1871, William Dean Howells published *Suburban Sketches*,[1] a collection of vignettes of Cambridge and its environs[2] most of which had previously appeared in the *Atlantic*. One of the sketches, hitherto unpublished and laconically titled "Scene," reports the suicide by drowning of an Irish girl, a "Fallen Woman." Written twenty years before Stephen Crane began his first draft of *Maggie* in a Syracuse fraternity house, it anticipates the subject if not the theme of Crane's Bowery novel and (whether or not Crane knew of it) may have some relevance to the not entirely easy association of the "Dean" and his professed disciple.[3] The sketch is short enough to reproduce *in toto*.

Scene.

On that loveliest autumn morning, the swollen tide had spread over all the russet levels, and gleamed in the sunlight a mile away. As the contributor moved onward down the street, luminous on either hand with crimsoning and yellowing maples, he was so filled with the tender serenity of the scene, as not to be troubled by the spectacle of small Irish houses standing miserably about on the flats ankle deep, as it were, in little pools of the tide, or to be aware at first, of a strange stir of people upon the streets: a fluttering to and fro and lively encounter and separation of groups of bareheaded women, a flying of children through the broken fences of the neighborhood, and across the vacant lots on which the insulted

† From *The New England Quarterly*, XXXVIII (March 1965), 85–90. William Dean Howells (1837–1920), considered the major American novelist in the 1880s and 1890s, was also the prime mover of the modern realistic tradition in literature, as reflected in his *Criticism and Fiction* (1891). Garland mentioned Crane to Howells. They corresponded and met for the first time in March–April 1893. Howells looked upon Crane as a writer "fully armed" and tried to find a publisher for the 1893 *Maggie*, without success. While Crane named Howells one of his "literary fathers," he was basically too naturalistic (especially in his use of profanity in *Maggie*) for Howells' taste. Later Howells was probably disenchanted with Crane's bohemianism. For Howells' review of the 1896 *Maggie*, see "New York Low Life in Fiction," below.

1. (Cambridge, Massachusetts, 1871).
2. Howells moved from Boston to Cambridge in 1866. His house was on Sacramento Street, "a bucolic and unfashionable outskirt of Cambridge." E. H. Cady, *The Road to Realism. The Early Years 1832–1885 of William Dean Howells* (Syracuse, N.Y., 1956), 131.
3. See T. A. Gullason, "New Light on the Crane-Howells Relationship," *The New England Quarterly*, XXX (September, 1957), 389–92.

sign-boards forbade them to trespass; a sluggish movement of men through all, and a pause of different vehicles along the sidewalks. When a sense of these facts had penetrated his enjoyment, he asked a matron whose snowy arms, freshly taken from the wash-tub, were folded across a mighty chest, "What is the matter?"

"A girl drowned herself, sir-r-r, over there on the flats, last Saturday, and they're looking for her."

"It was the best thing she could do," said another matron grimly.

Upon this answer that literary soul fell at once to patching himself up a romantic story for the suicide, after the pitiful fashion of this fiction-ridden age, when we must relate everything we see to something we have read. He was the less to blame for it, because he could not help it; but certainly he is not to be praised for his associations with the tragic fact brought to his notice. Nothing could have been more trite or obvious, and he felt his intellectual poverty so keenly that he might almost have believed his discomfort a sympathy for the girl who had drowned herself last Saturday. But of course, this could not be, for he had but lately been thinking what a very tiresome figure to the imagination the Fallen Woman had become. As a fact of Christian civilization, she was a spectacle to wring one's heart, he owned; but he wished she were well out of the romances, and it really seemed a fatality that she should be the principal personage of this little scene. The preparation for it, whatever it was to be, was so deliberate, and the reality had so slight relation to the French roofs and modern improvements of the comfortable Charlesbridge which he knew, that he could not consider himself other than as a spectator awaiting some entertainment, with a faint inclination to be critical.

In the mean time there passed through the motley crowd, not so much a cry as a sensation of "They've found her, they've found her!" and then the one terrible picturesque fact, "She was standing upright!"

Upon this there was wilder and wilder clamor among the people, dropping by degrees and almost dying away, before a flight of boys came down the street with the tidings, "They are bringing her—bringing her in a wagon."

The contributor knew that she whom they were bringing in the wagon, had had the poetry of love to her dismal and otherwise squalid death; but the history was of fancy, not of fact in his mind. Of course, he reflected, her lot must have been obscure and hard; the aspect of those concerned about her death implied that. But of her hopes and her fears, who could tell him anything? To be sure he could imagine the lovers, and how they first met, and where, and who he was that was doomed to work her shame and death; but here his fancy came upon something coarse and common: a man of her own race and grade, handsome after that manner of beauty which is so much more hateful than ugliness is; or, worse still, another kind of man whose deceit must have been subtler and wickeder; but whatever the person, a presence defiant of sympathy or even interest, and simply horrible. Then there were the details of the affair, in great degree common to all love affairs, and not varying so widely in any condition of life; for the passion which is so rich and infinite to those within its charm, is apt to seem a little tedious and monotonous in its character, and poor in resources to the cold looker-on.

Then, finally, there was the crazy purpose and its fulfillment: the headlong plunge from bank or bridge; the eddy, and the bubbles on the current that calmed itself above the suicide; the tide that rose and stretched itself abroad in the sunshine, carrying hither and thither the burden with which it knew not what to do; the arrest, as by some ghastly caprice of fate, of the dead girl, in that upright posture, in which she should meet the quest for her, as it were defiantly.

And now they were bringing her in a wagon.

Involuntarily all stood aside, and waited till the funeral car, which they saw, should come up toward them through the long vista of the maple-shaded street, a noiseless riot stirring the legs and arms of the boys into frantic demonstration, while the women remained quiet with arms folded or akimbo. Before and behind the wagon, driven slowly, went a guard of ragged urchins, while on the raised seat above sat two Americans, unperturbed by anything, and concerned merely with the business of the affair.

The vehicle was a grocer's cart which had perhaps been pressed into the service; and inevitably the contributor thought of Zenobia, and of Miles Coverdale's belief that if she could have foreboded all the *post-mortem* ugliness and grotesqueness of suicide, she never would have drowned herself. This girl, too, had doubtless had her own ideas of the effect that her death was to make, her conviction that it was to wring one heart, at least, and to strike awe and pity to every other; and her woman's soul must have been shocked from death could she have known in what a ghastly comedy the body she put off was to play a part.

In the bottom of the cart lay something long and straight and terrible, covered with a red shawl that drooped over the end of the wagon; and on this thing were piled the baskets in which the grocers had delivered their orders for sugar and flour, and coffee and tea. As the cart jolted through their lines, the boys could no longer be restrained; they broke out with wild yells, and danced madly about it, while the red shawl hanging from the rigid feet nodded to their frantic mirth; and the sun dropped its light through the maples and shone bright upon the flooded flats.

ii

James Russell Lowell, reviewing *Suburban Sketches*, did not hear the somber passages occasionally sounding through the genial and gossipy commentary on Negro cooks, unreliable Irishmen, and crowded horsecars. He spoke instead of Howells' delicacy and humor, of his Chaucerian ease, "the supreme gift of the poet . . . to rim the trivial things of our ordinary and prosaic experience with an ideal delight," and he praised Howells for maintaining his "breadth and sympathy" without sacrificing refinement.

> Let us make the most of Mr. Howells (he concluded) for in the midst of our vulgar self-conceits and crudenesses, and noisy contempt of those conventions which are the safeguards of letters, and the best legacy of culture, we have got a gentleman and artist worthy to be ranked with Hawthorne in sensitiveness of observation, with Longfellow in perfection of style.[4]

Lowell correctly gauged Howells as the gentleman reporter (the reader is never permitted to forget the social distance separating the observer from the observed), but "Scene," with its Maupassant touches, hardly can be said to blend the ideal with the prosaic.

Howells' ostensible purpose, I suspect, was to brush aside the romantic folderol surrounding tales of abandoned females and to dramatize the "*post-mortem* ugliness and grotesqueness" of the squalid actuality. His imagination balked at the prospect of filling in the sordid background, so "rich and infinite to those within its charm," so "tedious and monotonous . . . to the cold looker-on." Nonetheless, the anger and revulsion flickering through his description of the suicide's untriumphant return—frozen in an ungainly posture like the ill-fated Zenobia, her legs bobbing over the tail gate of the wagon—upset his pose of detachment. The sketch, as I read it, betrays a moral uncertainty, as if Howells were withholding his compassion at some emotional cost. He can neither convince himself nor his readers why he should not have reflected a little longer on the girl's "obscure" and "hard" lot.

Crane in *Maggie* suffered no such inhibitions. Whereas Howells stubbornly refused to "romanticize" what was for him a tiresome and unpleasant incident, Crane sought to explain Maggie's fate, to fit her suicide into a logical context, and to make it the text for one of his profane moral judgments. Maggie's nemesis is not simply "a man of her own race and grade" but a pug-nosed hooligan whose "patent leather shoes looked like weapons." He is not "subtle" or "wicked" or "simply horrible"; he is an organism of the Bowery, hardy enough to survive for the moment in his primitive habitat. The grim matrons in "Scene"[5] are translated by Crane into an obscene chorus of harridans.

Although Howells honored Crane for his "faithful rendering of those semi-savage natures," and declared *Maggie* (whose publication he had supported) the "best thing" Crane had written, he had no

4. *The North American Review*, CCXXX (January, 1871), 236–37.
5. O. W. Firkins describes "Scene" as "over- wrought and perhaps underfelt tragedy." *William Dean Howells: A Study* (Cambridge, Mass., 1924), 57.

relish for the "inarticulate and blasphemous life" Crane portrayed.[6] Crane, in turn, sensed this fastidiousness on the part of the man he had publicly and privately praised and at the end of his short life condemned him for failing to live up to his own realistic credo. Apparently Howells himself came to regret his inability to follow his own recommendations, to go (as he put it) "into the dark places of the soul, the filthy and squalid places of society, high and low." So he said, at least, one year before Crane died. "The novelist," he asserted then, "must endeavor to give exactly the effect of life. I believe he will yet come to this. I can never do it, for I was bred in a false school whose trammels I have never been quite able to burst; but the novelist who begins where I leave off, will yet write the novel which has been my ideal."[7]

Disqualified by temperament and conditioning from dragging "hidden things" into the sun, Howells made it easier for later novelists who could. A sketch like "Scene" may be read as a promise of the more relentless realism of the future, but it would be hard to match the power of his final paragraph in the fiction of his naturalistic successors.

ERIC SOLOMON

[*Maggie* and the Parody of Popular Fiction]†

*   *   *

In *The Red Badge of Courage* Crane employs real war to shatter the hero's romantic dreams of battle, and in so doing creates a new and finer form of war fiction; in "The Open Boat" his correspondent comments on the way matters *should* be, and in the process of the narration Crane rejects the familiar conception of the confrontation of man against nature on the sea and also writes a marvelous sea adventure. Similarly in the novels *Maggie* and *George's Mother* he parodies the accepted forms of slum fiction and, with the same materials, makes fresh and powerful slum novels. The critical and creative method exemplified in "In the Tenderloin"[1] is operative throughout his fiction.

In *Maggie*, his earliest novel (1893), Crane reacts sharply to some familiar modes of popular fiction. *Maggie* is about novels, as well as

6. William Dean Howells, "Frank Norris," *The North American Review*, CLXXV (December, 1902), 770.
7. William Dean Howells, "Novel-Writing and Novel Reading. An Impersonal Explanation," edited by W. M. Gibson in *Howells and James: A Double Billing* (New York, 1958), 21.

† From Chapter I, "Love and Death in the Slums," in *Stephen Crane: From Parody to Realism*, by Eric Solomon (Cambridge: Harvard University Press, 1966), pp. 22–26.
1. This is a New York City sketch by Crane, published October 1, 1896. [*Editor*.]

being a novel, and, as Frank Kermode has said about another writer's book, this technique is simply part of the work's "perfectly serious way of life."[2]

Maggie involves a complete reversal of the sentimental themes of the nineteenth-century best sellers that dealt with the life of a young girl. These novels, from such active pens as those of Susan Warner, Maria Cummins, E. D. E. N. Southworth, and E. P. Roe, displayed a manifest religious bias; Maggie is scorned by a clergyman and Jimmie finds organized religion abhorrent. The conventional novels treated romantic love and the salvation of female honor; Crane's heroine is sexually betrayed and falls to the lower depths. A key scene in the sentimental novel was the slow, beautiful death of the heroine's mother; here Maggie herself dies, off stage, and her drunken, blaspheming mother survives. The villain in the sentimental novel was generally regenerated by the heroine's good influence; Crane's Pete the bartender becomes increasingly degraded and ends in a drunken stupor, mocked by thieving streetwalkers. The essential lesson of the sentimental novel was that happiness (and wealth) came from submission to suffering; suffer Maggie does, but the result of her pangs is only further misery, poverty, and death.[3]

The sentimentalist's approach extended into the slum novel itself. In Walter F. Taylor's words, "In 1890 appeared the key-book of the entire anti-slum movement, Jacob Riis's *How the Other Half Lives* . . . . Thence-forward—and especially for the next five years— the slum was in effect a fresh literary field . . . and both writers and readers appear to have explored the new area with an intense curiosity in which were mingled compassion, morbid fascination, and something akin to horror."[4] While there were many writers who saw life in the big city as full of charm and adventure—Richard Harding Davis, Bayard Taylor, and H. C. Bunner, for example—others with more active social consciences, like Howells or H. H. Boyesen, were aware of the city's dangers but treated the slum dwellers only in passing. The life of the poor, according to Bunner, writing in 1896, was enjoyable because of the "pitiful petty schemes for the gaining of daily bread that make up for them ["Bohemians"] the game and comedy of life." Bunner could view casually "the daily march of the mob of drunks, detectives, butcher's boys, washerwomen, priests, drunken women . . . "[5] because he never probed beneath the surface of these lives. And for the writers of melodrama the slum girl was a creature of romance, sure to rise above her situation, as did the dime novel heroines of *Orphan Nell, the Orange Girl; or The Lost Heir*

2. Frank Kermode, "The Prime of Miss Muriel Spark," *New Statesman*, 66 (1963), 397.
3. I have drawn on Alexander Cowie's excellent discussion of sentimental fiction in his *The Rise of the American Novel* (New York, 1948), pp. 412ff.
4. Walter F. Taylor, *The Economic Novel in America* (Chapel Hill, 1942), pp. 79–80.
5. "The Bowery and Bohemia," *The Stories of H. C. Bunner* (New York, 1916), pp. 370, 336.

118 · *Eric Solomon*

(1880) and *The Detective's Ward; or The Fortunes of a Bowery Girl* (1871). Whatever stresses life might present to the slum heroine, she was proof against temptation: "I am but a poor shop-girl; my present life is a struggle for a scanty existence; my future a life of toil; but over my present life of suffering there extends a rainbow of hope . . . Life is short, eternity endless—the grave is but the entrance to eternity. And you, villain, ask me to change my present peace for a life of horror with you. No, monster, rather may I die at once!"[6]

The same combinations of humor, melodrama, and sentiment marked the novels of Edward Townsend, who invented Chimmie Fadden, one of the early vernacular heroes. In his *A Daughter of the Tenements* (1895) the life of the poor was shown in some detail—more than exists in Crane's *Maggie*, just as De Forest included more combat reality than Crane did in his war novel—and there was liberal irony directed toward people of other classes who could not understand that the poor might have feelings. But the heroine rises from her slum background of sweatshops and fruitstands to become a ballet dancer, the hero becomes a newspaper illustrator, and they live happily ever after—on Long Island. Only a minor character is permitted to be ruined by drink and opium, and even he manages to perform a shining good deed before he dies. Crane's remark is worth noting: "My good friend Edward Townsend—have you read his 'Daughter of the Tenements'?—has another opinion of the Bowery, and it is certain to be better than mine."[7] The slums in these novels were grim and dangerous, but hard work finally conquered them, and the basic passage was from rags to riches. For those trapped there, the authors sustained a tone of pity and humor that reminds one of a famous *Life* cartoon of the period that showed two ragged tots staring at the sky and remarking that the stars were as thick as bedbugs. From these studies of the depths of the city came the work of O. Henry and Damon Runyon, not of Theodore Dreiser, James Farrell, and Nelson Algren.

Perhaps closest to *Maggie* in theme and texture was Edgar Fawcett's tale of a poor girl's betrayal and destruction, *The Evil That Men Do* (1889). The miseries of the working girl, the loathsomeness of drunken, fighting parents, the assumption that innocence is only temporary, get the novel off to a serious start. But the confrontations of the heroine and her would-be seducers are hysterical, and the sufferings of the working girl at the hands of the rich are overdone.[8]

6. Quoted in Mark Sullivan, *Our Times* (New York, 1926), I, 218–19.
7. Crane, letter to Catherine Harris, November 12? 1896, *Stephen Crane: Letters*, ed. R. W. Stallman and Lillian Gilkes (New York: New York University Press, 1960), p. 133.
8. The novel fits into the category called by Friedrich Engels the "old, old story of the proletarian girl seduced by a man of the middle class." Letter to Margaret Harkness, April 1888, quoted in *Documents of Modern Literary Realism*, ed. George F. Becker (Princeton, 1963), p. 483. Crane avoids, as Fawcett did not, the trap that Engels noticed in such fiction: "a mediocre writer would have attempted to disguise the trite character of the plot under a heap of artificial details and embellishment."

Fawcett created a world of corruption, venality, and weakness, true; and his heroine is not saved at the end—rather she declines from housemaid to kept woman to drunken whore and dies in an alley at the hands of her equally degraded working-class lover. But two hundred sixty-two pages of bombast must pass before she finally gives in to her seducer, and much of the novel is given over to the depiction of wealthy cardboard villains.[9]

I believe that Stephen Crane's *Maggie* is in part a reaction to these "realistic" city novels that were as sentimental and melodramatic, finally, as was the other traditional popular fiction of Crane's time.[1]   *   *   *

9. It is interesting to note that in this novel there is a character named Maggie who goes bad: Townsend's *A Daughter of the Tenements* also has a fallen Maggie.

1. "In plot, Crane's book is the most faithful of all to the stereotype . . . [and involves] travesties." Leslie Fiedler, *Love and Death in the American Novel* (Cleveland, 1960), pp. 238–39.

The Author and the Novel

Birth Notices, Letters, and Inscriptions: The 1893 *Maggie*

FRANK W. NOXON

The Real Stephen Crane†

One of Stephen Crane's characteristics was a haunting solicitude for the comforts and welfare of other people, especially those of narrow opportunity. He thought about it as one thinks about an art or craft, developing a style and inventing original methods.

* * *

No doubt some of our acquaintances in those days[1] as well as critics and readers since have ascribed Crane's interest in unfortunate women to another instinct than sympathy and compassion. Nobody can be sure. But knowing him pretty well and seeing him a good deal in the company of girls, toward whom he showed respect and deference, I have no difficulty in believing that when he wrote about scarlet sisters or vehemently defended one as later he did in a New York police court,[2] the dominant impulse was a desire to serve the helpless. *Maggie, a Girl of the Streets*, at least in its early form, was wholly or in part written at Syracuse.[3] With typical carelessness the author left the sheets lying about in the front corner room which he shared with Norton Goodwin.[4] Some of these pages were picked up and read by droppers-in. The other day a '93 man whom I had not seen for many years asked me what I thought of Crane as a man at the time, knowing that he was writing that sort of thing. Had it been my observation, as it had been his, that Crane's own conduct seemed to contrast with his choice of literary themes? In 1927 this sounds primitive. It was 1890,[5] and it was a Syracuse much more Methodist

† From *The Step Ladder* [Chicago], XIV (January 1928), 4, 5. This entire article is reprinted in *Stephen Crane: Letters*, ed. R. W. Stallman and Lillian Gilkes (New York: New York University Press, 1960), pp. 334–39.
1. At Syracuse University. [*Editor*.]
2. This is a reference to Dora Clark, who was accused of prostitution. For a full study of this incident, see Olov W. Fryckstedt, "Stephen Crane in the Tenderloin," *Studia Neophilologica*, XXXIV (1962), 135–63. [*Editor*.]
3. This is corroborated by another Syracuse University student, Clarence Loomis Peaslee. See his "Stephen Crane's College Days," *The Monthly Illustrator and Home and Country*, XIII (August 1896), 27–30. [*Editor*.]
4. Now a judge in Chicago. [His first name was Clarence.—*Editor*.]
5. Noxon and Crane were in the Class of 1894 and they belonged to the Delta Upsilon Fraternity. Crane transferred to Syracuse University in January 1891; he had spent the previous semester at Lafayette College. In all, he completed one year as a college student. [*Editor*.]

and very much more "divinity" than now. By the way, in after years Crane told me about the publication of *Maggie*. He had vainly peddled it among the publishers, though to his delight the gentle realist, Howells, reading it for somebody (Harpers?) had written an enthusiastic memorandum. Finally he paid for bringing it out himself, using the pseudonym "Johnston Smith." The cover was yellow paper with the title in large black letters. Four men were hired to sit all day one in front of another in New York elevated trains, reading intently and holding up the volume so that passengers would think the metropolis was *Maggie*-mad.

* * *

WILLIS FLETCHER JOHNSON

The Launching of Stephen Crane†

* * *

One day in the summer of 1891 he brought me a big bundle of manuscript, and asked me to read it and tell him what to do with it. I found it to be not a Sullivan County sketch, but a tale of the slums of New York; the first draft of "Maggie: A Girl of the Streets."[1] It was in some respects crude, but powerful and impressive. Three features were conspicuous. One was the writer's mastery of the speech and manners of the denizens of the New York slums, altho he had spent little time in that city and had enjoyed little opportunity for observation of its ways. The second was the throbbing vitality and dynamics of the story; every line seemed alive and active. And the third was, despite the stark brutality and astounding frankness of it, the absolute lack of prurience, of erotic suggestiveness, of the "sex-motive," which nowadays dominates so much of our fiction. Compared, let us say, with the novels of Hall Caine, which I mention because they were just then in great vogue, "Maggie" seemed almost Puritanical. The notion that it was "obscene" was grotesque in its silliness. Its chief fault was in that exuberance and extravagance of adjectives which Stephen never was able wholly to outgrow.

---

† From *The Literary Digest International Book Review*, IV (April 1926), 289. Willis Fletcher Johnson (1857–1931), day editor of the *New York Tribune*, had been a student at Pennington Seminary, Pennington, New Jersey—he graduated in 1875—where Stephen Crane's father was once principal (1849–58). This tie aided the newspaper careers of other Cranes: J. Townley, Stephen's older brother, ran a news bureau at Asbury Park and worked for the *Tribune* as early as 1878; Stephen Crane's mother also reported for the *Tribune*, covering the Methodist activities at Ocean Grove; and Stephen himself contributed items to the *Tribune* as early as 1888. It was Johnson who personally accepted several of Stephen Crane's Sullivan County, New York, sketches for publication in the *Tribune* in 1892.
1. Johnson's dating in this article has been questioned; several dates are indeed faulty. See Donald Pizer's introduction to *Maggie: A Girl of the Streets* (San Francisco: Chandler Publishing Co., 1968), p. xiv. Pizer thinks that Johnson first saw *Maggie* in early 1893, not 1891. It is still possible, however, that Johnson was shown the Syracuse version of *Maggie* in the summer of 1891. [*Editor.*]

I told him that the book, with some revision, would be worth publishing, and ought to be successful. But I warned him that it would be difficult to find a reputable publisher who would dare to bring it out; and that if it were published it would so shock the Podsnaps and Mrs. Grundys[2] as to bring upon him a storm of condemnation. At that he suggested that in order not to compromise his future it might be well to print it under an assumed name; and he discust the same point also with Mr. Post Wheeler,[3] then a leading New York journalist, and with some others. The outcome was that he put upon the title page the name of "Johnston Smith," suggested by the two names which were most numerous in the city directory— he first made it "Johnson Smith," but finally inserted the "t" in the former name, in order that, as he whimsically explained to me when he told me of it, neither Mr. Podsnap nor Mrs. Grundy might suspect him of being the guilty author!

The crux was to find a publisher. The book was quite "out of the line" of the house which had produced my books, and there was no use in trying it. The man whom I knew best in the New York publishing trade was my very dear friend and former colleague, Ripley Hitchcock, then literary adviser of D. Appleton & Co.; so I sent Stephen to him. He appreciated the merits of the book, but hesitated to recommend its acceptance. He told me, however, that "That boy has the real stuff in him," and a few years later eagerly accepted for publication Stephen's next work, "The Red Badge of Courage." *   *   *

STEPHEN CRANE

Howells Discussed at Avon-by-the-Sea†

Avon-by-the-Sea, Aug. 17 (Special).—At the Seaside Assembly the morning lecture was delivered by Professor Hamlin Garland, of Bos-

2. Mr. and Mrs. Podsnap, though leaders of society, were pompous, ignorant, narrow-minded, without culture or taste; they appear in Charles Dickens' *Our Mutual Friend* (1864–65). Mrs. Grundy was the priggish and strait-laced symbol of social conventions in Thomas Morton's comedy, *Speed the Plow* (1800). [*Editor*.]
3. Post Wheeler (1869–1956), who knew Stephen Crane in childhood, was a newspaperman and for a brief period (1896–1900) editor of the *New York Press*. Later he became a career diplomat. Wheeler recalled (with his wife, Hallie Erminie Rives) his relationship with Crane in *Dome of Many-Coloured Glass* (New York: Doubleday & Co., 1955). [*Editor*.]
† From *New York Tribune*, August 18, 1891, p. 5. This item was first reprinted in full by Donald Pizer, "Crane Reports Garland on Howells,"

Modern Language Notes, LXX (January 1955), 37–39. For a discussion of Howells, see Daniel Aaron, "Howells' 'Maggie,'" above. Hamlin Garland (1860–1940), whose *Main-Travelled Roads* was published in June 1891, was one of the new "realists" and named by Stephen Crane as one of his "literary fathers" (the other being William Dean Howells). Their first meeting was at Avon-by-the-Sea, New Jersey, in August 1891. Garland tried to find a publisher for *Maggie* and encouraged Crane in his poetry and his war novel, *The Red Badge of Courage*. Crane may have learned something about impressionism and realism ("veritism") from Garland, whose articles between 1890–93 became his book of literary theory, *Crumbling Idols* (1894). Later Garland was disenchanted with Crane's bohemianism.

ton, on W. D. Howells, the novelist. He said: "No man stands for a more vital principle than does Mr. Howells. He stands for modern-spirit, sympathy and truth. He believes in the progress of ideals, the relative in art. His definition of idealism[1] cannot be improved upon, 'the truthful treatment of material.'[2] He does not insist upon any special material, but only that the novelist be true to himself and to things as he sees them. It is absurd to call him photographic. The photograph is false in perspective, in light and shade, in focus. When a photograph can depict atmosphere and sound, the comparison will have some meaning, and then it will not be used as a reproach. Mr. Howells' work has deepened in insight and widened in sympathy from the first. His canvas has grown large, and has thickened with figures. Between "Their Wedding Journey" and "A Hazard of New Fortunes" there is an immense distance. "A Modern Instance" is the greatest, most rigidly artistic novel ever written by an American, and ranks with the great novels of the world. "A Hazard of New Fortunes" is the greatest, sanest, truest study of a city in fiction.[3] The test of the value of Mr. Howells' work will come fifty years from now, when his sheaf of novels will form the most accurate, sympathetic and artistic study of American society yet made by an American. Howells is a many-sided man, a humorist of astonishing delicacy and imagination, and he has written of late some powerful poems in a full, free style. He is by all odds the most American and vital of our literary men to-day. He stands for all that is progressive and humanitarian in our fiction, and his following increases each day. His success is very great, and it will last."

* * *

STEPHEN CRANE

The Broken-Down Van†

The gas lamps had just been lit and the two great red[1] furniture vans with impossible landscapes on their sides rolled and plunged

1. Misprint for "realism." [*Editor*.]
2. This is a key definition of Howells' concept of realism as elaborated in his *Criticism and Fiction*, published in May 1891. See W. D. Howells, *Criticism and Fiction and Other Essays*, ed. and introd. Clara Marburg Kirk and Rudolf Kirk (New York: New York University Press, 1959), p. 38. *Criticism and Fiction* was made up of essays from Howells' column, "Editor's Study," in *Harper's Monthly*, beginning in 1886. Crane may have been influenced by Howells' literary theories and practices in his 1893 *Maggie*. [*Editor*.]
3. The first major American novel to deal with New York City; Howells does make reference to the slums. *A Hazard of New Fortunes* first ap-

peared as a serial in *Harper's Weekly* (March–November 1889) and was published as a novel (in America) in 1890. [*Editor*.]
† From *New York Tribune*, July 10, 1892, part I, p. 8. No one knows exactly how long Stephen Crane was in New York City (presumably he was in the city as early as 1891) before he wrote the 1893 *Maggie*. This sketch forecasts many things in the novel, though here Crane is far more naturalistic (with close details) and more openly comic.
1. Note Crane's early use of color in this sketch, which is more suggestively employed in *Maggie*. [*Editor*.]

slowly along the street. Each was drawn by four horses, and each almost touched the roaring elevated road above. They were on the uptown track of the surface road—indeed the street was so narrow that they must be on one track or the other.

They tossed and pitched and proceeded slowly, and a horse car with a red light came up behind. The car was red, and the bullseye light was red, and the driver's hair was red. He blew his whistle shrilly and slapped the horse's lines impatiently. Then he whistled again. Then he pounded on the red dash board with his car-hook till the red light trembled. Then a car with a green light crept up behind the car with the red light; and the green driver blew his whistle and pounded on his dash board; and the conductor of the red car seized his strap from his position on the rear platform and rung such a rattling tattoo on the gong over the red driver's head that the red driver became frantic and stood up on his toes and puffed out his cheeks as if he were playing the trombone in a German street-band and blew his whistle till an imaginative person could see slivers flying from it, and pounded his red dash board till the metal was dented in and the car-hook was bent. And just as the driver of a newly-come car with a blue light began to blow his whistle and pound his dash board and the green conductor began to ring his bell like a demon which drove the green driver mad and made him rise up and blow and pound as no man ever blew or pounded before, which made the red conductor lose the last vestige of control of himself and caused him to bounce up and down on his bell strap as he grasped it with both hands in a wild, maniacal dance, which of course served to drive uncertain Reason from her tottering throne in the red driver,[2] who dropped his whistle and his hook and began to yell, and ki-yi,[3] and whoop harder than the worst personal devil encountered by the sternest of Scotch Presbyterians ever yelled and ki-yied and whooped on the darkest night after the good man had drunk the most hot Scotch whiskey; just then the left-hand forward wheel on the rear van fell off and the axle went down. The van gave a mighty lurch and then swayed and rolled and rocked and stopped; the red driver applied his brake with a jerk and his horses turned out to keep from being crushed between car and van; the other drivers applied their brakes with a jerk and their horses turned out; the two cliff-dwelling men on the shelf half-way up the front of the stranded van began to shout loudly to their brother cliff-dwellers on the forward van; a girl, six years old, with a pail of beer crossed under the red car horses' necks; a boy, eight years old, mounted the red car with the sporting extras of the evening papers; a girl, ten years old, went in front of the van horses with two pails of beer; an unclassified boy poked his

2. Compare to Jimmie's throne in *Maggie* (Chapter IV). [*Editor.*]

3. A howl or yelp (like a dog). [*Editor.*]

finger in the black grease in the hub of the right-hand hind van wheel and began to print his name on the red landscape on the van's side; a boy with a little head and big ears examined the white rings on the martingales[4] of the van leaders with a view of stealing them in the confusion; a sixteen-year-old girl without any hat and with a roll of half-finished vests under her arm crossed the front platform of the green car.[5] As she stepped up on to the sidewalk a barber from a ten-cent shop said "Ah! there!"[6] and she answered "smarty!" with withering scorn and went down a side street. A few drops of warm summer rain began to fall.

Well, the van was wrecked and something had got to be done. It was on the busiest car track on Manhattan Island. The cliff-dwellers got down in some mysterious way—probably on a rope ladder. Their brethren drove their van down a side street and came back to see what was the matter.

"The nut is off," said the captain of the wrecked van.

"Yes," said the first mate, "the nut is off."

"Hah," said the captain of the other van, "the nut is off."

"Yer right," said his first mate, "the nut is off."

The driver of the red car came up, hot and irritated. But he had regained his reason. "The nut is off," he said.

The drivers of the green and of the blue car came along. "The nut," they said in chorus, "is off."

The red, green and blue conductors came forward. They examined the situation carefully as became men occupying a higher position. Then they made this report through the chairman, the red conductor:

"The nut is gone."

"Yes," said the driver of the crippled van, who had spoken first, "yes, the damned nut is lost."

Then the driver of the other van swore, and the two assistants swore, and the three car drivers swore and the three car conductors used some polite but profane expressions.[7] Then a strange man, an unknown man and an outsider, with his trousers held up by a trunk-strap, who stood at hand, swore harder than any of the rest. The others turned and looked at him inquiringly and savagely. The man wriggled nervously.

"You wanter tie it up," he said at last.

---

4. Part of a harness, connecting the head gear with the bellyband, that prevents a horse from throwing back its head. [*Editor.*]
5. An early hint of Maggie, who works in a collar and cuff factory. [*Editor.*]
6. An echo of Maggie's "line" in *Maggie*.

Chapter XVII. [*Editor.*]
7. The references to "damned" and to "swore" indicate that the publishers of the newspapers of the day were not as cautious as publishers of magazines and novels, but this is still far removed from the full-scale swearing in *Maggie*. [*Editor.*]

"Wot yo' goin' to tie it to, you cussed fool?" asked the assistant of the head van scornfully, "a berloon?"

"Ha, ha!" laughed the others.

"Some folks make me tired," said the second van driver.

"Go and lose yourself with the nut," said the red conductor, severely.

"That's it," said the others. "Git out, 'fore we t'row you out."

The officiously profane stranger slunk away.

The crisis always produces the man.

In this crisis the man was the first van driver.

"Bill," said the first van driver, "git some candles." Bill vanished.

A car with a white light, a car with a white and red light, a car with a white light and a green bar across it, a car with a blue light and a white circle around it, another car with a red bullseye light and one with a red flat light had come up and stopped. More were coming to extend the long line. The elevated trains thundered overhead, and made the street tremble. A dozen horse cars went down on the other track, and the drivers made derisive noises, rather than speaking derisive words at their brother van-bound drivers. Each delayed car was full of passengers, and they craned their necks and peppery old gentlemen inquired what the trouble was, and a happy individual who had been to Coney Island began to sing.

Trucks, mail-wagons and evening paper carts crowded past. A jam was imminent. A Chatham Square cab fought its way along with a man inside wearing a diamond like an arc-light. A hundred people stopped on either sidewalk; ten per cent of them whistled "Boom-de-ay." A half dozen small boys managed to just miss being killed by passing teams. Four Jews looked out of four different pawnshops. Pullers-in for three clothing stores were alert. The ten-cent barber eyed a Division-st. girl who was a millinery puller-in and who was chewing gum with an earnest, almost fierce, motion of the jaw. The ever-forward flowing tide of the growlers flowed on. The men searched under the slanting rays of the electric light for the lost nut, back past a dozen cars; scattering drops of rain continued to fall and a hand-organ came up and began an overture.

Just then Bill rose up from somewhere with four candles. The leader lit them and each van man took one and they continued the search for the nut. The humorous driver on a blue car asked them why they didn't get a fire-fly; the equally playful driver of a white car advised them of the fact that the moon would be up in the course of two or three hours. Then a gust of wind came and blew out the candles. The hand-organ man played on. A dozen newsboys arrived with evening paper extras about the Presidential nomination. The passengers bought the extras and found that they contained nothing new. A man with a stock of suspenders on his arm began to look into the trade situation. He might have made a sale to the profane man with the trunk-strap but he had disappeared. The leader again asserted himself.

"Bill," he shouted, "you git a lager beer-keg." Bill was gone in an instant.

"Jim," continued the leader, in a loud voice, as if Jim were up at the sharp end of the mainmast and the leader was on the deck, "Jim, unhitch them hosses and take out the pole."

Jim started to obey orders. A policeman came and walked around the van, looked at the prostrated wheel, started to say something, concluded not to, made the hand-organ man move on, and then went to the edge of the sidewalk and began talking to the Division-st. girl with the gum, to the infinite disgust of the cheap barber. The trunk-strap man came out of a restaurant with a sign of "Breakfast, 13 cents; Dinner, 15 cents," where he had been hidden and slunk into the liquor store next door with a sign of "Hot spiced rum, 6 cents; Sherry with a Big Egg in it, 5 cents." At the door he almost stepped on a small boy with a pitcher of beer so big that he had to set it down and rest every half block.[8]

Bill was now back with the keg. "Set it right there," said the leader. "Now you, Jim, sock that pole under the axle and we'll h'ist 'er up and put the keg under."

One of the horses began kicking the front of the van. "Here, there!" shouted the leader and the horse subsided. "Six or seven o' you fellers git under that pole," commanded the leader, and he was obeyed. "Now all together!" The axle slowly rose and Bill slipped under the chime of the keg. But it was not high enough to allow the wheel to go on. "Git a paving block," commanded the leader to Bill. Just then a truck loaded with great, noisy straps of iron tried to pass. The wheels followed the car track too long, the truck struck the rear of the van and the axle went down with a crash while the keg rolled away into the gutter. Even great leaders lose their self-control sometimes; Washington swore at the Battle of Long Island; so this van leader now swore. His language was plain and scandalous. The truckman offered to lick the van man till he couldn't walk. He stopped his horses to get down to do it. But the policeman left the girl and came and made the truckman give over his warlike movement, much to the disgust of the crowd. Then he punched the suspender man in the back with the end of his club and went back to the girl. But the second delay was too much for the driver of the green car, and he turned out his horses and threw his car from the track. It pitched like a skiff in the swell of a steamer. It staggered and rocked and as it went past the van plunged into the gutter and made the crowd stand back, but the horses strained themselves and finally brought

8. A first glimpse of Jimmie, who performs a sim-   ilar task in *Maggie* (Chapter III). [*Editor*.]

it up and at last it blundered on to its track and rolled away at a furious rate with the faces of the passengers wreathed in smiles and the conductor looking proudly back. Two other cars followed the example of the green and went lumbering past on the stones.

"Tell them fellers we'll be out of their way now in a minute," said the leader to the red conductor. Bill had arrived with the paving block. "Up with 'er, now," called the leader. The axle went up again and the keg with the stone on top of it went under. The leader seized the wheel himself and slipped it on. "Hitch on them hosses!" he commanded, and it was done. "Now, pull slow there, Bill," and Bill pulled slow. The great red car with the impossible landscape gave a preliminary rock and roll, the wheel which had made the trouble dropped down an inch or two from the keg and the van moved slowly forward. There was nothing to hold the wheel on and the leader walked close to it and watched it anxiously. But it stayed on to the corner, and around the corner, and into the side street. The red driver gave a triumphant ki-yi and his horses plunged forward in their collars eagerly. The other drivers gave glad ki-yis and the other horses plunged ahead. Twenty cars rolled past at a fast gait. "Now, youse fellys, move on!" said the policeman, and the crowd broke up. The cheap barber was talking to a girl with one black eye, but he retreated to his shop with the sign which promised "bay rum and a clean towel to every customer." Inside the liquor store the trunk-strap man was telling a man with his sleeves rolled up how two good men could have put their shoulders under the van and h'isted it up while a ten-year-old boy put on the wheel.

STEPHEN CRANE

Summer Dwellers at Asbury Park and Their Doings†

* * *

The thousands of summer visitors who have fled from the hot, stifling air of the cities to enjoy the cool sea breezes are not entirely forgetful of the unfortunates who have to stay in their crowded tenements. Jacob Riis, the author of "How the Other Half Lives," gave an illustrated lecture on the same subject in the Beach Audi-

† From *New York Tribune*, July 24, 1892, p. 22. For background, see Jacob Riis, *How the Other Half Lives*, above, and Thomas A. Gullason, "A Minister, a Social Reformer, and *Maggie*," also above.

torium on Wednesday evening. The proceeds were given to the tenement-house work of the King's Daughters.[1] Over $300 was cleared, which, at $2 each, will give 150 children a two-weeks outing in the country.

*   *   *

STEPHEN CRANE

Letters and Inscriptions†

17.[1] To Hamlin Garland

[March? 1893]

[Inscribed across the cover of a copy of *Maggie*][2]

It is inevitable that you will be greatly shocked by this book but continue please with all possible courage to the end. For it tries to show that environment is a tremendous thing in the world and frequently shapes lives regardless. If one proves that theory one makes room in Heaven for all sorts of souls (notably an occasional street girl) who are not confidently expected to be there by many excellent people.

It is probable that the reader of this small thing may consider the Author to be a bad man, but, obviously, this is a matter of small consequence to   *The Author*

23. To William Dean Howells

1064 Ave A./March 28, 93

My dear Mr. Howells: I sent you a small book some weeks ago.[3] Mr. Garland had, I believe, spoken to you of it. Having recieved [*sic*] no reply I must decide then that you think it a wretched thing? Yours faithfully   *Stephen Crane*

---

1. A woman's club that performed volunteer service in tenement neighborhoods and with Jacob Riis's encouragement founded a settlement house. [*Editor.*]
† From *Stephen Crane: Letters*, ed. R. W. Stallman and Lillian Gilkes (New York: New York University Press, 1960), pp. 14, 16, 20–22, 59, 79, 125–26, 129.
1. This number and the ones that begin each letter or inscription are those used by the editors of *Stephen Crane: Letters*. [*Editor.*]
2. A note about this inscribed copy of *Maggie* in the holograph of Hamlin Garland reads: "The first copy Crane sent to me, probably about Oct. '92 H. G." Garland has misdated it, since *Maggie* was not published until early 1893. Crane re-

peated this inscription almost word for word in inscribing *Maggie* copies for [Dr. Lucius L.—*Editor*] Button (1893?) and Dixon (1895). He probably inscribed a batch of copies with this same message upon receiving the books from the printer in 1893 and had some remaining in 1895, at least the one he sent the Reverend Thomas Dixon early in 1895.
3. *Maggie*. It was the literary creed of Howells and Hamlin Garland that influenced Crane to reconstruct *Maggie*, an influence that he acknowledged—"a certain re-adjustment of his point of view victoriously concluded some time in 1892" (see Letters 34, 80). Howells wrote an Appreciation of *Maggie* for Heinemann's 1896 edition.

Anne Arundel County
Public Library
Crofton
410-222-7915

Library name: CRO

Title: TUXEDO PARK - A
WALL STREET TYCOON AND
THE SECRET
Author: JENNET CONANT
Item ID: 39856001036540
Date due: 6/25/2018,23:59

Title: MAGGIE, A GIRL OF
THE STREETS - (A STORY
OF NEW Y
Author: STEPHEN CRANE
Item ID: 21982005391192
Date due: 6/25/2018,23:59

To renew your materials:
Go to the Library's
Website at www.aacpl.net,
or call any branch.
****

Did you know we offer
free online tutoring
for all ages? Check out
www.aacpl.net/homework

28. *To Lily Brandon Munroe*[4]

1064 Ave. A. NYC [April, 1893]

Dearest L. B.
                                   *   *   *

Well, at least, I've done something. I wrote a book.[5] Up to the present time, I think I can say I am glad I did it. Hamlin Garland was the first to over-whelm me with all manner of extraordinary language. The book has made me a powerful friend in W. D. Howells. B. O. Flower[6] of the "*Arena*" has practically offered me the benefits of his publishing company for all that I may in future write. Albert Shaw of the "Review of Reviews" wrote me congratulations this morning and to-morrow I dine with the editor of the "Forum."

So I think I can say that if I "watch out," I'm almost a success. And "such a boy, too," they say.

I do not think, however, that I will get enough applause to turn my head. I don't see why I should. I merely did what I could, in a simple way, and recognition from such men as Howells, Garland, Flower and Shaw, has shown me that I was not altogether reprehensible.

Any particular vanity in my work is not possible to me. I merely write you these things, to let you know why I was silent for so long.

I thought if I could measure myself by the side of some of the great men I could find if I was of enough value to think of you, L. B.

They tell me I did a horrible thing, but, they say, "its great."

"And it's style," said Garland to Howells, "Egad, it has no style! Absolutely transparent! Wonderful—wonderful."

And I? I have merely thought of you and wondered if you cared that they said these things. Or wether [*sic*] you have forgotten?

---

4. Parts of this letter and of No. 29 were reprinted in *Omnibus* [*Stephen Crane: An Omnibus*, ed. R. W. Stallman (Knopf, 1952); hereafter *Omnibus.—Editor*] from *Stephen Crane*, by John Berryman (William Sloane Associates, 1950), p. 45. Berryman also used fragments of Letter 34, and Melvin H. Schoberlin reproduced about one-third of it in his Introduction to the *Sullivan County Sketches* (Syracuse University Press, 1949), p. 19. The complete text of these three letters to Lily Brandon Munroe is from the originals in the possession of Frederick B. Smillie.
5. *Maggie.* Since Howells had not read *Maggie*

all March, this letter must be dated for April, 1893, rather than for March (as Berryman [*Stephen Crane—Editor*] has it, pp. 45, 52).
6. Benjamin Orange Flower, editor of *The American Sentinel* (a literary and social weekly), established *The American Spectator*, which subsequently merged into *The Arena*. Founder of *The Arena*, he was an extensive contributor to leading magazines and periodicals and was editor of *The Coming Age* (Boston), one of the editors of *New Time* (Chicago), an editor of *Twentieth Century Magazine*, and president of Menace Publishing Company.

29. *To Lily Brandon Munroe*

c/o R. G. Vosburgh/143 E. 23ᵈ/N.Y. [Winter of 1893–1894?]

Dearest:

*   *   *

The *Arena Co.* brings out a book of mine this winter.[7] I wish you to get it, for it will show you how much I have changed. The Boston critics and Mr Howells think it quite extraordinary. I could prattle on here of the men who are now my friends and of the things I now hear—I am foolish enough to desire to tell you, for I wish you to think well of the man you have made—still[.]

*   *   *

74. *To Copeland and Day*

#126 Williams [*sic*] St. [Lantern Club]/New York City/

[June? 1895]

Dear sirs/ I cant seem to light on a copy of Maggie.[8]

*   *   *

Yours sincerely   *Stephen Crane*

111. *To an Editor of* Leslie's Weekly

[About November, 1895]

*   *   *

But, personally, I was unhappy only at times during the period of my struggles. I was always looking forward to success. My first great disappointment was in the reception of "Maggie, a Girl of the Streets." I remember how I looked forward to its publication, and pictured the sensation I thought it would make. It fell flat. Nobody seemed to notice it or care for it. I am going to introduce Maggie again to the world some time, but not for a good while.[9] Poor Maggie! she was one of my first loves.

*   *   *

---

7. The book was *Maggie*; evidently the Arena Company considered reissuing the 1893 edition. Nothing came of this, nor—as we shall see—of the trip to Europe.
8. This statement suggests that Copeland and Day was interested in reissuing the 1893 *Maggie*. It was an avant-garde Boston publishing house which issued Crane's iconoclastic volume of poetry, *The Black Riders*, in March 1895. [*Editor.*]

9. J. Herbert Welch published this letter on May 28, 1896, in *Leslie's Weekly*: "The Personality and Work of Stephen Crane." Welch reported that Crane had said this much "the other day," but Crane must have written this letter much earlier because *Maggie* was in the press during May, 1896—it was published in June. *Maggie* was in process of revision in February. Crane's letter was again published in *Omnibus*, pp. 627–29.

163. *To DeWitt Miller*[1]

Mr. DeWitt Miller/July 3d, 96

[Inscribed in a copy of *Maggie*][2]

It is indeed a brave new binding and I wish the inside were braver.
Stephen Crane

164. *To H. P. Taber: Editor of* The Philistine

[Undated]

[Inscribed in a copy of *Maggie*][3]

My dear Tabor: I wrote this book when I was very young so if you dont like it, shut up. But my best wishes go with it. *Stephen Crane*

173. *To an unknown recipient*

New York/Aug. 29, 1896

[Inscribed in a copy of *Maggie*, 1893 edition]

And the wealth of the few shall be built upon the patience of the poor/Prophecy not made B.C. 1090[4] *Stephen Crane*

1. Identity not known.
2. The 1896 edition of *Maggie: A Girl of the Streets*, published by D. Appleton and Company, was announced in the *Publishers' Weekly*, June 13. [This inscription was in a copy of the 1893, not the 1896, *Maggie*. See "DeWitt Miller's *Maggie*: A Correction," *Stephen Crane Newsletter*, II (Winter 1967), 4—*Editor*.]
3. Crane sent Taber this inscribed copy of the 1893 edition some time subsequent to the honorary dinner tendered him by the Society of the Philistines in December, 1895. Until then Crane had not met Taber, and his first appearance in the *Philistine* was in June, 1895, with the poem "I stood upon a high place," reprinted from *The Black Riders* (1895). The *Philistine* published in February, 1896, "What says the little sea-shell," and in March the sketch "Great Mistake," and in October "An Ominous Baby," reprinted from the *Arena* (1894). That Crane sent Taber this 1893 *Maggie* sometime during the first half of 1896 or at the end of 1895 is evidenced also by the contents of his inscription. That he knew him only slightly is shown by his misspelling Taber's name. This copy of *Maggie*, in original wrappers, is in the Houghton Library.
4. There are a few hints in *Maggie* of Crane's hostility toward the indifference of the well-to-do for the plight of the poor. [*Editor.*]

Rebirth and Revisions: The 1896 *Maggie*

STEPHEN CRANE

Letters†

138.[1] *To Ripley Hitchcock*

Hartwood, N.Y./February 2ᵈ [1896]

Dear Mr Hitchcock: I am very glad to hear you speak as you do concerning *Maggie*.[2] I will set to work this month rewriting it. I have no more pictures until they come from New York where I sat the last time I was down.[3] They should reach me soon. I was very much delighted with Frederick's [*sic*] letter in the Times.[4] I see also that they are beginning to charge me with having played base ball. I am rather more proud of my base ball ability than of some other things. I am coming down to New York this month and will come to see you first thing.

Yours sincerely   *Stephen Crane*

140. To Ripley Hitchcock

[Hartwood, N.Y., February 4–6? 1896]

Dear Mr. Hitchcock: I am working at *Maggie*. She will be down to you in a few days. I have dispensed with a goodly number of damns. I have no more copies of the book or I would have sent you one.

I want to approach Appleton & Co on a delicate matter. I dont care much about money up here save when I have special need of

† From *Stephen Crane: Letters*, ed. R. W. Stallman and Lillian Gilkes (New York: New York University Press, 1960), pp. 110, 112, 113–14, 122, 133.

1. This number and the ones that begin each letter or inscription are those used by the editors of *Stephen Crane: Letters*. [*Editor*.]

2. Ripley Hitchcock was an editor at D. Appleton & Company, who earlier accepted *The Red Badge of Courage* for book publication, and who now would publish a revised *Maggie* in order to capitalize on the war novel's phenomenal success. [*Editor*.]

3. The photograph was taken at the Lantern Club, as is shown by Crane's reply to the editor of *The Critic*, who also asked for a photograph (Letter 146). When [Elbert—*Editor*] Hubbard requested a picture, Crane promised that he would take one to Buffalo; and when [John Northern—*Editor*] Hilliard asked him for one the following December, Crane replied that he had no recent one at hand. In Letters 141, 142 he begs off on requests for photographs. In his letter to Nellie Crouse (No. 129) he said that the *Bookman* and *Echo* were publishing his photograph.

4. The London *Times Supplement* for January 26: "Stephen Crane's Triumphs."

it and just at this time there is a beautiful riding-mare for sale for a hundred dollars. The price will go up each week, almost, until spring and I am crazy to get her now. I dont want to strain your traditions but if I am worth $100. in your office, I would rather have it now.[5]
[*Incomplete*]

143. To Ripley Hitchcock

Hartwood/Monday [February 10, 1896]

Dear Mr Hitchcock: I am delighted with your prompt sympathy in regard to the saddle horse. It is a luxury to feel that some of my pleasures are due to my little pen. I will send you *Maggie* by detail. I have carefully plugged at the words which hurt. Seems to me the book wears quite a new aspect from very slight omissions.[6] Did you know that the book is very short? Only about 20000 words? Yours sincerely   *Stephen Crane*

156. To Ripley Hitchcock

165 W 23d/Thursday [April 2, 1896]

Dear Mr Hitchcock: I am engaged on the preface.[7] Dont let anyone put chapter headings on the book. The proofs make me ill. Let somebody go over them—if you think best—and watch for bad grammatical form & bad spelling. I am too jaded with Maggie to be able to see it.
Yours   *Crane*

178. To Miss Catherine Harris

[Jacksonville, Florida/November 12? 1896]

[*No salutation*] Thank you very much for your letter on Maggie. I

5. During December, 1895, when Crane visited Elbert Hubbard, he fell in love with a little brown horse, Peanuts, and, according to letters of the Crane family, he purchased him with money earned from the sale of a short story. On the other hand, here he is writing [Ripley—*Editor*] Hitchcock in February and asking for an advance of $100 for the purchase of a horse. Peanuts was clever, playful, and tricky; one never knew what he was going to do next. And that was perhaps why Crane had special affection for him—he was as unpredictable as his master. Crane was an excellent horseman. [Thomas Beer, *Hanna, Crane and the Mauve Decade* (Knopf, 1941); hereafter Beer.—*Editor*.]

Beer (p. 305) has Crane riding Peanuts in January, but Crane did not leave Hartwood all that month, and his letter to Hubbard (No. 147) inquiring about the noble horse indicates that he had not yet obtained Peanuts—not until mid-Feb-

ruary. In any case, the mare he asks Hitchcock money for is not Peanuts.

6. The omissions include the portrait of a character who appears only in the 1893 edition of *Maggie* and who provides thus an addition to the nine persons Maggie encounters on her predestined journey to the river. The omitted character is "a huge fat man in torn and greasy garments." See R. W. Stallman, "Stephen Crane's Revisions of *Maggie: A Girl of the Streets*," *American Literature*, XXVI (January, 1955). On the genesis and designed intention of *Maggie* see *Stephen Crane: An Omnibus*, ed. R. W. Stallman (Knopf, 1952), pp. 3–20. For an analysis of the novel see R. W. Stallman, "Stephen Crane's Primrose Path," *New Republic*, September 19, 1955, p. 133.

7. The preface to *Maggie* never materialized, at least not in print.

will try to answer your questions properly and politely. Mrs. Howells was right in telling you that I have spent a great deal of time on the East Side and that I have no opinion of missions. That—to you—may not be a valid answer since perhaps you have been informed that I am not very friendly to Christianity as seen around town.[8] I do not think that much can be done with the Bowery as long as the [*word blurred*] are in their present state of conceit. A person who thinks himself superior to the rest of us because he has no job and no pride and no clean clothes is as badly conceited as Lillian Russell. In a story of mine called "An Experiment in Misery" I tried to make plain that the root of Bowery life is a sort of cowardice. Perhaps I mean a lack of ambition or to willingly be knocked flat and accept the licking. The missions for children are another thing and if you will have Mr. Rockefeller give me a hundred street cars and some money I will load all the babes off to some pink world where cows can lick their noses and they will never see their families any more. My good friend Edward Townsend—have you read his "Daughter of the Tenements"?—has another opinion of the Bowery and it is certain to be better than mine. I had no other purpose in writing "Maggie" than to show people to people as they seem to me. If that be evil, make the most of it.

8. Nor was he friendly to temperance leaders, although his own father—author of *The Arts of Intoxication*—subscribed to the cause, and his mother, Helen Peck Crane, was an active participant in the work of the organization headed by Miss [Frances—*Editor*] Willard, the Woman's Christian Temperance Union. "Frances Willard," he told Miss Harris, "is one of those wonderful people who can tell right from wrong for everybody from the polar cap to the equator. Perhaps it never struck her that people differ from her. I have loved myself passionately now and then but Miss Willard's affair with Miss Willard should be stopped by the police" (Beer, p. 359).

Contemporary Reviews

American Reviews: 1893

From the *Port Jervis* [New York] *Union* †

The *Union* has been favored with a copy of a recently published novel entitled, "Maggie, a Girl of the Streets," by Stephen Crane of New York city [*sic*]. The writer is a son of the late Rev. J. T. Crane and a brother of Judge Wm. H. Crane, which facts, apart from the merits of the publication, will invest it with a certain degree of local interest.[1]

The plot is laid in the slums and dives of the great metropolis and the characters depicted are all, without exception, creatures of the slums. The evident object of the writer is to show the tremendous influence of environment on the human character and destiny. Maggie, the heroine, or central figure of the tale, grows up under surroundings which repress all good impulses, stunt the moral growth and render it inevitable that she should become what she eventually did, a creature of the streets. The pathos of her sad story will be deeply felt by all susceptible persons who read the book.

The slum life of New York city is treated with the frank fidelity of the realist, and while the unco guid[2] and ultra pious may be shocked by the freedom of his descriptions and the language in which the dialogues are carried on, sensible people will read the book in the spirit in which it was written and will derive therefrom the moral lesson which it is the author's aim to inculcate.

The literary merits of the work are considerable.

The author, although scarcely yet out of his teens, is the master of a vigorous style and uses the English language with precision, force and fluency. He has humor, originality and a wonderful power of depicting life as he sees it. He has a positive genius for description and great skill in the analysis of human character and motive.

The dialect of the New York slums, which is reproduced in this volume with absolute accuracy, is, we take it, something new in

† From the *Port Jervis* [New York] *Union*, March 13, 1893, p. 3.
1. Thomas Beer, *Stephen Crane* (New York: Alfred A. Knopf, 1923), pp. 245–46, quotes Stephen Crane's brother, William, who "tells me [Beer] that after *Maggie* appeared in 1896 several ladies of Port Jervis solemnly consulted him as to the propriety of receiving Stephen Crane in their homes. . . ." Yet it is interesting to note that the harsher 1893 *Maggie* was sensitively and intelligently reviewed in a Port Jervis newspaper and Crane's hometown did follow his career with some pride. See Thomas A. Gullason, "The First Known Review of Stephen Crane's 1893 *Maggie*," *English Language Notes*, V (June 1968), 300–302. [*Editor.*]
2. Very or remarkably good. [*Editor.*]

literature. It is certainly as legitimate a subject of literary and artistic treatment as the dialect of the Georgia negro or Tennessee mountaineer and even more interesting to the average New Yorker.

The volume before us is a very clever and most creditable achievement for so young a man and we congratulate the author most heartily on the success of his first attempt at book making.

HAMLIN GARLAND

An Ambitious French Novel and a Modest American Story†

* * *

"Maggie; A Story of New York."[1] This is of more interest to me,[2] both because it is the work of a young man, and also because it is a work of astonishingly good style. It deals with poverty and vice and crime also, but it does so, not out of curiosity, not out of salaciousness, but because of a distinct art impulse, the desire to utter in truthful phrase a certain rebellious cry. It is the voice of the slums. It is not written by a *dilettante*; it is written by one who has lived the life. The young author, Stephen Crane, is a native of the city,[3] and has grown up in the very scenes he describes. His book is the most truthful and unhackneyed study of the slums I have yet read, fragment though it is. It is pictorial, graphic, terrible in its directness. It has no conventional phrases. It gives the dialect of the slums as I have never before seen it written—crisp, direct, terse. It is another locality finding voice.

It is important because it voices the blind rebellion of Rum Alley and Devil's Row. It creates the atmosphere of the jungles, where vice festers and crime passes gloomily by, where outlawed human nature rebels against God and man.

The story fails of rounded completeness. It is only a fragment. It is typical only of the worst elements of the alley. The author should delineate the families living on the next street, who live lives of heroic purity and hopeless hardship.

The dictum is amazingly simple and fine for so young a writer. Some of the words illuminate like flashes of light. Mr. Crane is only twenty-one years of age, and yet he has met and grappled with the actualities of the street in almost unequalled grace and strength.

† From *The Arena*, VIII (June 1893), xi–xii.
1. "Maggie." By Stephen Crane. Published by the author.
2. Than Paul Bourget's *Cosmopolis*, the other book Garland is reviewing. [*Editor*.]
3. Stephen Crane was born in Newark, New Jersey, in 1871 and grew up in Port Jervis, New York, and Asbury Park, New Jersey, before he came to New York City in 1891. [*Editor*.]

With such a *technique* already at command, with life mainly *before him*, Stephen Crane is to be henceforth reckoned with. "Maggie" should be put beside "Van Bibber"[4] to see the extremes of New York as stated by two young men. Mr. Crane need not fear comparisons so far as *technique* goes, and Mr. Davis will need to step forward right briskly or he may be overtaken by a man who impresses the reader with a sense of almost unlimited resource.

The Author-Artist Will Soon Issue a Book— Stephen Crane's "Maggie"†

"Maggie: a Girl of the Streets," Stephen Crane's book, to which Mr. W. D. Howells pays such an astonishing tribute in the interview published in another part of this paper,[1] is a study of tenement house life in this city. It tells two stories—those of a brother and sister. It begins in this way:*   *   *

*   *   *

Such is the environment which Mr. Crane gives the brother and Maggie. It is from it that she goes out to become "a girl of the streets." He tells his story—or, rather, makes his study—with merciless accuracy. There is unquestionably truth in it; the kind of truth that no American has ever had the courage (or is it bravado?) to put between book covers before. It is a question if such brutalities are wholly acceptable in literature. Perhaps, as Mr. Howells says, they will be before long. Perhaps there will always be certain phases of life which we will not want to have woven with entire realism into our reading matter.

This writer, however, deserves praise for one thing, surely. He has not failed to touch vice in his book where he has found it in real life; but he has not gilded it. He has painted it as it is; he has not made it clandestinely attractive. In this he rises far above such other Americans—Edgar Fawcett and Edgar Saltus, notably—as have endeavored to gain recognition in somewhat similar fields.

Throughout the book the quaint and graphic descriptive powers of the young author are shown as strongly as in the portions quoted. Whether or not we can be entertained by the book, it certainly must command our respect. "Maggie" is published by the Arena Company of Boston.[2]

*   *   *

4. By Richard Harding Davis. [*Editor.*]

† From the *New York Press*, April 15, 1894, part III, p. 2.

1. A reference to Edward Marshall, "Greatest Living American Writer," *New York Press*, April 15, 1894, part II, p. 2. Crane was working for the *Press* at this time. His "An Experiment in Misery" appeared on April 22 and "An Experiment in Luxury" on April 29, 1894. [*Editor.*]

2. In more than one place, it was announced that the *Arena* had published the privately printed *Maggie*, which it did not. This remains one of the many mysteries of Crane's career. The novel was officially published by D. Appleton and Company in 1896. [*Editor.*]

From *The Bookman* [New York]†

You will look in vain through the pages of the *Trade Circular* for any record of a story of New York life entitled *Maggie: A Girl of the Streets*, which was published three or four years ago in this city.[1] At the moment of going to press the timorous publishers withdrew their imprint from the book, which was sold, in paper covers, for fifty cents. There seems to be considerable difficulty now in securing copies, but the fact that there is no publisher's name to the book, and that the author appears under the *nom de plume* of "Johnston Smith," may have something to do with its apparent disappearance. The copy which came into the writer's possession was addressed to the Rev. Thomas Dixon a few months ago, before the author went West on a journalistic trip to Nebraska, and has these words written across the cover: "It is inevitable that this book will greatly shock you, but continue, pray, with great courage to the end, for it tries to show that environment is a tremendous thing in this world, and often shapes lives regardlessly. If one could prove that theory, one would make room in Heaven for all sorts of souls (notably an occasional street girl) who are not confidently expected to be there by many excellent people." The author of this story and the writer of these words is Stephen Crane, whose "Lines" (he does not call them poems) have just been published by Copeland and Day, and are certain to make a sensation.

Stephen Crane is not yet twenty-four years old, but competent critics aver that his command of the English language is such as to raise the highest hopes for his future career. The impression he makes on his literary co-workers is that he is a young man of almost unlimited resource. The realism of his *Maggie*—a story that might have taken a greater hold on the public than even *Chimmie Fadden*,[2] had the publishers been less timid—is of that daring and terrible directness which in its iconoclasm is the very characteristic of rugged undisciplined strength in a youth of genius.   *   *   *

† From *The Bookman* [New York], I (May 1895), 229.
1. This is not a "legitimate" review of the 1893 *Maggie* but an announcement of the publication of Crane's volume of poetry, *The Black Riders*. It shows that the novel still had an underground reputation among critics two years after its initial publication. This review was presumably written by Harry Thurston Peck, editor of *The Bookman*. [*Editor*.]
2. By Edward W. Townsend. [*Editor*.]

CHELIFER [RUPERT HUGHES]

The Justification of Slum Stories†

*   *   *

But probably the strongest piece of slum writing we have is "Maggie," by Mr. Stephen Crane, which was published some years ago with a pen-name for the writer and no name at all for the publishers.[1] But merit will out, and the unclaimed foundling attracted no little attention, though by no means as much as it deserves. The keenness of the wit, the minuteness of the observation, and the bitterness of the cynicism resemble Morrison's work.[2] The foredoomed fall of a well-meaning girl reared in an environment of drunkenness and grime is told with great humanity and fearless art, and there is a fine use of contrast in the conclusion of the work, where the brutal mother in drunken sentimentality is persuaded with difficulty to "forgive" the dead girl whom she compelled to a harsh fate by the barren cruelty of home-life.

*   *   *

† From *Godey's Magazine*, CXXXI (October 1895), 431–32.
1. This is another late review of the 1893 *Maggie*. R. W. Stallman, in *Stephen Crane: A Critical Bibliography* (Ames: The Iowa State University Press, 1972), p. 112, wrongly lists it as a review of the 1896 *Maggie*. [*Editor.*]
2. A reference to Arthur Morrison's *Tales of Mean Streets*. [*Editor.*]

American Reviews: 1896

From the *New York Tribune* †

Mr. Stephen Crane in "Maggie" studies New-York tenement-house life with the pretence of aggressive realism. He puts on paper the grossness and brutality which are commonly encountered only through actual contact with the most besotted classes. Oaths, drunkenness, rags, stained walls, cut heads, black eyes, broken chairs, delirious howlings, the flat staleness of a police report are his properties. In his finished book they are still raw material with the edge of their offensiveness in no way taken off; for Mr. Crane entirely lacks the ability which has enabled some other men to deal with sordid, disgusting and vicious themes in a way that made them at least entertaining. He has no charm of style, no touch of humor, no hint of imagination. His story is one of unrelieved dulness in which the characters interest neither by their words nor acts, are depraved without being either thrilling or amusing, are dirty without being picturesque. There is nothing enticing in their lives nor uplifting in the contemplation of their sorrows. There is nothing alluring in the evils they exhibit. They are not even piquantly wicked, and their talk is as dreary as their lives are empty. Mr. Crane has attempted the accurate reproduction of the tenement dialect, but has succeeded in presenting only its brutal side. He has learned its billingsgate.[1] He does not know anything of the quaint idiom and odd inflection which made Mr. Townsend's slum talk[2] at once alive and pleasing. Nor does he show any knowledge of the interesting human traits, the quick wit, the self conceit, the local sense of the cockney which make the Bowery Boy a character. He sees only dulness and dirt. The book shocks by the mere fact of its monotonous and stupid roughness. To read its pages is like standing before a loafer to be sworn at and have one's face slapped twice a minute for half an hour.

Mr. Crane was ill-advised to allow the present publication of this story. Three years ago he printed and circulated it as the work of Johnston Smith, and it attracted almost no attention. Now it is reissued to take advantage of the talk concerning his later work.[3] It

† From the *New York Tribune*, May 31, 1896, p. 26.

1. Vulgar, foul-mouthed language. [*Editor.*]

2. A reference to Edward W. Townsend's *Chimmie Fadden*. [*Editor.*]

3. Specifically *The Red Badge of Courage* (1895). [*Editor.*]

has been rendered somewhat less disgusting than formerly by the evident aid of some friendly editor who realizes that there might be limits to the public appetite for profanity. About three "great crimson oaths" have been eliminated from each page. People now "trow fits" part of the time instead of "raising hell," and the small boy threatens to "paste yeh" rather than "club hell outa yeh." Plentiful dashes have also been judiciously introduced. The same hand might well have suppressed the whole book.[4]

From *The Nation*†

* * *

Taking all three stories together,[1] we should classify Mr. Crane as a rather promising writer of the animalistic school. His types are mainly human beings of the order which makes us regret the power of literature to portray them. Not merely are they low, but there is little that is interesting in them. We resent the sense that we must at certain points resemble them. Even the old mother[2] is not made pathetic in a human way; her son disgusts us so that we have small power of sympathy with her left. Maggie it is impossible to weep over. We can feel only that it is a pity that the gutter is so dirty, and turn in another direction. In short, Mr. Crane's art is to us very depressing. Of course, there is always the crushing reply that one who does not love art for the sake of art is a poor devil, not worth writing for. But we do not; we do not even love literature for its own sake.

It is only fair to say that what we have called animalism others pronounce wonderful realism. We use the word animalism for the sake of clearness, to denote a species of realism which deals with man considered as an animal, capable of hunger, thirst, lust, cruelty, vanity, fear, sloth, predacity, greed, and other passions and appetites that make him kin to the brutes, but which neglects, so far as possible, any higher qualities which distinguish him from his four-footed relatives, such as humor, thought, reason, aspiration, affection, morality, and religion. Real life is full of the contrasts between these conflicting tendencies, but the object of the animalistic school seems always to make a study of the *genus homo* which shall recall the menagerie at feeding-time rather than human society.

4. This negative review in the *Tribune* may have been prompted by Crane's firing for his sardonic news report about the parading Junior Order of United American Mechanics (*New York Tribune*, August 21, 1892, p. 22). Melvin Schoberlin, in his edition of *The Sullivan County Sketches of Stephen Crane* (Syracuse: Syracuse University Press, 1949), p. 1, says that after Crane was fired the *Tribune* directed against him "its interminable and frequently pointless attacks." [*Editor*.]

† From *The Nation*, LXIII (July 2, 1896), 15.

1. *The Red Badge of Courage*, *Maggie*, and *George's Mother*. [*Editor*.]

2. In *George's Mother*. [*Editor*.]

FRANK NORRIS

Stephen Crane's Stories of Life in the Slums: *Maggie* and *George's Mother*†

In *Maggie, a Girl of the Streets*, Stephen Crane has written a story something on the plan of the episode of Nana in *L'Assomoir*,[1] the dialect and local color being that of the Bowery. Mr. Crane strikes no new note in his picture of the other half. Most of his characters are old acquaintances in the world of fiction and we know all about— or, at least, certain novelists have pretended to tell us all about the life of the mean streets[2] of a great city. In ordinary hands the tale of "Maggie" would be "twice told." But Mr. Crane is, of course, out of the ordinary. I think that the charm of his style lies chiefly in his habit and aptitude for making phrases—short, terse epigrams struck off in the heat of composition, sparks merely, that cast a momentary gleam of light upon whole phases of life. There are hundreds of them throughout this tale of "Maggie." Indeed, it is the way Mr. Crane tells his story. The picture he makes is not a single carefully composed painting, serious, finished, scrupulously studied, but rather scores and scores of tiny flashlight photographs, instantaneous, caught, as it were, on the run. Of a necessity, then, the movement of his tale must be rapid, brief, very hurried, hardly more than a glimpse.

One of the best of these "flash-lights" is that of the "truck driver."[3] At first one is tempted to believe that it is a "long exposure," but on second thought I conclude that it is merely a great number of snapshots taken at the same subject. * * *

Good though the story is and told in Mr. Crane's catching style, the impression left with the reader is one of hurry, the downfall of Maggie, the motif of the tale, strikes one as handled in a manner almost too flippant for the seriousness of the subject.

* * *

But though these stories[4] make interesting reading, the reader is apt to feel that the author is writing, as it were, from the outside. There is a certain lack of sympathy apparent. Mr. Crane does not seem to *know* his people. You are tempted to wonder if he has ever studied them as closely as he might have done. He does not seem to

---

† From *The Wave* [San Francisco], XV (July 4, 1896), 13.
1. Zola's *L'Assommoir*. [*Editor*.]

2. An allusion to Arthur Morrison's *Tales of Mean Streets* (1894). [*Editor*.]
3. That is, Jimmie. [*Editor*.]
4. *Maggie* and *George's Mother*. [*Editor*.]

me to have gotten down *into* their life and to have written from what he saw around him. His people are types, not characters; his scenes and incidents are not particularized. It is as if Mr. Crane had merely used the "machinery" and "business" of slum life to develop certain traits or to portray certain emotions and passions that might happen anywhere. With him it is the broader, vaguer, *human* interest that is the main thing, not the smaller details of a particular phase of life.

EDWARD BRIGHT

A Melodrama of the Streets†

A novel by Stephen Crane, entitled "Maggie: A Girl of the Streets," has just been published by D. Appleton & Co. It is the last of the talented young author's works to see the light, but it is the first in point of composition. I base this inference on the fact that it was put in type and copyrighted three years ago. Now, allowing six months for the writing, this ought to take us back to the dawn of a career still in its infancy.

I have thought it best to emphasize this circumstance, because I wish to be absolutely just to the author. I have done so, furthermore, because I have found it extremely difficult to reconcile my undisguised admiration for Mr. Crane's "The Red Badge of Courage" with my dissatisfaction with "Maggie." The difference between these two books is so great that, were I to neglect chronology, I should have to confess that Mr. Crane's talents are in a process of degeneration.[1]

My objection might be phrased differently—and perhaps more accurately—were I to say that as between "The Red Badge of Courage" and "Maggie," the dissimilarity is mainly noticeable in the greater conventionality of the latter. This is extraordinary, considering the well-known character of the author's work, and, according to my view, can be explained only on the ground that "Maggie" is an immature effort in a most ambitious field of literary art.

In further explanation of my meaning, let the reader reflect that the slums presents itself to the imagination of most prosperous and well-bred people under one of two aspects: Either it is a locale replete with the raw material of sentiment, or it is a battle-ground of unspeakable sordidness, a loathsome pit infested by monsters in human form, who pass their lives preying on one another—a menace to

---

† From *The Illustrated American*, XX (July 11, 1896), 94.
1. Other critics of the day voiced this response. Some did not know that *Maggie* had been issued ·

earlier (1893) than *The Red Badge of Courage* (1895) and so presumed that Crane was indeed in a "process of degeneration." [*Editor.*]

respectable society, a source of dread even to the well-armed police-man.

Now, it is because, knowing somewhat of the slums of New York and having arrived at certain definite conclusions from my experi-ence, I have for several years contended that Richard Harding Davis's sentimental slum sketches[2] are as false to the actual conditions as I am now reluctantly forced to own is Mr. Crane's presentation of the life of the same locality. There is little to choose between hollow sentimentality and lurid melodrama.

In the bare facts of Maggie's career I am able to believe. Credulity is not taxed by learning that her home—or the miserable tenement which passed for a home—was sordid; neither am I surprised to be told that she drifted easily into a still more hapless life. There is something shocking but quite natural in the fact that Pete was the instrument of her ruin.

Yes! Mr. Crane has used his note-book to good effect; his story bears unmistakable evidences of being observed, and observed on the spot. I will go so far as even to admit that there are a few scenes and passages of dialogue in Mr. Crane's story of masterly vigor and convincing reality. I make no objection to the details—or to most of them. My quarrel with the author begins and ends with his general conception of the life of the slums.

To change the form of expression, he might be likened to an artist who knows how to draw but cannot paint. He has "laid in" an admirable sketch, which raises one's hopes high for the success of the finished picture. But the moment he begins to lay on his colors it is evident that he is a caricaturist, not an artist; and, to make matters worse, he is a caricaturist without humor.[3]

Space does not permit me to prove my indictment by quotations, but I would call the reader's attention to the fight with which the book opens, and would ask that special attention be given to the adjectives employed in describing the affray. There are gentler modes of exercise than an East-Side fight, but I protest that even the sturdy children of the tenements are maligned by Mr. Crane's adjectives.

2. Probably a reference to *Van Bibber and Others* (1892). [*Editor.*]
3. Many of his critics—from the 1890s to the present—have missed Crane's comedy in *Maggie* and in his work generally. [*Editor.*]

WILLIAM DEAN HOWELLS

New York Low Life in Fiction†

* * *

There is a curious unity in the spirit of the arts; and I think that
what strikes me most in the story of "Maggie" is that quality of fatal
necessity which dominates Greek tragedy. From the conditions it all
had to be, and there were the conditions. I felt this in Mr. Hardy's
"Jude,"[1] where the principle seems to become conscious in the writer;
but there is apparently no consciousness of any such motive in the
author of "Maggie." Another effect is that of an ideal of artistic
beauty which is as present in the working out of this poor girl's
squalid romance as in any classic fable. This will be foolishness, I
know, to the foolish people who cannot discriminate between the
material and the treatment in art, and who think that beauty is
inseparable from daintiness and prettiness, but I do not speak to
them. I appeal rather to such as feel themselves akin with every kind
of human creature, and find neither high nor low when it is a
question of inevitable suffering, or of a soul struggling vainly with an
inexorable fate.

My rhetoric scarcely suggests the simple terms the author uses to
produce the effect which I am trying to report again. They are
simple, but always most graphic, especially when it comes to the
personalities of the story: the girl herself, with her bewildered wish
to be right and good; with her distorted perspective; her clinging and
generous affections; her hopeless environments; the horrible old
drunken mother, a cyclone of violence and volcano of vulgarity; the
mean and selfish lover, a dandy tough, with his gross ideals and
ambitions; her brother, an Ishmaelite[2] from the cradle, who, with his
warlike instincts beaten back into cunning, is what the b'hoy[3] of
former times has become in our more strenuously policed days. He is
indeed a wonderful figure in a group which betrays no faltering in
the artist's hand. He, with his dull hates, his warped good-will, his
cowed ferocity, is almost as fine artistically as Maggie, but he could
not have been so hard to do, for all the pathos of her fate is rendered
without one maudlin touch.

So is that of the simple-minded and devoted and tedious old

† *New York World*, July 26, 1896, p. 18. With
minor changes, this review appeared as "An Appreciation" in the first English edition of *Maggie*,
which was subtitled *A Child of the Streets* (London: William Heinemann, 1896), pp. v–vii.

1. Thomas Hardy's *Jude the Obscure*, published
in 1895. [*Editor*.]
2. One at odds with society. [*Editor*.]
3. Slang for "rowdy" or "tough." [*Editor*.]

woman who is George's Mother in the book of that name. This is scarcely a study at all, while Maggie is really and fully so. It is the study of a situation merely: a poor, inadequate woman, of a commonplace religiosity, whose son goes to the bad. The wonder of it is the courage which deals with persons so absolutely average, and the art that graces them with the beauty of the author's compassion for everything that errs and suffers. Without this feeling the effects of his mastery would be impossible, and if it went further or put itself into the pitying phrases it would annul the effects. But it never does this; it is notable how in all respects the author keeps himself well in hand. He is quite honest with his reader. He never shows his characters or his situations in any sort of sentimental glamour; if you will be moved by the sadness of common fates you will feel his intention, but he does not flatter his portraits of people or conditions to take your fancy.

* * *

English Reviews: 1896

From *The Bookman* [London]†

Mr. Stephen Crane impresses us with the conviction that he tells the truth as he knows it. "The Red Badge of Courage" showed his refusal to sentimentalise. Sentimentality is so far away from the story of "Maggie" that one expects every moment to come on some exaggeration of sordidness, some morbid revelling in the ugly and the brutal; yet nothing of the kind happens. His mind is as unusually restrained as it is watchful. Romance is not wanting. It is shining bright when Pete, the elegant bar-tender, condescends to visit Maggie's brother, and sit on the table and give a glowing account of how he deals with troublesome persons in his master's public-house. "As Jimmie and his friend exchanged tales descriptive of their prowess, Maggie leaned back in the shadow. Her eyes dwelt wonderingly and rather wistfully upon Pete's face. The broken furniture, grimy walls, and general disorder and dirt of her home of a sudden appeared before her and began to take a potential aspect. Pete's aristocratic person looked as if it might soil. She looked keenly at him, occasionally wondering if he was feeling contempt. But Pete seemed to be enveloped in reminiscence.

" 'Hully gee!' said he, 'dose mugs can't phase me. Dey knows I kin wipe up d' street wid any tree of dem.'

"Maggie perceived that he was the ideal man. Her dim thoughts were often searching for far-away lands where the little hills sing together in the morning."

There is running through the miserable story the fair light of a trustful, grateful nature, a "blossom in a mud-puddle," gentle even when cruelty and treachery have done their worst. And as such, Maggie is as real as the redoubtable savage Jimmie, or the terrible mother, nearly as real as the magnificent Pete. There Mr. Crane surpasses nearly all his models of the sternly realistic school, who fail so often in their finer, their more beautiful portraits. New York life— nearly at its lowest, surely—is the material of the book, and the material is used by a daring and a relentless hand. But Mr. Crane has reticence and sympathy, and these, as much as his astonishing cleverness, have given him the high rank he holds already in America and England.

† From *The Bookman* [London], XI (October 1896), 19–20.

From *The Athenœum*†

The author of 'The Red Badge of Courage,' Mr. Stephen Crane, publishes through Mr. Heinemann *Maggie, a Child of the Streets.*[1] This little story will make a powerful impression on those who are not repelled by the strange oaths in which the story is for the most part told. Maggie, a factory hand, the child of a drunken woman and sister of a rough in an American town, is seduced by a barman (the patron of her brother), and dies. The telling of the tale is so strong that it produces on the reader an impression of absolute truthfulness, and yet, we are convinced, it is not true to life. Such a case as is described may, indeed, be met with; but far more usual would be either the moral destruction of the girl by her mother's influence at an earlier age, or, on the other hand, the development of a harder type, helped along by the extreme kindness to one another of the very poor. To this kindness there is only one allusion in the book, yet it is the most striking feature of low life in the United Kingdom, and is probably not lacking in the low life of the United States.

H. G. WELLS

Another View of "Maggie"†

The literature of the slum multiples apace; and just as the mud of the Port of London has proved amenable to Mr. Whistler, so the mud of the New York estuary has furnished material for artistic treatment to Mr. Crane. Mr. Crane, in "Maggie," shows himself the New York equivalent of Mr. Morrison,[1] with perhaps a finer sense of form and beauty and a slenderer physique. He is the light weight of the two. He is far more alert for what the industrious playwright calls the effective "line," and every chapter cocks its tail with a point to it. He sketches, for instance, the career of Maggie's brother James, and tells of his lusts and brutality. "Nevertheless," ends the chapter, "he had on a certain starlit evening said wonderingly and quite reverently, 'Dah moon looks like h——l, don't it?'" And with that the chapter, rather self-consciously, pauses for your admiration. Of Mr. Morrison's "Dick Perrott" it is not recorded that he ever saw the beauty of moonlight or the stars. But one may doubt, even after the chromatic tumult of the "Red Badge of Courage," whether Mr.

---

† From *The Athenæum*, No. 3600 (October 24, 1896), 562.
1. William Heinemann, the English publisher of *Maggie*, changed the subtitle of the novel to *A Child of the Streets*. [*Editor*.]

† From *The Saturday Review* [London], LXXXII (December 19, 1896), 655.
1. A reference to Arthur Morrison and his English slum fiction, *Tales of Mean Streets* (1894). [*Editor*.]

Crane is anywhere equal to Mr. Morrison's fight between Perrott and Leary. To read that and to turn to Mr. Crane's fight between Maggie's brother and her seducer is to turn from power to hysterics. The former is too strong and quiet to quote—it must be read; but of the latter:—

"The arms of the combatants whirled in the air like flails. The faces of the men, at first flushed to flame-coloured anger, now began to fade to the pallor of warriors in the blood and heat of a battle. Their lips curled back, stretched tightly over the gums in ghoul-like grins. Through their white, gripped teeth struggled hoarse whisperings of oaths. Their eyes glittered with murderous fire. . . . Blows left crimson blotches upon the pale skin. . . . The rage of fear shone in all their eyes, and their blood coloured fists whirled. . . . The pyramids of shimmering glasses, that had never been disturbed, changed to cascades as heavy bottles were flung into them. Mirrors splintered to nothing. The three frothing creatures on the floor buried themselves in a frenzy for blood. . . . The quiet stranger had sprawled very pyrotechnically out on the sidewalk."

Which is very fine, no doubt, but much more suggestive of a palette dipped in vodki than of two men fighting. Yet, on the other hand, the emotional power of that concluding chapter of "Maggie" seems a little out of Mr. Morrison's reach—the old woman, drink sodden and obese, stricken with the news of her daughter's death and recalling her one vivid moment of maternal pride.

"Jimmy, boy, go get yer sister! Go get yer sister an' we'll put dah boots on her feet!"

The relative merits of the "Red Badge of Courage" and "Maggie" are open to question. To the present reviewer it seems that in "Maggie" we come nearer to Mr. Crane's individuality. Perhaps where we might expect strength we get merely stress, but one may doubt whether we have not been hasty in assuming Mr. Crane to be a strong man in fiction. Strength and gaudy colour rarely go together; tragic and sombre are well nigh inseparable. One gets an impression from the "Red Badge" that at the end Mr. Crane could scarcely have had a gasp left in him—that he must have been mentally hoarse for weeks after it. But here he works chiefly for pretty effects, for gleams of sunlight on the stagnant puddles he paints. He gets them, a little consciously perhaps, but, to the present reviewer's sense, far more effectively than he gets anger and fear. And he has done his work, one feels, to please himself. His book is a work of art, even if it is not a very great or successful work of art—it ranks above the novel of commerce, if only on that account.

Novels of American Life†

* * *

Mr. Crane is too young to have written a good novel, and 'The Third Violet,' his only attempt at the ordinary story of familiar life, is simply amazing in its futility. But he has written a short study of New York slums which may compare with Mr. Arthur Morrison's Jago sketches and Mr. Maugham's 'Liza of Lambeth.' 'Maggie' appears with a prefatory commendation from Mr. Howells. We have no objection to stories of slum life; Mr. R. H. Davies's[1] 'Gallegher' is a wonderful and attractive picture of the New York street-arab. But 'Maggie' does not seem to us to justify its existence. Given a drunken father, a drunken mother, and their children, a pretty girl and a boy, stunted but as brave as a weasel; this is very likely how the lives will shape themselves. Tragic pathos there certainly is in the girl's devotion to her swaggering lover, a fighting bartender, who deserts her without the shadow of compunction. But it seems as if one needed more than this to repay one for wading through such a mass of revolting details—street fights of little boys, fights of grown men in bars, scenes in dirty beer saloons, and everywhere the dialect of the Bowery, which, as Mr. Crane writes it, is the most hideous representation of human speech that we have ever met with. One may read a book like this as a tract, to keep one alive to the misery existent somewhere in the world; but we can conceive no other motive for reading it. As a work of art we disbelieve in it. Take Mr. Maugham's 'Liza,' a work equally unsparing and in some ways more revolting; here you have at least credible human beings, with natural affections. In Mr. Crane's book Maggie's passion for Pete is the one trace of human coherence; there is no other tie between any two of the characters. It is an impression; that is to say, a study made to emphasise certain traits; and an impression of sheer brutality. The admiration for work of this sort savours of the latest modern cant, which preaches that to see things artistically you must see them disagreeably. Mr. Crane has seen a piece of life in a hard superficial way, and rendered it in the spirit of a caricaturist. That is the true formula for producing what, in the cant of the day, is called uncompromising realism.

* * *

† From *The Edinburgh Review*, CLXXXVII (April 1898), 413–14.

1. This is Richard Harding Davis, not Davies. [*Editor*.]

Criticism

JOHN BERRYMAN

[Crane's Art in *Maggie*]†

* * *

Several remarks are to be made of this little book, and first in regard to its *art*, which is an effect of intense pressure and nearly perfect detachment. No American work of its length had driven the reader so hard; in none had the author remained so persistently invisible behind his creation. The incongruity of these qualities forces our attention to the strangeness—the daring and ambition—of Crane's attempt. Everything here was incongruous also. He was describing a modern slum-world, ferocious and sordid, with a fidelity that reached down to Pete's amiable reminiscence: "I met a chump deh odder day way up in deh city. . . . When I was a-crossin' deh street deh chump runned plump inteh me, an' den he turns aroun' an' says, 'Yer insolen' ruffin!' he says, like dat. 'Oh, gee!' I says, 'Oh, gee! git off d' eart'!' I says, like dat. See? 'Git off d' eart'!' like dat. Den deh blokie he got wild. He says I was a contempt'ble scoun'el, er somethin' like dat, an' he says I was doom' teh everlastin' pe'dition, er somethin' like dat. 'Gee!' I says, 'gee! Yer joshin' me,' I says. 'Yer joshin' me.' An' den I slugged 'im. See?" But dialogue aside (in Pete's jawing, for that matter, we hear a rhythm of the artist), Crane was to describe this world with an Alexandrian stylization; with imagery ranging from the jungle up through war to medieval and hieratic imagery; with the last possible color, force, succinctness—without destroying the illusion of fidelity. The banal story, that is, had to be given heroic and pathetic stature and yet not falsified. At the same time, its melodramatic character called for disguise under an air of flatness and casualness. Furthermore Crane had to rely on loose, episodic structure—except once or twice he would never use any other. And no passion such as revenge or love or greed could dominate the fable. If in these unpropitious circumstances he achieved in *Maggie* a sense of inevitability, one may well wonder how he did it. The word Howells[1] was to use for this triumph of Crane was a good one, namely, "Greek."

Not Maggie's fate alone but the fates of the others are inevitable, given their misconceptions of each other, themselves, and their world. These misconceptions register as astonishment and rage. Pete and then another man are astonished when Maggie repulses them;

---

† From *Stephen Crane*, by John Berryman (New York: William Sloane Associates, 1950), pp. 58–61.
1. William Dean Howells. [*Editor.*]

her mother is astonished when she succumbs. Jimmie is astonished to learn that his own sister, like others', can be seduced. She is astonished by leonine Pete's sudden submissiveness (to Nell), then by his desertion. Everything is exactly what we expect but not at all what they expect. It is not that they lack moral ideas but that these ideas either are the perverted ones common to their conditions or are simply unable to make headway against their conditions' weight. The first moral idea in the book is introduced in the first sentence and the last is fulfilled in the last sentence, and the delicacy and completeness of the deterioration from one to the other, Crane standing aside, account for the fable's power. The small boy standing on a heap of gravel for the "honour" of Rum Alley impresses us as natural; loyalty and bravery may begin so. But this defiance and an attempt later the same evening to prevent his father from stealing a can of beer (with which, empty, his father then hits him on the head) represent the highest point Jimmie's morality will touch. His parents are far below this already, and the saturnine parody of a forgiveness-scene with which *Maggie* ends concludes a sort of demonstration in the geometry of needless agony.

Self-indulgent, brutal, self-pitying, none of these people can help each other. Even when a decent action is advocated, the reason is wrong. "Why deh blazes don'cher try teh keep Jim from fightin'?" the mother bellows at the father, and why? "Because he tears 'is clothes, yeh fool!" Shamefacedly one day Jimmie tries to get her to let him bring Maggie home, because "dis t'ing queers us! See?" One note of sentimentality or reproof, by the author, would destroy the work, but Crane never falters or insists. "It seemed that the world had treated this woman very badly. . . . She broke furniture as if she were at last getting her rights." The characters are left to their illusion that they are working out their own fates, and the reader is left to draw his own conclusions. In the brilliant analysis of Jimmie's progress towards nihilism, all Crane says is: "He became so sharp that he believed in nothing." If the mother's self-pity apes affection, crooning drunkenly to her children about "yer poor mudder" just before she beats them up again, Crane does not explain that it does. At most, over certain moments of their aspiration, irony permits the tone to lift. The young man wanders hilariously into a mission and comments freely, but confuses the speaker with Christ: "Momentarily, Jimmie was sullen with thoughts of a hopeless altitude where grew fruit." And for all his police record, his seductions and desertions, "he had, on a certain star-lit evening, said wonderingly and quite reverently, 'Deh moon looks like hell, don't it?'"

Of the compassion that plays unseen over the story, we catch glimpses only once or twice, as toward the "meek freaks" in a dime museum Pete takes Maggie to—and at once we learn that Maggie "contemplated their deformities with awe, and thought them a sort of chosen tribe," for his heroine's misconceptions are spared as little as anyone else's by Crane in this confident and stern little work. Only her good faith distinguishes her from the others, who deceive themselves with their simulations of good faith. And after her fall, the timid girl "imagined a future rose-tinted because of its distance from all that she had experienced before. . . . Her life was Pete's, and she considered him worthy of the charge. . . . She did not feel like a bad woman. To her knowledge she had never seen any better." Nervously leaving the music-hall with him then, because other men eye her, she shrinks aside passing two painted women and draws back her skirts; very much as, after her suicide (but not because of it), Pete drunk in a saloon "laid stress upon the purity of his motives in all dealings with men in the world, and spoke of the fervour of his friendship for those who were amiable. Tears welled slowly from his eyes. . . . 'I'm goo' f'ler, ain' I, girlsh?'" Crudity in stylistic detail *Maggie* sometimes shows, but in originality of conception, energy, instinct for exclusion and for the tacit, consistency of ironic execution, it as little solicits allowance on the score of its author's youth as the *Disparates* of Goya do on the score of his deafness and age. *Maggie* is like a *Disparate*.[2]

* * *

CHARLES CHILD WALCUTT

[Hallucination and Hysteria in *Maggie*]†

* * *

In telling this story, Crane fuses elements of poverty, ignorance, and intolerance in a context of violence and cruelty to create a nightmarish world wavering between hallucination and hysteria. The language establishes this tone through violent verbs, distorted scenes, and sensory transfer. A sampling of the first three pages discovers such terms as "howling," "circling madly about," "pelting," "writhing," "livid with the fury of battle," "furious assault," "convulsed," "cursed in shrill chorus," "tiny insane demon," "hurling," "barbaric," "smashed," "triumphant savagery," "leer gloatingly," "raving," "shrieking," "chronic sneer," "seethed," and "kicked, scratched and tore," which immediately suggest that the people are hurled through

2. One of a series of etchings by the Spanish painter Francisco Goya (1746–1828), which projected nightmare visions, distorted images, symbolism, and cynical, despairing moods. [*Editor.*]
† From Chapter IV, "Stephen Crane: Naturalist and Impressionist," in *American Literary Naturalism: A Divided Stream*, by Charles Child Walcutt (Minneapolis: University of Minnesota Press, 1956), pp. 67–72.

a nightmare. The device of sensory transfer appears in "lurid alter-
cations," "red years," "dreaming blood-red dreams," and "various
shades of yellow discontent." When Maggie's brother comes in
bloody from fighting, "The mother's massive shoulders heaved with
anger. Grasping the urchin by the neck and shoulder she shook him
until he rattled. . . . The babe sat on the floor watching the scene,
his face in contortions like that of a woman at a tragedy. The father . . . bellowed at his wife. 'Let the kid alone for a minute, will
yeh, Mary? Yer allus poundin' 'im. When I come nights I can't get
no rest 'cause yer allus poundin' a kid. Let up, d'yeh hear? Don't be
allus poundin' a kid.'"[1]

In the same vein, Maggie's parents are depicted in insanely drunken battles during which they break up whole roomfuls of furniture
and crockery several times during the brief story. After one such
battle, "A glow from the fire threw red hues over the bare floor, the
cracked and soiled plastering, and the overturned and broken furniture. In the middle of the floor lay his mother asleep. In one corner
of the room his father's limp body hung across the seat of a chair."
And a bit later, Maggie's "mother drank whiskey all Friday morning.
With lurid face and tossing hair she cursed and destroyed furniture
all Friday afternoon. When Maggie came home at half-past six her
mother lay asleep amid the wreck of chairs and a table." Now, such
people would not have more than one set of furniture, and it is
improbable that they would in an ordinary drunken quarrel reduce
it to matchwood, although of course one grants the likelihood of a
table overturned or a chair smashed. The rather fantastic but obviously intentional exaggeration of these passages renders Crane's
sense that this world is so warped as to be mad. His tone unites
despair and moral outrage with the self-protection of a sort of wild
humor.

A dominant idea that grows from this landscape of hysteria is that
these people are victimized by their ideas of moral propriety which
are so utterly inapplicable to their lives that they constitute a social
insanity. Maggie is pounced upon by the first wolf in this jungle and
seduced. When she is abandoned and returns home, her mother's
outraged virtue is boundless:

> "Ha, ha, ha!" bellowed the mother. "Dere she stands! Ain't she
> purty? Look ut her! Ain't she sweet, deh beast? Look ut her! Ha,
> ha! Look ut her!" She lurched forward and put her red and seamed

1. *Maggie: A Girl of the Streets* (New York, 1893) was published under the pseudonym John-ston Smith. The only complete edition of Crane's prose and poetry is *The Work of Stephen Crane*, ed. Wilson Follett (New York, 1925–27), in 12 volumes. His letters have not been collected. [A new edition of Crane's works, in 10 volumes, is *The Works of Stephen Crane*, ed. Fredson Bow-ers (Charlottesville: University Press of Virginia, 1969–75). A first collection of Crane's letters is *Stephen Crane: Letters*, ed. R. W. Stallman and Lillian Gilkes (New York: New York University Press, 1960)—*Editor.*]

hands upon her daughter's face. She bent down and peered keenly up into the eyes of the girl. "Oh, she's jes' dessame as she ever was, ain't she? She's her mudder's putty darlin' yit, ain' she? Look ut her, Jimmie. Come here and look ut her."

Maggie is driven forth with jeers and blows and presently commits suicide. Crane tells how her mother responds to the lugubrious consolations of her neighbors in this classic paragraph:

The mourner essayed to speak, but her voice gave way. She shook her great shoulders frantically, in an agony of grief. The tears seemed to scald her face. Finally her voice came and arose in a scream of pain. "Oh, yes, I'll fergive her! I'll fergive her!"

The impressions that these people are not free agents, and that their freedom is limited as much by their conventional beliefs as by their poverty, are naturalistic concepts completely absorbed into the form of the story. One might object upon sociological grounds that Crane's ideas of the family are unsound, but his literary technique here is a triumph. It creates a coherent if terrible world, and there are no serious loose ends—no effect of tension or contradiction between abstract theory and human event. Crane's hallucinatory inferno is a gift of his style. What he says and what he renders are one. Indeed, he does not comment because the whole work is one grand roar of mockery and outrage. The hysterical distortions symbolize, image, and even dramatize the confusion of values which puts these social waifs in a moral madhouse.

The discrepancy between the Victorian pieties and the jungle reality of the slums is conscientiously explored. At a play to which Maggie is taken by her seducer, "Shady persons in the audience revolted from the pictured villainy of the drama. With untiring zeal they hissed vice and applauded virtue. Unmistakably bad men evinced an apparently sincere admiration for virtue. The loud gallery was overwhelmingly with the unfortunate and the oppressed. They encouraged the struggling hero with cries and jeered the villain, hooting and calling attention to his whiskers." "Maggie always departed with raised spirits from these melodramas. She rejoiced at the way in which the poor and virtuous eventually overcame the wealthy and wicked."

Another interesting passage begins when Maggie's mother is evicted, drunk, from a bar; the brother, Jimmie, tries to take her home, and a great battle ensues:

She raised her arm and whirled her great fist at her son's face. Jimmie dodged his head, and the blow struck him in the back of the neck . . .
"Keep yer hands off me!" roared his mother again.
"Say, yeh ol' bat! Quit dat!" yelled Jimmie . . .

And presently he defeats her. Whereupon the conquered mother, in high moral dudgeon, evicts his erring sister: "Yeh've gone t' d' devil, Mag Johnson. . . . Yer a disgrace t' yer people. . . . Git out. I won't have sech as youse in me house!" The next time she is drunk, the pity of it overcomes her:

> "She's d' devil's own chil', Jimmie. . . . Ah, who would t'ink such a bad girl could grow up in our fambly, Jimmie, me son. Many d'hour I've spent in talk wid dat girl an' tol' her if she ever went on d' streets I'd see her damned. An' after all her bringin'-up, an' what I tol' her and talked wid her, she goes teh d' bad, like a duck teh water."

Confused by the fact that it was he who brought the seducer to the house, Jimmie curses manfully but does nothing until he finds that the fall of Maggie is causing rude comment from the neighbors; then he proposes to salvage the family's reputation by bringing Maggie back home. But the mother screams with indignation, "What! Let 'er come an' sleep under deh same roof wid her mudder again? . . . Shame on yehs . . . dat ye'd grow up teh say sech a t'ing teh yer mudder—yer own mudder." Sobs choke her and interrupt her reproaches.

Jimmie does not renew his suggestion, "But, arguing with himself . . . he, once, almost came to a conclusion that his sister would have been more firmly good had she better known how. However, he felt that he could not hold such a view. He threw it hastily aside." Here Crane's technique flags for a moment and betrays his tone, even though he does not fall into inconsistency. Elsewhere the tone is complicated, beyond the needs of his thesis, into further impressionisms which demonstrate virtuosity of auctorial impression (and style) rather than exploration of the subject. In the dirty street, for example, Maggie—as a little girl—is dragging her infant brother Tommie along: "He fell on his face, roaring . . . He made *heroic* endeavors to keep on his legs, *denounced* his sister, and consumed a bit of orange peeling which he chewed between the times of his *infantile orations*." The italicized words come from a world of reference beyond this grisly slum. They convey a stylistic exuberance; they introduce humor and psychic distance, or what Joyce terms aesthetic *stasis*. But to call a grubby child's screams infantile orations is to deflect the impact of the scene and make us aware of the writer. The deflection is studiously grotesque: there is just enough truth in the pictorial comparison between a child waving its arms and opening its mouth to scream and an orator with hand raised and mouth wide in campaign eloquence to elicit a flash of recognition. But the comparison makes a comment on the orator, not on the child. One thinks of the current fad of infant portraits with subtitles pointing to adult conduct. With this abrupt wrenching of the attention the effect of hysteria and wild confusion spreads out from the scene itself into the world that includes the writer and the reader, suggesting that if our world includes Maggie's world then it is insane too. Thus the impressionism renders the scene as it strikes the observing author, giving his involvement with this impression and uttering the comment that this scene outrages the sense of order and decency to the point where—like Hamlet jumping into the grave and outboasting Laertes—one responds in self-defense with an outburst of wild mockery.

But we have not done. A still further effect is attained because Crane's detachment motivates the reader to an involvement which he might otherwise resist, and we come finally to sense the horror of this life when, after a climactic drunken brawl between the horrible parents, "The father had not moved, but lay in the same death-like sleep. The mother writhed in a uneasy slumber, her chest wheezing as if she were in the agonies of strangulation. Out at the window a florid moon was peering over dark roofs, and in the distance the waters of a river glimmered pallidly."

A perennial controversy about naturalism concerns whether it is optimistic or pessimistic—whether it dwells in the horrors it portrays or believes it can correct them. The problem achieves an epitome in *Maggie*: however stark the horror, no reader can feel that Crane is scientifically disinterested or unconcerned. Where his method does, through its fascinated concern with detail, achieve a ghastly fixation, it is the quality of Goya rather than the cold form of Velasquez.[2] The story shows that nothing can be done for Maggie and her family, for they are lost; but it presents the exact reality with an intensity that defies indifference. I say the exact reality. It seems exact, but it would be more accurate to say that Crane objectifies and renders exactly his spirited and intentional distortion of the grotesque world that he has exactly seen.

* * *

2. The Spanish painter Francisco Goya (1746–1828) relied on grotesque symbolism and pessimism in his etching suites, *Disasters of War* and *Disparates*. Diego Velásquez (1599–1660), another Spanish painter, was a forerunner of nineteenth-century French impressionism. [*Editor*.]

WILLIAM BYSSHE STEIN

New Testament Inversions in Crane's *Maggie*†

The rigid naturalistic interpretations of *Maggie*, so popular in some critical circles today, obscure the universal implications of Crane's dramatic re-creation of Bowery existence. It is not enough, for instance, to say that the novel is the sum of "innocence thwarted and betrayed by environment."[1] Such a categorical statement implies that Crane's view of reality is unalterably objective, concerned only with the transcription of calculable sociological data. Actually his creative imagination is deeply stirred by religious aspects of the setting. This is seen in a recurrent pattern of symbolic moral situations which is inspired by the New Testament.

Here, of course, Crane's background is the point at issue. Reared in a confining religious atmosphere (his father was a Methodist minister and his mother a newspaper reporter of church activities), he unconsciously was trained to think in the ideological framework of Christianity. Even in rebellion against its expression in institutional religion, he could not completely subdue its incontrovertible ethical affirmations. We can see, for example, his patent detestation of mission evangelism in *Maggie*, and we can understand his impatience with its blatant self-righteousness. But, on the other hand, he introduces certain scenes and incidents which, though they do not beg attention, are nevertheless manifestations of an intuitive loyalty to the redemptive love of the Gospels. In the opening chapter of the book there is, I think, evidence of this. His juxtaposition of the violent scuffle in the alley with the tableau of human callousness illustrates what I mean: "From a window of an apartment-house that uprose from amid squat stables there leaned a curious woman. Some labourers, unloading a scow at a dock at the river, paused for a moment and regarded the fight. The engineer of a passive tugboat hung lazily over a railing and watched. Over on the island a worm of yellow convicts came from the shadow of a building and crawled slowly along the river's bank." These phlegmatic onlookers, so carefully foreshortened against the background of a prison, epitomize the indifference of a society familiar with violence and crime. But at the same time their moral unconcern represents the degradation of the values of love and compassion in their daily lives. This is to say

† From *Modern Language Notes*, LXXIII (April 1958), 268–72.

1. *Stephen Crane: Stories and Tales*, ed. Robert W. Stallman (New York: Vintage Books, 1955), p. 7, introduction to the Bowery Tales.

that Crane's visualization of the heartlessness of human relationships in this scene takes note of the paralysis of Christianity in this environment and in the world.

In effect, his scenic logic argues that human nature is depraved; but he counterpoints this attitude with an argument to the contrary which promises a deliverance from this amoral state. The complete title of the novel, *Maggie: A Girl of the Streets*, constitutes an initiation into the function of this device of irony. The name Maggie is deliberately equated with the practice of prostitution, but it is also, in context at least, suggestively proposed as a diminutive of Magdalene. This etymology, of course, is not correct, but here the association is almost instinctive for anyone acquainted with the parables. Since Crane presupposes, as all of us must, that in our culture man has been taught to make sense out of his experience in terms of the Christian myth, then the title should excite our sympathy instead of indignation. The heroine, in other words, is entitled to forgiveness like her counterpart in the New Testament. Crane has in mind, I think. Maggie's quite pardonable sin of assuming that love will redeem all, and at this juncture she metamorphoses into Magdalene: "Wherefore I say unto Thee, Her sins which are many, are forgiven; for she loved much: but to whom little is forgiven, the *same* loveth little."[2] This interpretation may seem to run counter to the opinions about Christ expressed by Crane in his poetry; yet his quick sympathy with prostitutes is an impulse of his moral conditioning—a much sounder gauge of his spiritual values, it seems to me, than the sophomoric heresies which dialectically shape some of his poems. Then, too, the novel was written before he began to connect his aggressive moral impatience with the scientific naturalism which enveloped the literary world of his day.

In any event, without too much difficulty this interpretive approach to the title can be applied to certain crucial episodes in the narrative. Jimmie's attempt to convince his mother that Maggie ought to be permitted to return home after her seduction results in a depressing burlesque of the Prodigal Son. By treating the incident humorously, Crane horrifyingly enhances the sadism of the mother. Unable to explain rationally his instinctive desire to protect his sister, Jimmie can only justify it by disclaiming its connection with Christian morality: "'Well, I didn't mean none of dis prod'gal bus'ness anyway.'" She, however, triumphantly refutes the validity of this precedent with the crushing rejoinder: "'It wa'n't no prod'gal daughter, yeh fool.'" And reducing Jimmie to impotent silence, she proceeds to revel in the opportunity for abuse which Maggie's inevitable return promises: "The mother's eyes gloated on the scene which her imag-

2. Luke 7:47.

ination called before her." This inversion and its implications are obvious, but they lend sanction to my belief that the unvoiced inspiration of the novel is Crane's distressed insight into the abandonment of Christian love by his culture.

This perception is forcefully embodied in another important segment of the action. It involves Maggie's quest for salvation after her rejection by Pete, and is an adaptation of another New Testament motif. The minister's lack of mercy in this case parallels the response of the priest in the parable of the Good Samaritan. Maggie, seeking the "grace of God," decides to accost "a stout gentleman in a silk hat and chaste black coat," but he makes "a convulsive movement and save[s] his respectability by a vigorous side-step." A glance at the circumstances of the parable will suffice to establish their relationship with this episode: "A certain man . . . fell among thieves, which stripped him of his raiment, and wounded *him*, and departed, leaving him half dead. And by chance there came a certain priest that way; and when he saw him, he passed by on the other side."[3] Ordinarily one would, I think, tend to limit this parody to Crane's contempt for the clergy and their fastidiously cultivated piety. But the satirical probe strikes deeper. It penetrates to the real cause of the degeneration of love in human affairs—the betrayal of Christ by his ministry.

Still another episode evolves out of the religious matrix of the artist's inspiration, the last scene in the novel. Mary's affected sorrow over Maggie's death is made painfully obvious, but once again Crane assumes that the reader will associate the travesty of bereavement with its archetypal counterpart. I refer, of course, to the conventional representation of the Virgin lamenting over the body of Christ after the crucifixion. Crane's re-creation of the depraved Pietà of the slums is contrived to comment ironically upon the mother's name, but it also functions to cast the black pall of an irredeemable Good Friday upon the culture which he criticizes. For, contrary to the critics who argue that Maggie is a victim of her environment, he dramatizes the key scenes of her pathetic fate against the background of man's defection from the redemptive love of Christianity as it is crystallized in John's record of the Savior's conversation after his betrayal by Judas: "A new commandment I give unto you, That ye love one another; as I have loved you, that ye also love one another."[4] Maggie, in short, is crucified by the same forces of hate in human nature that destroyed Christ. Fittingly the concluding chapter of the novel is characterized by the repetition of the word black in contrast with the violent colors of life in the earlier chapters. In this way Crane emphasizes the advent of the Black Friday which can become

3. Luke 10:30–31.   4. John 13:34.

Good Friday only when it ensures salvation. But, in his perspective, this miraculous transformation cannot occur. The darkness of hate is fixed for ever in time.

And considering the symbolic function of the names of Maggie and Mary, it may not be farfetched to ascribe a similar meaning to the names of Pete and Jimmie. Simon Peter and James were the two disciples who accompanied Christ on the road to Calvary. Even the young Tommie who dies in his infancy may be a vague reflection of his doubting namesake in the New Testament. His death, in any event, seems to prove that Thomas intuitively foresaw the failure of the law of love as in later history it is interpreted by the new Marys, and Peters, and Jameses. Confirmation of Crane's preoccupation with the nature of human and divine love is sardonically recorded in the name he chooses for the unscrupulous prostitute, Nell. The new Helen of Troy mocks the meaning of love in her scarlet arrogance, reversing the downfall not only of her Greek congener but of the Whore of Babylon in The Revelation, the prototypal scarlet woman. She sheds no tears, she wastes no pity, she shows no remorse. She lives in the spirit of the new law of venal love which Crane proclaims to rule the world.

This conviction, enhanced by immersion in the destructive element of personal experience, perhaps explains why in his later fiction religious images, for the most part, serve as simple correlatives of irony. Crane seems to lose even his provisional faith in the symbolic machinery of Christian salvation. When Maggie's innocent dream of love died, something may be said to have died in his soul.

JOSEPH X. BRENNAN

Ironic and Symbolic Structure in Crane's *Maggie* †

It is rather symptomatic of the scant attention scholars have accorded Stephen Crane that in the sixty-seven years since its publication no adequate formal analysis has yet appeared of his telling short novel *Maggie: A Girl of the Streets*.[1] This seems the more difficult to explain in view of *Maggie's* persistent vitality and the general agreement among literary historians respecting its significance in the development of American letters. Of its continued

† From *Nineteenth-Century Fiction*, XVI (March 1962), 303–15.
1. Since the present study was completed and submitted for publication, R. W. Stallman's article, "Crane's *Maggie*: A Reassessment," has appeared in the special Crane issue of *Modern Fic-* *tion Studies*, autumn, 1959. As the title suggests, however, Stallman's article is more summary and discursive than closely analytical, and hence fundamentally different in scope and intention from what follows here.

interest to readers there can be no real question, for since its appearance in 1893 it has advanced from near total neglect, through some seventeen new editions, to its present modest but assured and growing reputation;[2] since 1945 it has appeared in seven different collections. Perhaps no critic since Howells has had the temerity to call this compact little narrative "great," though several critics have echoed with approval Howells's equally flattering comment that it is "Greek," evincing the same "fatal necessity which dominates Greek tragedy." Scholars, nevertheless, are in more general agreement that the story of *Maggie* is something of a literary landmark. In the *Literary History of the United States* (p. 1022), for example, R. E. Spiller asserts that with the republication of *Maggie* in 1896, "modern American fiction was born," and in his introduction to the Crane *Omnibus* (p. xix), R. W. Stallman comments that "the then sordid realism of that work" initiated "the literary trend of the next generation," opening "the door to the Norris-Dreiser-Farrell school of sociological realism."

In view of what appears to be both the historical importance and intrinsic interest of Crane's *Maggie*, it seems desirable that it should receive something more than the generalized assessments it has heretofore received. For beneath the excessive violence and inept diction, the melodramatic posturing and grotesque characterization—weaknesses critics have been prompt enough to recognize—there is a degree of subtlety and calculated artistry in this narrative that existing critical estimates have generally overlooked. In the present study attention is focused on the ironic and symbolic structure of *Maggie*, an aspect any discriminating critical evaluation of the work must seriously take into account.

Perhaps the most remarkable single characteristic of *Maggie* is its insistent, and at times even oppressive, ironic tone. In its sustained and vehement irony *Maggie* was as much without precedent in American fiction as in its daring subject matter, and even today, in spite of all that the school of naturalism has produced in this manner, Crane's short narrative still marks something of the limits to which that method can go. In *Maggie*, indeed, the irony is so all-pervasive, ranging from the inversion of a single word or phrase to the thematic idea itself, that it is at once the most striking and yet most elusive aspect of the novel. In order to illustrate better how far-reaching this irony is, I shall proceed generally from its more overt and localized

2. For the years 1893-1946 twelve editions and two reprintings of *Maggie* are listed in *Stephen Crane: A Bibliography*, ed. A. W. Williams and V. Starrett (Glendale, Calif., 1948), pp. 106-07. Since then *Maggie* has also appeared in the following editions: *Stephen Crane: Selected Prose and Poetry*, ed. W. M. Gibson (New York, 1950); *Stephen Crane: An Omnibus* (New York, 1952) and *Stephen Crane: Stories and Tales* (New York, 1955), both edited by R. W. Stallman; *The Red Badge of Courage and Other Writings*, ed. Richard Chase (Boston, 1960); and *American Short Novels*, ed. R. P. Blackmur (New York, 1960).

to its more complex manifestations, from the ironic cast of the single word or phrase to the ironic manipulation of theme and character.

Of the ironic inversion of the single term one might cite numerous instances; Chapter IV, however, provides several of the more interesting examples. In the second paragraph of this chapter we read that Jimmie "studied human nature in the gutter, and found it no worse than he thought he had reason to believe it." Where we would ordinarily expect "no better" Crane overreaches our expectations to emphasize not only Jimmie's cynicism but the inversion of his scale of values as well: in his world there is no concept of good and bad; there is only bad or worse. This ironic twist is reinforced in the next sentence as well: "He never conceived a respect for the world, because he had begun with no idols that it had smashed." And later in this chapter, when Jimmie, by his premeditated indifference, had successfully snarled traffic, we read that "some blue policeman turned red and began . . . to . . . beat the soft noses of the responsible horses." Quite clearly the responsibility was not the horses'; Crane achieves an ironic effect here, however, not by a mere arbitrary inversion of the expected but by momentarily abandoning his usual objectivity and letting, as it were, the policeman's red point of view prevail. The same might be said for Crane's ironic use of the term "reverently" in the last sentence of this chapter: "Nevertheless, he had, on a certain starlit evening, said wonderingly and quite reverently, 'Deh moon looks like hell, don't it?'" This entire passage, indeed, following immediately upon a terse review of Jimmie's brawlings and seductions, is itself a trenchant ironic commentary upon his soulfulness and sensitivity.

More interesting yet, in Chapter XVI, is Crane's use of the word "respectability" as a kind of ironic motif; the term is repeated six times, each time with broadening implications and heightened ironic effect. There is a very deliberate progression here from Pete's apprehension lest Maggie should compromise the "atmosphere of respectability upon which the proprietor insisted"—the term being used three times in this association—to his confused impression that the respectability of the barroom now being threatened is really his own respectability. Having driven Maggie away at last, Pete then returns "with an air of relief, to his respectability," so that the psychological transference from the barroom to himself is now complete. In the last paragraph this motif reappears when a picture of benevolence and kind-heartedness to whom Maggie makes a gesture of appeal for help draws back from her convulsively to save his respectability. Thus in the brief course of this scene, by means of an ironic manipulation of the term, Crane reduces respectability to a hypocritical sham, a convenient justification for cruelty, irresponsibility, and indifference.

In the delineation of the main characters, moreover, Crane employs with telling effect a technique of ironically leveling the reader's normal assumptions and expectations. When we first encounter Jimmie in Chapter I, for example, he is the "little champion," fighting against overwhelming odds for the honor of Rum Alley. But lest by his initial display of courage he should too seriously engage our sympathies, a short while thereafter he turns his fists with unabated fury upon his defenseless sister. In Chapter III, when the father snatches the can of beer which Jimmie had just bought for the leathery old woman downstairs, he protests as though from a certain sense of justice, "Ah, come off! I got dis can fer dat ol' woman, an' it 'ud be dirt teh swipe it. See?" But a moment thereafter we perceive that he is really more concerned with the difficulties this creates for himself: "Look at deh dirt what yeh done me. . . . Deh ol' woman 'll be t'rowin' fits." Similarly one might be led to expect that the mother's objection to Jimmie's fighting springs from some dim instinct of solicitude for his physical well-being, yet, as it turns out, the real reason for her objection is that he tears his clothes. One wonders, too, when the father shouts at Jimmie, "Leave yer sister alone on the street," whether it is to Jimmie's pounding of Maggie or to the publicity of it that he is really objecting. In short, Crane has a real flair for this sort of ironic qualification of proper appearances with improper and unexpected motives; by means of this device he can deeply compromise his characters with one deft economical stroke.

Equally important, but somewhat more subtle, is Crane's device of interlinking his chapters by an ironic inversion of some key phrase or circumstance. In Chapter X the incredulity—in itself sufficiently ironic—with which the mother greets Jimmie's statement, "Well, Maggie's gone teh d' devil!" takes on another dimension of meaning when we remember that in the previous chapter, after having cursed and calumniated Maggie sanctimoniously from a position of drunken prostration, the mother had then driven her out with the words, "Git th' devil outa here." The point of it all, of course—and this scarcely needs such insistence—is that it is really the mother who is ultimately responsible for Maggie's seduction by Pete.

More effective is the ironic inversion which interlocks Chapters X and XI. Outraged by the news of Maggie's seduction, Jimmie sets out to trounce the culprit Pete singlehandedly; but he does not hesitate, in spite of his claims to superiority, to annex the assistance of a friend whom he encounters on the way. The ironic twist comes at the end of Chapter XI when Jimmie escapes and the friend who had sought to dissuade him from his purpose—"What's deh use! Yeh'll git pulled in! . . . An' ten plunks! Gee! . . . What's d'use?"—is himself hauled off by the policeman, evidently to pay the "ten plunks." Though Jimmie has a momentary urge to run to the rescue, he finally consigns his friend to his fate, ironically with that poor fool's very words, "Ah, what's deh use?" Crane uses this ironic inversion, however, not merely for the verbal sport of it, but in order to give firm emphasis to the essential cowardice that sinews all these boastful characters, and Jimmie in particular.

Also striking is the manner in which Chapters XV and XVI are thematically tied together. Within the immediate confines of Chapter XV, the initial scene of Jimmie's harsh repudiation of the forlorn woman whom he had brought to ruin serves to highlight ironically his self-righteous repudiation of his own sister shortly thereafter, but this scene functions even more importantly to reduce the next meeting between Pete and Maggie to ironic parody. In particular the dialogue of the one scene directly mimics that of the other. "Ah, don't bodder me!" Jimmie complains to Hattie; "Don' be allus bodderin' me," echoes Pete to Maggie. "But Jimmie," protests Hattie, "yeh tol' me yeh—"; "Why, Pete!" exclaims Maggie, "yehs tol' me—" Jimmie: "Yehs makes me tired, allus taggin' me. See?" Pete: "Say, yehs makes me tired! See? What d'yeh wanna tag aroun' after me fer?" Jimmie: "Ain' yehs got no sense?" Pete: "Ain' yehs got no sense?" Even Jimmie's parting advice to Hattie, "Oh, go teh blazes!" is echoed by Pete, but with less indirection, "Oh, go teh hell!" By means of this grotesque parody, the author not only magnifies the irony of Maggie's situation, but points more deliberately to the dismal round, the universality, of this kind of viciousness in the moral void of these slums.

Closely connected with this ironic repetition and inversion of a given word or phrase is Crane's use of the ironic, and even symbolic, gesture. The fear of contamination, for example, with which in Chapter XV the neighboring women recoil from Maggie is really the ironic reversal of her own gesture, at the end of Chapter XII, where she draws back her skirts in revulsion from two painted prostitutes. We have already commented upon Pete's repudiation of Maggie in Chapter XVI and his return, after that encounter, to his "respectability," but it is somewhat consoling to note how later in Chapter XVIII the very women whom Pete has treated royally all evening, prostitutes all apparently, scream in disgust and draw back their skirts when he falls to the floor in drunken insensibility. Thus all the accumulated ironies of that gesture, by now clearly a symbol of self-righteous aversion for moral degeneracy, are heaped with a kind of poetic justice upon the prostrate figure of Pete. In order to understand the full significance of that repudiation, however, it is necessary to look more closely at the previous chapter, for the two are closely connected in symbolism and meaning.

Chapter XVII, wherein Maggie is briefly seen plying her trade as a streetwalker, is certainly one of the most skillfully and economically constructed in the story. Unlike many sections of the book, this one states its meaning and conveys a sense of stark inevitability without any overt insistence. After close study, moreover, one realizes that a mere literal reading of this episode, as an unsuccessful evening's ramble that leads to the waterfront, raises certain difficulties. From the description of her clothes—she sports a "handsome cloak" and her feet are "well-shod"—Maggie has evidently prospered in her activity. Obviously successful after a few months' experience, why on this particular evening should she commit suicide? And if she is really seriously interested in engaging profitable attention, why does she enter into "darker blocks than those where the crowd traveled" to solicit less numerous and less well-to-do customers? Why is it also that after Maggie has left the glittering avenues with their tossing sea of umbrellas, there is no further mention of the rain? And in this connection, are we to take as literal or ironic the laborer's response to her overtures, "It's a fine evening, isn't it?"

Clearly this whole passage makes sense only when this evening's venture is taken as a drastic foreshortening or symbolic telescoping of the inevitable decline and ruination to which Maggie and all the women of her order must come. Especially significant in this respect is the pattern of Maggie's encounters: at first she engages the eye of a tall young man in evening dress, one evidently from the social upper crust, but he passes her by when he notices she is no longer "new"; then in order she meets a stout gentleman, he too apparently well off; a business man, who recognizes her and calls her "old girl" rather patronizingly; a young dandy, who addresses her more disparagingly as "old lady"; a laboring man; a mere boy; a drunk; a man with blotched features; and finally a "ragged being with shifting bloodshot eyes and grimy hands." Concomitant with this deliberate regression from wealth and well-being to poverty and physical degeneration, from the most to the least profitable and desirable prospect, there is also a steady shift in the symbolic light, from the brilliant and gay main avenues to the deadly black hue of the river. To have prolonged Maggie's plight over a much more extensive period of time would have quite obviously destroyed the dramatic impact of her story, but in order to point up the more universal implications of her situation, Crane has astutely focused into the range of this particular evening a panoramic and symbolic view of the prostitute's career. These implications he had strengthened also by identifying the subject of this chapter only as "a girl of the painted cohorts" and never specifically as Maggie.

So construed, this section strongly reinforces the meaning of the next and is in turn reinforced by it. Superficially it would seem that the glimpse we receive of Pete, proclaiming to six rapacious women that he is one fine fellow, functions merely as an ironic contrast to what immediately precedes, but upon closer examination one perceives that in its real meaning and implications this chapter reaches much further. It is significant, first of all, that once Pete falls into drunken paralysis, the women upon whom he has lavished his funds abandon him in the saloon compartment, the exit from which is now obscured by the stifling smoke from the lamps. Looking back to the various beer-hall scenes from this point, one finds that there is a steady retrogression here as well, from the bowery version of the de luxe—the great hall in Chapter VII—to the shabbiness of the hall of irregular shape in Chapter XII, to the unabashed sordidness of the hilarious hall in Chapter XIV. Commensurate with this movement from one level of vulgarity to another lower still, there is also a spatial contraction, an increased density of smoke, and an intensification of drunken hilarity. In the present scene, accordingly, it is surely symbolic that Pete is abandoned by a pack of professionals in a narrow saloon compartment from which the way out becomes progressively less apparent. More important, however, is the last sentence of this chapter, where Crane adumbrates in the posture of Pete's present debasement his inevitable and complete degeneration: "The wine from an overturned glass dripped softly down upon the blotches on the man's neck." In the wine drops upon the blotches, Pete's end in drunkenness and disease, one condition leading to and aggravating the other, is thus pointedly symbolized. This meaning is reinforced if one recalls now the previous section where on the lowest level of her inexorable descent to destruction Maggie encounters first a drunkard, then "a man with blotched features," and finally the "ragged being with shifting bloodshot eyes and grimy hands." Nor is this the only verbal tie-up between the two chapters. Just as Maggie had been addressed earlier in Chapter XVII as "old girl" and then "old lady," the woman of brilliance and audacity speaks to Pete in the same patronizing manner: "Never you mind, old boy"; and later, "And we're not goin' back on you, old man." By the end of this chapter, at any rate, Pete has reached the point where even women of no high standing pick up their skirts and recoil from him in disgust. Thus Crane would have us understand that Pete's fate is as inevitable as Maggie's and certainly more pitiless, since unlike Maggie he lacks both the conscience and the objectivity to perceive the hopeless waste of his existence.

In the last few pages we have been concerned with various modes of symbolism whose function is primarily or very largely ironic. Before turning to other aspects of Crane's ironic method, it may be well at this point to examine other symbolic passages whose function is only less pointedly related to that device. One of the most unobtrusive but thematically important of these is the following tightly compressed paragraph which appears in the first chapter:

> From a window of an apartment-house that uprose from amid squat ignorant stables there leaned a curious woman. Some labourers, unloading a scow at a dock at the river, paused for a moment and regarded the fight. The engineer of a passive tugboat hung lazily over a railing and watched. Over on the island a worm of yellow convicts came from the shadow of a grey ominous building and crawled slowly along the river's bank.

This passage serves first of all to give a sweeping view of the dismal environment, the "ignorant stables," in which these brawling little savages proliferate. But more importantly, it sounds a significant and pervasive theme of the novel, human indifference to human suffering: the bloody fight of the back-alley gangs may provide some momentary distraction for the curious or the bored, but it apparently touches these human spectators no more deeply than that. Most important of all, however, in this panoramic sweep of the scene, is the final focusing of the reader's attention upon the "worm of yellow convicts" and the "ominous" prison in the distance—the inevitable destiny, apparently, of a large number of these urchins. That prison fortress, accordingly, is fitly characterized as "ominous" for it portends the ultimate desolation and insensate degradation towards which this abandoned segment of society tends. In this connection it should be noted that these youngsters are described just before and following this passage as wearing "the grins of true assassins" and leering gloatingly at the blood upon Jimmie's face.

More curious is the symbol of the horse-drawn fire engine which appears in Chapter IV. Earlier in this chapter it was said of Jimmie that "He was afraid of nothing," yet some seven paragraphs later we learn that the mere sight or sound of a fire engine could strike absolute panic into his soul:

> As one charged toward his truck he would drive fearfully upon a sidewalk, threatening untold people with annihilation. When an engine struck a mass of blocked trucks, splitting it into fragments as a blow annihilates a cake of ice, Jimmie's team could usually be observed high and safe, with whole wheels, on the sidewalk. . . . A fire-engine was enshrined in his heart as an appalling thing that he loved with a distant, dog-like devotion. . . . Those leaping horses, striking sparks from the cobbles in their forward lunge, were creatures to be ineffably admired. The clang of the gong pierced his breast like a noise of remembered war.

Taken in isolation the fire engine may be regarded simply as a symbol of irresistible brute force, the only fact which Jimmie can either respect or admire, for that alone can touch his soul with fear. The ambivalence of Jimmie's attitude, however, is particularly interesting here, for it brings this passage into close relationship with the previous chapter, where the mother's character is dramatized in all its fright and vehemence.

Especially significant in Chapter III is the extreme and curious terror the mother inspires in Jimmie. Though he stands up with dauntless courage to all the abuse of the neighboring roughnecks, and responds on occasion with kicks and curses to his father's violence, he dodges from his mother in abject terror, screaming more from panic than from pain, it seems, once she takes hold of him. So much in dread does he live of her violent outbursts he has even learned to detect their ominous approach: "He cast furtive glances at his mother. His practised eye perceived her gradually emerge from a mist of muddled sentiment until her brain burned in drunken heat. He sat breathless." Once the outburst comes, though it is immediately directed at Maggie, Jimmie runs out of the flat "shrieking like a monk in an earthquake." When at last the battle subsides and his parents collapse in drunken stupor, the mother in the middle of the floor, the father across the seat of a chair, Jimmie enters the room stealthily, still trembling with fear. What follows upon this is particularly interesting. "A glow from the fire threw red hues over the bare floor," and in this symbolically suggestive light, half hypnotized between dread and fascination, Jimmie studies the grotesque figure of his mother:

> His mother's great chest was heaving painfully. Jimmie paused and looked down at her. . . . He was fearful lest she should open her eyes, and the dread within him was so strong that he could not forbear to stare, but hung as if fascinated over the woman's grim face. Suddenly her eyes opened. The urchin found himself looking straight into an expression which, it would seem, had the power to change his blood to salt. He howled piercingly and fell backward.

Though the mother sinks again into drunken sleep, Maggie and Jimmie clutch one another and huddle in a corner, to spend an all-night vigil gazing with expectant horror at the mother's prostrate form:

> The eyes of both were drawn, by some force, to stare at the woman's face, for they thought she need only to awake and all the fiends would come from below. They crouched until the ghost mists of dawn appeared at the window, drawing close to the panes, and looking in at the prostrate, heaving body of the mother.

This passage serves to rivet the reader's attention, at the very threshold of the adult histories of these children, upon the drunken figure of the mother, the strongest formative force in their lives, and in that sense the chief symbol of the novel. For symbolically embodied in the mother—brutal yet hopelessly maudlin, irresistibly aggressive and invulnerably self-righteous—are all the evil forces of this society that work Maggie's and eventually its own destruction.

The connection between this passage and that of the fire engine can be more readily perceived now in the pattern of Jimmie's psychology. Towards both his mother and the fire engine his attitude is clearly ambivalent; both command that incontestable brute force which fascinates him because it overawes, and wins his respect because it overwhelms. It is also noteworthy that, whether intentionally or not, the mother is frequently described in terms strongly suggestive of the fire engine: she is "immense," "rampant," "chieftain-like," "crimson," "puffing and snorting," "fervent red," and "inflamed." Nor is it any wonder, when one recalls the scenes of her drunken rampages, that "the clang of the fire gong pierced Jimmie's breast like a noise of remembered war." Like the fire engine, the mother smashes everything in her path once her drunken rage runs wild; but whereas the fire engine symbolizes in Jimmie's psychology an ideal of destructive brute force, her outrageous physical strength betokens something more, the devastating moral and psychological might by which she smashes the minds and the souls of her children. As the fire engine symbolizes overpowering physical force in Jimmie's brutal world, the mother represents its destructive spiritual counterpart. Taken together thus these passages reciprocally enrich each other's meaning.

Another set of symbols worth attention is the lambrequin and blue ribbons with which Maggie rather pathetically attempts to improve the appearance of her home. When we study the several passages in which these items appear, it becomes clear that they are intended as symbols of Maggie herself, of her essentially feminine but somewhat romantically distorted sensibility. Although Maggie has worked upon the lambrequin "with infinite care" in order to attract Pete's attention, he fails completely to look at, let alone admire it: symbolically, Pete cannot even discern, much less value, the real virtues of Maggie's nature. One must have a soul in order to recognize one, and Pete, there can be no doubt, has none. Shortly thereafter we read that the mother "had vented some phase of drunken fury upon the lambrequin. It lay in a bedraggled heap in the corner. . . . the knots of blue ribbons appeared like violated flowers." This passage corroborates symbolically what was said earlier, that it is the mother who is really culpable for Maggie's seduction and ruin, for it is the mother who has most ruthlessly outraged Maggie, who has violated her soul repeatedly and trampled her sensibilities.

In the final use of these symbols in Chapter X there are several interesting implications concerning Maggie herself. The night before, in the height of her drunken fury, the mother had driven Maggie out of the house and into the willing arms of Pete. Before leaving her home the next day, however, in order to live with Pete, Maggie first attempts to restore appearances.

> The rooms showed that attempts had been made at tidying them. . . . The floor had been newly swept. The blue ribbons had been restored to the curtains, and the lambrequin, with its immense sheaves of yellow wheat and red roses of equal size, had been returned, in a worn and sorry state, to its place at the mantel. Maggie's jacket and hat were gone from the nail behind the door.

Though repeatedly abused and trampled upon, Maggie constantly picks up the remnants of her life and tries to restore them, even if "in a worn and sorry state," to some semblance of decency. When she leaves home to live with Pete, she does so in the full conviction that under the circumstances what she is doing is expedient rather than immoral; now that she has been driven from her home and seduced, going to live with Pete is, from her point of view, the only decent restoration of her life possible. "She did not feel like a bad woman," we are informed further on; "to her knowledge she had never known any better."

It seems likely too that in the lambrequin's "immense sheaves of yellow wheat and red roses of equal size," Crane is suggesting something further about Maggie: the romantic distortion of her sensibility, which beguiles her into regarding a patent vulgarian like Pete as a "golden sun," a "knight" and "ideal man," the "lover . . . under the trees of her dream-gardens." For Maggie is no more spared by Crane's irony than the rest of his characters. Indeed, however sympathetically in other respects she may be portrayed, her tastes and mental perceptions are sometimes absurd to the point of exasperation. When, for example, Pete shouts at a waiter, "Ah, git off d' eart!" and from this evidence Maggie infers that "Pete brought forth all his elegance and all his knowledge of high-class customs for her benefit," one might well wonder whether any kind of moral light could pierce such density.

But if Crane did not spare Maggie's intelligence, he did at least intend to spare her soul, to depict her as the innocent victim of the brutal forces around her, a flower which "blossomed in a mud-puddle," only to be sullied and broken and trampled back into it. This fact is certainly clear enough in the novel, but it is interesting to note how Crane himself phrased it in an inscription copy he sent to Hamlin Garland:

> It is inevitable that you will be greatly shocked by the book but continue, please, with all possible courage, to the end. For it tries to show that environment is a tremendous thing in the world and frequently shapes lives regardless. If one proves that theory one makes room in Heaven for all sorts of souls, notably an occasional

street girl, who are not confidently expected to be there by many excellent people.

Although the story itself, fortunately, is nowhere so explicit about heaven and salvation, it nevertheless dramatizes quite forcefully this central thematic irony: the self-righteous condemnation of a woman who is good by the very society responsible for her downfall. From this thematic center extends the whole labyrinthian structure of particular ironies briefly surveyed above.

Maggie, then, is a much more intricately structured work of art than its more obvious infelicities of style and emphasis might lead one to suspect. Though the vehemence of Crane's ironic vision undoubtedly accounts for much that is excessive in *Maggie*, to that same force, whenever he succeeded in harnessing it to his artistic instincts, is due most of its artistic strength as well. Crane's irony, moreover, is generally more subtle and successful when rendered in large deliberate patterns; when such patterns were also fused into symbol, for which Crane has a much surer instinct, the effects are truly brilliant.

JANET OVERMYER

The Structure of Crane's *Maggie* †

Stephen Crane's first novelette is often considered worth-while only because its author later went on to write *The Red Badge of Courage*. While *Maggie* has several faults, it also has several virtues which indicate plainly that its author, even at twenty, was a skilled craftsman. One of its most noticeable virtues is the relation of structure to theme.

Maggie's structure is often regarded as being flimsy. John Berryman says, "Crane had to rely on loose, episodic structure."[1] While Robert Wooster Stallman feels that *Maggie* has a definite pattern, he says that "not logic but mood defines the relationship by the images and episodes."[2] It is my contention that the novelette has a decided controlling structure that combines with the theme to form a pleasing whole.

The structure, which serves as an encircling frame for the plot, is that of the familiar "play within a play." The very first scene is Jimmie fighting the Devil's Row children with an audience of "a curious woman," "some laborers," and "the engineer of a passive

† From *The University of Kansas City Review*, XXIX (Autumn 1962), 71–72.
1. *Stephen Crane* (New York: William Sloane

Associates, 1950), p. 59.
2. "Crane's 'Maggie': A Reassessment," *Modern Fiction Studies*, V (Autumn 1959), 251–52.

tugboat." Not one of them moves to interfere; they might as well be an audience at a theater. The same is true, to a heightened degree, of the Johnsons' neighbors. Not only do they not interfere in the family's quarrels, even when bodily injury is imminent, but they crowd into the hall and hurl comments at the combatants, much as spectators at a prize fight cheer on their favorite. Again, the fights serve as entertainment. The final, disgustingly ironic comment of Maggie's mother—"I'll fergive her!"—would not have been uttered at all but for the neighbors' prodding. As they repeatedly ask if the mother will forgive, she senses that it would be a fine gesture to make; it would make her out a martyr. The neighbors have gotten their money's worth.

To emphasize this theatrical unreality still further, three scenes are set in a beer hall that presents stage shows, where Pete takes Maggie on their dates. On their first date (Section 7) Maggie has a fine time; she sees a wonderful world hitherto completely unknown to her. The second beer hall scene (Section 12) takes place after Maggie has left home to be with Pete, and is becoming used to such evenings. The stage show is therefore described in less detail than previously, and Maggie, while enjoying herself, has a less pleasant time. On the way out she prophetically sees two street walkers. The third such scene (Section 14) gives very little description of the entertainment and is saddened for Maggie by Pete's desertion of her. Maggie's downward slide is set against the make-believe backdrop to further emphasize the story's theme.

The theme may be stated as being that an unreal view of life precipitates tragedy, or at least unhappiness. None of the four main characters sees life clearly and honestly. Pete correctly views his affair with Maggie as a pleasant interlude for him and nothing more, but he hopes mightily for a satisfactory relationship with Nell, who sees him as a fool. Jimmie is at a loss to understand his sister's fall and, incapable of seeing any relation between his own seduction of various women and Pete's seduction of his sister, damns his sister mercilessly for thus disgracing the family. Once he "almost came to a conclusion that his sister would have been more firmly good had she better known how," but he discards this idea. Neither he nor his mother can understand Maggie's desire for a better life or see how her environment helped to propel her into Pete's arms.

But it is Maggie's view of reality that proves, finally, the most saddening. She sees life as she wishes it to be; to her, Pete is "the ideal man," and the plays she sees represent "transcendental realism." It is quite proper to her that in the theater the villain is punished and the hero is rewarded; she fails to realize that this is not necessarily the way of the world. She believes her love affair with Pete will last forever; when it does not, she is utterly lost.

The play within a play structure thus reinforces the idea that life must be viewed realistically, even if painfully. It is far more painful to fool oneself. Crane begins and ends his story with the emphasis on unreality, and includes several overt references at intervals throughout. It can thus be seen that structure and theme are firmly and complementarily wedded to give the story unity.

As a postscript, it may be added that *Maggie* is further kept from flying apart by the number of parallel incidents. In the following examples, the first even foreshadows the second:

1. Jimmie's fight as a child and his fight with Pete, his early rescuer.
2. The drunkenness of Mr. Johnson and Jimmie.
3. The death of Tommie, an innocent child, and Maggie, an "innocent" girl.
4. The casual seductions by Jimmie and Pete.
5. Maggie's pulling back from the painted women and the minister's pulling back from her.

In addition, there are the following parallels:

1. Two fallen women, Nell and Maggie.
2. The souls of Jimmie and Maggie.
3. The powerlessness of the mission church and of the minister.

There is also a careful alternation of places and people throughout; scenes in the beer hall alternate with scenes of home as scenes of Maggie and Pete alternate with scenes of Jimmie and his mother. All of which shows that while the structure of *Maggie* may be episodic, it is not loose, but tightly controlled; for all his faults, Crane, even at an early age, knew how to structure a story.

DONALD PIZER

Stephen Crane's *Maggie* and American Naturalism†

Stephen Crane's *Maggie: A Girl of the Streets* has often served as an example of naturalistic fiction in America. Crane's novel about a young girl's fall and death in the New York slums has many of the distinctive elements of naturalistic fiction, particularly a slum setting and the theme of the overpowering effect of environment. Crane himself appeared to supply a naturalistic gloss to the novel when he wrote to friends that *Maggie* was about the effect of environment on human lives. Yet the novel has characteristics which clash with its

† From *Criticism, a Quarterly for Literature and the Arts*, VII (Spring 1965), 168–75.

neat categorization as naturalistic fiction. For one thing, Crane's technique of an intense verbal irony is foreign to the naturalistic vision; for another, Maggie herself, though she becomes a prostitute, is strangely untouched by her physical environment. She functions as an almost expressionistic symbol of inner purity uncorrupted by external foulness. There is nothing, of course, to prevent a naturalist from using verbal irony and expressionistic symbolism, just as there is nothing to prevent him from introducing a deterministic theme into a Jamesian setting. But in practice the naturalist is usually direct. He is concerned with revealing the blunt edge of the powerful forces which condition our lives, and his fictional technique is usually correspondingly blunt and massive. When Zola in *L'Assommoir* and *Nana* wished to show the fall into prostitution of a child of the slums, his theme emerged clearly and ponderously from his full description of the inner as well as outer corruption of Nana and from his "realistic" symbolism. Crane's method, on the other hand, is that of obliqueness and indirection. Irony and expressionistic symbolism ask the reader to look beyond literal meaning, to seek beyond the immediately discernible for the underlying reality. Both are striking techniques which by their compelling tone and their distortion of the expected attempt to shock us into recognition that a conventional belief or an obvious "truth" may be false and harmful. Perhaps, then, *Maggie* can best be discussed by assuming from the first that Crane's fictional techniques imply that the theme of the novel is somewhat more complex than the truism that young girls in the slums are more apt to go bad than young girls elsewhere.[1]

The opening sentence of *Maggie* is "A very little boy stood upon a heap of gravel for the honor of Rum Alley." The sentence introduces both Crane's theme and his ironic technique. By juxtaposing the value of honor and the reality of a very little boy, a heap of gravel, and Rum Alley, Crane suggests that the idea of honor is inappropriate to the reality, that it serves to disguise from the participants in the fight that they are engaged in a vicious and petty scuffle. Crane's irony emerges out of the difference between a value which one imposes on experience and the nature of experience itself. His ironic method is to project into the scene the values of its participants in order to underline the difference between their values and reality.

---

1. The interpretation of *Maggie* which follows has been evolving in criticism of the novel for some years, though it has not been pursued as fully or pointedly as I do here. Both R. W. Stallman, in "Crane's *Maggie*: A Reassessment," *Modern Fiction Studies*, V (Autumn 1959), 251–59, and Charles C. Walcutt, in *American Literary Naturalism, A Divided Stream* (Minneapolis, 1956), pp. 67–72, touch briefly on the theme of *Maggie* somewhat as I do. I have also been aided by Edwin H. Cady, *Stephen Crane* (New York, 1962), pp. 102–11; Joseph X. Brennan, "Ironic and Symbolic Structure in Crane's *Maggie*," *Nineteenth-Century Fiction*, XVI (March 1962), 303–15; and Janet Overmyer, "The Structure of Crane's *Maggie*," *University of Kansas City Review*, XXIX (Autumn 1962), 71–72. [See the essays by Walcutt, Brennan, and Overmyer, above.—*Editor*.]

So the scene has a basic chivalric cast. The very little boy is a knight fighting on his citadel of gravel for the honor of his chivalrous pledge to Rum Alley. Crane's opening sentence sets the theme for *Maggie* because the novel is essentially about man's use of conventional but inapplicable abstract values (such as justice, honor, duty, love, and respectability) as weapons or disguises. The novel is not so much about the slums as a physical reality as about what people believe in the slums and how their beliefs are both false to their experience and yet function as operative forces in their lives.

Let me explore this idea by examining first the lives of the novel's principal characters and then the moral values which control their thinking about their lives. Crane uses two basic images to depict the Bowery. It is a battlefield and it is a prison. These images appear clearly in the novel's first three chapters, which describe an evening and night in the life of the Johnson family during Maggie's childhood. The life of the family is that of fierce battle with those around them and among themselves. The novel opens with Jimmie fighting the children of Devil's Row. He then fights one of his own gang. His father separates them with a blow. Maggie mistreats the babe Tommie; Jimmie strikes Maggie; Mrs. Johnson beats Jimmie for fighting. Mr. and Mrs. Johnson quarrel. Mrs. Johnson beats Maggie for breaking a plate; Mr. Johnson strikes Jimmie with an empty beer pail. Mr. Johnson comes home drunk and he and Mrs. Johnson fight—all this in three rather short chapters. Crane's fundamental point in these chapters is that the home is not a sanctuary from the struggle and turmoil of the world but is rather where warfare is even more intense and where the animal qualities encouraged by a life of battle— strength, fear, and cunning—predominate. The slum and the home are not only battlefields, however, but are also enclosed arenas. Maggie's tenement is in a "dark region," and her apartment, "up dark stairways and along cold, gloomy halls," is like a cave. Crane's description of the Johnson children eating combines both the warfare and cave images into one central metaphor of primitive competition for food.

> The babe sat with his feet dangling high from a precarious infant's chair and gorged his small stomach. Jimmie forced, with feverish rapidity, the grease-enveloped pieces between his wounded lips. Maggie, with side glances of fear of interruption, ate like a small pursued tigress.

By means of this double pattern of imagery, Crane suggests that the Johnsons' world is one of fear, fury, and darkness, that it is a world in which no moral laws are applicable, since the Johnsons' fundamental guide to conduct is an instinctive amorality, a need to feed and to protect themselves.

Once introduced, this image of the Bowery as an amoral, animal world is maintained throughout *Maggie*. Mr. Johnson dies, Jimmie assumes his position, and the Johnsons' family warfare continues as before. Maggie and Jimmie go to work, and each finds that struggle and enclosure mark his adult world. Jimmie becomes a belligerent truck driver, imprisoned by his ignorance and his distrust. He respects only strength in the form of the red fire engine which has the power to crush his wagon. Maggie works in a prison-like sweat shop where she is chided into resentment by her grasping employer. Theirs are lives of animal struggle and of spiritual bleakness in which they only faintly realize their own deprivation. Maggie sits with the other girls in her factory workroom in a vague state of "yellow discontent," and Jimmie, the brawling teamster, "nevertheless . . . , on a certain starlit evening, said wonderingly and quite reverently, 'Deh moon looks like hell, don't it?'"

The moral values held by the Johnsons are drawn almost entirely from a middle class ethic which stresses the home as the center of virtue, and respectability as the primary moral goal. It is a value system oriented toward approval by others, toward an audience. In the opening chapter of the novel, Jimmie hits Maggie as Mr. Johnson is taking them home. Mr. Johnson cries, "'Leave yer sister alone *on the street*'" (my italics). The Johnsons' moral vision is dominated by moral roles which they believe are expected of them. The roles bring social approbation, and they are also satisfying because the playing of them before an audience encourages a gratifying emotionalism or self-justification. The reaction to Maggie's fall is basically of this nature. She is cast out by her mother and brother for desecrating the Home, and her seducer, Pete, rejects her plea for aid because she threatens the respectability of the rough and tumble bar in which he works. The moral poses adopted by the Johnsons and by Pete have no relation to reality, however, since the home and the bar are parallel settings of warfare rather than of virtue.

The key to the morality of the Bowery is therefore its self-deceiving theatricality. Those expressing moral sentiments do so as though playing a role before a real or implied audience. Crane makes the dramatic nature of Bowery morality explicit in scenes set in dance halls and theatres. In a dance hall, an audience of Maggies, Jimmies, and Petes listens enraptured to a song "whose lines told of a mother's love, and a sweetheart who waited, and a young man who was lost at sea under harrowing circumstances." Later, Maggie and Pete see plays

> in which the dazzling heroine was rescued from the palatial home of her treacherous guardian by the hero with the beautiful sentiments. . . . Maggie lost herself in sympathy with the wanderers swooning in snowstorms beneath happy-hued church windows,

while a choir within sang "Joy to the World." To Maggie and the rest of the audience this was transcendental realism. Joy always within, and they, like the actor, inevitably without. Viewing it, they hugged themselves in ecstatic pity of their imagined or real condition.

The audience identifies itself with maligned and innocent virtue despite the inapplicability of these roles to their own lives. "Shady persons in the audience revolted from the pictured villainy of the drama. With untiring zeal they hissed vice and applauded virtue. Unmistakably bad men evinced an apparently sincere admiration for virtue."

This same ability to project oneself into a virtuous role is present in most of the novel's characters. Each crisis in the Johnson family is viewed by neighbors who comprise an audience which encourages the Johnsons to adopt moral poses. In the scene in which Maggie is cast out, both Jimmie and Mrs. Johnson are aware of their need to play the roles of outraged virtue in response to the expectations of their audience. Mrs. Johnson addresses the neighbors "like a glib showman," and with a "dramatic finger" points out to them her errant daughter. The novel's final scene is a parody of Bowery melodrama. Mrs. Johnson mourns over the dead Maggie's baby shoes while the neighbors cry in sympathy and the "woman in black" urges her to forgive Maggie. In the midst of her exhortations, "The woman in black raised her face and paused. The inevitable sunlight came streaming in at the window." Crane in this scene connects the sentimental morality of melodrama and the sanctimoniousness of Bowery religion. Both the theatre and the mission purvey moral attitudes which have no relation to life but which rather satisfy emotional needs or social approval. The heroes and heroines of melodrama cannot be confronted with reality, but the church is occasionally challenged. When it is, as when the mission preacher is asked why he never says "we" instead of "you," or when Maggie seeks aid from the stout clergyman, its reaction is either non-identification with reality ("'What?'" asks the preacher) or withdrawal from it (the clergyman sidesteps Maggie). It is as though the church, too, were a sentimental theatre which encouraged moral poses but which ignored the essential nature of itself and of its audience.

Both of these central characteristics of the Bowery—its core of animality and its shell of moral poses—come together strikingly in Mrs. Johnson. There is a bitter Swiftian irony in Crane's portrait of her. Her drunken rages symbolize the animal fury of a slum home, and her quickness to judge, condemn, and cast out Maggie symbolizes the self-righteousness of Bowery morality. In a sense she symbolizes the entire Bowery world, both its primitive amorality and its sentimental morality. It is appropriate, then, that it is she who literally drives Maggie into prostitution and eventual death. Secure in her moral role, she refuses to allow Maggie to return home after her seduction by Pete, driving her into remaining with Pete and then into prostitution. Maggie is thus destroyed not so much by the physical reality of slum life as by a middle class morality imposed on the slums by the missions and the melodrama, a morality which allows its users both to judge and to divorce themselves from responsibility from those they judge.

Crane's characterization of Maggie can now be examined. His description of her as having "blossomed in a mud-puddle" with "none of the dirt of Rum Alley . . . in her veins" is not "realistic," since it is difficult to accept that the slums would have no effect on her character. Zola's portrait of Nana dying of a disfiguring disease which symbolizes her spiritual as well as physical corruption is more convincing. Crane's desire, however, was to stress that the vicious deterministic force in the slums was its morality, not its poor housing or inadequate diet, and it is this emphasis which controls his characterization of Maggie. His point is that Maggie comes through the mud-puddle of her physical environment untouched. It is only when her environment becomes a moral force that she is destroyed. Maggie as an expressionistic symbol of purity in a mud-puddle is Crane's means of enforcing his large irony that purity is destroyed not by concrete evils but by the very moral codes established to safeguard it.

But Maggie is a more complex figure than the above analysis suggests. For though her world does not affect her moral nature, it does contribute to her downfall by blurring her vision. Her primary drive in life is to escape her mud-puddle prison, and she is drawn to Pete because his strength and elegance offer a means of overcoming the brutality and ugliness of her home and work. Her mistaken conception of Pete results from her enclosed world, a world which has given her romantic illusions just as it has supplied others with moral poses. Her mistake warrants compassion, however, rather than damnation and destruction. She is never really immoral. Throughout her fall, from her seduction by Pete to her plunge into the East River, Crane never dispels the impression that her purity and innocence remain. Her weakness is compounded out of the facts that her amoral environment has failed to arm her with moral strength (she "would have been more firmly good had she better known how"), while at the same time it has blinded her with self-destructive romantic illusions ("she wondered if the culture and refinement she had seen imitated . . . by the heroine on the stage, could be acquired by a girl who lived in a tenement house and worked in a shirt factory").

There is considerable irony that in choosing Pete Maggie flees into the same world she wished to escape. Like Mrs. Johnson, Pete desires to maintain the respectability of his "home," the bar in which he works. Like her, he theatrically purifies himself of guilt and responsibility for Maggie's fall as he drunkenly sobs "'I'm good f'ler, girls'" to an audience of prostitutes. And like Maggie herself, he is eventually a victim of sexual warfare. He is used and discarded by the "woman of brilliance and audacity" just as he had used and discarded Maggie. In short, Maggie can escape the immediate prison of her home and factory, but she cannot escape being enclosed by the combination of amoral warfare (now sexual) and moral poses which is the pervasive force in her world.

In his famous inscription to *Maggie*, Crane wrote that the novel "tries to show that environment is a tremendous thing in the world and frequently shapes lives regardless." But he went on to write that "if one proves that theory one makes room in Heaven for all sorts of souls (notably an occasional street girl) who are not confidently expected to be there by many excellent people."[2] The second part of the inscription contains an attack on the "many excellent people" who, like Maggie's mother, immediately equate a fallen girl with evil and hell. Crane is here not so much expressing a belief in heaven as using the idea of salvation and damnation as a rhetorical device to attack smug, self-righteous moralism. The entire novel bears this critical intent. Crane's focus in *Maggie* is less on the inherent evil of slum life than on the harm done by a false moral environment imposed on that life. His irony involving Mrs. Johnson, for example, centers on the religious and moral climate which has persuaded her to adopt the moral poses of outraged Motherhood and despoiled Home.

Maggie is thus a novel primarily about the falsity and destructiveness of certain moral codes. To be sure, these codes and their analogous romantic visions of experience are present in Maggie's environment, and are in part what Crane means when he wrote that environment shapes lives regardless. But Crane's ironic technique suggests that his primary goal was not to show the effects of environment but to distinguish between moral appearance and reality, to attack the sanctimonious self-deception and sentimental emotional gratification of moral poses. He was less concerned with dramatizing a deterministic philosophy than in assailing those who apply a middle class morality to victims of amoral, uncontrollable forces in man and society. *Maggie* is therefore very much like such early Dreiser novels as *Sister Carrie* and *Jennie Gerhardt*, though Dreiser depends less on irony and more on an explicit documentation and discussion of the discrepancy between an event and man's moral

2. *Stephen Crane: Letters*, ed. R. W. Stallman   and Lillian Gilkes (New York, 1960), p. 14.

evaluation of an event. *Maggie* is also like *The Red Badge of Courage*, for the later novel seeks to demonstrate the falsity of a moral or romantic vision of the amorality which is war.

Crane, then, is a naturalistic writer in the sense that he believes that environment molds lives. But he is much more than this, for his primary concern is not a dispassionate, pessimistic tracing of inevitable forces but a satiric assault on weaknesses in social morality. He seems to be saying that though we may not control our destinies, we can at least destroy those systems of value which uncritically assume we can. If we do this, a Maggie (or a Jennie Gerhardt) will at least be saved from condemnation and destruction by an unjust code.

Writers who seek greater justice, who demand that men evaluate their experience with greater clarity and honesty, are not men who despair at the nature of things. They are rather critical realists. Like William Dean Howells, Crane wishes us to understand the inadequacies of our lives so that we may improve them. Although Crane stresses weaknesses in our moral vision rather than particular social abuses, there is more continuity between Howells' critical realism and Crane's naturalism than one might suspect. This continuity is not that of subject matter or even of conception of man and society. It is rather that of a belief in the social function of the novel in delineating the evils of social life. If one sees such a writer as Crane in this light, the often crude and out-dated determinism of early American naturalism lessens in importance. One begins to realize that American naturalism, like most vital literary movements, comprised a body of convention and assumption about the function and nature of literature which unprescriptively allowed the writer to mold this shared belief into a personally expressive work of art. Crane's fiction is therefore permanently absorbing and historically significant not because he was a determinist or fatalist writing about the slums or about the chaos of war. His fiction still excites because his ironic technique successfully involves us in the difference between moral appearance and reality in society. His fiction is historically important because his expression of this theme within the conventions of naturalistic fiction reveals the relationship between critical realism and naturalism. But his fiction is perhaps even more significant historically because he revealed the possibility of a uniquely personal style and vision within naturalistic conventions. Our writers have responded to the critical spirit and the fictional sensationalism and freedom of naturalism without a sense of being burdened by doctrinaire precepts and forms. And it is no doubt this invigorating freedom within continuity which has been one of the principal reasons for the strength and influence of the naturalistic movement in America, from Crane and Dreiser to our own times.

JOSEPH KATZ

[Art and Compromise: The 1893 and the 1896 *Maggie*]†

* * *

The original objection to *Maggie* was that it was too brutal. "Cruel," Richard Watson Gilder had called it when he turned it down for the *Century*.[1] William Dean Howells half agreed: "There is so much realism of a certain kind in it that unfits it for the general reading, but once in a while it will do to tell the truth as completely as 'Maggie' does."[2] In rewriting the novel, Crane was to temper the brutality and to subdue the coarseness of the original. His method of achieving this was the series of omissions—and another of revisions and additions—to which he referred in his letter to Hitchcock. Evidently working over a copy of the 1893 edition,[3] Crane carefully deleted goodly numbers of damns and hells, changed others into more innocuous exclamations, and rendered those that remained as "d——n" and "h——l." Most references to swearing he softened, and he transformed many invocations of the Deity into less offensive expressions ("Gee!" and "Great Heavens!"). When Crane finished, the Appleton editors continued. Hitchcock may have believed that he was supervising the removal of unnecessarily antagonizing appendages; Crane knew that he was patching together "quite a new aspect."

Three directions of the 1893 *Maggie* were in this way modified or completely removed in the 1896. Both R. W. Stallman and William Gibson considered that the tinkering with the "hells," "damns," and "Gawds" was unimportant, but this tinkering greatly affected all three. Both William Dean Howells and Hamlin Garland were astonished by the language of the characters: "the dialect of the slums as I have never before seen it written,—crisp, direct, terse," Garland had commented. "It is important because it gives voice to the blind rebellion of Rum Alley and Devil's Row. It creates the atmosphere of the jungles, where vice festers and crime passes gloomily by, where outlawed human nature rebels against God and man."[4]

† From "The *Maggie* Nobody Knows," *Modern Fiction Studies*, XII (Summer 1966), 203–12.

1. Thomas Beer, *Stephen Crane: A Study in American Letters* (New York, 1923), p. 85.
2. W. D. Howells, *New York Press*, 15 April 1894; quoted by R. W. Stallman in "Crane's *Maggie* in Review," *The Houses that James Built* (East Lansing, Michigan, 1964), p. 64.
3. "Evidently" because of the peculiar inconsistencies in rendering the word "hell" in the 1896 edition. Most frequent is "h——l," but on occasion it is "h—ll" (1896, pp. 4, 136). No well-trained editor would produce both, but one might easily pass over the variant in reading authorial revisions.
4. Hamlin Garland, "An Ambitious French Novel and a Modest American Story," *Arena*, VIII (June 1893), xii. [See excerpt above—*Editor*.]

The language of the novel and of the characters in it delineated the world within which *Maggie* operated. In 1893, this was good slum dialect: it was crisp, direct, and terse, but it was also coarse, vulgar, and brutal. "Naw," said Jimmie when he was told to flee the battle which opens the book (1893, p. 3), "dese micks can't make me run." The boy was using the language of prejudice directed against the Irish of the "old immigration" by the community outside. The word specifies the people in the slum, but it also demonstrates the workings of environment. When, in 1896, Jimmie called his enemies "mugs," (1896, p. 1), his language was still vulgar, but it was less brutal. This linguistic brutality is present in the language of the 1893 edition: Mother curses father, parents curse children, children curse parents and all within hearing. In 1896, the brutality is all but gone; coarseness remains.

If this function of the "hells" and "damns" is minor, and I believe that it is not, there are two further functions which are undeniably important. The first, indeed, concerns the theme of the novel. A reader of the 1896 edition will agree that the novel is still brutal; there are enough indications remaining from the earlier edition. But why did Gilder believe it to be cruel? The opening game of "King of the Mountain" begins a metaphor of war that extends throughout the novel, but it is a game of equals. For cruelty, one would expect an exertion of unequal forces.

When Crane received the ugly yellow copies of *Maggie* from the printer in 1893, he inscribed many copies and sent them off. The inscriptions to close friends and to acquaintances vary much as one would expect. On Holmes Bassett's copy, for example, he said "This work is a mudpuddle, I am told on the best authority. Wade in and have a swim," while to the daughter of his tobacconist, Crane wrote, "This story will not edify or improve you and may not even interest you but I owe your papa $1.30 for tobacco."[5] But the inscriptions on the copies that Crane mailed to men of influence conform to a pattern that suggests a carefully conceived design: "It is inevitable that you be greatly shocked by this book but continue, please, with all possible courage to the end. For it tries to show that environment is a tremendous thing in the world and frequently shapes lives regardless. If one proves that theory, one makes room in Heaven for all sorts of souls (notably an occasional street girl) who are not confidently expected to be there by many excellent people."[6]

The suggestion is that environment is more powerful in directing lives than, say, either individual will or the wishes of God. Crane is

5. R. W. Stallman and Lillian Gilkes, *Stephen Crane: Letters* (New York, 1960), p. 15. Hereafter *Letters*.
6. This is the inscription on Hamlin Garland's copy in the Lilly Library of Indiana University.

It appears, with minor errors in transcription, in *Letters*, p. 14. See also the similar inscriptions in *Letters*, pp. 14, 49, and compare those in *Letters*, pp. 69, 126.

quite logical: If one were to prove this, even an occasional street girl could be admitted to Heaven. This had happened before. One of Maggie's predecessors, Mary Magdalene (*Luke* 7:37–50, 8:2), was admitted to Heaven over the protests of excellent people. "Wherefore I say unto thee, Her sins, which are many, are forgiven; for she loved much: but to whom little is forgiven, *the same* loveth little." The difficulty in *Maggie* is greater than that in the Bible: there is no one save the reader to forgive the transgressor. In several of the poems in *The Black Riders* (1895)—"My aim was to comprehend in it the thoughts I have had about life in general," Crane said of it—that comment is explicit:

> God fashioned the ship of the world carefully.
> With the infinite skill of an all-master
> Made He the hull and the sails,
> Held He the rudder
> Ready for adjustment.
> Erect stood He, scanning His work proudly.
> Then—at fateful time—a wrong called,
> And God turned, heeding.
> Lo, the ship, at this opportunity, slipped slyly,
> Making cunning noiseless travel down the ways.
> So that, forever rudderless, it went upon the seas
> Going ridiculous voyages,
> Making quaint progress,
> Turning as with serious purpose
> Before stupid winds.
> And there were many in the sky
> Who laughed at this thing. (6)[7]

A poem in *War Is Kind* (1899) makes Crane's existential attitude even more clear:

> A man said to the universe:
> "Sir, I exist!"
> "However," replied the universe,
> "The fact has not created in me
> A sense of obligation." (96)

I am suggesting, of course, that the cruelty in the book is God's indifference to man.

When Jimmie is kicked home by his father from the heap of gravel, Mary Johnson waits brutal attendance first on Jimmie, then on the father. After she forces the father into the street—in much the same manner that she later forces Maggie into the street—she croons to the terrified children "about their 'poor mother' and 'yer fader, damn

7. The comment on *The Black Riders* is from a letter written by Crane to an editor of *Leslie's Weekly*, [November 1895]: in *Letters*, p. 78. The poems are identified by number in my edition of Crane's poetry. [Joseph Katz, *The Poems of Stephen Crane* (New York, 1966)—*Editor*.]

'is soul'" (1893, p. 20). When the father is next revealed, it is apparent that his soul is indeed damned: "During the evening he had been standing against a bar drinking whiskies and declaring to all comers, confidentially: 'My home reg'lar livin' hell! Damndes' place! Reg'lar hell! Why do I come an' drin' whisk' here thish way? 'Cause home reg'lar livin' hell!'" (1893, p. 25). The father has been caught in an adult version of the battle between Rum Alley and Devil's Row. The intention here is clear enough. There are really only three swear-words—out of the entire range available to Crane—used in the novel: "hell," "damn," and "Gawd" (or metonymic references to the Deity). By the process of repetition, these hells, damns, and pleas to God are turned through the funnel of the opening chapters, the confrontations with Christian respectability, and the references to fiends, imps, devils, and the other paraphernalia of repressive religiosity, from the level of simple swearing to the suggestion that the world of *Maggie* is a hell on earth. Despite their calls to "Gawd" these people are damned, for "Gawd" never responds.

In the *Maggie* of 1893, then, there is a coherent development of a world in which religion is inoperable. All of the characters are caught in the battle between Rum Alley and Devil's Row. In their excursions into the world of religion, they meet with frustration. There is Jimmie, who "never conceived a respect for the world, because he had begun with no idols that it had smashed. He clad his soul in armor by means of happening hilariously in at a mission church where a man composed his sermons of 'yous.' . . . Jimmie and a companion sat in a rear seat and commented upon the things that didn't concern them with all the freedom of English gentlemen. When they grew thirsty and went out their minds confused the speaker with Christ. . . . His companion said that if he should ever meet God he would ask for a million dollars and a bottle of beer" (1893, pp. 31–33). And there is Maggie, who "blossomed in a mud puddle. . . . None of the dirt of Rum Alley seemed to be in her veins. The philosophers up-stairs, down-stairs and on the same floor, puzzled over it" (1893, p. 41). After her affair with Pete is suddenly ended, she asks him: "But where kin I go?" . . . "Oh, go teh hell," cried he. He slammed the door furiously and returned, with an air of relief, to his respectability." (1893, p. 140). She walks aimlessly away, and her aimlessness is taken to be the attitude of the street-walker engaged in soliciting.

> Suddenly she came upon a stout gentleman in a silk hat and a chaste black coat, whose decorous row of buttons reached from his chin to his knees. The girl had heard of the Grace of God and she decided to approach this man.
>
> His beaming, chubby face was a picture of benevolence and kind-heartedness. His eyes shone good-will.

But as the girl timidly accosted him, he gave a convulsive movement and saved his respectability by a vigorous side-step. He did
not risk it to save a soul. For how was he to know that there was
a soul before him that needed saving? (1893, pp. 141–142)

Maggie's only relief from the hell within which she has lived is the
river, her final baptism.

In the 1896 edition the religious overtones are present but the
coherence is lost. No longer do the characters invoke in their speech
the suggestions of hell, damnation, and the futility of calling upon
God. When the father stands against the bar, declaiming to all, the
omission of two sentences that appeared in his 1893 declamation
serves to lower the level of applicability of the metaphor: "My home
reg'lar livin' h——l! Why do I come an' drin' whisk' here thish way?
'Cause home reg'lar livin' h——l!" (1896, p. 22). The omission seems
minor but it is not. The repetition of "Reg'lar hell!" and "Damndes'
place!" helped establish the pattern of the novel in 1893. In 1896, the
series of omissions—of which this is one example—makes the pattern
defective.

But if the world of *Maggie* is a "reg'lar hell," it is a hell with a
singular torment for its inhabitants. This is an aspect of the novel
which the excisions of 1896 almost completely removed. None of the
damned can communicate effectively on any but the most primitive
level. Pete, Maggie, Jimmie, Mary, the neighbors, all are inarticulate,
unable to express any but the most coarse emotions. This quality is
communicated through their language. When Pete asks Jimmie the
reason for the battle on the heap of gravel, he uses the question
with which he meets all situations: "What deh hell, Jimmie?" (1893,
p. 7). With the same phrase he orders beer (1893, p. 58), expresses
his astonishment at artifacts in the Museum (1893, p. 69), and coaxes
Maggie for a kiss:

"Naw, Pete," she said, "dat wasn't in it."
"Ah, what deh hell?" urged Pete.
The girl retreated nervously.
"Ah, what deh hell?" repeated he. (1893, p. 64)

His language must serve him equally for love, for admiration, for
utility, and for war. But in 1896, this quality is destroyed by the
"slight omissions." Pete now asks of the battle, "What's wrong wi'che,
Jimmie?" (1896, p. 5); of the waiter, "what's eatin' yeh?" (1896, p. 54);
of the "little jugs," "Aw!" (1896, p. 65); and coaxes Maggie with more
variety (if with less textual consistency on the part of the narrator):

"Ah, why wasn't it?" urged Pete.
The girl retreated nervously.
"Ah, go ahn!" repeated he. (1896, p. 60)

Of greater length, but possibly of less ultimate significance in the texture of the novel, is an omission first noted by R. W. Stallman.[8] Chapter XVII opens immediately after the "stout gentleman in a silk hat and a chaste black coat" has sidestepped Maggie. The scene is a "prominent side-street" in the theater district; the time is "several months after the last chapter." "A girl of the painted cohorts of the city went along the street" (1893, p. 144) meeting, as Mr. Stallman has outlined, "(1) a 'tall young man,' (2) a 'stout gentleman, with pompous and philanthropic whiskers,' (3) a 'belated man in business clothes,' (4) a 'young man in light overcoat and Derby hat,' (5) a 'labouring man,' (6) a boy with 'blond locks,' (7) a 'drunken man, reeling in her pathway,' (8) 'a man with blotched features,' (9) 'a ragged being with shifting, bloodshot eyes and grimy hands.'" In 1893, Maggie "exchanges words with the man 'with blotched features.' . . . '"Ah, there," said the girl. "I've got a date," said the man.' In the 1893 text, the 'ragged being with shifting, bloodshot [*sic*] eyes and grimey hands' utters a comment of no small sociological import: '"Ah, what deh hell? Tink I'm a millionaire?"' His retort—economically sound but aesthetically irrelevant—was spared from the second edition."

But in the 1893 edition, Mr. Stallman continued, is the "single saving discovery" that resulted from his collation. This was a tenth man Maggie met on her journey in 1893, one who is absent in 1896:

The 1893 edition:
She went into the blackness of the final block. The shutters of the tall buildings were closed like grim lips. The structures seemed to have eyet [*sic*] that looked over her, beyond her, at other things. Afar off the lights of the avenues glittered as if from an impossible distance. Street car bells jingled with a sound of merriment.

When almost to the river the girl saw a great figure. On going forward she perceived it to be a huge fat man in torn and greasy garments. His grey hair straggled down over his forehead. His small, bleared eyes, sparkling from amidst great rolls of red fat, swept eagerly over the girl's upturned face. He laughed, his brown, disordered teeth gleaming under a grey, grizzled moustache from which beer-drops dripped. His whole body gently quivered and shook like that of a dead jelly fish. Chuckling and leering, he followed the girl of the crimson legions.

At their feet the river appeared a deathly black hue. Some hidden factory sent up a yellow glare, that lit for a moment the waters lapping oilily against timbers. The varied sounds of life, made joyous by distance and seeming unapproachableness, came faintly and died away to a silence.

8. R. W. Stallman, "Stephen Crane's Revisions   *Literature,* XXVI (January 1955), 533–36.
of *Maggie: A Girl of the Streets," American*

The 1896 edition:

She went into the blackness of the final block. The shutters of the tall buildings were closed like grim lips. The structures seemed to have eyes that looked over them, beyond them, at other things. Afar off the lights of the avenues glittered as if from an impossible distance. Street-car bells jingled with a sound of merriment.

At the feet of the tall buildings appeared the deathly black hue of the river. Some hidden factory sent up a yellow glare, that lit for a moment the waters lapping oilily against timbers. The varied sounds of life, made joyous by distance and seeming unapproachableness, came faintly and died away to a silence.

Mr. Stallman continued: "The leering fat man represents a mockery of Maggie's plight, and his attribute of 'dead jelly fish' prepares for the death by drowning that occurs subsequent to Maggie's encountering him. That he is a 'dead jelly fish' anticipates, to put it another way, the death of Maggie. On both accounts, as I see it, this unreproduced passage from the 1893 edition of *Maggie* deserves to be incorporated into future editions on the grounds of its artistic relevance to what precedes and follows it."

William Gibson's objections to Mr. Stallman's conclusions are also worth reproducing exactly:

The portrait is exaggerated and Crane might well have cut it for this reason alone, but the omitted passage also makes the suggestion—perhaps an improvisation of the moment—that Maggie, whose face is "upturned" rather than averted, may accept this loathsome customer after refusals from nine other men. The reader is to be left in suspense for another chapter. Such a hinted reversal he came to see in revising was appropriate only to a writer of "the clever school" which he had abandoned; it was false and melodramatic because it did not naturally follow from the action of the chapter or from Maggie's state of mind so far as it is suggested, and it did not lead clearly to his predetermined end.

Crane's intention in changing his text at this point is further substantiated by his cutting two bits of dialogue which immediately precede. The first of these was:

"Ah, there" said the girl [to the man with "blotched features"].
"I've got a date," said the man.

The second, which is the reply only of a "ragged being with shifting bloodshot eyes and grimy hands," was:

"Ah, what deh hell? Tink I'm a millionaire?"

Thus in Crane's revised text, Maggie no longer solicits the last two men she meets, and the "huge fat man" whom she might accept has wholly disappeared; she has, plainly, made up her mind to drown herself. The ambiguity is gone and the logic of Crane's chapter and his whole story is improved, or remains unimpaired. One may of course question that logic on larger grounds, but if one accepts Maggie as a girl who "blossomed in a mud puddle" and was capable of deep shame and remorse, the last events of Crane's story in its final version seems inevitable.[9]

Actually, the exaggeration of "the great figure" was probably intentional. As Edwin H. Cady has suggested,[1] Chapter XVII telescopes Maggie's path of degradation. The journey is linear: Maggie travels from the higher class places of entertainment through to the squalid reaches of the city. Each of the men she meets on her journey represents a further stage in the descent. The journey can provide this telescoping because of the geography of New York City. The numbered streets in the vicinity of the theater district run east to west, from river to river; the avenues from north to south. One might begin at the theater district and walk down a numbered street to encounter representatives of each level on Maggie's descent. The grotesque great figure that she meets at the river certainly does suggest the end that she will meet. It is quite significant that this "dead jelly fish" scans her "upturned face" with eagerness, and follows her to the end. The suggestion that Maggie has upturned her face as a technique for soliciting the man is no improvisation. She learned that this was an invitation as soon as Pete told her to "go teh hell."

> Soon the girl discovered that if she walked with such apparent aimlessness, some men looked at her with calculating eyes. She quickened her step, frightened. As a protection, she adopted a demeanor of intentness as if going somewhere.
> After a time she left rattling avenues and passed between rows of houses with sterness [*sic*] and stolidity stamped upon their features. She hung her head for she felt their eyes grimly upon her. (1893, p. 141).

On her final journey, she turns what she had learned to protect her innocence into a method for selling it. It is a measure of the depth of her fall that she averts her face from all but boys, drunks, and the disreputable; this is the level to which she has descended. It is a further measure of that level for her offer to be rejected by all but the dead jelly fish of a man. She has reached her end. If one is to seek for a reason for this omission, one must go back to the circumstances behind the 1896 revision: Maggie's soliciting was simply too specific for the house of Appleton; her acceptance by the disgusting "great figure"—her only acceptance on the journey—the exchange with the man "with blotched features," and the financial comment of the "ragged being" make the fact of her prostitution inescapable. All went.

9. William M. Gibson, ed. *The Red Badge of Courage and Selected Prose and Poetry* (New York, 1956), pp. xvii–xviii.

1. Edwin H. Cady, *Stephen Crane* (New York, 1962), pp. 105–06.

Unfortunately, Crane's were not the only tamperings with the novel. "The proofs make me ill," he wrote Hitchcock. "Let somebody go over them—if you think best—and watch for bad grammatical form & bad spelling. I am too jaded with Maggie to be able to see it."[2] With this *carte blanche*, the Appleton editors proceeded to impose house styling on the novel.

To a degree, this editorial review was necessary. From the legend of the 1893 printing of *Maggie*, one would expect to find a textual record of a job undertaken by printers more interested in speed than in faithfully rendering the manuscript of a literary work. That record may be found in compositorial errors such as "oblgied" (p. 67), "had'n'" (p. 46), "boat" (p. 97), and "eyet" (p. 148). Since these clearly were not in Crane's manuscript, they should have been set to rights (all but "boat"—for "bote"—were corrected in 1896). Furthermore, orthographical errors produced by Crane were recorded in the 1893 *Maggie*. Such originals as "begrimmed hands" (p. 92), "missles" (pp. 100, 101), and "sterness" (p. 141) needed the attention that the Appleton men gave them. Unfortunately, they exceeded the demands of the situation.

Crane was a notorious speller, but he was working—albeit loosely—in an American tradition of orthography. The house styling of D. Appleton and Company, however, was based generally on the English tradition. When "valor" became "valour," "honor" was changed to "honour," and Crane's inconsistent "theatre" remained, *Maggie* became a strange mutant, an American novel on an American theme in a local dialect—in English orthography. But more important, the Appleton house styling interfered with Crane's stylistic effects. Crane was fond of compounds, and often used them as he did in *The Red Badge of Courage*, as epithets. The contrast between the epic language of the narrator and the exclamation of the warrior stresses the irony of Pete's entrance into the battle before the heap of gravel: "'Ah, what deh hell,' he said, and smote the deeply-engaged one on the back of the head." (1893, p. 6). Disjoint the compound and the Homeric epithet is lost. But the compound was disjuncted in 1896. Similarly, Crane frequently retained a hyphen in a compound to emphasize the elements of the compound: "Chieftain-like" (1893, p. 17) is not the same as "chieftainlike" (1896, p. 13) in referring to the stride of Mary Johnson. Occasionally, Crane created hyphenated compounds where none existed before: In 1893, the father smoked a "newly-ladened" pipe (p. 16); in 1896, it became a "newly ladened" pipe (p. 13). Still less forgivable, is the Appleton destruction of Crane's experiments in rendering dialect. Pete is describing for Jimmie and Maggie his encounter with a drunk:

2. Crane to Hitchcock [2 April 1896]; in *Letters*, p. 122.

"Well, deh blokie he says: 'T'hell wid it! I ain' lookin' for no scrap,' he says (See?) 'but' he says, 'I'm spectable cit'zen an' I wanna drink an' purtydamnsoon, too.' See? 'Deh hell,' I says. Like dat! 'Deh hell,' I says. See? 'Don' make no trouble,' I says. Like dat. 'Don' make no trouble.' See? Den deh mug he squared off an' said he was fine as silk wid his dukes (See?) an' he wanned a drink damnquick. Dat's what he said. See?" (1893, pp. 45–46)

In 1896, the rhythm is gone:

"Well, deh blokie he says: 'T' blazes wid it! I ain' lookin' for no scrap,' he says—see? 'but,' he says, 'I'm 'spectable cit'zen an' I wanna drink, an' quick, too.' See? 'Aw, goahn!' I says, like dat. 'Aw, goahn,' I says. See? 'Don' make no trouble,' I says, like dat. 'Don' make no trouble.' See? Den d'mug he squared off an' said he was fine as silk wid his dukes—see? an' he wanned a drink—quick. Dat's what he said. See?" (1896, p. 43)

But these are merely indicative of the more than three hundred variants between the 1893 and 1896 editions.

* * *

ERIC SOLOMON

[*Maggie* as a Three-Act Drama]†

* * *

The structure of the novel itself is that of a three-act drama with an appended conclusion; the technique is that of ironic counterpoint. A further parodic element appears in the characterization of the heroine, who is barely sketched and has only the faintest of emotions, in contrast to the stock heroine's catalogue of fading charms and hysterical passages. To be sure, Crane's controlling idea enforces this method. Maggie is a victim, bearing the brunt of others' lusts and hypocrisies. Everyone else seems to swirl around her. They are always in motion, while she is passively dragged in their currents until, at the end, she floats along the gutters of the city streets, impelled by the force of others' vigor—and then slips quietly into the waters of the East River, her stillness at last become permanent obscurity.

The first act encompasses three chapters and establishes the detail and color of slum life. Street urchins war against a stolid background: "From the window of an apartment house that uprose from amid squat ignorant stables . . . labourers, unloading a scow at a dock at

† From Chapter I, "Love and Death in the Slums," in *Stephen Crane: From Parody to* *Realism*, by Eric Solomon (Cambridge: Harvard University Press, 1966), pp. 35–44.

the river . . . The engineer of a passive tugboat . . . Over on the island a worm of yellow convicts came from the shadow of a grey ominous building and crawled slowly along the river's bank." Here are all the strands of the novel—the river, the indifferent observers, the street battles, the squalor of a great city. All the important characters are introduced in these first pages, the brawling Jimmie, the swaggering sixteen-year-old Pete (already muttering "Ah, what d' Hell"), the sullen, brutal, drunken father, and the savage, hysterical, massive mother. Maggie, "the heroine," is barely present. She is a product of the others' emotions, a tiny recipient of their blows, "a small pursued tigress." Her attempts to care for her infant brother, to soothe the mauled Jimmie, to help her intoxicated mother, all meet with the curses and cuffs of the hostile world that will eventually destroy her. The stereotypes of parental or brotherly love are ruthlessly reversed; emotions are as crude as the environment. "Long streamers of garments fluttered from fire-escapes. In all unhandy places there were buckets, brooms, rags and bottles. . . . A thousand odours of cooking food came forth to the street. The building quivered and creaked from the weight of humanity stamping about in its bowels." Crane carries the ugliness of his scene to naturalistic limits. The various fights are overdone, as is the passage where Jimmie, sent out for a can of beer by the mendacious old lady beggar who serves as a Hardyesque choral figure, is set upon by his father, robbed of the beer, and then hit on the head with the empty can. Yet the first act ends on a note of peace, Maggie quivering with fear, watching the prostrate, heaving body of her drunken mother. "Out at the window a florid moon was peering over dark roofs, and in the distance the waters of a river glimmered pallidly."

Act II starts with a chapter completely given over to a careful and fairly interesting character study of Jimmie, who is analyzed much more acutely than Maggie. Crane explains the brother's cynical temperament, his motivation, and indicates that, despite his sins, he is not totally depraved. "Nevertheless, he had, on a certain star-lit evening, said wonderingly and quite reverently, 'Deh moon looks like hell, don't it?'" All we learn of Maggie appears in a short paragraph saying that by some rare chance of alchemy, she grew up to be a pretty girl. Crane seems to be more interested in describing the mother's rise to fame in the police courts. The relationship between Maggie and Pete, the slum flower and the uncouth bartender, is ironic, too heavily so. Here Crane's parody gets out of hand. After Pete describes his brawls in filthy language, "Maggie perceived that here was the ideal man. Her dim thoughts were often searching for far-away lands where the little hills sing together in the morning. Under the trees of her dream-gardens there had always walked a lover." The counterpoint is thunderous, as in the next line where

Pete responds to the girl: "Say, Mag, I'm stuck on yer shape. It's outa sight." To Maggie, "He was a knight." The only motivation for Maggie's perverse romanticizing of this oaf, quixotically converting him from a brute into a knight, is the ugliness of her dark, dusty home that clouds her vision. Pete represents a way of escape to a world of finer quality, at least in her estimation, and when he does take her out, it is from a home once more crumbled by her mother. "The curtain at the window had been pulled by a heavy hand and hung by one tack, dangling to and fro in the draught through the cracks at the sash. . . . The remnants of a meal, ghastly, lay in a corner. Maggie's mother, stretched on the floor, blasphemed, and gave her daughter a bad name."

Pete takes Maggie to a dance hall that seems to her, in contrast to her home, to be the height of elegance. Crane lovingly describes this Bowery institution, the first of three to which Pete will take Maggie. This establishment is bourgeois, numbers only a very few tipsy men among the customers, and presents fairly wholesome entertainment. While Crane views the crowd with some irony, particularly during their warm response to an anti-British song, his description is mixed with affection. And from this respectable place Maggie emerges a respectable girl, refusing to kiss Pete. The second act of Maggie's little drama ends with an emphasis on her honesty and goodness. She seems impervious to her lover's temptations, even that of a life filled with visits to theaters and museums.

The final act commences immediately after the melodramatic play discussed earlier. In contrast to the events of the play, Maggie's descent into sin is casual. There is no villain and no heroine. Driven out of her home by a vilely intoxicated mother, accused of sin while still virginal, forced, as it were, into Pete's arms, Maggie goes—"falls." "'Git th' devil outa here.' Maggie went." Her "ruin," of course, must be handled obliquely, and Crane treats this problem of Victorian reticence with great skill. The old beggarwoman with relish tells Jimmie of Maggie's tears and pleas for the assurances of Pete's love, as if these were uproariously funny. "'Oh, gee, yes,' she called after him. She laughed a laugh that was like a prophetic croak." Crane's comedy is effective here; so much so that the pathos inherent in this traditional situation catches the reader unawares. The reader familiar with sentimental fiction must be amused at Jimmie's commonplace responses to the hackneyed situation of the fall from grace of the innocent daughter and sister—but with laughter comes also a measure of real pity for Maggie. This pathetic parody, this travesty of the mother and the son—far more sinful themselves than Maggie—lamenting over her damnation, calls to mind a similar mockery of parental affection in John Gay's *The Beggar's Opera*. The parody of bourgeois standards is superb. "'May she be cursed for ever!' she shrieked. 'May she eat nothin' but stones and deh dirt in deh street. May she sleep in deh gutter an' never see the sun shine again. D' bloomin'—.'" Their mutual hypocrisy and self-congratulation is as harrowing as it is comic, so that the scene that starts in parody ends in seriousness. This response, Crane says, is the blindness and hypocrisy of society—and he underlines the terrible lack of insight on the part of Maggie's relatives by calling forth the same rapid, unjust condemnation of the girl's character from the other slum dwellers who accuse Maggie of years of licentious behavior. The reader not only feels a sense of pity for Maggie, who, as usual, is not on the scene, but also attains a genuine sense of the absurdity of moral pretension. That these reprobates should judge Maggie on the basis of their loss of "respectability" because of her love affair is a cruel commentary on the ways of the social animal. Later Jimmie will be embarrassed because Maggie's new role "queers" him and his mother. As for the mother, she rapidly learns how to use her daughter's fall to excuse her own drinking habits. Yet the words of a cynical police judge help to sustain the needed antisentimental tone: "Mary, the records of this and other courts show that you are the mother of forty-two daughters who have been ruined." Jimmie, finally, is not as bad as his mother. He does have a brief flash of insight, as he did on the night when he noticed the moon's beauty. He is able to understand, for a moment, that Maggie might have been better had she known how. "However, he felt that he could not hold such a view. He threw it hastily aside."

A second dance-hall scene establishes the distance Maggie has fallen, although this device seems rather strained. Now the singer wears a scarlet gown and does a strip tease; more drinking takes place; Maggie is totally submissive and the object of stares, as if she were not a person, but a thing. "Grey-headed men, wonderfully pathetic in their dissipation, stared at her through clouds. Smooth-cheeked boys, some of them with faces of stone and mouths of sin, not nearly so pathetic as the grey heads, tried to find the girl's eyes in the smoke wreaths. Maggie considered she was not what they thought her." She is not, for she is merely a cipher, a victim; Maggie is not now, and she never has been, an identity. In a passage at the end of this section she shrinks from two painted women, harbingers of her future in which she must become what people—parents, brothers, lovers, society—make of her. The most delicate aspect of Crane's achievement in the novel is this facelessness of his heroine that at once makes his point about her victimization and allows him to crush her pitilessly without falling into sentiment or bathos. The ironic mode prevails.

The third dance-hall scene transpires three weeks after Maggie has left home. It is a wild scene, a Walpurgisnacht[1] of noise, alcohol, savage music. Maggie loses Pete to Nellie, an old flame, a more sophisticated woman of the (under) world. Pete goes off with Nellie as if Maggie does not exist. Nellie's date, "a mere boy," discusses this unfair action as if Maggie does not exist. He even condescends to offer to sleep with her: "You look bad longsider her, but by y'self ain't so bad. Have to do anyhow. Nell gone. O'ny you left"—as if Maggie does not exist.[2] And she *does* not exist. There are no persons or places available for her to use as a mirror for her identity. Her attempt to return home is thwarted by her mother's cruel and indignant rebuff, "Look ut her! Ain' she a dandy? An' she was so good as to come home teh her mudder, she was!" Jimmie echoes the mother's jeers. "Radiant virtue sat upon his brow, and his repelling hands expressed horror of contamination." The neighbors who rescue their children from Maggie's path echo again the taunts. Only the old beggar realizes that Maggie, if not a human, is at least a thing: "Well, come in an' stay wid me t'-night. I ain' got no moral standin'."

Since her family and her lover have failed to recognize her identity, Maggie must assume the only role available, the traditional role of fallen woman in which they have cast her. The third act ends with one of the finest passages of sustained power and restraint in all of Crane's writing, the chapter (XVII) that indirectly treats Maggie's death. Crane showed his realization of the importance of this chapter by paying more attention to it than to any other section of the novel when he revised his privately printed 1893 version for commercial publication in 1896. He describes a wet evening several months later; the Tenderloin[3] aglow with lights and people as the theaters empty; an atmosphere of pleasure and prosperity, of misery and horror. Then: "A girl of the painted cohorts of the city went along the street." She has no name, no identity, for, as we have seen, whatever individuality she had possessed was denied her by those who should have cared. Now the uncaring men whom she meets, in the cleverly foreshortened series of encounters that represents the complete pattern of her decline and fall, merely repeat the rejections by Maggie's clan. Down the chain of being she goes. A handsome young man in evening dress scorns her because she is neither new, Parisian, nor theatrical. A stout gentleman, a businessman, a city tough in a derby hat, a laboring man, a nervous boy—down the path of whoredom

1. A reference to Walpurgis Night, something nightmarish. [*Editor.*]
2. Crane often remarks on the difficult position of the woman who is loyal, whom the more brutal male often deserts. In "The 'Tenderloin' As It Really Is" (1896), he depicts a girl gallantly helping her man in a barroom brawl; in "Yen-Nock Bill and His Sweetheart" (1896), the faithful girl helps an opium-wrecked, pneumonia-wracked wretch back to health, and he later bullies, abuses, and rages at her.
3. A district in New York City (between 24th and 40th Streets, from Fifth Avenue to Seventh Avenue) where night life (theaters, bars, restaurants), vice, and crime flourished. [*Editor.*]

Maggie hurries. A drunk without cash, a man with blotched features (who, in a cut passage, says that he has another date), complete her attempts at assignations. (In the earlier version she meets one more, a revolting, obese pig of a man who follows her, chuckling. Crane probably removed this character because, no matter how disgusting, he at least *sees* Maggie, in order to follow her, and for Crane's purposes she is, metaphorically, invisible.) The section ends, and Maggie's life ends, as was inevitable from the beginning, and Crane returns to the water images of the novel's start. "At the feet of the tall buildings appeared the deathly black hue of the river. Some hidden factory sent up a yellow glare, that lit for a moment the waters lapping oilily against timbers. The varied sound of life, made joyous by distance and seeming unapproachableness, came faintly and died away to a silence."[4]

The novel does not end yet, even though Maggie's life is played out. Since she has never been a subject, only an object, the final section of the book rightfully concentrates on the responses to her death. Chapter XVIII is a long treatment of Pete's degradation. He is slobbering, incoherent, maudlin. He mumbles about his pure motives while a gang of whores, led by Nellie, hover about, only waiting for him to pass out so they can roll him. Too much like a woodcut of "The Corrupter Corrupted," the barroom scene is anticlimactic. The final section is also pictorial—"a woman sat at a table eating like a fat monk in a picture"—but wretchedly effective. To Jimmie's remark, "Mag's dead," her mother responds, "'Deh blazes she is!' . . . She continued her meal." Fitting as this sentence is as an obituary for Maggie, Crane must end the novel on the parodic note that has informed most of the work. The faked sentimentality of the mother's subsequent hysterical sobbing and her maudlin emphasis on the memory of Maggie's wearing worsted boots is an obscene—if pitiful—parody of mother love, of the familiar excesses of the fiction of domestic sentiment. With vocabulary "derived from mission churches" the mourners join the mother's laments. For all the satire, Crane's wake is effective in its own right. When the mother begs Jimmie to go and get Maggie so they can put the little boots on her feet, the narration transcends parody—without turning away from the form—and touches upon genuine anguish. And the book closes to the choir of old ladies begging the mother to forgive Maggie her sins. The final words highlight the novel's terms, as the mother weeps and screams in real pain. The parody remains operative; this

4. See Crane's bitter little "Legends," ii, *Bookman* (New York), 3 (1896), 206: "When the suicide arrived at the sky, the people there asked him, 'Why?' He replied: 'Because no one admired me.'" The water image often stands for Crane's idea of city death. In "A Street Scene in New York" (1894) a body on the pavement is like "a bit of debris sunk in this human ocean," a "human bit of wreckage at the bottom of the sea of men" (*The Work of Stephen Crane*, ed. Wilson Follett [New York: Alfred A. Knopf, 1925–27], XI, 191–92).

version of mourning is grotesque. The ironic tone is still present—
she should be begging Maggie's forgiveness. Somehow, through Stephen Crane's art, the scene attains a fine fictional effect: the Maggie
who never existed as a person in her own self, when alive, is passively
made into a figure to justify the society that has ignored her. "Oh,
yes, I'll fergive her! I'll fergive her!" As he rejects the society's cheap
lies, Crane's sympathy, controlled by his irony, becomes ours.

JAY MARTIN

[*Maggie* and Satire]†

* * *

Near the beginning of *The Red Badge of Courage* Crane has Henry
Fleming meditate on the possibility of heroism in the machine age:
"He had long despaired of witnessing a greeklike struggle. Such
would be no more, he had said. Men were better, or more timid.
Secular and religious education had effaced the throat-grappling
instinct." But in *Maggie* he had already proved that men in the
present are no less savage than in the past: they are rather worse
than better. Like Twain, Crane relied on the recapitulation theory
of human development for his irony. Apparently confirmed in the
'90s by embryological experiments, this theory suggested that the
human embryo, from the fertilization of the cell through to birth,
recapitulated all the stages of human development. Generalizing this
sequence, psychologists saw childhood as the savage stage of the
race. Thus, in the beginning of *Maggie*, Crane presents his young
savages engaged in a mock-Homeric battle—one, however, totally
devoid of the Homeric virtues.[1] Like the heroes before Troy, Jimmie
throws stones in defense of his gravel heap. He too delivers great
war-crys—but they are only curses. He too fights for honor—but
only for that of Rum Alley against the equally grotesque Devil's
Row. His opponents are "barbaric," "true assassins"—yet they are
only the children of the slum. The Achilles who comes to Jimmie's
aid, called Pete, wears a "chronic sneer" and tilts his cigar "at an
angle of defiance" as proofs of his manhood. Entering the conflict
with his battle oath—"Ah, what d' hell,"—he "smites" (in the cliché
of chivalry) a boy on the *back* of the head. All this is to say that in
Maggie Crane superimposes a vague memory of the heroic past upon

† From *Harvests of Change: American Literature 1865–1914*, by Jay Martin (Englewood Cliffs,
New Jersey: Prentice-Hall, 1967), pp. 57–59.
1. On the influence of Homer on Stephen Crane,
see Warren D. Anderson, "Homer and Stephen

Crane." *Nineteenth-Century Fiction*, XIX (June
1964), 77–86; and Robert Dusenbery, "The Homeric Mood in the 'Red Badge of Courage,'"
Pacific Coast Philology, III (April 1968), 31–37.
[*Editor.*]

210 · *Jay Martin*

a savage present. The heroic world has given way to the slums. This novel is his *Maggie Agonistes*.

Crane's modern world, then—in *Maggie* no less than in *The Red Badge*—is ruled by war. A sense of fear and trembling, the stunned receptivity of the soldier, hangs over it. Crane's irony, however, cuts both ways. By recalling the Homeric world he reveals us to ourselves as savage and cowardly. But at the same time, his satire, like most forceful satire, criticizes the romance and chivalry of his heroic world as well. His vision is contrary—set against itself. He is comfortable with neither the ideal nor the real, but alienated from both. The conventional ideal that he uses to illustrate the decline of modern man he must, therefore, expose as hopelessly idealistic. In *Maggie*, then, he parallels his mock-heroic satire against the slum world with three other ironically treated themes: (1) the mock-chivalric satire on the courtly lover; (2) the mock-sentimental satire on the happy American family; and (3) the mock-genteel satire on the angelic-child figure.

Pete, of course, with his elaborately "oiled bang," his checkered pants, his "red puff tie," and his patent leather shoes, is a grotesque mockery of the courtier. He had been the warrior; soon he becomes the lover. Helen (Maggie) becomes Guinevere. Pete's manners are now ridiculously sophisticated: he surveys the world with "valor and contempt," and pronounces his judgment upon it. "Rats!" he says gloriously. He had, after all, "seen everything." Maggie thinks him "a very 'elegant' bartender"—a detail that Dreiser would borrow to attribute to Hurstwood. To Maggie, Pete looks "aristocratic," "as if he might soil." In short, he is her "ideal man." Ironically, Crane spells out the tragedy of the "Ragged Girl" about which Howells had wanted to write a happy novel.[2] Although Maggie is uncontaminated by her environment, she is deficient in knowledge. And the very innocence which allows her to flourish into womanhood is then the reason for her betrayal. Although Pete can court no more elegantly than to announce, "Say Mag, I'm stuck on yer shape. It's outa sight," and to boast of his victories in street fights like the childish courtiers in *A Connecticut Yankee*, still, in her innocence, Maggie concludes: "He was a knight."

Crane develops his other mock-conventional themes in a similar fashion. The theme of the happy American family had been popularized by several well known writers, among them Louisa May Alcott, in *Little Women* (1868), *Little Men* (1871), and *Jo's Boys* (1886). In this convention, the family usually is threatened with not

2. This allusion is in Stephen Crane, "Fears Realists Must Wait: An Interesting Talk with William Dean Howells," *New York Times*, October 28, 1894, p. 20; and reprinted in *The Works of Stephen Crane*, ed. Fredson Bowers (Charlottesville: The University Press of Virginia, 1973), VIII, pp. 635–38. [*Editor*.]

only a series of minor disappointments, but also with dissolution. At the end, however, the family is joyfully unified. This literary convention, to be sure, had strong emotional appeal in an America that was undergoing a significant breakdown in family relations. With transportation making all parts of the country more accessible and familiar, with the cities draining the countryside of its sons, the family dissolved. The year after *Maggie* appeared, tramp armies marched across the country. The family was obviously breaking down. Howells, Twain, Dreiser, Norris, Edith Wharton, Crane—all felt strong compulsions to reject their fathers.

Refusing to allow his novels to compensate for life's losses, Crane, in *Maggie*, violently shatters the literary convention of the happy family. Maggie's mother is hardly more than an animal, characterized by red fists, tossing hair, curses, massive shoulders, huge arms, immense hands, grunts or screams of hatred, and muddled sentiments. Her home is always spoken of as "gruesome." Crane ironically concludes this theme by making the half-witted mother wish hysterically to possess Maggie's corpse so that she might put her baby booties on her adult feet. Thus Crane symbolizes the foolish hope for miracles in the conventional theme. For Maggie there is *no* redemption. Her betrayed adulthood can never be renewed. As Jimmie says to her mother, "Dey [the booties] won't fit her now, yeh fool."

Crane's satire on the innocent-eye theme of childhood occupies the early part of the story and is an aspect of his narrative of Maggie's growth to maturity. Several books portraying childhood as ways of reviving the past had appeared after the war—from Aldrich's *The Story of a Bad Boy* (1870) to Twain's *Huckleberry Finn* (1885). These had formed the convention of the child making mischief because of his romantic adventurousness. Tom and Becky lost in the cave, the discovery of buried treasure, and the discovery of Injun Joe are all really illustrations of how appealingly devilish the American Boy was. Add to this the book that was sensationally popular shortly before *Maggie* appeared, Frances Hodgson Burnett's *Little Lord Fauntleroy* (1886). Crane was so violently antagonized by this book that he refused to attend a dinner at which Mrs. Burnett was present. Beginning with *Maggie*, Crane satirized the genteel child, writing a series of tales about Maggie's young brother, Tommie, including two brilliant ones, *An Ominous Baby* and *A Dark Brown Dog*, about the savage cunning of a child. And even as late as his *Whilomville Stories* (1900)—describing his own youth and insisting, by his title, that this was a stage of existence to which he could never return—he portrayed brilliantly a diabolical young girl called the "angel-child."

✻ ✻ ✻

DONALD B. GIBSON

[The Flawed *Maggie*]†

* * *

Crane's intention in *Maggie, A Girl of the Streets* was neither to support nor to refute Darwinism as he understood it. Rather, his central concern was in railing against the nature of things, raging against the universe which Darwin describes, but raging against it as one might rage against the daily rising of the sun. He accepted the Darwinian scheme so far as he understood it, with no question as to its truth or its adequacy for defining the life situation.[1]

Maggie manifests a considerable change in attitude from that apparent in *The Sullivan County Sketches*. In the earlier work there is at least the possibility of free action, action resulting from a decision on the part of a character. But in *Maggie* no such possibility exists. Even if we decide that the little man does not actually perform heroic action, we yet must grant that he is not determined in his actions. No one in *Maggie* is free.[2]

The hypothesis of Darwin, unless qualified, leads the artist into a morass of inconsistency and contradiction, a morass from which young Stephen Crane was unable to extract himself. *Maggie*, Crane inscribed in one copy of the book, ". . . tries to show that environment is a tremendous thing and shapes lives regardless."[3] Crane carries this idea to its extreme by making his characters "nothing but" animals, apparently not recognizing that in so doing he relinquishes his prerogative as author to judge them. If Maggie is simply a victim of her environment, then so are all of the other characters and so is the rest of society. Nobody is to blame for anything and we cannot help but cringe when Crane attempts with irony to condemn Maggie's fellow victims.

If we consider the matter closely enough, then it becomes obvious that on the ideational level the tale is entirely inadequate. For not only has Crane surrendered his right to judge, he has likewise denied

† From Chapter II, "Crane Among the Darwinians," in *The Fiction of Stephen Crane*, by Donald B. Gibson (Carbondale and Edwardsville: Southern Illinois University Press, 1968), pp. 26–34.

1. This view is supported by David Fitelson in "Stephen Crane's *Maggie* and Darwinism," *American Quarterly*, XVI (Summer 1964), 182–94. This article as well as other major articles on *Maggie* is reprinted in Maurice Bassan, ed., *Stephen Crane's Maggie: Text and Context* (San Francisco, 1966). [See Fitelson's essay, reprinted above—*Editor*.]

2. Edward Garnett in *Friday Nights, Literary Criticism and Appreciation* (New York, 1922): "The Bowery inhabitants, as we, can be nothing other than what they are; their human nature responds inexorably to their brutal environment," p. 214. [The "little man" appears in *The Sullivan County Sketches—Editor*.]

3. Crane made the same essential inscription in several copies of the book. See R. W. Stallman and Lillian Gilkes, eds., *Stephen Crane: Letters* (New York, 1960), Nos. 18 (p. 14) and 58 (p. 49). See also 14 n. [Hereafter *Letters—Editor*.]

this right to the reader. Unless the reader is sufficiently wary, then he too will fall into the inconsistency inherent in the conception of the book. He will find himself judging characters who have absolutely no responsibility for their shortcomings nor, indeed, for any virtues that they might have.

It should be recognized in all fairness that Crane did not intend that we examine too closely the implications of his premises. Continuing the inscription cited above, Crane wrote, "If one proves that theory [the influence of environment upon the individual], one makes room in heaven for all sorts of souls, notably an occasional street girl, who are not confidently expected to be there by many excellent people." Crane obviously intended to elicit sympathy for Maggie, though at the expense of the other characters in the novel who, all together, represent the whole of society. The inadequacy of the basic conception of the tale becomes even more apparent when we note that the terms of Crane's statement, without reservation, tell us that there is room in heaven not only for Maggie, but for her lover, Pete, her brother, Jimmie, and her reprehensible, repugnant, disgusting mother, Mrs. Johnson. But Crane, becoming subject to the very same shortcoming which he criticizes in others, is not willing to "make room in heaven" (whatever that means) for the other characters. Hence, the disparity occurring between his achievement and his intention in *Maggie* emerges when we compare his statement of intention with his actual accomplishment. The inconsistency indicated by such a comparison, and the ramifications of the basic error in conception reveal in large measure why the book is less than a first-rate work of art.

The severe irony with which the characters are treated exists because Crane renders judgment of his characters through that means though he cannot legitimately do so, at least according to his initial assumptions. But even if we overlook the contradiction, we can see without great difficulty that Crane's irony betrays him in other ways. Because the characters, Maggie included, are treated with such devastating irony, the reader is likely to find it difficult to involve his sympathies with anyone in the story.[4] Aside from Maggie herself there is only one other character in the story who could conceivably elicit the least bit of sympathy, Jimmie, Maggie's brother. From time to time he has a flickering awareness that he should not judge Maggie so harshly. But such awareness only flickers weakly, so weakly in fact that when Maggie returns home he joins Mrs. Johnson in driving her from the apartment. "'Well, now, yer a t'ing, ain' yeh?' he said, his lips curling in scorn. Radiant virtue sat upon his brow, and his

4. Compare Walter Sutton, "Pity and Fear in 'The Blue Hotel,'" *American Quarterly*, IV (Spring 1952), 76. "The very choice of theme and situation indicates an attitude of protest against social injustice which must have sprung from compassion," p. 77. [See footnotes 6 and 7 below—*Editor.*]

repelling hands expressed horror of contamination."[5] Ironically—the irony here is too explicit to be a reasonable approximation of the illusion of reality, a matter to be discussed later—Jimmie has only a few moments before told Hattie, a girl who bears the same relationship to him that Maggie bears to Pete, "Oh, go teh blazes!" Jimmie cannot engage our sympathies for long.

In responding positively to Maggie, we are likely to be responding to an idea rather than to a seemingly live character.[6] Since Maggie is so deficient in knowledge, intelligence, judgment, sensibility, even common sense, she has only her simplicity to recommend her to us. She is beautiful we are told, but we never *see* her beauty; she is supposedly kind, but since we never see any evidence of her kindness except in her youth, there is no reason to believe that she is any more kind than the vegetable which is incapable of either good or evil. What we are intended to see is the most simple and innocent humanity at the mercy of predatory beasts. What reader with the least reading experience can become seriously involved with a conflict between these cruel, vicious, animalistic people and Maggie, who "blossomed in a mud-puddle," and had "none of the dirt of Rum Alley . . . in her veins"? The sympathy we have for Maggie is little more than that which we could have for *any* helpless person or animal overwhelmed by devastating forces. Crane elicits a stock response. In treating Maggie with such irony—especially in dwelling on her completely inadequate ability to cope with the simplest life problems—he compounds his failure to create a sympathetic character. He might have shown us her deficiencies without the irony, without seeming himself to scorn her.[7]

But Crane scorned her because he found it impossible to like any of the characters in his work very well. In forgetting through the course of the work that his statement, ". . . environment is a tremendous thing and frequently shapes lives regardless" applies to everyone in the book, he reverted to the feelings that prompted a sentiment he expressed in a letter in 1896, "The root of bowery life is a sort of cowardice."[8] What has seemed to some critics to be

5. This and subsequent quotations from *Maggie* are taken from William Gibson's edition of *The Red Badge of Courage and Selected Prose and Poetry* (New York, 1960). [Gibson's edition reprints the 1896 *Maggie*—Editor.]

6. Maxwell Geismar agrees: Maggie "is a curiously wooden, graceless and unsympathetic figure when compared with Carrie Meeber or even Trina of *McTeague*." See his *Rebels and Ancestors* (Boston, 1953), p. 77. William T. Lenehan also agrees in "The Failure of Naturalistic Techniques in Stephen Crane's *Maggie*," Bassan, pp. 166–73. [See footnote 1 for Bassan reference. Carrie Meeber is from *Sister Carrie*—Editor.]

7. Cf. Oscar Cargill's statement, "He [Crane] is wholly devoid of any sympathy for Maggie, but

this comes not from a scientific detachment, rather from ignorance." *Intellectual America* (New York, 1941), p. 85.

8. In the same letter Crane writes, "A person who thinks himself superior to the rest of us because he has no job and no pride and no clean clothes is as badly conceited as Lillian Russell." *Letters*, p. 133. Crane's lack of sympathy for slum dwellers is likewise indicated in one of his war dispatches sent from Cuba during the Spanish American War, "Hunger Has Made Cubans Fatalists": "Everyone knows that the kind of sympathetic charity which loves to be thanked is often grievously disappointed and wounded in tenement districts, where people often accept gifts as if their own property had turned up after a short

"objectivity" or "ironic detachment" is not that at all, but loathing and disgust for the depraved characters of whom he writes.[9]

Crane's attitude toward his characters created a conflict between what he wanted to say in *Maggie* and what he found himself saying through the course of the work. His irony betrayed him to the extent that Maggie herself appeared just as crude and unattractive as the other characters. Crane, either consciously or unconsciously, dealt with this problem in a rather simple way. In order to differentiate Maggie from the other characters in the story he gradually withdrew her from participation in the events of the narrative. Her character is not revealed in action as are the characters of the other major participants; she seldom speaks directly as do others. Between the eighth chapter and the last, Chapter XIX, Maggie utters only two sentences, "Dis is outa sight!" (Chapter VIII) and "I'm going home" (Chapter XIV), which she repeats once. She leaves home only when coerced by Pete or ordered out by her mother. Even when she commits suicide, her only act of any consequence in the story, she seems to be in a somnambulate state, hovering somewhere above the plot, not in the same context as the other characters. Maggie's position in the novel is a direct result of the inconsistency noted above: since there is no "room in heaven" for the other characters, Maggie must be differentiated from them, though Crane paid the price of committing the same error that those who wouldn't admit Maggie to heaven committed.

It is questionable whether the sustained irony of *Maggie* is as successful as it might have been at the hands of a more experienced Crane. This question too points back toward the problem of the basic conception of the novel. When the irony here is most artificial, most contrived, it seems to intend to point out the baseness of the characters, to censure them further for being the result of their environment. Usually the irony is overdone to the extent that it becomes unintentionally humorous, destroying the illusion of reality. Such is the case when Mrs. Johnson says of Maggie: "Ah, who would t'ink such a bad girl could grow up in our family, Jimmie, me son," and when the mother is outraged by Jimmie's suggestion that Maggie be returned home: "What! Let 'er come an' sleep under deh same roof wid her mudder agin? . . . Little did I t'ink when yehs was a

---

absence." R. W. Stallman and E. R. Hagemann, *The War Dispatches of Stephen Crane* (New York, 1964), p. 163.

William Graham Sumner stated this attitude in more extreme terms: "The weak who constantly arouse the pity of humanitarians and philanthropists are the shiftless, the imprudent, the negligent, the impractical, and the inefficient, or they are the idle, the intemperate, the extravagant, and the vicious." "The Forgotten Man," *The Forgotten Man and Other Essays by William Graham Sumner* (New Haven, 1919), p. 475.

9. Berryman (John Berryman, *Stephen Crane* [New York, 1950]—*Editor*) disagrees saying that in no American work "had the author remained so persistently invisible behind his creation," p. 59. Cf. Granville Hicks, *The Great Tradition* (New York, 1933), p. 161. Hicks observes that Crane feels less than kind toward Maggie.

baby playin' about me feet dat ye'd grow up teh say sech a t'ing teh yer mudder—yer own mudder." It is a bit difficult to believe that the hypocritical Mrs. Johnson would likely muster such false sentiments. Likewise the final scene where Mrs. Johnson learns of Maggie's death is hardly credible and very humorous.

> "Well," said he, "Mag's dead."
> "What?" said the woman, her mouth filled with bread.
> "Mag's dead," repeated the man.
> "Deh blazes she is!" said the woman. She continued her meal. When she finished her coffee she began to weep.

Though many of the problems of style in *Maggie* are attributable to the inexperience of the author, several of the stylistic deficiencies are directly traceable to the problem of point of view, which is simply another way of referring to the imperfection of the original conception of the story. The great gulf separating the language of the Bowery characters from that of Crane reflects the author's lack of sympathetic involvement with his people. Crane's preference for words of a learned character and for overly formal sentence structure suggests condescension toward the Bowery inhabitants, the distance between the two levels of usage being a measure of the distance between author and subject.

> There came a time, however, when the young men of the vicinity said, "Dat Johnson goil is a putty good looker." About this period her brother remarked to her: "Mag, I'll tell yeh dis! See? Yeh've eeder got t' go on d' toif er go t' work!" Whereupon she went to work, having the feminine aversion to the alternative.

At best Crane's style in *Maggie* is uneven. All too often his meaning is obscured by tortured sentence structure or by vague, imprecise diction. At worst his self-conscious and tortured diction abuses the language, distorting whatever thought he intended to convey.

> The quiet stranger had sprawled very pyrotechnically out on the sidewalk.

> He had an evening dress, a moustache, a chrysanthemum, and a look of *ennui*, all of which he kept carefully under his eye.

> There was given to him the charge of a painstaking pair of horses and a large rattling truck.

> At last the father pushed a door, and they entered a lighted room in which a large woman was rampant.

> He had been in quite a number of miscellaneous fights, and in some general barroom rows that had become known to the police.   ("miscellaneous"?)

There followed in the wake of missiles and fists some unknown prayers, perhaps for death.   ("unknown"?)

From a window of an apartment house that uprose from amid squat ignorant stables there leaned a curious woman.   (What are "ignorant" stables?)

She wore no jewelry and was painted with no apparent paint.   (Was she painted or not?)

Anyone who has paid attention to Crane's style in *Maggie* should be able to recall that there are many other examples of stylistic infelicity which might have been selected. Likewise there are instances in which Crane's sentences are ambiguous, violate common logic, or are unclear because their meaning is incomplete. Such is the case when Crane tells us that ". . . Maggie blossomed in a mud-puddle. She grew to be a most rare and wonderful production of a tenement district, a pretty girl." Surely there is no correlation between social environment and the physical structure of one's face and body. Why is it odd that a pretty girl should be produced in a tenement district? Crane also tells us that Maggie worked ". . . turning out collars with a name which might have been noted for its irrelevancy to anything connected with collars." Aside from the fact that this statement is not relevant to its context or to the context of the novel, it suggests that there should necessarily be some relationship between collars and their brand names. Even if the name of the collar is entirely unrelated to the collar itself, what is the point?

Another stylistic problem in *Maggie* involves the metaphors and similes throughout the book. As is the case with much of the diction, the figures of speech represent attempts on Crane's part to get beyond the barriers of traditional literary style and though sometimes his unusual comparisons are effective, most often they seem merely peculiar and do not go very far in conveying a clear, sharp image or in revealing a new or more meaningful way of seeing objects. Usually when Crane's metaphors fail in *Maggie* it is because the vehicle is not within the realm of ordinary experience and thus the reader finds it difficult to establish the relationship between tenor and vehicle. When he does establish the relationship, it is only after having gone through much effort, having created for himself an image which Crane only suggests.

His wan features looked like those of a tiny insane demon.   (Who has seen "a tiny insane demon"?)

The babe sat on the floor watching the scene, his face in contortions like that of a woman at a tragedy.   (Do women contort their faces at tragedies more so than men? If so, in what way do they contort their faces?)

Her bare red arms were thrown out above her head in an attitude of exhaustion, something, mayhap like that of a sated villain.   ("Sated" with what?)

Pete at intervals gave vent to low, labored hisses that sounded like a desire to kill.   (What does the desire to kill sound like?)

A baby falling down in front of the door wrenched a scream like that of a wounded animal from its mother.   (Even if wounded animals scream, certainly various ones scream differently.)

Overwhelmed by a spasm of drunken adoration, he drew two or three bills from his pocket and, with the trembling fingers of an offering priest, laid them on the table before the woman.   (Do the offering fingers of priests often tremble?)

In a room a woman sat at a table eating like a fat monk in a picture.   (Why "in a picture"? Is this a religious figure or a monkey?)

Probably many of these figures were quite meaningful to Crane; he likely knew very well what he meant when he compared a woman eating to "a fat monk in a picture." But whatever response the figure aroused in him remained private, for I doubt that the image of a fat monk in a picture has very particularized meaning to most people.

* * *

ARNO KARLEN

[Lapses and Craft in Crane's *Maggie*†]

* * *

In his earliest fiction, Crane already showed his gifts and weaknesses clearly. He had a brilliant, unorthodox ear for far-flung analogies. Friends recorded that he spoke of an old egg having a "snarling smell," and that he called *A Connecticut Yankee* "as inappropriate as a drunken bride." In the opening pages of his short first novel, *Maggie*, he produced such unpredictable beauties as:

Over on the island a worm of yellow convicts came from the shadow of a gray ominous building and crawled slowly along the river's bank.

The little boy ran to the halls, shrieking like a monk in an earthquake.

† From "The Craft of Stephen Crane," *The Georgia Review*, XXVIII (Fall 1974), 473–77.

He became a young man of leather. He lived some red years without laboring.

Within the same pages, Crane produced such strained and inaccurate sentences as:

Blows dealt in the fight were enlarged to catapultian power.

The broken furniture, the grimy walls . . . appeared before her and began to take on a potential aspect.

In front of the gruesome doorway he met a lurching figure.

Crane could not resist modifiers. Some were brilliant, some appalling—poor verbal shortcuts and hasty guesses—but almost always there were too many:

He glanced over into the vacant lot in which the little raving boys from Devil's Row seethed about the shrieking and tearful child from Rum Alley.

As the sullen-eyed man, followed by the blood-covered boy, drew near, the little girl burst into reproachful cries.

Maggie also shows a weakness for words that tell instead of show—dead wood of the "nice" and "bad" variety. When Crane didn't have something inspired, he used whatever was handy, especially superlatives. The words "lurid," "gruesome," "formidable," "tremendous," "furious," crowd the tumid sentences. Desperate to convince, Crane produced an atmosphere of grotesquerie in which everything was bigger than life, like a violent shadow play. No one speaks in the opening pages of *Maggie*; everyone shouts, bellows, roars. Yet amid all this *grand guignol*[1] lie sentences that are little masterpieces of the most subtle and difficult prose effects—rhythm, assonance, alliteration—and full of premeditated irony or menacing beauty:

He paced placidly along with the applewood emblem of serenity clenched between his teeth.

Above all things he despised obvious Christians and ciphers with the chrysanthemums of aristocracy in their buttonholes.

The building quivered and creaked from the weight of humanity stamping about in its bowels.

Such beautiful rhythms, though, are often succeeded by clanking monotony, especially when several sentences in a row have the same structure, length, and cadence:

1. Allusion to a Parisian theater whose productions were basically melodramatic. [*Editor.*]

The urchin raised his voice in defiance to his parent, and continued his attacks. The babe bawled tremendously, protesting with great violence. During his sister's hasty maneuver, he was dragged by the arm.

Crane often strung together passive verbs and past tenses that leave the verb "to be" droning in one's ear:

He was throwing stones at howling urchins from Devil's Row, who were circling madly about the heap and pelting him. His infantile countenance was livid with the fury of battle. His small body was writhing in the delivery of oaths.

Sometimes the references and time sequence are confusingly tangled:

Once, when a lady had dropped her purse on the sidewalk, the gnarled woman had grabbed it and smuggled it with great dexterity beneath her cloak. When she was arrested she had cursed the lady into a partial swoon, and with her aged limbs, twisted from rheumatism, had kicked the breath out of a huge policeman whose conduct upon that occasion she referred to when she said, "The police, damn 'em!"

And then all the glories and all the fumbling combine in one long sentence:

Above the muffled roar of conversation, the dismal wailing of babies at night, the thumping of feet in unseen corridors and rooms, and the sound of varied hoarse shoutings in the street and the rattling of wheels over cobbles, they heard the screams of the child and the roars of the mother die away to a feeble moaning and a subdued bass muttering.

Crane's writing always suffered from occasional lapses into wooden clumsiness or rigidity, and often the cause was pompous diction. The Naturalists inherited more from their Romantic forebears than they could admit. The intrigue with local color, dialect, and street language was an extension of Romantic exoticism; the taste for the strange, the brutal, the frankly sexual, moved from Gipsy camps and South Sea islands to the industrial slums. The Goncourt brothers,[2] students of Oriental art and eighteenth-century courtesans, went walking the poor quarters of Paris to collect details of squalor, vulgarity, and violence, then went home to polish their notes with *frissons*[3] not only of compassion but of fascinated disgust. The works of many great Naturalists, including Crane's, abound with sentimentality and vague, passionate effusions. Their very unconcern about

2. French novelists who used close documentation, as in *Germinie Lacerteux* (1865), and were considered precursors of Zola's scientific naturalism. [*Editor.*]

3. Shivers, shudders. [*Editor.*]

techniques was Romantic, an assumption that powerful feelings and deep truths could be conveyed by the brute force of their being, almost despite craft. After all, it was a Romantic who said, long before Zola or Howells, that truth is beauty, beauty truth.[4]

When one word mars in mid-course the suppleness and glitter of one of Crane's sentences, the reason is often that the word is self-consciously literary. Changing the highfalutin word to idiomatic speech rescues the sentence, as in these parenthetical substitutions in sentences from *Maggie*:

> As he neared the spot where the little boys strove (fought), he regarded them listlessly.

> His infantile countenance (childish face) was livid with the fury of battle.

> The old woman was a gnarled and leathery personage (was gnarled and leathery). . . .

Perhaps another reason for this inflated diction was Crane's desire to keep a good Naturalist's scientific distance from his subject. The result of such a tone tends to be the sort of stuff social scientists indulge in so often—saying "overt expressions of interpersonal attitudes in societal interaction" when they mean "the way people act."

But Crane sometimes used diffidence and high diction to achieve some of his finest effects. His pose of neutrality and his polysyllables could be tools of irony, mocking the trivial by forcing it into full-dress costume. Again, from *Maggie*:

> He sat on the table of the Johnson home, and dangled his checked legs with an enticing nonchalance. His hair was curled down over his forehead in an oiled bang. His pugged nose seemed to revolt from contact with a bristling moustache of short, wire-like hairs. His blue double-breasted coat, edged with black braid, was buttoned close to a red puff tie, and his patent leather shoes looked like weapons.

> His mannerisms stamped him as a man who had a correct sense of his personal superiority. There were valor and contempt for circumstances in the glance of his eye. He waved his hands like a man of the world who dismisses religion and philosophy, and says "Rats." He had certainly seen everything, and with each curl of his lip he declared that it amounted to nothing. Maggie thought he must be a very "elegant" bartender.

One character after another becomes pathetically comical when Crane presents him with dispassionate, formal voice. The word "reverent" may have never held as much vitriol and pathos as in the last

---

4. A reference to John Keats (1795–1821) and to his poem "Ode on a Grecian Urn." [*Editor*.]

sentence of the chapter devoted to Maggie's brother Jimmie, the truck driver who "menaced mankind at the intersections of streets."

Nevertheless, he had, on a certain star-lit evening, said wonderingly and quite reverently, "Deh moon looks like hell, don't it?"

Finally, *Maggie* leaves a memory of brilliant effects and glaring failures jumbled together, of heavy-handed irony, telegraphed punches, exquisite humor, melodrama, and verbal audacity. Crane begins fortissimo[5] and then keeps straining for a crescendo, confusing volume with the power of harmony. But you can get no louder than your loudest. Typically, when Crane had a chance to revise *Maggie* for a second edition, he hesitated on the grounds that improving it on a second try was "dishonest." As usual he confused sincerity and craft.

* * *

KATHERINE G. SIMONEAUX

Color Imagery in Crane's *Maggie: A Girl of the Streets*†

Color imagery is an important part of Stephen Crane's impressionistic writing. His unusual use of color was noted by his contemporaries and continues today to fascinate and sometimes to frustrate his readers. Using color with great variety, Crane associates it with his characters, with these characters' hopes and fears, and with aspects of the environment he creates. His color imagery contributes forcefully to his ideology and the themes in his work. *Maggie: A Girl of the Streets* strongly reflects Crane's deterministic, fatalistic philosophy which is evident in its themes. One of the important themes in the novel is man's isolation not only from an unsympathetic society but from nature which is indifferent to his problems. The colors used, usually strong and pure, heighten the emotions that surround the characters, their environment, and their problems.

The predominant color used in *Maggie* is red, followed by black, yellow, and blue. It is interesting to note that while most of the colors used are pure and strong, Crane *suggests* color in such expressions as "many-hued," "happy-hued," and "painted"; words like "wan," "blackness," and "glittering" reveal his awareness of the importance of light and shadows.

A tabulation of color-words in *Maggie* is as follows:

RED: Sub-total 29
    (Red 18, Flaming Scarlet, Flame-colored 5, Crimson
    3, Florid 1, Pink 1, Rose tinted 1)
BLACK: Sub-total 23
    (Black 13, Darkness, Shadows, Blackness 10)
YELLOW: Sub-total 16
    (Yellow 10, Golden 2, Gilt 2, Straw Colored 1, Brass
    1)
BLUE: Sub-total 7
GRAY: Sub-total 7
    (Gray 6, Mouse colored 1)
WHITE: Sub-total 7
    (White 4, Wan, Pale 3)
GREEN: Sub-total 5
    (Green 4, Olive 1)
BROWN: Sub-total 3
    (Brown 1, Tan 1, Bronze 1)
PURPLE: Sub-total 1
LIVID: Sub-total 1
LIGHT: Sub-total 11
    (Light, Dawn, Glare, Star-lit, Sun-light, Glittering
    11)
PAINTED, Many-hued, Happy-hued: Sub-total 3
    TOTAL .... 113[1]

Although color is used symbolically, much of it is used realistically and some of it is used realistically with symbolic overtones. These uses of color are evident in *The Red Badge of Courage*[2] and most of Crane's work.

Color images surround each character in *Maggie*. It is significant that Crane uses red sparingly in the images surrounding Maggie although the color is traditionally associated with prostitutes. The reader's introduction to Maggie is: "A small ragged girl dragged a red, bawling infant along the crowded ways." The reader, however, notices that it is the infant and not Maggie who is red. Near the end of the novel when Maggie returns home and is condemned by her mother, neighbors crowd the doorway to glimpse the "fallen" girl. "A baby, overcome with curiosity concerning this object at which all were looking, sidled forward and touched her dress, cautiously, as if

1. In *Maggie: A Girl of the Streets*, a novel of approximately 20,000 words, Crane uses color-words 113 times or one color-word per 177 words. By contrast Emile Zola, Crane's French naturalist contemporary, in *Germinal*, a novel of approximately 188,000 words, uses color-words 467 times or one color-word per 402 words. See Philip Walker, "Zola's Use of Color Imagery in *Germinal*," *PMLA*, LXXVII (1962), 442–49.
2. Claudia C. Wogan, "Crane's Use of Color in 'The Red Badge of Courage,'" *Modern Fiction Studies*, VI (1960), 169.

investigating a red-hot stove." The angry red face of Maggie's crying infant brother has kinship to the mother whose anger is often described in shades of red. That another infant should regard Maggie "cautiously" as if she were "a red hot stove" is ironic. In the cautious approach to the symbolic danger, the child, in essence, does not want to be burned; society does not want to be contaminated by the soiled Maggie. The irony is all the more emphatic when one considers the screaming, raving mother. Symbolically, she is society's contaminating force, not the innocent Maggie.

While red is used in only one image, the colors white and black contribute largely to imagery associated with Maggie. When Jimmie, Maggie's brother, creeps silently into the tenement rooms in order not to arouse his drunken parents, Maggie is described: "The thin white face of his sister looked at him from the doorway of the other room." This realistic use of white, because Maggie is fearful, has symbolic overtones signifying her innocence.

Another realistically accurate description of Maggie, but again with symbolic connotations, is made by Nellie. She comments that Maggie is "a little pale thing with no spirit." Maggie's paleness contrasts, however, with the intensity of her death; in committing suicide she escapes the hopelessness of her environment, but for Nellie and Pete there is no escape. Pete is the butt of Nellie's deception, and she must constantly seek men to victimize.

Musing over her first date with Pete, Maggie fears that "she might appear small and mouse-coloured." That she sees herself "mouse-coloured," gray, indicates her inability to survive. When Pete calls for her, Maggie, "in a worn black dress, was waiting for him in the midst of a floor strewn with wreckage." Her mother in a drunken rage had flung the furniture about. "The fire in the stove had gone out. The displaced lids and open doors showed heaps of sullen grey ashes." Like Maggie's dress, the reader can assume that the stove was worn and black. Its displaced lids find correspondence in Maggie who is later displaced by society and whose escape, her "open doors," with Pete from her unhappiness turns to despair, "sullen grey ashes."

Maggie's rival, Nellie, is in a black dress, also, when the reader meets her for the first time. In contrast to Maggie's worn black dress, Nellie's "black dress fitted her to perfection." One feels that her prostitution "fits" her; she seems at ease with her position in life. In fact, she appears successful in it. Maggie, although forced to prostitution, is repulsed by it, fails, and remains in Crane's presentation an innocent. Unlike her brother Jimmie, Maggie is "a victim rather than a product of her environment."[3]

She does not survive because, unlike Jimmie who is a realist,

3. Lars Åhnebrink, *The Beginnings of Natural-ism in American Fiction* (Upsala, 1950), p. 191. [See Åhnebrink's essay, reprinted above— *Editor.*]

Maggie is a romantic. Being romantic, she "perceived" that Pete "was the ideal man." Dreaming of her first date with Pete "she saw the golden glitter of the place where Pete was to take her." In reality, the "golden glitter" turns out to be only "dull gilt": "Clouds of tobacco smoke rolled and wavered high in air above the dull gilt of the chandeliers." The only other mention of golden is again associated with Pete as Maggie sees him, but again it is ironically used. Pete "swaggering . . . loomed like a golden sun to Maggie." Like the sun, he is Maggie's life-giving force. But he is only "golden" in Maggie's illusions; in reality he is false gold, a gilded god who abandons rather than saves her.

Used only once in the novel, the color rose connotes happiness. Maggie, still the dreamer, "imagined a future rose-tinted because of its distance from all that she had experienced before." Ironically, the happiness is not attainable. There is no future for Maggie, and the rose-tinted dream contrasts sharply with her present drab life. The rose-tint, like the gold, exists only in Maggie's mind.

Maggie's descent to the river is, itself, symbolically depicted. Her walk to the river and her death are viewed in terms of light and shade. Increasing blackness envelops her as she nears the water. Crane juxtaposes society's indifference to the individual by a contrast of darkness and light. As a prosperous and well-dressed group of people emerge from the theaters, Maggie, now a prostitute, walks in the rain. Frightened, she meets a minister and approaches him. He was "a stout gentleman in a silk hat and a chaste black coat, whose decorous row of buttons reached from his chin to his knees." He is repulsed by the street walker and does not help her. The passage seems to be an ironic comment on religion: his coat is, hypocritically, "chaste black" and, like his buttons, his compassion stretched just so far, but not far enough to include Maggie. Like Pete, he possesses the power to "save" Maggie, but he does not understand how to use it.

As she nears the river, Maggie enters "darker blocks than those where the crowd traveled." When she proceeds farther into the gloomy blackness, "the tall black factories shut in the street" as events of her past "shut" her in the hopeless environment and "shut" out a future. That she goes into "the blackness of the final block" is prophetic; it is the final block before one comes to the river. It is Maggie's "final block." She never emerges from the darkness. Instead, "the deathly black hue of the river" claims her.

"Fittingly the concluding chapter of the novel is characterized by the repetition of the word black in contrast with the violent colors of life in the earlier chapters."[4] After Maggie's death, a neighbor "in a

4. William Bysshe Stein, "New Testament Inversions in Crane's *Maggie*," *Modern Language Notes*, LXXIII (1958), 271. [See Stein's essay, reprinted above—*Editor*.]

black gown" eagerly comforts the mother. The neighbor is referred to five times as the "woman in black" in slightly more than five paragraphs. That "her vocabulary was derived from mission churches" seems to be, like the scene with the minister, a criticism of religion, one of society's pitiless institutions as Crane presents it. That she is dressed in black reflects Crane's criticism of society in general, which she symbolizes. Crane saw society's cruelty, ignorance, and lack of compassion for the individual as black sin.

In contrast to Maggie, the colors most often associated with her mother are red and yellow. Both have unpleasant connotations. Although used mostly for descriptive purposes, these colors also have symbolic suggestions. Red describes her skin as well as her emotional state. Her red skin connotes not only the harshness of her physical being and personality, but of her world.

Her anger is reported in terms of red. "The fervent red of her face turned almost to purple" describes her rage when Maggie breaks a plate while washing dishes. The change, darkening from red to purple, represents the intensity of her anger. That it is over such a minor event, one broken dish, imparts a sense of brutality.

Mary Johnson's sleep is usually associated with inebriation. In one drunken stupor "her yellow brows shaded eyelids that had grown blue." Her puffed face and her outflung red arms coupled with yellow brows and blue eyelids complete her demonic appearance.

Like his parents, Jimmie, Maggie's brother, degenerates into a drunkard. At one and the same time, he both fights society and conforms to it. Images associated with him mirror this ambivalence. He is jealous of the illusion of his honor, he sometimes has moments of pity for Maggie, he fights when he thinks he ought and compromises when he must. The colors red and blue as well as contrasts of light and shade help define his character. The color most often associated with him is red, suggesting anger, violence, and sex.

The novel opens with warring factions of Bowery society: Jimmie, alone, fights "for the honour of Rum Alley" against a group representing Devil's Row. That he fights the group single-handedly contributes to one of the underlying themes in much of Crane's work, the individual pitted against hostile masses.

As he fights the urchins from Devil's Row, Jimmie's "infantile countenance was livid with the fury of battle." Unlike the mother whose anger is viewed in terms of red, Jimmie's is "livid." A few paragraphs later "his wan features looked like those of a tiny insane demon." By fighting the devils from Devil's Row, he becomes a demon himself. Thus does Jimmie conform to his society.

Although he fights the group, he becomes like them. He "publicly damned" Maggie to appear "on a higher social plane." Even though he felt that Maggie "would have been more firmly good" if she could, he "felt that he could not hold such a view" and "threw it hastily aside." He does not risk opposing the group. Ultimately, like his mother, he stays within the limits of society.

The color red explains Jimmie's adolescent years. "He lived some red years without labouring." His "occupation for a long time was to stand at street corners and watch the world go by, dreaming blood-red dreams at the passing of pretty women." This is one of the *few* sexual images in all Crane's canon. Because Jimmie is a hardened young man, the red connotes animal power, like that of his mother, plus contempt for the world, indolence, and impiety.

A variation of red, flame-color, is prominent in a mythical image surrounding Jimmie. As a truck driver he views the world, from his high driver's seat, with contempt. Pedestrians risk their lives and other drivers fume in anger because he slows traffic. In defiance of all, Jimmie remains resolute. "And if the god-driver had a desire to step down, put up his flame-coloured fists, and manfully dispute the right of way, he would have probably been immediately opposed by a scowling mortal with two sets of hard knuckles." This is another image of Jimmie's struggling alone, this time against "the god driver." Jimmie, the "scowling mortal," symbolizes in this image man's struggle against fate, "the god driver."

Crane often uses such contrasts of colors as red and green or red and blue. One image, using the contrast of red and blue, reflects Jimmie's contempt for the world. "Multitudes of drivers might howl in his rear, and passengers might load him with opprobrium, but he would not awaken [move on] until some blue policeman turned red . . ."

Contrasts of shadows and light are used less frequently with Jimmie than with Maggie. Nevertheless, one example helps in understanding his character. As Pete has "ruined" Maggie, Jimmie has "ruined" other men's sisters. One woman follows him and pleads with him, as Maggie pleads in the next chapter with Pete, not to leave her. Jimmie sends the woman "teh blazes" and seeks refuge in a saloon. A little later, he emerges "into the shadows" as he sees the "forlorn woman" walking "on the brilliantly lighted avenue." That he escapes "into the shadows" while the woman is seen on a "brilliantly lighted" street seems to be a comment on the double standard of morality popular at the end of the century. In a conversation with an Englishman named Bassett, Crane commented that women "were hunted animals anyhow."[5]

The colors red, blue, black, and white are associated with Pete. He is the ultimate product of the Bowery's society. Though Jimmie may occasionally rebel against the "god-driver," Pete is the high

5. Thomas Beer, *Stephen Crane* (New York, 1923), p. 106.

priest of that god. He presides over the institution which has replaced the church for those in the Bowery—the bar.

He is Maggie's "ideal man," her "knight." In reality, he is the Bowery bartender who seduces her. Like Jimmie, there is the aura of battle about him; "his patent shoes looked like weapons." He demonstrates his prowess with his fists, and he brags about it. "He walked to and fro in the small room which seemed then to grow even smaller and unfit to hold his dignity, the attribute of a supreme warrior."

Because Maggie sees him as a "knight," the traditional colors of heraldry can be used to interpret color images in association with him. When he visits the Johnson household for the first time, "his blue double-breasted coat, edged with black braid, was buttoned close to a red puff tie . . ." This image of Pete dressed in his best clothes is reminiscent of the attire of a courtier or of a knight dressed for pagaentry. Blue and red, in heraldry, signify sincerity and bravery respectively. Both are used ironically: Pete behaves neither bravely nor sincerely in his relationship with Maggie. Black represents grief and sorrow. Like the black braid, a trim, his coming into Maggie's life brings pleasure and happiness; later, he is the cause of her grief and sorrow.

Pete, in his duties as bartender, wears a white jacket and apron, the symbols of his profession. Measured in prestige and money, Pete's is the highest achievement in the novel. When Jimmie enters the saloon looking for Pete and a fight, "Pete, in a white jacket," was attending the bar. When Maggie seeks him out in the saloon and pleads with him not to desert her, he "was immaculate in white jacket and apron . . ." The white jacket and apron, used realistically, have symbolic implications. Bartenders do often wear white jackets and aprons. However, white traditionally signifies purity and innocence and, associated with Pete, may be used ironically: the white jacket and apron are in contrast to his black deed. Or, one can see him innocent of Maggie's unhappiness, as he believes himself to be. Family, society, and environment are responsible for her ruin. He is only the instrument of that ruin. Hers was an impossible situation before she met Pete.

Aside from aiding the reader in the understanding and evaluation of principal characters, color in Crane is an important factor present in nearly all minor characters and fringe situations. Yellow, a color easily sullied, describes the ugliness of Bowery life and the unhappiness of its inhabitants. As Jimmie fights the gang from Devil's Row, disinterested persons watch while "over on the island a worm of yellow convicts came from the shadow of a grey ominous building and crawled slowly along the river's bank." As Jimmie resembles an "insane demon," the convicts resemble a yellow worm that emerges from the shadows. Both Jimmie and the convicts are dehumanized, one by members of society, the other by an institution of that society. When Maggie goes to work in the collar-and-cuff factory, "she received a stool and a machine in a room where sat twenty girls of various shades of yellow discontent." The "various shades" mirror the degrees of dissatisfaction that is countenanced in the workers.

Images that suggest infernal regions surround the Johnson's tenement house as the inhabitants, like the convicts, are reduced to crawling insects. The father, Jimmie, Maggie, and the bawling Tommie "entered a dark region" and "crawled up dark stairways." The autumn wind "raised yellow-dust . . . and swirled it" reminding one of the yellow, sulphuric flames that swirl in the fire lakes of Hell. After his parents are asleep, "Jimmie crawled back into the shadows" while "a glow from the fire threw red hues over" the room.

When Maggie is a child, the river "glimmered pallidly" in the distance under "a florid moon." When its waters claim her life, "a yellow glare . . . lit for a moment the waters . . ." The yellow glare, caused by a factory like the stifling collar-and-cuff factory, contrasts with the pallid glimmer caused by the moon: sordid man-made institutions contrast with the beauty of nature.

One of the underlying themes in Crane's work is Nature's indifference to the problems of men. Crane often suggests this indifference in terms of light (sun or star) and shade. In the closing scenes of the novel after Maggie's suicide, "the inevitable sunlight came streaming in at the window and shed a ghastly cheerfulness upon the faded hues of the room" where Mrs. Johnson and neighbors are mourning the girl's death. That human events do not stop or retard processes of nature is explicit in the word "inevitable." Crane's use of the oxymoron, "ghastly cheerfulness," is a characteristic device to communicate the author's impression of the scene. Cheerfulness should not be ghastly. Even Nature with her "inevitable sunlight" cannot bring true cheer to the "faded hues" of the lives of these characters who are restricted by standards of morality that are not operable for them.

Color, then, is not only a vital part of Crane's work but an aspect of it which is of primary importance, indispensable to an understanding of his art. To convey emotional or sense impressions, Crane depends on color-words which, though perhaps not always realistically accurate, cause the reader to appreciate and remember characters and events. Thus Crane associates black primarily with Maggie; red with her mother and her brother; red, blue, black, and white with Pete; and yellow with the environment. Black in *Maggie* is related to death; red to anger and violence; and yellow to the harshness of the grim environment and the discontent of its inhabitants. Crane's philosophy found little use for delicate colors such as green, pink, or blue except when these colors are used for irony or for contrast with the harsh world that the strong, plain colors portray. The frequent use of color creates a poetic texture in Crane's prose and contributes to the power of his impressionistic writing.

FRANK BERGON

[The Framework of *Maggie*†]

* * *

The whole work is encased, like a parody, in popular attitudes and depends on a reader's own capacity to sort these attitudes out; but he must be guided by the framework Crane provides to evaluate these attitudes. This same framework is the means by which the novel's events can transcend their specific situation and refer to a general scheme of experience. Certainly if *Maggie* is to retain the shock value it once had, it must do more than show that environment is a tremendous thing, or that people in the Bowery are moral cowards, or that a girl can blossom in a mud puddle, or that Maggie's error is to live by fantasies. The pattern emerging from *Maggie* is important not just for the unity it might give the work, but because it provides frames of reference whose contradictions implicate the reader and cause him to question his own conceptions of morality and culture.

Efforts to describe the structure of *Maggie* have usually done little more than make the novel less episodic than it appears to be. Thus *Maggie* has been called a "three-act drama with an appended conclusion"; and it has been quite differently divided into "four major 'perspectives.'"[1] Once when Crane was writing about social form, he said that "form really is truth," and he added that it is "simplicity."[2] A similar simplicity is evident when *Maggie* is seen as falling not into three or four parts, but simply into two.[3] It might be worthwhile to think momentarily of the novel conceived in the shape of a reclining hourglass. It opens with a black vision of the savagery, sordidness, desperation, and terror that characterize life in and around Rum Alley.[4] These qualities, presented in the first three chapters in terms

† From Chapter Three, "Crane's Sense of Story," in *Stephen Crane's Artistry*, by Frank Bergon (New York and London: Columbia University Press, 1975), pp. 71–76.

1. Eric Solomon, *Stephen Crane: From Parody to Realism* (Cambridge: Harvard University Press, 1966), p. 35; Edwin Cady, *Stephen Crane* (New York: Twayne, 1962), p. 104.

2. *Stephen Crane: Letters*, ed. R. W. Stallman and Lillian Gilkes (New York: New York University Press, 1960), p. 115.

3. See Milne Holton, *Cylinder of Vision* (Baton Rouge: Louisiana State University Press, 1972), p. 43. Unlike other critics, Holton has noticed this simple division of "rude [*sic*] symmetry in the novel."

4. *Maggie: A Girl of the Streets . . . A Facsimile Reproduction of the 1893 Edition*, ed. Joseph Katz (Gainesville: Scholars' Facsimiles and Reprints, 1966). For this discussion of the novel proper, the original *Maggie* has been chosen over the 1896 revision.

of a gruesome fairy tale, inform life in the major institutions of this realm, the tenement, the factory, and the bar. In contrast to this environment are Maggie's vague fantasies of love, serenity, freedom, and power—which she identifies with money, clothes, and the society of Pete, her "knight." From a broad, expressionistic panorama of Rum Alley the novel spirals in toward its middle chapter as Pete and Maggie move toward each other. In chapter 10 they become offstage lovers, and we see the first reactions to her "fall." The novel spirals out again as Pete and Maggie move apart. The novel closes with another broad, scenic presentation, this time of the conceptualizations, rationalizations, moralisms, and false expectations with which society disguises and perpetuates the conditions of existence presented in the opening chapters.

The ironic relation between the chaos of the first chapters and the after-the-fact assertions of the last is Crane's essential subject. The emphasis of the first half is upon the terrible physical and emotional realities of slum life. The narrator keeps his distance; explicit moral concerns are absent. All the furniture broken in *Maggie* is broken in the first half of the novel; and with the exception of the barroom brawl in chapter 11, all the seemingly incessant slaps, slugs, scratches, and kicks occur before the middle chapter.

In the second half of the book the emphasis is upon the moral orderings people use to boost their egos and assert their social positions. Hints of an operative social code appear in an early chapter when Jimmie's father shouts, "Leave yer sister alone on the street," but not until the second half is the idea of "respectability" introduced directly and repeated, as often as five times in chapter 16. In the second half Maggie's mother has stopped using physical destruction to vent her rage against the universe and instead turns it into moralist invectives against Maggie; and "Of course Jimmie publicly damned his sister that he might appear on a higher social plane."[5] This moral posturing is matched by the "cultural" deceptions of the dance halls in which Maggie appears in the second half as a changed person; she is now realistic about "Pete's strong protecting fists." He is no longer a knight who will lead her to "elegance and soft palms," but only a safeguard against her falling back into the grotesque world of the novel's first half. These two general perspectives of the Bowery are not simply to be seen as moral appearance, on the one hand, juxtaposed against an amoral reality on the other. The two are really aspects of the same thing. The moral and cultural attitudes are part

5. General criticism of the dialogue in *Maggie* states that the characters make only verbal pronouncements without communicating. Despite its particular manifestations, this aspect of the dialogue, at least in the first half of the novel, may reflect the spirit of actual Bowery talk. See Edmund Leach, "Mythical Inequalities," *New York Review of Books*, 28 Jan. 1971, p. 44: "As a restricted code, which tends to be characteristic of working-class homes in which the parents have only limited educational equipment, language is a device which constantly reinforces the speaker's ideas about his own position in the total structure of society."

of that vicious reality and they are partly the reason for its continuing existence. This is why the exposure of Pete, Jimmie, and Maggie's mother as cowards, liars, and fools is less interesting than Crane's complex depiction of the manner in which self-interest motivates moral passion, and the manner in which the confused linkage of self-interest with social status produces unsocial actions in the name of virtue.

Lurking inchoately in *Maggie* is the formal organization Crane would perfect in "The Blue Hotel." Maggie's sin and death are indeed "the result of a collaboration,"[6] but who will accept responsibility? Like the cowboy, each Bowery character implicitly cries, "Well, I didn't do anythin', did I?" Yet blame for Maggie's fate cannot be placed on the other characters alone. If she were only in her world and not of it, as she is initially presented, Crane might have used her as a catalyst—as he later used Henry Johnson in "The Monster"— and based the structure of the whole novel around the polarities of society and hell. Such an arrangement allows a monster and fire to rip apart the social artificialities that screen the chaos society does not want to see, let alone touch. But Maggie is not just a catalyst. Like the Swede in "The Blue Hotel," she ironically collaborates in her own fate, and both characters are in the sway of romantic notions. By the end of the novel, then, the reader is caught in the position of realizing that it is as absurd to forgive Maggie as it is to damn her. Her only transgression is against moral and social codes that are in themselves transgressions of moral and social reality. Yet Maggie shares these codes with other characters whom the reader would never forgive. Like them, she is a victim of self-deception; and like them, she adopts moral poses so as to appear on a higher social plane. Her errors are so perfectly those of her society that forgiveness of Maggie should be extended to others. The forgiving reader is caught in a moral contradiction, or like Maggie's mother, becomes bound to noble sentiments that are in themselves self-serving deceptions.

Denied a normal response to events and characters, the reader is also refused the comfort of those values that he may most deeply cherish. The episodic method itself shocks and upsets normal order through its lack of transitions and its use of juxtaposition, which Roger Shattuck describes as a "great diversity employed to suggest and delimit a point in another dimension."[7] *Maggie* likewise takes its comment into another dimension, for the reader comes to see that the real thing is as unreal as its Bowery imitations. There are theaters, for instance, "giving to the Bowery public the phantasies of the

6. *The Works of Stephen Crane*, ed. Fredson Bowers (Charlottesville: University Press of Virginia, 1970), V, 170.

7. Charles Shattuck, *The Banquet Years*, rev. ed. (New York: Knopf-Vintage, 1968), p. 342.

aristocratic theatre-going public, at reduced rates," but the second half of the novel indicates that Crane's ironic attack is actually directed toward the "aristocratic theatre-going public" itself. The "soft palms," "smiles of serenity," money, and "adornments of person"— all that Maggie desires—are no guarantee of love or the serenity they seem to promise. They are merely the outer trappings of a life based on illusion. The Bowery people are much like their counterparts in a more sophisticated society. A minister, representative of that society, rejects Maggie for the same reasons as do Pete and her family; and the theater-going crowd of New York emerges from a performance with their "hearts still kindling from the glowings of the stage," just as Maggie once did. When Maggie becomes a successful whore she has a "handsome cloak" and "well-shod feet," and she daintily lifts her skirts as do those women in the crowd who "shrugged impatient shoulders in their warm cloaks and stopped to arrange their skirts." All Crane's indictments of the society crowd's values are implicit except for one sentence in which he directly comments on the illusory basis of their lives: "An atmosphere of pleasure and prosperity seemed to hang over the throng, born, perhaps, of good clothes and two hours in a place of forgetfulness." Maggie is familiar with Bowery places of forgetfulness; the most that good clothes and a cloak can give her are additional illusions. Through a series of juxtapositions Crane thus directs his final comment toward that society from which Maggie draws her fantasies and from which the Bowery adopts its moral and social codes. The reader is presumably a member of this society, whose culture, like the Bowery theater and the mission, must be seen for what it really is. Ortega y Gasset bluntly describes the nature of such ideals:

> Justice and truth, too, all work of the spirit, are mirages produced on matter. Culture—the ideal side of things—tries to set itself up as a separate and self-sufficient world to which we can transfer our hearts. This is an illusion, and only looked upon as an illusion, only considered as a mirage on earth, does culture take its proper place.[8]

Although *Maggie* does not have the weight and force of some of Crane's other investigations of conventional values, it does sketch a basic conflict between reality perceived as chaos and reality conceived in terms of certain moral and cultural orderings. Crane will suggest later with greater force that though such orderings may be illusionary, they still may be necessary—if only for survival. As a well-dressed whore, Maggie acquires the manners and adornments of the socially successful; she lacks only status. The rest of the novel

---

8. José Ortega y Gassett. "The Nature of the Novel." *Hudson Review*, 10 (Spring 1957), 29.

shows status to be as hollow as clothes or manners, and those who do have it are not that much different from Maggie, but they are accepted by their peers. They do not go to the river. If rules or communal conceptions are not accepted, then there is no way out except through isolation or death.

Crane may have shared his basic story with the Reverend Thomas de Witt Talmage,[9] yet what must have first shocked readers of the 1890s was not that *Maggie* attacked cherished values but that it totally lacked the condescension with which crusaders of the times approached such characters. Crane was to present for the first time this lower class of society from a seriously rendered, insider's point of view. This perspective is most successfully achieved in the first half of the novel; in the second half, however, when the characters parody middle-class terminology and moral postures to excess, at times they become hybrids who represent neither class realistically. And in his effort to evoke the sensations of slum life, Crane often lets his prose attempt to stimulate more response than the situations themselves seem to warrant. The violence and terror of the first half become repetitious and extreme. It is true that *Maggie* gave Crane a shadowy realistic framework which his earlier stories and sketches never had. He was writing in an accepted and popular genre, but as with the Sullivan County tales, he still pumped more feeling into events than the novel's dramatic structure could support.

* * *

HERSHEL PARKER and BRIAN HIGGINS

Maggie's "Last Night": Authorial Design and Editorial Patching†

After his manuscript of *Maggie* was turned down by various publishers in 1892 or early 1893 because it was "too honest," Stephen Crane paid to print the story himself.[1] It went almost unreviewed, but it won him the approval and friendship of Hamlin Garland and William Dean Howells. In this 1893 edition Chapter 17 is brilliantly contrived. The frightened Maggie of Chapter 16 has in the passing

9. A reference to Reverend Thomas De Witt Talmage's *The Night Sides of City Life*. See Bergon, p. 70. [*Editor*.]

† From *Studies in the Novel*, Vol. 10, No. 1 (Spring 1978), 64–75.

1. According to Thomas Beer, *Stephen Crane: A Study in American Letters* (New York: Alfred A. Knopf, 1923), p. 86, Crane offered the manuscript to Richard Watson Gilder, the editor of the *Cen-*

tury, who insultingly condemned its cruelty of subject and then itemized errors and awkwardnesses of style until Crane interrupted him with, "'You mean that the story's too honest?'" Confident of his achievement, Crane sank his inheritance into paying—grossly overpaying—to have *Maggie* printed by a firm specializing in religious and medical books.

months become so totally one of the anonymous prostitutes of the
city that Crane refers to her only as "a girl," never by name. This
girl is a well-dressed and self-assured professional who casually and
knowingly adapts her approach to prospective customers. Still we
find that during the course of the evening there is not limit beneath
which she will not descend. Failing to attract any of the men she
solicits along many blocks of a "prominent side-street" (1893, p. 143)
filled with noisy crowds, she walks past glittering avenues into "darker
blocks" (1893, p. 146) where four more men successively reject her,
the last a drunken man who roars at her "'I ain' ga no money,
dammit'" (1893, p. 147). Then she goes "into gloomy districts near
the river" (1893, p. 147), where she solicits a man "with blotched
features" (1893, p. 148). When he says "'I've got a date,'" she goes
further on "in the darkness" and meets "a ragged being with shifting,
blood-shot eyes and grimey hands," who also rejects her. Then instead of returning to the comparative safety of the lighted streets,
she walks on into "the blackness of the final block" before the river.
When "almost to the river" she sees "a great figure," and goes "forward" (1893, p. 148) toward this "huge fat man in torn and greasy
garments" (1893, p. 149). His "small, bleared eyes" sweep eagerly
over her "upturned face" and his whole body quivers and shakes "like
that of a dead jelly fish." "Chuckling and leering," he follows her to
the edge of the black river.[2] The brightness and noise of the opening
scenes of the chapter are gone. Now the only light is the momentary
"yellow glare" sent up by some "hidden factory" and the dominant
sound is that of "the waters lapping oilily against timbers" (1893, p.
149). For all her subtle calculation at the start of the evening, the
girl is last seen in obvious degradation and danger; her descent is
swift and horrifying.

Powerful as an implacable narrative unit, Chapter 17 in 1893 de-
rives much of its strength from reciprocal illumination with other
chapters, earlier and later. The girl who had shrunk from the
"painted" women at the end of Chapter 12 (1893, p. 108) has herself
become one of the "painted cohorts of the city" (1893, p. 144). Her
purposeful walk, as she throws "changing glances" (1893, p. 144) at
men she meets, startlingly contrasts with the aimlessness which had
marked her movements after Pete turned her away for the last time;
in that earlier scene the "glances of the men, shot at Maggie," had
made her tremble (1893, p. 108), while now one young man receives

2. Here is the paragraph (1893, pp. 148–49), which is still not well enough known: "When almost to the river the girl saw a great figure. On going forward she perceived it to be a huge fat man in torn and greasy garments. His grey hair straggled down over his forehead. His small, bleared eyes, sparkling from amidst great rolls of red fat, swept eagerly over the girl's upturned face. He laughed, his brown, disordered teeth gleaming under a grey, grizzled moustache from which beer-drops dripped. His whole body gently quivered and shook like that of a dead jelly fish. Chuckling and leering, he followed the girl of the crimson legions."

"a glance shot keenly" from Maggie's own eyes (1893, p. 146). Toward the end of Chapter 16 Maggie had guiltily read reproach into the faces of the houses (1893, p. 141), but now toward the end of Chapter 17 the tall, unoccupied buildings near the river emphasize how rejected and isolated a person she has become, since these structures seem to have eyes that look not at her but "over her, beyond her, at other things" (1893, p. 148). The "great figure" Maggie meets in the blackness recalls by his size the respectable "stout gentleman" (obviously a clergyman) who had rebuffed her at the end of Chapter 16, while the "torn and greasy garments" contrast with the earlier man's "silk hat" and "chaste black coat whose decorous row of buttons reached from his chin to his knees" (1893, p. 141); the parallel diffuses blame for Maggie's ruin, inviting the reader to feel renewed contempt for Christians who fail to be Christlike, and reminding him that there is no saving grace, religious or social, for this girl of the Bowery. After the last glimpse of Maggie offered by the 1893 version, Pete's drunken benevolence toward the half dozen women in the "partitioned-off section of a saloon" (1893, p. 150), and toward the universe at large, Hottentots included, is grimly ironic. Crane's refusal to use Pete's name (he is simply "a man," "the man," or "he," except when others address him or talk about him) recalls the avoidance of Maggie's name in Chapter 17, thereby emphasizing their comparable loss of identity. Furthermore, the end of Chapter 18 vividly reminds the reader that Pete's own deterioration has kept close pace with Maggie's: after just showing Maggie's overtures to the man with blotched features, Crane reveals that Pete's neck now has blotches, onto which wine is dripping (1893, p. 158); now he too is in the grip of the devils of their environment.

When Crane had the chance in 1896 to republish *Maggie* with D. Appleton and Company, neither he nor Ripley Hitchcock, the editor who always dealt with Crane for the firm, gave much thought to the literary quality of the 1893 *Maggie*, in Chapter 17 or elsewhere. On 6 January 1896 Hitchcock wrote Crane, who was in Hartwood, New York, accepting *The Third Violet* but making it plain that he wanted Crane to come into the city to discuss changes Hitchcock had in mind.[3] Crane obliged promptly, and the timing of the next events suggests that reprinting *Maggie* just then was Hitchcock's brainstorm, a tough professional gamble by which *The Red Badge* could be followed by another sensational, if dangerous, book, not the tepid *Third Violet*. When he decided to publish *Maggie*, Hitchcock did not have a copy, but he knew what it was like because he had been one of the

---

3. Henry Binder called our attention to this letter, which is at the Baker Library of Dartmouth College. Fredson Bowers does not mention it in the Virginia Edition of *The Third Violet* (Charlottes- ville: University Press of Virginia, 1976), even though it is the best direct evidence of Hitchcock's tactful but determined guidance of Crane's texts.

editors who refused it three years or so before.[4] He remembered it well enough to apprise Crane at the outset that it had to be cleaned up. Surprised and happy at the prospect of having *Maggie* reprinted sooner than he had anticipated,[5] Crane set to work and by early February, 1896, had obediently "dispensed with a goodly number of damns," and on the tenth he assured Hitchcock that he had "carefully plugged at the words which hurt."[6] The cleaning-up process took weeks, off an on; from Washington in mid-March Crane wrote Hitchcock for "the edited Maggie,"[7] apparently pages which Hitchcock had *further* edited, though he may merely have wanted proofs if they were ready. In any case, neither Crane nor Hitchcock manifested any instinct for literary revision or even intelligent cobbling in the book as a whole or in particular Chapter 17, where the major alteration was the complete expurgation of Maggie's encounter with the fat man, by all odds the most powerful scene in the 1893 edition. What Appleton printed of the chapter, as we will show, was cynically reduced.

But not all oddities in the 1896 *Maggie* can be accounted for merely by recognizing that the basic motive was expurgative: it is also necessary to visualize the sort of copy the Appleton compositor was given to set from. Even allowing for the chance that a few of the 1896 alterations were compositorial or were made in proof, the setting copy must have been unusually messy. For the last third of Chapter 17, this setting copy consisted of pages 148 and 149 taken loose from the copy of the 1893 *Maggie* Crane had at Hartwood, and heavily marked. On page 148 the 1893 solecism "from whence came" was doctored to "whence came." The two lines of dialogue between Maggie and the man with blotched features were marked for deletion. In the first sentence of the middle paragraph on page 148 "bloodshot" and "grimey" were probably marked for alteration to "bloodshot" and "grimy." The last sentence of that paragraph—"'Ah, what deh hell? Tink I'm a millionaire?'"—was marked for total deletion.

4. Willis Fletcher Johnson, who knew both Crane and Hitchcock, is definite about Hitchcock's having rejected *Maggie* in manuscript: "The crux was to find a publisher. The book was quite 'out of the line' of the house which had produced my books, and there was no use in trying it. The man whom I knew best in the New York publishing trade was my very dear friend and former colleague, Ripley Hitchcock, then literary adviser of D. Appleton & Co.; so I sent Stephen to him. He appreciated the merits of the book, but hesitated to recommend its acceptance. He told me, however, that 'That boy has the real stuff in him,' and a few years later eagerly accepted for publication Stephen's next work, 'The Red Badge of Courage.'" See "The Launching of Stephen Crane," *Literary Digest International Book Review*, IV (April 1926), p. 289.

5. See *Stephen Crane: Letters*, eds. R. W. Stallman and Lillian Gilkes (New York: New York University Press, 1960), p. 79, Crane to an editor of *Leslie's Weekly* around November, 1895: "But, personally, I was unhappy only at times during the period of my struggles. I was always looking forward to success. My first great disappointment was in the reception of 'Maggie, a Girl of the Streets.' I remember how I looked forward to its publication, and pictured the sensation I thought it would make. It fell flat. Nobody seemed to notice it or care for it. I am going to introduce Maggie again to the world some time, but not for a good while. Poor Maggie! she was one of my first loves."

6. *Letters*, pp. 112, 113.

7. *Letters*, p. 119.

In the last full paragraph of page 148 the typo "eyet" for "eyes" was surely marked for correction, and the hyphen which the Appleton text put into "Street car" was probably marked on the page as well. The last two lines on page 148, the start of the paragraph containing the fat man, were marked for excision, as were the twelve lines which concluded that paragraph at the top of the 1893 page 149. In order to remove the last traces of the fat man, the opening of the last paragraph on page 149 ("At their feet the river appeared a deathly black hue.") was marked for alteration to "At the feet of the tall buildings appeared the deathly black hue of the river."

At best, even if we assume that a few of these changes were not marked on Crane's loose pages from the dismembered 1893 *Maggie* but were made by the compositor or in proof, and that all the changes were neatly indicated in the text and the margins of the loose pages and that no extraneous marks appeared, the printer would have found the copy hard enough to work from. Given the number of hands that fixed up the pages (Crane's own, since he would have seen a "hell" to be worried about, if nothing else; then Hitchcock's and perhaps other employees' at Appleton), there may well have been a good many additional marks, such as superseded queries and replies, which the printer was expected to ignore. Hitchcock may well have worked here in stages, such as getting rid of the fat man first, then easing the two previous men out of contact with Maggie; certainly the revision of *The Red Badge* under Hitchcock was accomplished in not one but two major stages. Crane may also have made some alteration to "what deh hell" (the words spoken by the man with "blood-shot eyes and grimey hands"), only to have Hitchcock expunge the whole speech.[8] These particular examples are merely the product of educated guessing, of course, but there is ample reason to suspect that the untidiness of the setting copy somehow resulted in the change of pronouns from "The structures seemed to have eyet that looked over her, beyond her, at other things." to "The structures seemed to have eyes that looked over them, beyond them, at other things." The 1896 reading is out of keeping with the nearby expurgations, for the word "them" must, in context, seem, at least momentarily, to suggest that someone is with Maggie, precisely the fact that the major expurgation in the passage was designed to remove. The 1896 reading is highly ambiguous, if not impossible, since it either makes the eyes of the structures look over the shutters of the tall buildings (that is, over their own lips or each other's lips, for

8. These 1893 leaves the Appleton printer set from were not large (a little less than eight inches by almost five and a half inches), and they were not mounted, since everything indicates that Crane was working with only one copy, not with the two it would have taken in order to mount each page on a larger sheet for the printer's more convenient handling. Since the text of pp. 147 and 150 in the 1893 edition was also expurgated, there may well have been some distracting show-through from any ink markings on *those* pages.

in 1896 the "shutters of the tall buildings" are still closed ("like grim lips"), or else over the tall buildings (that is, over themselves). Whether the perplexing "them" resulted from the messy printer's copy or not, no one at Appleton went out of the way to be certain that what got printed made sense. Someone, or more than one person, blundered in the cavalier reworking of the chapter, where the prime purpose was not the creation of a text intelligible in a *new* way but the production of a text which would *not* be intelligible in the old way. Hitchcock wanted something as little offensive as possible yet salably controversial; intelligibility could go by the boards.

While Chapter 17 in the 1893 edition is an overpowering climax to the story of Maggie, a girl of the streets, Chapter 17 in the Appleton version ultimately removes the focus from her degradation so that she hardly seems more than incidental to Crane's depiction of the evils of the Bowery. Nothing much happens in the chapter beyond Maggie's soliciting a few healthy and well-dressed men as she walks along brightly lighted streets filled with the sound of crowds just out of theatres or around restaurants and saloons. In the "darker blocks" the drunken man still rejects her, though without saying "dammit," and she still goes on "into gloomy districts near the river" where stands the man with blotched features. As far as the reader of the expurgated edition can tell, she does not notice him, much less address him. In the next paragraph she meets (but does not speak with) the ragged man. The 1893 descent into still more horrifying realities of prostitution is abruptly truncated, since the ragged man is the last person she meets in the Appleton text and her encounter with the fat man is entirely excised. Worse, Appleton's leaves no coherent motivation for Maggie's actions. After the drunken man turns her down, it is impossible to say whether she simply changes her mind about trying to find a customer that night or whether she decides that she does not want to solicit the next two men she passes (if she notices them at all). The point is that since the Appleton text lacks motivation the reader automatically begins supplying it: the men are too repulsive, the reader guesses, or Maggie does not solicit them because she knows they would not have any money. Most conspicuously, this now-unmotivated passage has proved open to the speculation that Maggie drowns herself—even though the 1896 text does *not* explicitly place her at the river, as the 1893 text graphically *does*. The Appleton changes which, as it turns out, have led some critics to think Maggie drowns herself were of course made with quite another purpose in mind, that of removing any indication that she would solicit such disfigured and frightening men as the last three she meets in the original version. The idea that she is meaning to commit suicide is not authorial but adventitious, projected by some sense-making readers onto the unintelligible 1896 text.

In addition to this absence of motivation which has naturally enough led readers to attribute any motivation they can find plausible, the Appleton edition betrays the attentive reader by bewilderingly juxtaposing two previously distinct stages in the progression throughout the chapter from bright lights and cheerful noises toward darkness and silence. In 1893 two short paragraphs (third from last and last) surround the longer paragraph in which Maggie meets the fat man. These two short paragraphs mark the difference between what she can see and hear at the beginning of the final block, before she meets the fat man, and what she can see and hear at the edge of the river, after she has walked down there ahead of him. Even in their 1896 placement as the last two paragraphs of the chapter, now that the excision of the fat man paragraph has left them collapsed together, these little paragraphs still seem, when carefully read, to refer to different locations, since in the last one the yellow glare on the waters replaces the lights of the avenues and the lapping of the waters helps to drown out the distant "sounds of life" such as the street-car bells (1893, p. 149; 1896, p. 144). But in Appleton's text there is no reference at all to Maggie's having *traveled* that implied distance. Indeed, neither Maggie nor any other possible witness to the sights and sounds is mentioned in the last paragraph of the Appleton version; she has vanished in the previous paragraph, just after she goes "into the blackness of the final block," well before she reaches the river. In this realm of haphazard publisher's conjuring under Hitchcock, it is cause for only minor wonder that the tall buildings (which in the Appleton next-to-last paragraph are apparently located near the beginning of the final block) abruptly move to the river's edge, so that the waters are at the "feet" of the buildings (not, as in 1893, at the feet of Maggie and the fat man). Such are some of the disastrous costs of making a few excisions and perfunctory splicings without reconceiving the chapter. Yet despite all the damage in the Appleton chapter, the final paragraph, in which the river is a "deathly black hue" and the "varied sounds of life" are seemingly unapproachable and die away "to a silence" (1893, p. 149; 1896, p. 144), still suggests that something very sad is to happen. But any pity and foreboding is undercut by the residue of bafflement any attentive reader brings to the last words of the expurgated Chapter 17.

Besides destroying Chapter 17 as a coherent narrative unit, the excisions and other changes of the Appleton version also damage its relationships with other chapters. The original point of the contrast between the houses which look grimly on Maggie in Chapter 16 and the tall buildings which seem to have eyes that look "over her, beyond her" in the 1893 Chapter 17 is lost in the now meaningless sentence: "The structures seemed to have eyes that looked over them, beyond them, at other things" (1896, p. 144). The role played in Maggie's ruin by the stout gentleman at the end of Chapter 16 receives less emphasis now as a result of the omission of the contrasted fat man: the reader no longer has any special impetus to think back on the unchristian clergyman. Then the irony of Pete's being surrounded by flattering women at the start of Chapter 18 is weakened or lost altogether when Maggie is no longer last seen alone at the river with the fat man; and since the man with blotched features is no longer important to Maggie's degradation (a reader of the 1896 edition could assume that she does not even notice him), the blotches on Pete's neck at the end of Chapter 18 signal no strong immediate connections to the reader. In terms of the book as a whole rather than just the surrounding chapters, the expurgation of the fat man removes the climactic instance in the set of out-sized characters who have in one way or another collaborated in Maggie's ruin: her mother (of the "massive shoulders," "great chest," and "immense hands"), the "fat foreigner" who owned the sweatshop where she worked, as well as the "stout gentleman" of Chapter 16: representatives of home, job, and church.[9] Taken all in all, the excisions in the Appleton Chapter 17 blur or destroy much of the vital structural coherence of the book as a whole.

Yet sadly, Fredson Bowers, the modern editor with the greatest chance to rescue Crane's intentions from his Appleton editor, chose to print basically the Appleton version of Chapter 17, with hardly more than two restorations of "dammit" to recapture any of the strength of what Crane wrote.[1] Bowers's primary editorial decision was apparently based on his general preference for most aspects of the tidied-up 1896 text over that of 1893, and his critical arguments too often have the air of after-the-fact justifications for prior editorial decisions. Insofar as Bowers defends his acceptance of the Appleton expurgations through analysis of what *Maggie* means, it is not by arguing from Crane's intentions and achievements in the first edition but by attempting to interpret the 1896 version (in which, as we have

9. The "fat foreigner" is in Chapter 8 (1893, p. 66) and the "stout gentleman," of course, is in Chapter 16 (1893, pp. 141–42). But the strongest similarity is between the fat man and Maggie's mother, who is a "large woman" (1893, p. 15), with "massive shoulders" (p. 15), "huge arms" (p. 16), "immense hands" (p. 17), a "great chest" (p. 27), "great fists" (p. 76), and a "huge back" (p. 78). By the time Jimmie and Maggie are grown she has "grey" (p. 43) or "gray" (p. 74) hair like the fat man, and like his straggling hair hers is "tossing" (p. 54), falling "in knotted masses" (p. 74), and "tangled" (p. 81); at one point her hair is said to have "straggled, giving her crimson features a look of insanity" (p. 76). The fat man's "great rolls of red fat" recall many places where Maggie's mother's face is "crimson" (p. 17, p. 74, and the one just cited on p. 76), "fervent red"

and almost purple (p. 21), as well as "lurid" (p. 54). She is referred to as "Maggie's red mother" (p. 55), shakes "red fists" (p. 75), and has a "red, writhing body" (p. 82). As usual, Crane knew what he was doing. The 1896 edition, where no one cared what he had achieved, decisively eliminated the parallel by expurgating the fat man, but it also incidentally toned down some of the mother's coloration, as in making her merely "Maggie's mother" instead of "Maggie's red mother" and making her have only a "writhing body" instead of a "red, writhing body."

1. *Bowery Tales: Maggie/George's Mother* (Charlottesville: University Press of Virginia, 1969), Vol. 1 in *The Works of Stephen Crane*, the Center for Editions of American Authors (CEAA) edition. Hereafter Va.

· *Hershel Parker and Brian Higgins*

seen, Chapter 17 was never intended to mean something new but merely *not* to mean what it too plainly meant in 1893). Working from the Appleton text, Bowers argues that Maggie's whole purpose in Chapter 17 is to commit suicide. His main reason for thinking so is a "foreshadowing sentence" (Va., p. lxxxii) in which Maggie hurries "through the crowd as if intent upon reaching.a distant home" (1893, p. 145; 1896, p. 141). Bowers finds these words "pregnant with meaning" (Va., p. lxxxi), especially the word "home," although whether he takes that "home" to be death or Heaven is hardly clear. However, the passage depends upon the parallel one in the previous chapter. There, cast off by Pete, Maggie wanders about until she discovers "that if she walked with such apparent aimlessness, some men looked at her with calculating eyes." Crane adds: "She quickened her step, frightened. As a protection, she adopted a demeanor of intentness as if going somewhere" (1893, p. 141; 1896, p. 137, with "demeanor" spelled "demeanour"). Maggie is *not* in fact going anywhere definite in Chapter 16: the demeanor of intentness is a stratagem for avoiding unwanted stares. Her hurrying in the next chapter "as if intent upon reaching a distant home" is likewise a stratagem, in no way an indication that she is not trying to attract a man. Any seeming contradiction is soon resolved: in Chapter 16, Maggie does not look like a whore, and therefore is protected by adopting a demeanor of intentness; in Chapter 17, she is obviously a whore, one of the "crimson legions" (1893, p. 149), and her purpose is understood by worldly men whether or not she walks as if intent on arriving anywhere in particular. Crane's language is clear, stressing as it does the discrepancy between what seems and what is, between acting from a given motive and acting "as if" one had that motive. Indeed, Crane's saying that Maggie walks "as if" intent on reaching a distant home pretty much amounts to saying that she is not in fact on her way to such a place, literally or metaphorically, and serves as an ironic reminder of the violence and squalor of her own Bowery "home."

In a related justification for printing the expurgated version of Chapter 17, Bowers insists that Maggie attempts to solicit only "unsophisticated or rural men" (Va., p. lxxx). On the contrary, she has two distinct roles or strategies: "She threw changing glances at men who passed her, giving smiling invitations to men of rural or untaught pattern and usually seeming sedately unconscious of the men with a metropolitan seal upon their faces" (1893, p. 144; "invitations to men" reads "invitations to those" in 1896, p. 140). The rural or untaught men cannot be trusted to know her profession, so she must give them smiling invitations. Men with the metropolitan seal know well enough what she is about, as the evaluation of the tall young man with the moustache soon shows. Although Maggie walks past him "as if such a young man as he was not in existence" (1893, p.

145; 1896, p. 141) he looks back transfixed with interest, but takes only a moment to discern "that she was neither new, Parisian, nor theatrical" (1893, p. 146; 1896, p. 142), and therefore not desirable to such a connoisseur as he is. After first arguing that Maggie is approaching only rural or untaught men, Bowers soon decides that soliciting "is not the primary purpose of her movement," that there is "no suggestion" she is "seriously seeking" customers (Va., p. lxxxii). But as Crane's description of her strategies shows, her purpose is clearly to attract a man. In her eagerness she even departs from her practice of letting "metropolitan" men make the first advance, a mistake which causes the young man in light overcoat and derby to mock her for sizing him up as a farmer (1893, pp. 146–147; 1896, pp. 142–143). Maggie indisputably makes some "remarks" to a laborer (1893, p. 147; 1896, p. 143). She smiles squarely into the face of a boy with blonde locks, who smiles back but waves his hands: "'Not this eve—some other eve!'" (1893, p. 147; 1896, p. 143). She perhaps speaks to the drunken man, who understands her purpose well enough to shout at her, "'I ain' ga no money, dammit'" (1893, p. 147; 1896, p. 143, without the "dammit" and repunctuated). In the unexpurgated edition she says "'Ah, there'" to the man with blotched features, who replies "'I've got a date'" (1893, p. 148). She apparently speaks to the "ragged being with shifting, blood-shot eyes and grimey hands," for he says "'Ah, what deh hell? Tink I'm a millionaire?'" (1893, p. 148). Far from rushing to drown herself, she turns her face up to the huge fat man in torn and greasy garments, who follows her to the river (1893, p. 149). In the first edition Maggie has unquestionably been soliciting, from the beginning to the end of the chapter; and in the expurgated edition she has been soliciting all along, although she seems to stop after the drunken man has rejected her. No matter how she dies in the interval between the close of Chapter 17 and the opening of Chapter 19, soliciting, not suicide, has been her motive during the time we have seen her, except that the Appleton excisions leave her without any motive at all after she meets the drunken man.[2]

The upshot of all Bowers's arguments, of course, is that he follows Hitchcock in expurgating the only customer to accept Maggie. This is his justification: "We may take it as at least a working hypothesis that by 1896 Crane had come to see the distracting effect, despite

---

2. Having convinced himself that "Maggie's mission" that night is to commit suicide, not primarily to solicit customers, Bowers has effectively boxed himself in: "If she is proposing suicide . . . why does she solicit?" (Va., pp. lxxxii–lxxxiii). He admits that "there is no literal answer that is wholly satisfying." But rather than admit a weakness in his theory of her mission, he decides that she does indeed, logic be damned, solicit on her way to commit suicide, and concludes that the book has a major fault, since the "literal details by which Crane describes Maggie's journey are absurd on their face" (Va., p. lxxxiii). Then Bowers slips out of this condemnation, deciding that the anomaly is only an "apparent paradox" after all, not a real one, and that there is only a "seeming clash between the superficial actions of this strangely impersonal girl and her secret intent" (Va., p. lxxxiv). According to Bowers, the "rationale" of Chapter 17 really rests upon a symbolic foundation.

the irony, of the fat man—what he does and what he stands for—and that he had concluded the total effect of the chapter was worth more than the sum of its parts" (Va., pp.lxxxviii–lxxxix). The most obvious objection to this is that the original "total effect" disappears in 1896, since the fat man is essential to the full view of Maggie's degeneration and since it is his presence which gave the horrific ominousness to the chapter's ending in 1893. The 1896 version of Chapter 17 has a "total effect," to be sure—a most puzzling one. But with the most powerful lines removed it cannot possibly have the same "total effect" it had in 1893. Such is the confusion that results from resorting to interpretive justifications for an indefensible textual decision. More to the point, such is the confusion that results from attempting to justify an unintelligible text.

All in all, Bowers's treatment of Chapter 17 provides a powerful warning about the dangers of editing by arbitrary impressionistic textual decisions, however elaborately buttressed, instead of by the most patient consideration of all the biographical, textual, and aesthetic evidence. Neither the Appleton edition nor Bowers's very similar one are worth the attention of critics who wish to confine their insights to what Crane wrote and meant. Literary czar that he was, Hitchcock could expurgate almost by fiat, however diplomatically he couched his desires, without thought for the possible unity of the book as Crane had first published it or for, in any profound sense, Crane's own artistic self-respect. In a kindred fashion, Bowers has operated in *Maggie* as an arbitrary editor and a highly subjective and erratic literary critic, in effect casting about for aesthetic reasons that might justify Hitchcock's purely commercial expurgations.

The best kind of editor, of course, will always be a thorough biographer and textual scholar as well as sensitive critic. Such an editor will carry in mind a comprehensive sense of the author's methods of writing and will understand the nature of his interaction with his publisher. From his familiarity with the writer's strategies for affecting the reader by words, passages, whole scenes, chapters, and larger units of the work as originally written, the true editor—the devoted textualist—will develop special alertness to the effects that any subsequent alterations, whether authorial or not, have on those intended responses. Indeed, one obvious way textualists can help free their colleagues from the lingering entanglements of the New Criticism is by focusing biographical and textual evidence directly on the problem of what a work of literature (or any part of it) means in any early form and what any later changes do to that meaning. Otherwise most English professors will continue to think that what textual scholars do all day is at best unthinking drudgery, irrelevant or even inimical to any aesthetic experience. With *Maggie* the textual scholar can easily be faithful to Crane and responsible to his readers: he has merely to reprint the 1893 edition in photographic facsimile,[3] or in a reset edition with misprints corrected, as the text readers should have in hand when they want to read Stephen Crane, not what his Appleton editor and Fredson Bowers left of him. Only such an edition will merit the attention that the best readers always lavish upon the text they are holding. For only the 1893 edition of *Maggie* may yet prove to be a masterpiece.

THOMAS A. GULLASON

Tragedy and Melodrama in Stephen Crane's *Maggie*†

Both tragedy and melodrama, with melodrama predominating, exist in Stephen Crane's *Maggie* (1893). On the surface, they suggest that Crane was working at cross-purposes. There is a limited sense of Aristotelian tragedy in the novel: in the representation of and the appeal to the emotions of pity and fear; in the compact, dramatic, and scenic structure. Tragic heroes and heroines, however—that is, people who are noble and "better"—are nowhere to be found. Moreover, there is no real movement from happiness to misery (Maggie's happiness is short-lived), only movement from misery to more misery. There is nothing to make one "marvel." Instead there is much that recalls melodrama: sensation, violence, terror, and shock, seemingly for their own sake; mawkish sentiment; vulgar rhetoric; stereotyped and one-dimensional people and situations; exaggerated actions and reactions that waver between the grotesque and the ludicrous.

Periodic references have been made to tragedy and melodrama in the criticism of Stephen Crane's first novel, yet little evidence has been presented to explain their positive values and strengths. No one has advanced the idea, for example, that Crane—a very precocious writer—was purposely mixing the two genres in the one work in order to reflect a tragicomic world. This perspective on the novel exposes finer and more subtle shades of Crane's talent; and while it does not transform *Maggie* into a great novel, it makes it more substantial.

All of Crane's early novels—*Maggie, The Red Badge of Courage* (1895), and *George's Mother* (1896)—have "dramatic" qualities. Like Henry James, Crane was expanding the province of fiction and the life of the novel by drawing on dramatic conventions (besides drawing on the painterly devices of impressionism), thereby moving beyond

---

3. As Joseph Katz did (Gainesville, Fla.: Scholars' Facsimiles & Reprints, 1966); as Donald Pizer did (San Francisco: Chandler Publishing Company, 1968); and as Philip D. Jordan did (Lexington: University of Kentucky Press, 1970). Few libraries have copies of the rare 1893 *Maggie* (the torn-apart and marked-up setting copy for the Appleton edition would be worth something now), but these facsimiles have made the first edition widely available in a form suitable for most scholarly purposes.

† Published for the first time in this volume.

the simple and traditional narrative forms. Crane refers specifically to drama in *Maggie*. "The babe [Tommie] sat on the floor watching the scene, his face in contortions like that of a woman at a tragedy." When Pete takes Maggie to the theater, they watch plays that have all the ingredients of the popular melodramas of the 1890s—"the brain-clutching heroine," the "hero with the beautiful sentiments," and "villains." Crane mentions that even "shady persons" in the audience "hissed vice and applauded virtue." The hero of the play marches "from poverty in the first act, to wealth and triumph in the final one . . ."

Interestingly, in his delineation of melodrama in *Maggie*, Crane represents it critically, that is, he is parodying and satirizing it even though the reader of the day (and the viewer like Maggie) took it all very seriously, expecting material success and moral victory to come inevitably. At the same time, Crane uses melodrama to provide one of the realistic dimensions of the novel where, like the children of the tenement building, the reader (the audience) views all as from "the front row at a theatre." Things are presented in stark terms and in planned disproportion for several reasons: to uncover and stress the real and basic elemental nature of the people of the slums, their spontaneous and uninhibited habits and ways; to shock the sensibilities of the "other half" of society by translating a foreign condition on native grounds, the life of the "lower half"; to control Crane's own sense of outrage at the "progress and poverty" of American civilization.

In drawing upon tragedy and melodrama, Stephen Crane was working to create the spirit of compassion on the one hand and the spirit of criticism on the other. There is compassion for the plight of the slum dwellers, especially for Maggie, who inherits the indifference, hopelessness, sterility, and cynicism of her parent world. There is criticism for the cowardice, meanness, and hypocrisy of the slum inhabitants generally, for the inanimate but hostile environment (the tenement building), and for the "other half"—those advancing an American civilization that seems indifferent and/or ineffective (note the mission preacher and the stout representative of the "Grace of God") in coping with a tragic condition. By mixing tragedy and melodrama, Crane was making his novel both timely—a contemporary protest against a contemporary problem—and timeless—a story about an age-old problem that simply would not go away.

Most Crane critics, however, refuse to see anything tragic in the novel, because there are no tragic heroes or heroines. Presumably it follows that if there are no tragic characters and a tragic action there can be no tragic spirit or vision. Yet Crane does generate a tragic spirit or vision in *Maggie*, especially when it is read in the context of the 1890s. The crusading newspapers of the day, like the

New York Press,[1] had vigorously exposed the terror and shame of slum existence. With the help of social reformers, like Jacob Riis, they were instrumental in the formation of the Tenement House Commission of 1884, followed by a second one in 1894 (the year after the publication of *Maggie*) to confront and correct the multifarious problems of slum life.[2]

In writing *Maggie*, Crane was fully aware of the tireless crusades of the newspapers, social reformers, ministers, and commissions; he was also aware of the little progress that was being made in dealing with the slums and their inhabitants. This tragic situation serves as the large backdrop to *Maggie*. For as Crane chooses to fix on one family, the Johnsons, he personalizes in small a large tragedy which affects and reflects on American society as a whole, not simply on New York City as an isolated case.

In other New York City sketches published after *Maggie*, Crane hinted at the indifference or ignorance of American civilization generally toward its existing social problems. In "An Experiment in Misery" (April 22, 1894), Crane, near the end of the sketch, interrupts the action:

> And in the background a multitude of buildings, of pitiless hues and sternly high were to him [the youth] emblematic of a nation forcing its regal head into the clouds, throwing no downward glances; in the sublimity of its aspirations ignoring the wretches who may flounder at its feet. The roar of the city in his ear was to him the confusion of strange tongues, babbling heedlessly; it was the clink of coin, the voice of the city's hopes which were to him no hopes.[3]

In "The Men in the Storm" (October 1894), Crane describes men waiting patiently for the doors of a "charitable house" to open:

> In this half-darkness, the men began to come from their shelter places and mass in front of the doors of charity. They were of all types, but the nationalities were mostly American, German and Irish. Many were strong, healthy, clear-skinned fellows with that stamp of countenance which is not frequently seen upon seekers after charity. There were men of undoubted patience, industry and temperance, who in time of ill-fortune, do not habitually turn to rail at the state of society, snarling at the arrogance of the rich and bemoaning the cowardice of the poor, but who at these times

1. As editor of the *New York Press* from 1890 to 1895, Edward Marshall did all he could in behalf of New York City's tenement house question. In 1894 he was named secretary of the Tenement House Committee. Marshall was probably responsible for the publication of excerpts from Stephen Crane's 1893 *Maggie* in the *Press* (April 15, 1894, part III, p. 2). He was impressed with Crane's talent (he published other pieces by him) and he sensed that the *Maggie* excerpts would further the cause of the Tenement House Committee.

2. For a sample of the work of these commissions, see *Report of the Tenement House Committee* (Albany, N.Y.: James B. Lyon, 1895).

3. *The Works of Stephen Crane*, ed. Fredson Bowers (Charlottesville: The University Press of Virginia, 1973), vol. VIII, p. 293.

are apt to wear a sudden and singular meekness, as if they saw the world's progress marching from them and were trying to perceive where they had failed, what they had lacked, to be thus vanquished in the race.[4]

The three-part title of the 1893 *Maggie* focuses on the social problem from individual to general to universal terms. The initial title is *Maggie*; the reference is to one person. The second title, *A Girl of the Streets*, reflects the occupation—prostitution—inevitably awaiting the girl, now a representative figure. The last title, *A Story of New York*, generalizes even more, placing the story within the framework of the large city, really any city. For in *Maggie* Crane does a characteristic thing, which he is very skillful with in *The Red Badge*. He avoids the typical and comprehensive naturalistic listing of specific names of streets and landmarks. Instead of "Blackwell's Island," for example, he simply says "Island"; instead of "East River" he says "river." Crane is more interested in the girl Maggie (and her tenement world) as a symbol and the city as a symbol. In the end, Crane is writing an exemplary novel, a novel that illustrates a large truth and a large moral, and he wants to present both artistically. One of his well-known pronouncements was: "Preaching is fatal to art in literature."

The girl Maggie is the only one in the entire novel who elicits genuine and continuous concern and sympathy. Some critics have complained, however, that she does not have enough of a personality in the novel to evoke reader sympathy for herself and her plight. She may be one of the most absent heroines in American literature, yet her presence is often felt by the reader through other characters like Mary Johnson, Jimmie, Pete, and Nellie. Besides, Crane did not intend his novel as a clinical case history of one person. (The same is true of two other famous novels dealing with women, *Madame Bovary* and *Anna Karenina*.) Maggie serves as a means to a larger end, as a paradigm of the continuing tragedy that exists in American life.

Within her brief time in the novel, Maggie generates not only pity but fear in the reader. She is not at all like her parents who have reached a dead end, who drink, fight, and abuse their children, but Maggie has very limited alternatives to their kind of life. Her brother Jimmie suggests this early when he serves her an ultimatum: "Yeh've edder got teh go teh hell [prostitution] or go teh work!" She goes to work. It does not take her long to realize the emptiness and mechanical drudgery in a collar and cuff factory.

The entrance of Pete gives Maggie the opportunity to fight inevitability and to "rise" above the slums. It is true that Maggie's actions take place mainly in her mind and thoughts, not in what she says, for she is barely articulate in the novel. But at least she "acts" to do

4. *Ibid.*, p. 317.

something about her condition, something the other characters in Rum Alley do not do. Her romantic illusions make her think Pete is a "knight," an "aristocratic person," when in fact he is a crude Bowery tough. She tries to impress him by prettying up her home. Maggie herself is seduced by materialism: by Pete's clothes and appearance, by the culture and refinement of the theater, by Nellie's garb. In visiting theaters, museums, and dance halls Maggie thinks she is "rising" away from her vicious Rum Alley environment when she is really "falling," though not immediately. Once she is seduced by Pete, she is totally dependent on him and his "strong protecting fists." Given the facts of life in the slums, Maggie does "not feel like a bad woman." This does not mean she is insensitive to right and wrong, the moral and the immoral. She is aware of "sin" and tries to avoid it:

> As they [Pete and Maggie] went out Maggie perceived two women seated at a table with some men. They were painted and their cheeks had lost their roundness. As she passed them the girl, with a shrinking movement, drew back her skirts.

Abandoned by Pete, Maggie attracts even more pity and fear as everyone else abandons her too. She returns home where she is rejected by her own "moral world," which has no morality: her mother, her brother, and the tenement dwellers. As a final act of desperation, Maggie reaches out toward the clergyman, who rejects her also: "For how was he to know that there was a soul before him that needed saving?" She has tried to save her soul but no one helps her.

When Maggie walks her telescoped "last mile" in Chapter XVII, from "glittering avenues" to the "blackness of the final block," Crane tactfully avoids sketching in a large-scaled and dramatic suicide because Maggie has reached bottom. At this point she is anonymous and dehumanized, "a girl of the painted cohorts" of the city. A last image, of "a huge fat man," as though from an expressionistic nightmare, is a grotesque and violent projection of Maggie's total degradation and victimization. There is no literal reference here to Maggie's death by drowning—this must be inferred by the reader—but Maggie's "action" proves many things. Though an ordinary rather than an extraordinary person, she has a conscience and personal dignity; she refuses to accept her inevitable fate. She refuses to accept her "material success" as a prostitute; her spiritual values triumph. In her death she "rises" above her Rum Alley environment and her social order. Crane presents this last scene (as he does others in the novel) in an unorthodox and effective way: it is like a dumb show, aimed directly at the audience, the reader, in the "front row at a theatre," who makes a final assessment of Maggie, her dreams and her reality.

Maggie has paid an awful price for trying to improve her lot in a world of cruelty and indifference. She is a victim whose punishment does not fit the crime, because she has committed none. She is the innocent—seduced and abandoned not only by Pete but by her family, her tenement, and society. True, she does not act heroically and tragically, like Sophocles' Antigone; but she acts and reacts, though naively and idealistically. True, the reader does not feel the "exaltation" of her struggle, for she suffers quietly and does not fight back. It is also true that "undeserved suffering in itself is not tragic," as Edith Hamilton states (in *The Greek Way*). As Maggie tries and fails to rise from her empty world, however, she never succumbs to self-pity, as her mother does. She faces her dilemma in the best way she knows how. Thus she becomes the representative figure of a collective tragic situation—the waste of human life and potential in the advancing world of civilization. Maggie's existence, her dreams, her reality, her treatment and destruction, Crane tells us, *is* an American tragedy. (Aristotle reminds us that there are other types of tragedy besides "tragedy of character"; he names four in all.) In the end, Maggie is "better" and "noble" compared to the others in Rum Alley, who are sometimes bathetic, sometimes pathetic. Physically they remain alive but spiritually they are dead.

To a far lesser degree and for a shorter period of time, Jimmie acts like the innocent Maggie. He is aware of right and wrong. When his father grabs the beer pail, Jimmie complains: "Ah, come off! I got dis can fer dat ol' woman an' it 'ud be dirt teh swipe it." For brief moments he shows his awareness of positive moral and spiritual values, for example, when he tries to avenge his sister's seduction by Pete. But Jimmie is rarely out of sync with his Rum Alley world. He respects only force—the fire engine, for example. He inherits his father's ways, for he drinks and quarrels. He is a measure of the difference between Rum Alley and Maggie. Though both he and she are members of the young generation and grow up in the same household in the same environment, only Maggie remains a flower in the mud puddle, because Jimmie adapts.

The tenement neighbors individually (the old woman) and collectively (the crowd that gathers to watch the "sinful" Maggie being condemned by her mother and brother) act as a naturalistic chorus. In classic Greek tragedy, the chorus often represents the community, as it does here. It also interprets the action, pities, consoles, takes sides, criticizes (sometimes justifiably), and moralizes. In *Maggie*, the chorus is belligerent: it damns and ostracizes; it is hypocritical; it does not have one iota of pity. Of course in this way more compassion and empathy build for Maggie, even when she is absent from the scene or scenes. Moreover, while the oft-repeated choric refrain—"Ah, what deh hell?"—underscores the helplessness, the cowardice, the hate, and cynicism of the slum dwellers, more sympathy is felt for Maggie who refuses to accept her fate, who seeks to find love and life in a world of brute force and fake morality.

II

Stephen Crane fixes far more on melodrama in *Maggie* than he does on tragedy. He employs melodrama critically, that is, satirically; this does not cancel out the tragic sense but enhances it. The one-dimensional Mary Johnson, her husband, Jimmie, Pete, Nellie, and the chorus more bluntly expose their elemental natures, their almost animal-like qualities. They are all human but far removed from a mature humanity. They act theatrically and melodramatically. On the one hand, their actions create shock, fear, and terror; on the other, grotesque comedy. They are symbols of the "dead end" that inevitably await those who dwell in the slum environment.

Mary Johnson sometimes indulges in self-pity; she never has pity for others. Early she reveals a strain of sentimentality:

> The mother sat blinking at them [her children]. She delivered reproaches, swallowed potatoes and drank from a yellow-brown bottle. After a time her mood changed and she wept as she carried little Tommie into another room and laid him to sleep with his fists doubled in an old quilt of faded red and green grandeur. Then she came and moaned by the stove. She rocked to and fro upon a chair, shedding tears and crooning miserably to the two children about their "poor mother" and "yer fader, damn 'is soul."

She repeats this sentimental strain on a grand scale in the last chapter of the novel, where she mourns for the dead Maggie and her "worsted boots." Mary Johnson hysterically insists that Jimmie produce his sister so that she can put the boots on her "child." By this action, Mary Johnson achieves the height of bathos and irrationalism. As she mourns in her "motherly" way, she exaggerates her nonexistent love and forgiveness. What Crane has done is to make her a grimly comic figure. In order to expose her ridiculousness and her stupidity, Crane draws on the classic device of *reductio ad absurdum*.

It is also the unmotherly Mary Johnson who falsely accuses Maggie of sin and then forces her to leave home. Later she assumes a moral posture and rationalizes. Her character may be flat and unsubtle but it is real and natural in animal-like cunning:

> He [Jimmie] found his mother raving. Maggie had not returned home. The parent continually wondered how her daughter could come to such a pass. She had never considered Maggie as a pearl dropped unstained into Rum Alley from Heaven, but she could not conceive how it was possible for her daughter to fall so low as to bring disgrace upon her family. She was terrific in denunciation of the girl's wickedness.

Other characters in the novel go through a similar ritual of *reductio ad absurdum*. Pete elaborates on his own "goodness" in Chapter

XVIII, when he has been partly responsible for Maggie's death. Now in his drunken stupor he is himself seduced and abandoned by Nellie and the other women. Jimmie continually rationalizes and reveals his double standards: he has seduced other women but wants to punish Pete for ruining his sister; he proposes to bring his disgraced sister home because he is worried about his moral standing. In the irrational jungle that is Rum Alley, justice and forgiveness and love and decency are really nonexistent.

Crane even treats inanimate objects in a melodramatic way. They may be, as previous critics have noted, implausible and inaccurate samples of literary naturalism, but Crane was intent on revealing the irrational, not the rational, world in *Maggie*. There is "comedy" in the fact that the parents continually break up the furniture in their home, though realistically the Johnsons would be too poor to afford new furniture or to repair it so expertly. Crane uses the furniture war to underscore the nightmare reality of the home environment of Maggie and Jimmie. Crane also personifies the tenement building, giving it the character of something human, grotesque, and ominous; he frequently uses the same word—"gruesome"—to describe the building.

The melodramatic style and melodramatic structure contribute to the irrational and absurd reality of Rum Alley and its people. Not one really tragic line exists in the entire novel. Typically the lines are stunted yet overblown (note the adverbs and adjectives), disjointed, ironic, and cacophonous. They reflect the tempo, the pace, the mood, the fragmented life in the slums. At times Crane does write awkwardly in the novel, but the style fits the lifestyle of the world he is presenting:

> He glanced over into the vacant lot in which the little raving boys from Devil's Row seethed about the shrieking and tearful child from Rum Alley.

> She returned and stirred up the room until her children were bobbing about like bubbles.

> He grovelled in the gloom, the eyes from out his drawn face riveted upon the intervening door.

Structurally, each chapter in the novel is like an impressionistic vignette, etched in broad and grotesque strokes. Each chapter is also episodic, usually ending in harsh irony. There are none of the smooth transitions common to the traditional novel. Like the melodramatic style of the novel, the chapters have blunt and jagged edges; they are separate islands, reflecting a world of chaos, without any order or peace. This is the way of the slums as envisioned by Crane.

Melodramatic characters and situations, style and structure—all together magnify the condition of the "lower half" of American life for the benefit of the "other half." This leads to the basic thrust in the novel—tragedy—which is mirrored in Crane's famous inscription: "It is inevitable that you will be greatly shocked by this book but continue please with all possible courage to the end. For it tries to show that environment is a tremendous thing in the world and frequently shapes lives regardless. If one proves that theory one makes room in Heaven for all sorts of souls (notably an occasional street girl) who are not confidently expected to be there by many excellent people."[5] By relying on the shock theory of disproportions, Crane makes his point. On the one hand, he shows the Rum Alley people as they really are; and on the other, he forces the reader of the novel to involve himself and right the balances, which can come only after reform. Crane demonstrates that without reforms future Maggies and future "dead end" slums will inevitably and predictably emerge. Crane's seeming cynicism is not really negative; as he presents an unrelenting and brutal reality he is questing for a new order and a new enlightenment in America.

Unfortunately, over the decades, Stephen Crane has been so closely identified with literary naturalism that almost everyone expects or demands that *Maggie* be read as a casebook of determinism and amoralism, where the characters lack free will and responsibility, where they are trapped animals in an indifferent and hostile universe. Though the novel begins with a fight and ends with a funeral dirge, it is nonetheless a tragedy-within-a-tragedy. The characters act and react.

Crane's approach to his subject is described in "The Blue Hotel." He writes: "We are all in it! . . .Every sin is the result of a collaboration." In *Maggie*, he shows the failed responsibilities, the helplessness, of the slum dwellers. He tries to impress on the reader (the audience) his responsibility for the existing conditions. He makes the reader see and feel the slum reality with suffocating closeness (not with naturalistic details but with redundant moods and scenes) in order to lead him from ignorance to awareness; to make him assess the "effects" of slum life and to review "causes"; to prove that Maggie and the families in Rum Alley are not isolated cases but part of a national American tragedy.

Both melodrama and tragedy serve Stephen Crane well. In an unorthodox and strikingly modern way, he unites the "absurd" and critical realism. *Maggie* is not really Greek (as William Dean Howells describes it in his review, "New York Low Life in Fiction," above). It is in the twentieth-century American tradition, a collective and general tragedy that prepares for later democratic tragedies of the common people, like Arthur Miller's *Death of a Salesman* (1949).

---

5. *Stephen Crane: Letters*, ed. R. W. Stallman and Lillian Gilkes (New York: New York University Press, 1960), p. 14.

Selected Bibliography

WRITINGS BY STEPHEN CRANE

Novels

Maggie: A Girl of the Streets (1893; 1896)
The Red Badge of Courage: An Episode of the American Civil War (1895)
George's Mother (1896)
The Third Violet (1897)
Active Service: A Novel (1899)
The O'Ruddy: A Romance (with Robert Barr) (1903)

Short Stories and Sketches

The Little Regiment and Other Episodes of the American Civil War (1896)
The Open Boat and Other Tales of Adventure (1898)
The Monster and Other Stories (1899; 1901)
Whilomville Stories (1900)
Wounds in the Rain (1900)
Last Words (1902)

Poetry

The Black Riders and Other Lines (1895)
War Is Kind (1899)

Collected Editions (in order of publication)

The Work of Stephen Crane. Edited by Wilson Follett. 12 vols. New York: Alfred A. Knopf, 1925–27. Reissued (6 vols.); New York: Russell & Russell, 1963.
Stephen Crane: Letters. Edited by R. W. Stallman and Lillian Gilkes. New York: New York University Press, 1960.
The Complete Short Stories and Sketches of Stephen Crane. Edited by Thomas A. Gullason. Garden City, New York: Doubleday & Co., 1963.
The Poems of Stephen Crane: A Critical Edition. Edited by Joseph Katz. New York: Cooper Square Publishers, 1966.
The Complete Novels of Stephen Crane. Edited by Thomas A. Gullason. Garden City, New York: Doubleday & Co., 1967.
The Notebook of Stephen Crane. Edited by Donald J. Greiner and Ellen B. Greiner. Charlottesville: The Bibliographical Society of the University of Virginia, 1969.
The Works of Stephen Crane. Edited by Fredson Bowers. 10 vols. Charlottesville: The University Press of Virginia, 1969–75.

WRITINGS ABOUT STEPHEN CRANE

Bibliographical

Beebe, Maurice and Thomas A. Gullason. "Criticism of Stephen Crane: A Selected Checklist with an Index to Studies of Separate Works." *Modern Fiction Studies*, V (Autumn 1959), 282–91.
Katz, Joseph. "Afterword: Resources for the Study of Stephen Crane." In *Stephen Crane in Transition: Centenary Essays*, edited by Joseph Katz. DeKalb: Northern Illinois University Press, 1972. Pp. 205–31.
Pizer, Donald. "Stephen Crane." In *Fifteen American Authors Before 1900: Bibliographic Essays on Research and Criticism*, edited by Robert A. Rees and Earl N. Harbert. Madison: The University of Wisconsin Press, 1971. Pp. 97–137.
———. "Stephen Crane: A Review of Scholarship and Criticism Since 1969." *Studies in the Novel*, X (Spring 1978), 120–45.
Stallman, R. W. *Stephen Crane: A Critical Bibliography*. Ames: The Iowa State University Press, 1972.
Wertheim, Stanley. "Stephen Crane." In *Hawthorne, Melville, Stephen Crane: A Critical Bibliography*, by Theodore L. Gross and Stanley Wertheim. New York: The Free Press, 1971. Pp. 203–95.

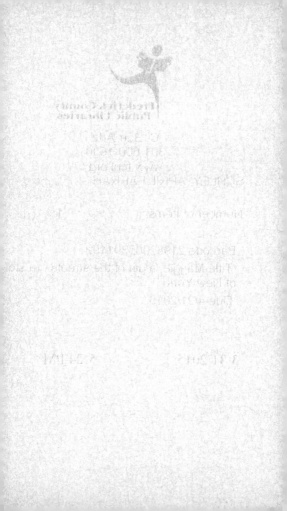

**Frederick County
Public Libraries**

C. Burr Artz
301-600-1630
www.fcpl.org

SCHLEY, APRIL FARRAH

Number of Items: 1

Barcode: 21982005391192
Title: Maggie, a girl of the streets : (a story of New York)
Due: 4/21/2015

3/31/2015   5:24 PM

. . .

———. "Stephen Crane." In "Guide to Dissertations on American Literary Figures, 1870–1910: Part One," compiled and edited by Noel Polk. *American Literary Realism, 1870–1910*, VIII (Summer 1975), 227–41.

Other present and future bibliographical information on Stephen Crane can be found in *Thoth* (published annually since 1963 by the Department of English, Syracuse University); *The Stephen Crane Newsletter*, edited by Joseph Katz (Fall 1966–Fall 1970); *American Literary Scholarship: An Annual*, edited by James Woodress (published since 1965, and beginning with 1963 scholarship); *MLA International Bibliography*, vol. 1 (published annually); *American Literature* (published quarterly).

Biographical

Beer, Thomas. *Stephen Crane: A Study in American Letters*. New York: Alfred A. Knopf, 1923. Reissued; New York: Octagon Books, 1972.
Berryman, John. *Stephen Crane*. New York: William Sloane Associates, 1950. Reissued; New York: Octagon Books, 1975.
Gilkes, Lillian. *Cora Crane: A Biography of Mrs. Stephen Crane*. Bloomington: Indiana University Press, 1960.
Linson, Corwin K. *My Stephen Crane*, edited by Edwin H. Cady. Syracuse, N.Y.: Syracuse University Press, 1958.
Solomon, Eric. *Stephen Crane in England: A Portrait of the Artist*. Columbus: Ohio State University Press, 1964.
Stallman, R. W. *Stephen Crane: A Biography*. New York: George Braziller, 1968.

Critical

Åhnebrink, Lars. *The Beginnings of Naturalism in American Fiction*. Upsala, Sweden: A.-B. Lundequistka Bokhandeln, 1950. Pp. 89–104, 150–55, 249–76, 328–32, 343–60, 378–81, *et passim*. Reissued; New York: Russell & Russell, 1961.
Anderson, Warren D. "Homer and Stephen Crane." *Nineteenth-Century Fiction*, XIX (June 1964), 77–86.
Bassan, Maurice. "Misery and Society: Some New Perspectives on Stephen Crane's Fiction." *Studia Neophiloligica*, XXXV (1963), 104–20.
———, ed. *Stephen Crane: A Collection of Critical Essays*. Englewood Cliffs, N.J.: Prentice-Hall, 1967.
Bates, H. E. *The Modern Short Story: A Critical Survey*. London: Thomas Nelson and Sons, 1941. Pp. 64–71, *et passim*. Reissued; Boston: The Writer, 1961.
Bender, Bert. "Hanging Stephen Crane in the Impressionistic Museum." *The Journal of Aesthetics and Art Criticism*, XXXV (Fall 1976), 47–55.
Bergon, Frank. *Stephen Crane's Artistry*. New York: Columbia University Press, 1975.
Berthoff, Warner. *The Ferment of Realism: American Literature, 1884–1919*. New York: The Free Press, 1965. Pp. 227–35, *et passim*.
Brennan, Joseph X. "Stephen Crane and the Limits of Irony." *Criticism*, XI (Spring 1969), 183–200.
Bridgman, Richard. *The Colloquial Style in America*. New York: Oxford University Press, 1966. Pp. 137–40, *et passim*.
Cady, Edwin H. "Stephen Crane and the Strenuous Life." *ELH*, XXVIII (December 1961), 376–82.
———. *Stephen Crane*. New York: Twayne Publishers, 1962.
Chase, Richard, ed. *The Red Badge of Courage and Other Writings*. Boston: Houghton Mifflin Co., 1960. Pp. vii–xxi.
Colvert, James B. "The Origins of Stephen Crane's Literary Creed." *The University of Texas Studies in English*, XXXIV (1955), 179–88.
———. "Structure and Theme in Stephen Crane's Fiction." *Modern Fiction Studies*, V (Autumn 1959), 199–208.
———. "Stephen Crane's Magic Mountain." In *Stephen Crane: A Collection of Critical Essays*, edited by Maurice Bassan (see above). Pp. 95–105.
———. "Stephen Crane: Style as Invention." In *Stephen Crane in Transition*, edited by Joseph Katz (see above). Pp. 127–52.
Dickason, David H. "Stephen Crane and *The Philistine*." *American Literature*, XV (November 1943), 279–87.
Edwards, Forest Carroll. "Decorum: Its Genesis and Function in Stephen Crane." *The Texas Quarterly*, XVIII (Summer 1975), 131–43.
Elconin, Victor A. "Stephen Crane at Asbury Park." *American Literature*, XX (November 1948), 275–89.
Frohock, W. M. "American Realism and the Elegiac Sensibility: Stephen Crane and Frank Norris." In *History and Fiction: American Prose in the 19th Century*, edited by Alfred Weber and Hartmut Grandel. Göttingen, Germany: Vandenhoeck & Ruprecht, 1972. Pp. 216–37.
Fryckstedt, Olov W. "Stephen Crane in the Tenderloin." *Studia Neophilologica*, XXXIV (1962), 135–63.

Garnett, Edward. *Friday Nights: Literary Criticisms and Appreciations*. First Series. New York: Alfred A. Knopf, 1922. Pp. 201–17, *et passim*.

Geismar, Maxwell. *Rebels and Ancestors: The American Novel, 1890–1915*. Boston: Houghton Mifflin Co., 1953. Pp. 69–136, *et passim*.

Gibson, Donald B. *The Fiction of Stephen Crane*. Carbondale and Edwardsville: Southern Illinois University Press, 1968.

Greenfield, Stanley B. "The Unmistakable Stephen Crane." *PMLA*, LXXIII (December 1958), 562–72.

Griffith, Clark. "Stephen Crane and the Ironic Last Word." *Philological Quarterly*, XLVII (January 1968), 83–91.

Gullason, Thomas A. "Introduction." In *The Complete Short Stories and Sketches of Stephen Crane* (see above). Pp. 19–45.

——. "Introduction." In *The Complete Novels of Stephen Crane* (see above). Pp. 3–97.

——, ed. *Stephen Crane's Career: Perspectives and Evaluations*. New York: New York University Press, 1972.

——. "Stephen Crane: In Nature's Bosom." In *American Literary Naturalism: A Reassessment*, edited by Yoshinobu Hakutani and Lewis Fried. Heidelberg, Germany: Carl Winter, 1975. Pp. 37–56.

Hoffman, Daniel G. *The Poetry of Stephen Crane*. New York: Columbia University Press, 1957.

Holton, Milne. *Cylinder of Vision: The Fiction and Journalistic Writing of Stephen Crane*. Baton Rouge: Louisiana State University Press, 1972.

Hough, Robert L. "Crane and Goethe: A Forgotten Relationship." *Nineteenth-Century Fiction*, XVII (September 1962), 135–48.

Katz, Joseph, ed. *Stephen Crane in Transition: Centenary Essays* (see above).

Knapp, Daniel. "Son of Thunder: Stephen Crane and the Fourth Evangelist." *Nineteenth-Century Fiction*, XXIV (December 1969), 253–91.

Kwiat, Joseph J. "Stephen Crane and Painting." *American Quarterly*, IV (Winter 1952), 331–38.

——. "The Newspaper Experience: Crane, Norris, and Dreiser." *Nineteenth-Century Fiction*, VIII (September 1953), 99–117.

——. "Stephen Crane and Frank Norris: The Magazine and the 'Revolt' in American Literature in the 1890's." *Western Humanities Review*, XXX (Autumn 1976), 309–22.

LaFrance, Marston. *A Reading of Stephen Crane*. New York: Oxford University Press, 1971.

Leaver, Florence. "Isolation in the Work of Stephen Crane." *The South Atlantic Quarterly*, LXI (Autumn 1962), 521–32.

Nelson, Harland S. "Stephen Crane's Achievement as a Poet." *Texas Studies in Literature and Language*, IV (Winter 1963), 564–82.

Noble, David W. *The Eternal Adam and the New World Garden: The Central Myth in the American Novel Since 1830*. New York: George Braziller, 1968. Pp. 101–105, 115–23.

Nye, Russel B. "Stephen Crane as Social Critic." *The Modern Quarterly: A Journal of Radical Opinion*, XI (Summer 1940), 48–54.

Overland, Orm. "The Impressionism of Stephen Crane: A Study in Style and Technique." In *Americana Norvegica: Norwegian Contributions to American Studies*, I, edited by Sigmund Skard and Henry H. Wasser. Philadelphia: University of Pennsylvania Press, 1966. Pp. 239–85.

Perosa, Sergio. "Naturalism and Impressionism in Stephen Crane's Fiction." In *Stephen Crane: A Collection of Critical Essays*, edited by Maurice Bassan (see above). Pp. 80–94.

Pizer, Donald. "Nineteenth-Century American Naturalism: An Essay in Definition." *Bucknell Review*, XIII (December 1965), 1–18.

Rogers, Rodney O. "Stephen Crane and Impressionism." *Nineteenth-Century Fiction*, XXIV (December 1969), 292–304.

Schneider, Robert W. *Five Novelists of the Progressive Era*. New York: Columbia University Press, 1965. Pp. 60–111, *et passim*.

Shroeder, John W. "Stephen Crane Embattled." *The University of Kansas City Review*, XVII (Winter 1950), 119–29.

Solomon, Eric. *Stephen Crane: From Parody to Realism*. Cambridge: Harvard University Press, 1966.

Stallman, R. W., ed. *Stephen Crane: An Omnibus*. New York: Alfred A. Knopf, 1952.

——. "Stephen Crane: A Revaluation." In *Critiques and Essays on Modern Fiction, 1920–1951*, selected by John W. Aldridge. New York: The Ronald Press Co., 1952. Pp. 244–69.

Stein, William Bysshe. "Stephen Crane's *Homo Absurdus*." *Bucknell Review*, VIII (May 1959), 168–88.

Taylor, Gordon O. *The Passages of Thought: Psychological Representation in the American Novel, 1870–1900*. New York: Oxford University Press, 1969. Pp. 110–35.

Trachtenberg, Alan. "Experiments in Another Country: Stephen Crane's City Sketches." *The Southern Review*, X (April 1974), 265–85.

Vanouse, Donald. "Popular Culture in the Writings of Stephen Crane." *Journal of Popular Culture*, X (Fall 1976), 424–30.

Walcutt, Charles Child. "Stephen Crane: Naturalist and Impressionist." In *American Literary Naturalism, A Divided Stream*. Minneapolis: University of Minnesota Press, 1956. Pp. 66–86, *et passim*.

Weatherford, Richard M., ed. *Stephen Crane: The Critical Heritage*. London: Routledge & Kegan Paul, 1973.

Weimer, David R. *The City as Metaphor*. New York: Random House, 1966. Pp. 52–64, *et passim*.

Wells, H. G. "Stephen Crane: From an English Standpoint." *The North American Review*, CLXXI (August 1900), 233–42.

Wertheim, Stanley. "Stephen Crane and the Wrath of Jehova." *The Literary Review*, VII (Summer 1964), 499–508.

West, Ray B., Jr. "Stephen Crane: Author in Transition." *American Literature*, XXXIV (May 1962), 215–28.

Westbrook, Max. "Stephen Crane: The Pattern of Affirmation." *Nineteenth-Century Fiction*, XIV (December 1959), 219–29.

———. "Stephen Crane and the Personal Universal." *Modern Fiction Studies*, VIII (Winter 1962/63), 351–60.

———. "Stephen Crane's Poetry: Perspective and Arrogance." *Bucknell Review*, XI (December 1963), 24–34.

Young, Philip. *Ernest Hemingway*. New York: Rinehart & Co., 1952. Pp. 161–69. Reissued; Pennsylvania State University Press, 1966.

Ziff, Larzer. "Outstripping the Event: Stephen Crane." In *The American 1890s: Life and Times of a Lost Generation*. New York: The Viking Press, 1966. Pp. 185–205, *et passim*.

Discussions of *Maggie: A Girl of the Streets*

Articles reprinted in this volume are not included here.

Bassan, Maurice, ed. *Stephen Crane's "Maggie": Text and Context*. Belmont, California: Wadsworth Publishing Company, 1966.

Beer, Thomas. "'Maggie: A Girl of the Streets.'" In *Stephen Crane* (see above). Pp. 78–107.

Begiebing, Robert J. "Stephen Crane's *Maggie*: The Death of the Self." *American Imago*, XXXIV (Spring 1977), 50–71.

Bowers, Fredson. "Textual Introduction." In *The Works of Stephen Crane*, edited by Fredson Bowers (see above), vol. I. Pp. liii–xcviii.

Bradbury, Malcolm. "Sociology and Literary Studies. II. Romance and Reality in *Maggie*." *Journal of American Studies*, III (July 1969), 111–21.

Bruccoli, Matthew J. "Maggie's Last Night." *The Stephen Crane Newsletter*, II (Fall 1967), 10.

Cady, Edwin H. *Stephen Crane* (see above). Pp. 102–11.

———. "Stephen Crane: Maggie: A Girl of the Streets." In *Landmarks of American Writing*, edited by Hennig Cohen. New York: Basic Books, 1969. Pp. 172–81.

Colvert, James B. "Introduction." In *The Works of Stephen Crane*, edited by Fredson Bowers (see above), vol. I. Pp. xxxiii–lii.

Fine, David M. "Abraham Cahan, Stephen Crane and the Romantic Tenement Tale of the Nineties." *American Studies* [University of Kansas], XIV (Spring 1973), 95–107.

Ford, Philip H. "Illusion and Reality in Crane's *Maggie*." *The Arizona Quarterly*, XXV (Winter 1969), 293–303.

Geismar, Maxwell. *Rebels and Ancestors* (see above). Pp. 74–77.

Graham, D. B. "Dreiser's Maggie." *American Literary Realism, 1870–1910*, VII (Spring 1974), 169–70.

Grau, Shirley Ann. "Introduction." In *Maggie: A Girl of the Streets*. Avon, Conn.: The Limited Editions Club, 1974. Pp. 5–11.

Gullason, Thomas A. "Thematic Patterns in Stephen Crane's Early Novels." *Nineteenth-Century Fiction*, XVI (June 1961), 59–67.

———. "Introduction." In *The Complete Novels of Stephen Crane* (see above). Pp. 55–65.

———. "The Prophetic City in Stephen Crane's 1893 *Maggie*." *Modern Fiction Studies*, XXIV (Spring 1978), 129–37.

Holton, Milne. "The Sparrow's Fall and the Sparrow's Eye: Crane's *Maggie*." *Studia Neophilologica*, XLI (1969), 115–29.

Ives, C. B. "Symmetrical Design in Four of Stephen Crane's Stories." *Ball State University Forum*, X (Winter 1969), 17–26.

Jackson, John A. "Sociology and Literary Studies. I. The Map of Society: America in the 1890s." *Journal of American Studies*, III (July 1969), 103–10.

Jordan, Philip D. "Introduction." In *Maggie: A Girl of the Streets*. Lexington: The University Press of Kentucky, 1970. Pp. v–xi.

Kahn, Sholom J. "Stephen Crane and Whitman: A Possible Source for 'Maggie.'" *Walt Whitman Review*, VII (December 1961), 71–77.

Kramer, Maurice. "Crane's *Maggie: A Girl of the Streets*." *The Explicator*, XXII (February 1964), item 49.

LaFrance, Marston. *A Reading of Stephen Crane* (see above). Pp. 38–43, 51–66.

———. "*George's Mother* and the Other Half of *Maggie*." In *Stephen Crane in Transition*, edited by Joseph Katz (see above). Pp. 35–53.

Lainoff, Seymour. "Jimmie in Crane's *Maggie*." *Iowa English Yearbook*, no. 10 (Fall 1965), 53–54.

Lenehan, William T. "The Failure of Naturalistic Techniques in Stephen Crane's *Maggie*." In *Stephen Crane's "Maggie": Text and Context*, edited by Maurice Bassan (see above). Pp. 166–73.

Martin, John C. "Childhood in Stephen Crane's *Maggie*, 'The Monster,' and *Whilomville Stories*." *The Midwestern University Quarterly*, II (1967), 40–46.

Noble, David W. *The Eternal Adam and the New World Garden* (see above). Pp. 116–21.

Pizer, Donald. "Introduction." In *Maggie: A Girl of the Streets*, edited by Donald Pizer. San Francisco: Chandler Publishing Company, 1968. Pp. vii–xxix.

Sansom, William. "Introduction." In *Maggie: A Girl of the Streets*, edited by Herbert Van Thal. London: Cassell & Co., 1966. Pp. vii–xiv.

Solomon, M. "Stephen Crane: A Critical Study." *Masses & Mainstream*, IX (January 1956), 26–30.

Stallman, R. W. "Stephen Crane's Revision of *Maggie: A Girl of the Streets*." *American Literature*, XXVI (January 1955), 528–36.

———. "Crane's 'Maggie': A Reassessment." *Modern Fiction Studies*, V (Autumn 1959), 251–59.

———. "Crane's *Maggie* in Review." In *The Houses That James Built and Other Literary Studies*. East Lansing: Michigan State University Press, 1961. Pp. 63–72. Reissued; Athens: Ohio University Press, 1977.

Taylor, Gordon O. *The Passages of Thought* (see above). Pp. 111–19.

Weimer, David R. *The City as Metaphor* (see above). Pp. 52–57.

Westbrook, Max. "Stephen Crane's Social Ethic." *American Quarterly*, XIV (Winter 1962), 587–96.

Ziff, Larzer. *The American 1890s* (see above). Pp. 190–93.